AMERICAN FOOTBALL

AMERICAN FOOTBALL

Willow Books
Collins
8 Grafton Street, London W 1
1987

MIKE DITKA *Chicago Bears*

FOREWORD

When I brought the Chicago Bears to play the Dallas Cowboys for the American Bowl, at Wembley in August, 1986, I immediately felt at home amidst the warmth and enthusiasm of British American Football fans. Back in the USA, it's good to know that so many people in the UK are now dedicated supporters of our great gridiron game.

Whether you are a firm fan or an interested newcomer, this book provides an in-depth look at what happens in NFL Football, plus details on all the teams, top players, tactics and great moments of the game I have loved since my childhood years.

Dedication and commitment are just two of the qualities needed to make a successful career in pro football. But you can't get to the top by relying on the physical aspects of the sport. You also need to know precisely what is going on, and base your decisions on detailed knowledge if you want to maintain a winning edge.

American Football is above all a game to enjoy. If I didn't enjoy it, I wouldn't have made it my life. In the pages that follow I hope you will share my pleasure in the best game on earth.

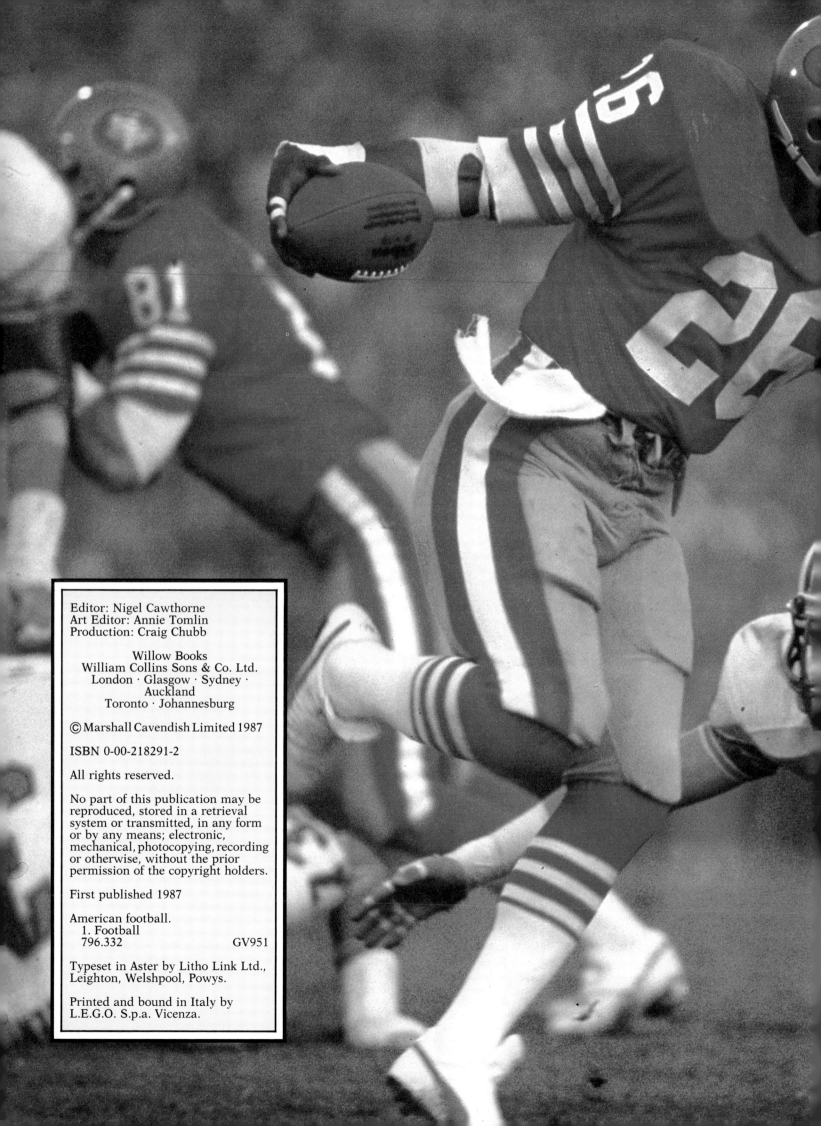

Editor: Nigel Cawthorne
Art Editor: Annie Tomlin
Production: Craig Chubb

Willow Books
William Collins Sons & Co. Ltd.
London · Glasgow · Sydney ·
Auckland
Toronto · Johannesburg

© Marshall Cavendish Limited 1987

ISBN 0-00-218291-2

First published 1987

American football.
  1. Football
796.332   GV951

Typeset in Aster by Litho Link Ltd.,
Leighton, Welshpool, Powys.

Printed and bound in Italy by
L.E.G.O. S.p.a. Vicenza.

CONTENTS

INTRODUCTION

There can be little doubt about what makes American Football so popular. Whether we look at the teams and players, history and behind the scenes, or the rules and strategy of the game itself, there is one aspect that constantly shines through to keep our attention – sheer excitement. Even team uniforms and the look of the players themselves strikes within each of us a note that says: Something big is about to happen!

But what is it precisely that makes American football so exciting – what makes it tick?

Well, the answer is quite simple – television. Since 1958, when the first NFL championship was televised to a national audience, Americans realised that professional football was here to stay. The fact is that Americans were already hooked on the sport, but on the college variety, with 70, 80, even 100,000 fans turning up to watch their teams play in fantastic stadiums. Even at high school, teams can draw as many as several thousand. In fact, high school is where most players begin their careers. While there, college coaches and their assistants watch the young players, and, if they see talent in the raw, attempt to lure the kids to play for the coach's university. This is known as scouting, and enormous budgets are set aside by the colleges each year specifically for this. The same scouting procedure is used by the NFL teams to find top college players. What's known as the college draft takes place, in which teams choose one player each at a time, the worst team getting first pick and the best last.

If you didn't go to college, however, or haven't played much but think you could, then all is not lost. Each year, NFL teams hold, before their summer training camps, special mini-camps, usually one-day affairs, where 'walk-ons' can show their stuff. The most famous walk-on was the legendary Johnny Unitas, who played for the Baltimore (now Indianapolis) Colts and went on to set career passing records in all major categories. So don't despair.

With full details of all 1986 results, this book should be especially useful going into the '87 season, but we hope that its thoroughness in all other areas of the game will make it stand on its own for many seasons to come as a reference book. Although the numbers change each year, the glamour and excitement of American football stay with us forever.

INSIDE THE GAME

Appreciating and enjoying American Football has as much to do with understanding the history of the sport, techniques, players and teams as it does with simply knowing the rules. With seven officials on the field at once, for example, it's more than worthwhile to find out exactly what they do and why certain officials only make certain calls.

The history of American Football is as lively as the game itself, and at no point was it more exciting than when the American Football League was formed as a rival to the NFL. For seven years, there were bitter battles between clubs from both leagues as each drafted the same players out of college. A decision was finally reached to amalgamate the two leagues in 1970, and for three years beforehand, the champions of the two leagues would meet in the newly created Super Bowl. The AFL remains today in the form of the American Football Conference, in which teams like Miami, Denver, the New York Jets and LA Raiders have won the Super Bowl and greatly enhanced the image of the NFL.

Analyses of the sport and playing the game by the NFL's top players provides us with a terrific insight into the intelligence and dedication needed to play in the NFL. San Francisco's Joe Montana and Seattle's Steve Largent, quarterback and wide receiver, respectively, comment openly and clearly about their game. Montana, for instance, explains which cornerbacks and safeties are most difficult to pass against, and what he looks for in running backs and wide receivers. Largent takes us on a trip through a wide receiver's thoughts as he prepares for games and assesses the talents of the league's top defensive backs. There's a lot more to catching passes than just running patterns correctly!

American Football stadiums are unparalleled in sport — huge capacity indoor battlefields with absolutely nothing lacking for the fan watching the game live. The Houston Astrodome, opened in 1966 and home of the Oilers, was the NFL's first indoor stadium, and also the world's. Since then, with the additions of other indoor venues in New Orleans, Detroit and Seattle, the league has taken on an image as both an innovator and leader in stadium design. With the Astrodome came the advent of artificial turf, more commonly known as AstroTurf; though AstroTurf is a trade name, it is still used twenty years later to describe any 'plastic' playing surface. With less than half the teams still playing on grass in their home fields, the initial, often adverse, reaction to artificial turf has long since settled. Both the players and the fans now accept the artificial playing surface — especially in winter.

One game that has been played on grass since 1980 is the annual Pro Bowl in Honolulu, Hawaii, in February. Following the Super Bowl and capping off the season, the game is a showcase of the league's best talent, with the NFC pitted against the AFC. Players are selected by their peers in their respective conferences, and though the game is effectively an 'all-star' game, the pride and enthusiasm of the players chosen does much credit to the sport.

GOING FOR GLORY

An NFL franchise since 1940, the Pittsburgh Steelers did not even make the playoffs until 1972. In 1974, however, they won their first of four Super Bowls – a turning point in the league's frantic history since 1960.

INSIDE THE GAME

Since the formation of the AFL in 1960, American Football has thrilled and entertained many millions of fans. The highlights and standings for each season tell their own magnificent story, as the game has developed into the mega-spectacular we know today

With the creation of the AFL in 1960, the resulting draft wars and ultimate joining with the NFL, American football has provided the fans with many great memories. The year 1960 was a watershed in American sport, and in football terms, a starting point for the modern game.

In this look at the National Football League since 1960, the NFL finds itself a serious rival in the American Football League. As Commissioner Pete Rozelle of the NFL takes charge, the drama takes on some dramatic turns.

1960

Conceived in 1959 by a group that includes Dallas businessman Lamar Hunt, the American Football League begins play with eight franchises representing Boston, Buffalo, Dallas, Denver, Houston, Los Angeles, New York and Oakland.

After marathon discussions and seemingly endless stalemates, NFL owners name Pete Rozelle, a former Los Angeles Rams general manager, the league's new commissioner. Rozelle succeeds Bert Bell, who died in 1959 during an NFL game at Philadelphia's Franklin Field.

At the NFL's annual meeting in January, Clint Murchison, Jr., and Bedford Wynne are awarded an expansion franchise for the city of Dallas. The new club begins play in September under head coach Tom Landry, and finishes with a 0-11-1 record.

Norm Van Brocklin ends his playing career with a bang, leading Philadelphia to a 17-13 victory over Green Bay in the NFL Championship Game.

In the first AFL Championship Game, the Eastern Division's Houston Oilers, led by quarterback George Blanda, defeat the Los Angeles Chargers, coached by Sid Gillman and quarterbacked by Jack Kemp, 24-16.

Home teams are indicated by capital letters.

1960 AFL

EASTERN CONFERENCE	W	L	T	Pct.	WESTERN CONFERENCE	W	L	T	Pct.
Philadelphia	10	2	0	.833	Green Bay	8	4	0	.667
Cleveland	8	3	1	.727	Detroit	7	5	0	.583
N.Y. Giants	6	4	2	.600	San Francisco	7	5	0	.583
St. Louis	6	5	1	.545	Baltimore	6	6	0	.500
Pittsburgh	5	6	1	.455	Chicago	5	6	1	.455
Washington	1	9	2	.100	L.A. Rams	4	7	1	.364
					Dallas Cowboys	0	11	1	.000

NFL Championship: PHILADELPHIA 17, Green Bay 13

1960 AFL

EASTERN DIVISION	W	L	T	Pct.	WESTERN DIVISION	W	L	T	Pct.
Houston	10	4	0	.714	L.A. Chargers	10	4	0	.714
N.Y. Titans	7	7	0	.500	Dallas Texans	8	6	0	.571
Buffalo	5	8	1	.385	Oakland	6	8	0	.429
Boston	5	9	0	.357	Denver	4	9	1	.308

AFL Championship: HOUSTON 24, L.A. Chargers 16

11

1961

NFL teams meet the AFL's draft challenge by signing all but two of their top picks. Only Syracuse fullback Art Baker and Auburn tackle Ken Rice get away (both to Buffalo). The expansion Vikings use their third choice on quarterback Fran Tarkenton.

Most backs and receivers use double-bar facemasks on their helmets as opposed to single-bar masks, while linemen and linebackers use birdcage-type masks.

George Blanda leads Houston to a second straight AFL Championship Game victory, kicking a field goal and throwing a 35-yard touchdown pass to halfback Billy Cannon as the Oilers defeat the San Diego (transplanted from Los Angeles) Chargers 10-3 at Balboa Stadium in San Diego.

The Green Bay Packers defeat the New York Giants 37-0 in the NFL Championship Game, initiating a string of title victories (five in seven years) that will establish head coach Vince Lombardi's club as a dynasty.

1961 NFL								
EASTERN CONFERENCE				**WESTERN CONFERENCE**				
	W	L	T	Pct.		W	L	T	Pct.
N.Y. Giants	10	3	1	.769	Green Bay	11	3	0	.786
Philadelphia	10	4	0	.714	Detroit	8	5	1	.615
Cleveland	8	5	1	.615	Baltimore	8	6	0	.571
St. Louis	7	7	0	.500	Chicago	8	6	0	.571
Pittsburgh	6	8	0	.429	San Francisco	7	6	1	.538
Dallas Cowboys	4	9	1	.308	Los Angeles	4	10	0	.286
Washington	1	12	1	.077	Minnesota	3	11	0	.214
NFL Championship: GREEN BAY 37, N.Y. Giants 0								

1961 AFL								
EASTERN DIVISION				**WESTERN DIVISION**				
	W	L	T	Pct.		W	L	T	Pct.
Houston	10	3	1	.769	San Diego	12	2	0	.857
Boston Patriots	9	4	1	.692	Dallas Texans	6	8	0	.429
N.Y. Titans	7	7	0	.500	Denver	3	11	0	.214
Buffalo	6	8	0	.429	Oakland	2	12	0	.143
AFL Championship: Houston 10, SAN DIEGO 3								

1962

Two southern California teams help shape their future in the NFL draft. The Rams use their two first-round picks on North Carolina State quarterback Roman Gabriel and Utah State defensive tackle Merlin Olsen. The San Diego Chargers select Kansas wide receiver Lance Alworth on the third round, then quarterback John Hadl.

The NFL takes a major safety precaution, ruling that a 15-yard penalty will be assessed when one player tackles another by the facemask.

ABC combines the broadcast experience of Curt Gowdy with the playing experience of former Chicago Cardinals' quarterback Paul Christman on AFL telecasts, the first extended use of a former player as a colour commentator.

Buffalo fullback Carlton (Cookie) Gilchrist becomes the AFL's first 1000-yard rusher, with 1096 yards in 14 games. Between 1965-67, he nurtures a lifestyle that includes a limousine with a driver who screens incoming phone calls.

Jim Taylor, the epitome of the basic, hard-grinding Lombardi style of football, wins the NFL rushing title with 1474 yards over a 14-game season. It marks the only time during the career of legendary Cleveland fullback Jim Brown (1957-1965) that Brown is not the league's leading rusher.

1962 NFL								
EASTERN CONFERENCE				**WESTERN CONFERENCE**				
	W	L	T	Pct.		W	L	T	Pct.
N.Y. Giants	12	2	0	.857	Green Bay	13	1	0	.929
Pittsburgh	9	5	0	.643	Detroit	11	3	0	.786
Cleveland	7	6	1	.538	Chicago	9	5	0	.643
Washington	5	7	2	.417	Baltimore	7	7	0	.500
Dallas Cowboys	5	8	1	.385	San Francisco	6	8	0	.429
St. Louis	4	9	1	.308	Minnesota	2	11	1	.154
Philadelphia	3	10	1	.231	Los Angeles	1	12	1	.077
NFL Championship: Green Bay 16, N.Y. GIANTS 7								

1962 AFL								
EASTERN DIVISION				**WESTERN DIVISION**				
	W	L	T	Pct.		W	L	T	Pct.
Houston	11	3	0	.786	Dallas Texans	11	3	0	.786
Boston Patriots	9	4	1	.692	Denver	7	7	0	.500
Buffalo	7	6	1	.538	San Diego	4	10	0	.286
N.Y. Titans	5	9	0	.357	Oakland	1	13	0	.071
AFL Championship: Dallas Texans 20, HOUSTON 17, sudden death overtime								

1963

The NFL Hall of Fame opens in Canton, Ohio. Cleveland's Jim Brown wins the NFL rushing title with a record 1863 yards, his highest annual contribution to a career total 12,312 yards between 1957-1965.

The New York Titans, formerly the property of sportscaster Harry Wismer, are sold to a five-man syndicate headed by David (Sonny) Werblin, who was chief executive for MCA. The team nickname is changed to the 'Jets'.

Lured by promises of tripled season-ticket sales and an improved stadium, Dallas Texans' owner Lamar Hunt moves his club to Kansas City, renaming it the 'Chiefs'.

The Cleveland Browns are the only AFL or NFL team without a helmet logo. In San Diego, Keith Lincoln amasses 334 yards of total offense, perhaps the greatest single-day performance of all time, as the Chargers defeat the Boston Patriots 51-10 in the AFL Championship Game.

CBS television producer Tony Verna, experimenting with videotape equipment, chooses the Army-Navy football game to introduce a new technique. When Rollie Stichweh runs for a touchdown late in the game, viewers are treated to a second show-

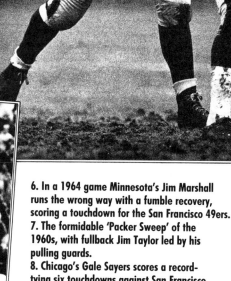

6. In a 1964 game Minnesota's Jim Marshall runs the wrong way with a fumble recovery, scoring a touchdown for the San Francisco 49ers.

7. The formidable 'Packer Sweep' of the 1960s, with fullback Jim Taylor led by his pulling guards.

8. Chicago's Gale Sayers scores a record-tying six touchdowns against San Francisco in 1965.

9. Olympic 100 metres champion Bob Hayes, sprinted into the NFL as a rookie flanker for the Dallas Cowboys in 1965.

ing of the play. Instant replay is born.

The New York Giants lose to the Chicago Bears 14-10 at Wrigley Field in what was coach George Halas's last NFL title.

1963 NFL								
EASTERN CONFERENCE				**WESTERN CONFERENCE**				
	W	L	T	Pct.		W	L	T	Pct.
N.Y. Giants	11	3	0	.786	Chicago	11	1	2	.917
Cleveland	10	4	0	.714	Green Bay	11	2	1	.846
St. Louis	9	5	0	.643	Baltimore	8	6	0	.571
Pittsburgh	7	4	3	.636	Detroit	5	8	1	.385
Dallas	4	10	0	.286	Minnesota	5	8	1	.385
Washington	3	11	0	.214	Los Angeles	5	9	0	.357
Philadelphia	2	10	2	.167	San Francisco	2	12	0	.143
NFL Championship: CHICAGO 14, N.Y. Giants 10								

1963 AFL								
EASTERN DIVISION				**WESTERN DIVISION**				
	W	L	T	Pct.		W	L	T	Pct.
Boston Patriots	7	6	1	.538	San Diego	11	3	0	.786
Buffalo	7	6	1	.538	Oakland	10	4	0	.714
Houston	6	8	0	.429	Kansas City	5	7	2	.417
N.Y. Jets	5	8	1	.385	Denver	2	11	1	.154
Eastern Division playoff: Boston 26, BUFFALO 8								
AFL Championship: SAN DIEGO 51, Boston 10								

1964

The New York Jets move from the old Polo Grounds to newly built Shea Stadium in Queens. Shea becomes the first automatically convertible stadium, able to accommodate both the Jets and baseball's Mets by rotating two sections of stands.

Many interior linemen and linebackers join most quarterbacks, running backs, and receivers in wearing lowcut, lightweight shoes. Houston end Charley Hennigan sets the all-time single-season reception record with 101.

Before 79,544 at Cleveland's Municipal Stadium, quarterback Frank Ryan of the Browns directs one of the major upsets in football history, a 27-0 victory over the Baltimore Colts in the NFL Championship.

Jack Kemp passes for 188 yards and Cookie Gilchrist rushes for 122 more, helping Buffalo to a 20-7 victory over San Diego in the AFL Championship Game.

1. From 1957-1965, Cleveland's Jim Brown was pro football's quintessential runner.
2. Buffalo's Cookie Gilchrist scores one of five TDs en route to a 243-yard rushing performance against the Jets in 1963.
3. In the 1964 NFL title game, Cleveland's Gary Collins broke clear for an 18-yard scoring pass, his first of three in a 27-0 upset of Baltimore.
4. In the Dallas Cowboys' inaugural season of 1960, they failed to win a single game, but tied the New York Giants 31-31.
5. Y. A. Tittle's seven touchdown passes tied an NFL record and helped the Giants to a 49-34 win over Washington in 1963.

1964 NFL								
EASTERN CONFERENCE				**WESTERN CONFERENCE**				
	W	L	T	Pct.		W	L	T	Pct.
Cleveland	10	3	1	.769	Baltimore	12	2	0	.857
St. Louis	9	3	2	.750	Green Bay	8	5	1	.615
Philadelphia	6	8	0	.429	Minnesota	8	5	1	.615
Washington	6	8	0	.429	Detroit	7	5	2	.583
Dallas	5	8	1	.385	Los Angeles	5	7	2	.417
Pittsburgh	5	9	0	.357	Chicago	5	9	0	.357
N.Y. Giants	2	10	2	.167	San Francisco	4	10	0	.286
NFL Championship: CLEVELAND 27, Baltimore 0								

1964 AFL								
EASTERN DIVISION				**WESTERN DIVISION**				
	W	L	T	Pct.		W	L	T	Pct.
Buffalo	12	2	0	.857	San Diego	8	5	1	.615
Boston Patriots	10	3	1	.769	Kansas City	7	7	0	.500
N.Y. Jets	5	8	1	.385	Oakland	5	7	2	.417
Houston	4	10	0	.286	Denver	2	11	1	.154
AFL Championship: BUFFALO 20, San Diego 7								

1965

In a memorable draft, the Chicago Bears take Illinois linebacker Dick Butkus and Kansas running back Gale Sayers.

The New York Jets secure the future of the AFL by outbidding the St. Louis Cardinals for Alabama quarterback Joe Namath.

San Francisco placekicker Tommy Davis misses a PAT, ending his all-time record consecutive string at 234.

Chicago's Gale Sayers becomes the third man in NFL history to score six touchdowns in one game. . .

Cleveland's Jim Brown is held to 50 yards by Green Bay. The Packers ease to a 23-12 NFL Championship Game victory. Buffalo dominates San Diego for the second straight year, winning 23-0 for the AFL.

1965 NFL								
EASTERN CONFERENCE				**WESTERN CONFERENCE**				
	W	L	T	Pct.		W	L	T	Pct.
Cleveland	11	3	0	.786	Green Bay	10	3	1	.769
Dallas	7	7	0	.500	Baltimore	10	3	1	.769
N.Y. Giants	7	7	0	.500	Chicago	9	5	0	.643
Washington	6	8	0	.429	San Francisco	7	6	1	.538
Philadelphia	5	9	0	.357	Minnesota	7	7	0	.500
St. Louis	5	9	0	.357	Detroit	6	7	1	.462
Pittsburgh	2	12	0	.143	Los Angeles	4	10	0	.286
Western Conference playoff: GREEN BAY 13, Baltimore 10								
NFL Championship: GREEN BAY 23, Cleveland 12								

1965 AFL								
EASTERN DIVISION				**WESTERN DIVISION**				
	W	L	T	Pct.		W	L	T	Pct.
Buffalo	10	3	1	.769	San Diego	9	2	3	.818
N.Y. Jets	5	8	1	.385	Oakland	8	5	1	.615
Boston Patriots	4	8	2	.333	Kansas City	7	5	2	.583
Houston	4	10	0	.286	Denver	4	10	0	.286
AFL Championship: Buffalo 23, SAN DIEGO 0								

1966

Secret meetings between Kansas City Chiefs' owner Lamar Hunt and Dallas Cowboys president Tex Schramm give way to Commissioner Pete Rozelle's stunning announcement on 8 June that the AFL and NFL will merge. The leagues announce that their champions will meet in a World Championship Game, the first one to be played following the 1966 season.

Built with a special emphasis on aesthetic appeal, Busch Memorial Stadium opens for business in St. Louis as the new home of the football and baseball Cardinals.

Completed in just 51 weeks for $18 million, multipurpose Atlanta Fulton County Stadium opens in time for the NFL's newest expansion franchise, the Atlanta Falcons. Atlanta's uniforms feature a Falcons logo on the sleeves with 'television' numbers on the top of the shoulders.

A new AFL team, the Miami Dolphins, opens play under the ownership of Minneapolis lawyer Joseph Robbie. George Wilson is the head coach. Dolphins' running back Joe Auer returns the opening kickoff 95 yards for a touchdown in the team's regular-season opener against Oakland, but the Raiders rally to win 23-14. The Dolphins finish the season with a 3-11 record.

Buffalo's bid for a third consecutive AFL title falls short as quarterback Len Dawson and rookie halfback Mike Garrett combine to lead Kansas City to a 31-7 rout in the Championship Game. The win puts AFL founder Lamar Hunt's team in the first Super Bowl.

Green Bay holds on in a classic shoot-out with Dallas to win 34-27 in the NFL Championship Game, giving them an historic chance to play in the first-ever Super Bowl.

1966 NFL

EASTERN CONFERENCE	W	L	T	Pct.	WESTERN CONFERENCE	W	L	T	Pct.
Dallas	10	3	1	.769	Green Bay	12	2	0	.857
Cleveland	9	5	0	.643	Baltimore	9	5	0	.643
Philadelphia	9	5	0	.643	Los Angeles	8	6	0	.571
St. Louis	8	5	1	.615	San Francisco	6	6	2	.500
Washington	7	7	0	.500	Chicago	5	7	2	.417
Pittsburgh	5	8	1	.385	Detroit	4	9	1	.308
Atlanta	3	11	0	.214	Minnesota	4	9	1	.308
N.Y. Giants	1	12	1	.077					

NFL Championship: Green Bay 34, DALLAS 27
Super Bowl I: Green Bay (NFL) 35, Kansas City (AFL) 10, at Memorial Coliseum, Los Angeles, California

1966 AFL

EASTERN DIVISION	W	L	T	Pct.	WESTERN DIVISION	W	L	T	Pct.
Buffalo	9	4	1	.692	Kansas City	11	2	1	.846
Boston Patriots	8	4	2	.677	Oakland	8	5	1	.615
N.Y. Jets	6	6	0	.500	San Diego	7	6	1	.538
Houston	3	11	0	.214	Denver	4	10	0	.286
Miami	3	11	0	.214					

AFL Championship: Kansas City 31, BUFFALO 7

1967

Attended by 63,035 fans, Super Bowl I is held at the Los Angeles Memorial Coliseum. Green Bay wins 35-10 as quarterback Bart Starr throws two touchdown passes to take MVP honours.

For the first time ever, the two leagues hold a combined draft as part of the merger agreement, and the NFL adds another franchise, the New Orleans Saints.

NFL and AFL teams meet for the first time in preseason play. With its 13-7 victory over Detroit, Denver becomes the first AFL team to defeat an NFL team.

Also for the first time, the NFL plays in four divisions: Capitol and Century in the Eastern Conference, and Coastal and Central in the Western Conference.

Joe Namath of the New York Jets becomes the first quarterback to throw for more than 4000 yards in a season, finishing with 4007, while St. Louis' Jim Bakken kicks an NFL-record seven field goals, to beat Pittsburgh single-handed.

1967 NFL

EASTERN CONFERENCE

Capitol Division	W	L	T	Pct.
Dallas	9	5	0	.643
Philadelphia	6	7	1	.462
Washington	5	6	3	.455
New Orleans	3	11	0	.214

Century Division	W	L	T	Pct.
Cleveland	9	5	0	.643
N.Y. Giants	7	7	0	.500
St. Louis	6	7	1	.462
Pittsburgh	4	9	1	.308

WESTERN CONFERENCE

Coastal Division	W	L	T	Pct.
Los Angeles	11	1	2	.917
Baltimore	11	1	2	.917
San Francisco	7	7	0	.500
Atlanta	1	12	1	.077

Central Division	W	L	T	Pct.
Green Bay	9	4	1	.692
Chicago	7	6	1	.538
Detroit	5	7	2	.417
Minnesota	3	8	3	.273

Los Angeles won division title on the basis of advantage in points (58-34) in two games vs Baltimore.
Conference championships: DALLAS 52, Cleveland 14; GREEN BAY 28, Los Angeles 7
NFL Championship: GREEN BAY 21, Dallas 17
Super Bowl II: Green Bay (NFL) 33, Oakland (AFL) 14, at Orange Bowl, Miami, Florida

1967 AFL

EASTERN DIVISION	W	L	T	Pct.	WESTERN DIVISION	W	L	T	Pct.
Houston	9	4	1	.692	Oakland	13	1	0	.929
N.Y. Jets	8	5	1	.615	Kansas City	9	5	0	.643
Buffalo	4	10	0	.286	San Diego	8	5	1	.615
Miami	4	10	0	.286	Denver	3	11	0	.214
Boston Patriots	3	10	1	.231					

AFL Championship: OAKLAND 40, Houston 7

1. Pittsburgh made a coaching change in 1969, hiring Chuck Noll.
2. Cincinnati head coach, Paul Brown inspected a variety of helmet designs for the new AFL team in 1968.
3. Pete Gogolak, shown here with the New York Giants, was pro football's first soccer-style kicker.
4. Green Bay's Jim Taylor joins the New Orleans Saints in 1967.
5. In 1967, Green Bay's Travis Williams is first player to return four kickoffs for touchdowns in a season.

part-owner and head coach.

With 1:05 remaining and the New York Jets leading the Oakland Raiders 32-29, NBC takes the game off the air to begin screening the movie *Heidi*. Fans go crazy. Meanwhile, the Raiders score twice in the closing minute to win 43-32. In response to the fans' outcry, NBC improvises by running the final score across the bottom of the screen during the movie. Even this fails, however, as the information crawls beneath the movie's most poignant scene.

In a meeting that lasts 35 hours and 45 minutes, NFL and AFL owners align the new NFL into two 13-team conferences. To balance the two, the Baltimore, Cleveland, and Pittsburgh franchises are included in the AFC, with the NFC retaining the other 13 NFL clubs.

On the field, the development of artificial turf and the influx of soccer-style kickers bring about the use of modified cleats on shoes. In Pittsburgh, Chuck Noll takes over as head coach of the hapless Steelers.

1968

Green Bay defends its world championship with a 33-14 thrashing of Oakland. Starr repeats as the game's most valuable player.

Another AFL franchise is born, this one in Cincinnati, nicknamed the Bengals. Paul Brown returns to football as the Bengals'

6. St. Louis' Jim Bakken kicks seven field goals against Pittsburgh in 1967 for an NFL record.
7. In 1968, the Chargers move to San Diego, and the excellent Jack Murphy Stadium.
8. Joe Kapp, Minnesota's enigmatic and ungainly quarterback, led his team to Super Bowl IV.
9. In 1969, Vince Lombardi switches clubs, moving to Washington as head coach and part-owner.

1968 NFL

EASTERN CONFERENCE				WESTERN CONFERENCE			
Capitol Division				**Coastal Division**			
	W	L	T	Pct.		W	L	T	Pct.
Dallas	12	2	0	.857	Baltimore	13	1	0	.929
N.Y. Giants	7	7	0	.500	Los Angeles	10	3	1	.769
Washington	5	9	0	.357	San Francisco	7	6	1	.538
Philadelphia	2	12	0	.143	Atlanta	2	12	0	.143
Century Division				**Central Division**			
	W	L	T	Pct.		W	L	T	Pct.
Cleveland	10	4	0	.714	Minnesota	8	6	0	.571
St. Louis	9	4	1	.692	Chicago	7	7	0	.500
New Orleans	4	9	1	.308	Green Bay	6	7	1	.462
Pittsburgh	2	11	1	.154	Detroit	4	8	2	.333

Conference championships: CLEVELAND 31, Dallas 20; BALTIMORE 24, Minnesota 14
NFL Championship: Baltimore 34, CLEVELAND 0
Super Bowl III: N.Y. Jets (AFL) 16, Baltimore (NFL) 7, at Orange Bowl, Miami, Florida

1968 AFL

EASTERN DIVISION				WESTERN DIVISION			
	W	L	T	Pct.		W	L	T	Pct.
N.Y. Jets	11	3	0	.786	Oakland	12	2	0	.857
Houston	7	7	0	.500	Kansas City	12	2	0	.857
Miami	5	8	1	.385	San Diego	9	5	0	.643
Boston Patriots	4	10	0	.286	Denver	5	9	0	.357
Buffalo	1	12	1	.077	Cincinnati	3	11	0	.214

Western Division playoff: OAKLAND 41, Kansas City 6
AFL Championship: N.Y. Jets 27, Oakland 23

1969

The New York Jets, led by quarterback Joe Namath, stun the heavily favoured Baltimore Colts 16-7 in Super Bowl III, striking a blow for AFL credibility.

1969 NFL

EASTERN CONFERENCE				WESTERN CONFERENCE			
Capitol Division				**Coastal Division**			
	W	L	T	Pct.		W	L	T	Pct.
Dallas	11	2	1	.846	Los Angeles	11	3	0	.786
Washington	7	5	2	.583	Baltimore	8	5	1	.615
New Orleans	5	9	0	.357	Atlanta	6	8	0	.429
Philadelphia	4	9	1	.308	San Francisco	4	8	2	.333
Century Division				**Central Division**			
	W	L	T	Pct.		W	L	T	Pct.
Cleveland	10	3	1	.769	Minnesota	12	2	0	.857
N.Y. Giants	6	8	0	.429	Detroit	9	4	1	.692
St. Louis	4	9	1	.308	Green Bay	8	6	0	.571
Pittsburgh	1	13	0	.071	Chicago	1	13	0	.071

Conference championships: Cleveland 38, DALLAS 14; MINNESOTA 23, Los Angeles 20
NFL Championship: MINNESOTA 27, Cleveland 7
Super Bowl IV: Kansas City (AFL) 23, Minnesota (NFL) 7, at Tulane Stadium, New Orleans, Louisiana

1969 AFL

EASTERN DIVISION				WESTERN DIVISION			
	W	L	T	Pct.		W	L	T	Pct.
N.Y. Jets	10	4	0	.714	Oakland	12	1	1	.923
Houston	6	6	2	.500	Kansas City	11	3	0	.786
Boston Patriots	4	10	0	.286	San Diego	8	6	0	.571
Buffalo	4	10	0	.286	Denver	5	8	1	.385
Miami	3	10	1	.231	Cincinnati	4	9	1	.308

Divisional playoffs: Kansas City 13, N.Y. JETS 6; OAKLAND 56, Houston 7
AFL Championship: Kansas City 17, OAKLAND 7

1970

The Kansas City Chiefs, led by quarterback Len Dawson, defeat the Minnesota Vikings 23-7 to win Super Bowl IV, levelling the AFL-NFL Super Bowl score at 2-2.

Pittsburgh owns the first pick of the draft and needs a quarterback. With Purdue's Mike Phipps available, the Steelers instead go for a strong-armed young man from little Louisiana Tech – Terry Bradshaw.

The Miami Dolphins get a new head coach, luring Don Shula from the Baltimore Colts. Don McCafferty replaces Shula as head coach of the Colts and will lead them to Super Bowl V, where they defeat Dallas.

After a year as part-owner, executive vice president, and head coach of the struggling Washington Redskins, Vince Lombardi dies of cancer at age 57.

1. 1970 saw Dallas win their first NFC championship. After beating the San Francisco 49ers 17-10, head coach Tom Landry greets star quarterback Craig Morton.
2. Buffalo's Marty Schottenheimer presented a real challenge when, as of 1970, all jerseys were made to bear the player's name. Schottenheimer became head coach of the Cleveland Browns 14 years later, to the chagrin of newspaper staff everywhere.
3. This carry in a 1973 game against the New York Jets put O. J. Simpson over the 2000-yard mark for the season.

1970

AMERICAN CONFERENCE EASTERN DIVISION					NATIONAL CONFERENCE EASTERN DIVISION				
	W	L	T	Pct.		W	L	T	Pct.
Baltimore	11	2	1	.846	Dallas	10	4	0	.714
Miami*	10	4	0	.714	N.Y. Giants	9	5	0	.643
N.Y. Jets	4	10	0	.286	St. Louis	8	5	1	.615
Buffalo	3	10	1	.231	Washington	6	8	0	.429
Boston Patriots	2	12	0	.143	Philadelphia	3	10	1	.231
CENTRAL DIVISION					**CENTRAL DIVISION**				
	W	L	T	Pct.		W	L	T	Pct.
Cincinnati	8	6	0	.571	Minnesota	12	2	0	.857
Cleveland	7	7	0	.500	Detroit*	10	4	0	.714
Pittsburgh	5	9	0	.357	Chicago	6	8	0	.429
Houston	3	10	1	.231	Green Bay	6	8	0	.429
WESTERN DIVISION					**WESTERN DIVISION**				
	W	L	T	Pct.		W	L	T	Pct.
Oakland	8	4	2	.667	San Francisco	10	3	1	.769
Kansas City	7	5	2	.583	Los Angeles	9	4	1	.692
San Diego	5	6	3	.455	Atlanta	4	8	2	.333
Denver	5	8	1	.385	New Orleans	2	11	1	.154

*Wild Card qualifier for playoffs
AFC divisional playoffs: BALTIMORE 17, Cincinnati 0; OAKLAND 21, Miami 14
AFC Championship: BALTIMORE 27, Oakland 17
NFC divisional playoffs: DALLAS 5, Detroit 0; San Francisco 17, MINNESOTA 14
NFC Championship: Dallas 17, SAN FRANCISCO 10
Super Bowl V: Baltimore (AFC) 16, Dallas (NFC) 13, at Orange Bowl, Miami, Florida

1971

Johnny Unitas forsakes his trademark – high-top black shoes – for one game – Super Bowl V – because of the need for special turf shoes.

In Super Bowl V at Miami's Orange Bowl, Dallas and Baltimore are tied 13-13 with nine seconds left. Colts placekicker Jim O'Brien lines up for a 32-yard field goal and nervously asks holder Earl Morrall about the wind. Morrall: 'There is no wind. Just kick the ball straight.' O'Brien does, and the Colts win.

Meanwhile, George Blanda, 43, puts together an incredible streak. He provides the tying or winning score in the closing seconds of four straight games.

Hailed as 'the first super stadium of the modern generation', Texas Stadium opens in the Dallas suburb of Irving. The stadium's distinction is a 2½ acre opening in its roof. The entire project costs a mere $15 million.

1971

AMERICAN CONFERENCE EASTERN DIVISION					NATIONAL CONFERENCE EASTERN DIVISION				
	W	L	T	Pct.		W	L	T	Pct.
Miami	10	3	1	.769	Dallas	11	3	0	.786
Baltimore*	10	4	0	.714	Washington*	9	4	1	.692
New England	6	8	0	.429	Philadelphia	6	7	1	.462
N.Y. Jets	6	8	0	.429	St. Louis	4	9	1	.308
Buffalo	1	13	0	.071	N.Y. Giants	4	10	0	.286
CENTRAL DIVISION					**CENTRAL DIVISION**				
	W	L	T	Pct.		W	L	T	Pct.
Cleveland	9	5	0	.643	Minnesota	11	3	0	.786
Pittsburgh	6	8	0	.429	Detroit	7	6	1	.538
Houston	4	9	1	.308	Chicago	6	8	0	.429
Cincinnati	4	10	0	.286	Green Bay	4	8	2	.333
WESTERN DIVISION					**WESTERN DIVISION**				
	W	L	T	Pct.		W	L	T	Pct.
Kansas City	10	3	1	.769	San Francisco	9	5	0	.643
Oakland	8	4	2	.667	Los Angeles	8	5	1	.615
San Diego	6	8	0	.429	Atlanta	7	6	1	.538
Denver	4	9	1	.308	New Orleans	4	8	2	.333

*Wild Card qualifier for playoffs
AFC divisional playoffs: Miami 27, KANSAS CITY 24, sudden death overtime; Baltimore 20, CLEVELAND 3
AFC Championship: MIAMI 21, Baltimore 0
NFC divisional playoffs: Dallas 20, MINNESOTA 12; SAN FRANCISCO 24, Washington 20
NFC Championship: DALLAS 14, San Francisco 3
Super Bowl VI: Dallas (NFC) 24, Miami (AFC) 3, at Tulane Stadium, New Orleans, Louisiana

1972

Despite a helping hand from President Richard Nixon, the Miami Dolphins are unable to solve the Dallas Cowboys' defense in Super Bowl VI. 'The Cowboys are a good defensive team,' Nixon told Miami coach Don Shula during the week before the game, 'but I think you can hit [wide receiver] Paul Warfield on that down-and-in pattern.' The Cowboys double-team Warfield, allowing him only four catches for 39 yards. The Dolphins' offense totals 185 yards, and Dallas wins 24-3.

Most running backs, quarterbacks, and wide receivers have switched to modified birdcage-type facemasks. One receiver, Don Maynard of the New York Jets, moves to the top of the NFL's all-time receiving list with catch number 632.

1972

AMERICAN CONFERENCE EASTERN DIVISION					NATIONAL CONFERENCE EASTERN DIVISION				
	W	L	T	Pct.		W	L	T	Pct.
Miami	14	0	0	1.000	Washington	11	3	0	.786
N.Y. Jets	7	7	0	.500	Dallas*	10	4	0	.714
Baltimore	5	9	0	.357	N.Y. Giants	8	6	0	.571
Buffalo	4	9	1	.321	St. Louis	4	9	1	.321
New England	3	11	0	.214	Philadelphia	2	11	1	.179
CENTRAL DIVISION					**CENTRAL DIVISION**				
	W	L	T	Pct.		W	L	T	Pct.
Pittsburgh	11	3	0	.786	Green Bay	10	4	0	.714
Cleveland*	10	4	0	.714	Detroit	8	5	1	.607
Cincinnati	8	6	0	.571	Minnesota	7	7	0	.500
Houston	1	13	0	.071	Chicago	4	9	1	.321
WESTERN DIVISION					**WESTERN DIVISION**				
	W	L	T	Pct.		W	L	T	Pct.
Oakland	10	3	1	.750	San Francisco	8	5	1	.607
Kansas City	8	6	0	.571	Atlanta	7	7	0	.500
Denver	5	9	0	.357	Los Angeles	6	7	1	.464
San Diego	4	9	1	.321	New Orleans	2	11	1	.179

*Wild Card qualifier for playoffs
AFC divisional playoffs: PITTSBURGH 13, Oakland 7; MIAMI 20, Cleveland 14
AFC Championship: Miami 21, PITTSBURGH 17
NFC divisional playoffs: Dallas 30, SAN FRANCISCO 28; WASHINGTON 16, Green Bay 3
NFC Championship: WASHINGTON 26, Dallas 3
Super Bowl VII: Miami (AFC) 14, Washington (NFC) 7, at Memorial Coliseum, Los Angeles, California

1973

The Miami Dolphins defeat the Washington Redskins 14-7 in Super Bowl VII at the Los Angeles Coliseum in January, completing the first 17-0 season ever.

In Washington, Congress adopts, for three years, experimental legislation requiring that any NFL game that has been declared a sellout 72 hours prior to kickoff be made available for local telecast.

In Green Bay, running back John Brockington finishes the season with 1144 yards rushing, becoming the only player to run for more than 1000 yards in each of his first three NFL seasons.

1973

AMERICAN CONFERENCE EASTERN DIVISION					NATIONAL CONFERENCE EASTERN DIVISION				
	W	L	T	Pct.		W	L	T	Pct.
Miami	12	2	0	.857	Dallas	10	4	0	.714
Buffalo	9	5	0	.643	Washington*	10	4	0	.714
New England	5	9	0	.357	Philadelphia	5	8	1	.393
Baltimore	4	10	0	.286	St. Louis	4	9	1	.321
N.Y. Jets	4	10	0	.286	N.Y. Giants	2	11	1	.179
CENTRAL DIVISION					CENTRAL DIVISION				
	W	L	T	Pct.		W	L	T	Pct.
Cincinnati	10	4	0	.714	Minnesota	12	2	0	.857
Pittsburgh*	10	4	0	.714	Detroit	6	7	1	.464
Cleveland	7	5	2	.571	Green Bay	5	7	2	.429
Houston	1	13	0	.071	Chicago	3	11	0	.214
WESTERN DIVISION					WESTERN DIVISION				
	W	L	T	Pct.		W	L	T	Pct.
Oakland	9	4	1	.679	Los Angeles	12	2	0	.857
Denver	7	5	2	.571	Atlanta	9	5	0	.643
Kansas City	7	5	2	.571	New Orleans	5	9	0	.357
San Diego	2	11	1	.179	San Francisco	5	9	0	.357

Wild Card qualifier for playoffs
Cincinnati won division title on the basis of a better conference record than Pittsburgh (8-3 to 7-4). Dallas won division title on the basis of a better point differential vs Washington (net 13 points)
AFC divisional playoffs: OAKLAND 33, Pittsburgh 14, MIAMI 34, Cincinnati 16
AFC Championship: MIAMI 27, Oakland 10
NFC divisional playoffs: MINNESOTA 27, Washington 20; DALLAS 27, Los Angeles 16
NFC Championship: Minnesota 27, DALLAS 10
Super Bowl VIII: Miami (AFC) 24, Minnesota (NFC) 7, at Rice Stadium, Houston, Texas

1974

The Miami Dolphins become the NFL's second repeat winners in the Super Bowl, defeating Minnesota (the Super Bowl's first two-time loser) 24-7 behind the record 145-yard performance of fullback Larry Csonka. The game is held on a cold, damp, and foggy day at Houston's Rice Stadium, and pregame complaints including Vikings' head coach Bud Grant's unhappiness at birds nesting in the locker room of his team's practice facility.

Johnny Unitas, arguably the finest quarterback ever, retires.

1974

AMERICAN CONFERENCE EASTERN DIVISION					NATIONAL CONFERENCE EASTERN DIVISION				
	W	L	T	Pct.		W	L	T	Pct.
Miami	11	3	0	.786	St. Louis	10	4	0	.714
Buffalo*	9	5	0	.643	Washington*	10	4	0	.714
New England	7	7	0	.500	Dallas	8	6	0	.571
N.Y. Jets	7	7	0	.500	Philadelphia	7	7	0	.500
Baltimore	2	12	0	.143	N.Y. Giants	2	12	0	.143
CENTRAL DIVISION					CENTRAL DIVISION				
	W	L	T	Pct.		W	L	T	Pct.
Pittsburgh	10	3	1	.750	Minnesota	10	4	0	.714
Cincinnati	7	7	0	.500	Detroit	7	7	0	.500
Houston	7	7	0	.500	Green Bay	6	8	0	.429
Cleveland	4	10	0	.286	Chicago	4	10	0	.286
WESTERN DIVISION					WESTERN DIVISION				
	W	L	T	Pct.		W	L	T	Pct.
Oakland	12	2	0	.857	Los Angeles	10	4	0	.714
Denver	7	6	1	.536	San Francisco	6	8	0	.429
Kansas City	5	9	0	.357	New Orleans	5	9	0	.357
San Diego	5	9	0	.357	Atlanta	3	11	0	.214

Wild Card qualifier for playoffs
St. Louis won division title because of a two-game sweep over Washington
AFC divisional playoffs: OAKLAND 28, Miami 26; PITTSBURGH 32, Buffalo 14
AFC Championship: Pittsburgh 24, OAKLAND 13
NFC divisional playoffs: MINNESOTA 30, St. Louis 14; LOS ANGELES 19, Washington 10
NFC Championship: MINNESOTA 30, Los Angeles 10
Super Bowl IX: Pittsburgh (AFC) 16, Minnesota (NFC) 6, at Tulane Stadium, New Orleans, Louisiana

5. Late in Super Bowl VII, Miami placekicker Garo Yepremian fumbles a passing attempt off a kick, and it's returned for a touchdown by Washington's Mike Bass.
6. Baltimore's Lydell Mitchell led the NFL in receptions in 1974 with 72, a new record for running backs.
7. After only five seasons as head coach of Pittsburgh, Chuck Noll leads his team to Super Bowl IX and comes away a winner.

4. New Orleans Saints' placekicker Tom Dempsey booms a record 63-yard field goal to beat Detroit in a 1970 game. Dempsey's defective foot was equipped with a specially made kicking boot.

THE POWER AND THE GLORY

The years since 1975 have seen football grow into a major world sport. In front of bigger crowds, the game keeps getting better, as it s players move to still greater heights of athletic prowess

A s they moved into the Pontiac Silverdome in 1975, the Detroit Lions became the first team to play under a Teflon roof. In the same year Walter Payton joined the Chicago Bears.

In this second section of a two-part look at the game since 1960, we chart the technology and the players that have taken football from strength to strength.

1975

Pittsburgh Steelers defeat Minnesota Vikings 16-6 in Super Bowl IX, the first of four NFL championships for the Steelers in a six-year span.

The Chicago Bears, drafting fourth, need a running back. After quarterback Steve Bartkowski (Atlanta), defensive tackle Randy White (Dallas), and guard Ken Huff (Baltimore) are picked, the Bears have to *settle* for Walter Payton.

As a service to spectators and television and radio audiences, NFL referees are equipped with small microphone and transmitter devices enabling them to announce, directly to fans, infractions and rules interpretations during the course of a game. A great aid to clarity.

1975

AMERICAN CONFERENCE
EASTERN DIVISION

	W	L	T	Pct.
Baltimore	10	4	0	.714
Miami	10	4	0	.714
Buffalo	8	6	0	.571
New England	3	11	0	.214
N.Y. Jets	3	11	0	.214

CENTRAL DIVISION

	W	L	T	Pct.
Pittsburgh	12	2	0	.857
Cincinnati*	11	3	0	.786
Houston	10	4	0	.714
Cleveland	3	11	0	.214

WESTERN DIVISION

	W	L	T	Pct.
Oakland	11	3	0	.786
Denver	6	8	0	.429
Kansas City	5	9	0	.357
San Diego	2	12	0	.143

NATIONAL CONFERENCE
EASTERN DIVISION

	W	L	T	Pct.
St. Louis	11	3	0	.786
Dallas*	10	4	0	.714
Washington	8	6	0	.571
N.Y. Giants	5	9	0	.357
Philadelphia	4	10	0	.286

CENTRAL DIVISION

	W	L	T	Pct.
Minnesota	12	2	0	.857
Detroit	7	7	0	.500
Chicago	4	10	0	.286
Green Bay	4	10	0	.286

WESTERN DIVISION

	W	L	T	Pct.
Los Angeles	12	2	0	.857
San Francisco	5	9	0	.357
Atlanta	4	10	0	.286
New Orleans	2	12	0	.143

*Wild Card qualifier for playoffs

Baltimore won division title on a two-game sweep over Miami.

AFC divisional playoffs: PITTSBURGH 28, Baltimore 10; OAKLAND 31, Cincinnati 28

AFC Championship: PITTSBURGH 16, Oakland 10

NFC divisional playoffs: LOS ANGELES 35, St. Louis 23; Dallas 17, MINNESOTA 14

NFC Championship: Dallas 37, LOS ANGELES 7

Super Bowl X: Pittsburgh (AFC) 21, Dallas (NFC) 17, at Orange Bowl, Miami, Florida

(Home teams in playoff games are indicated by capital letters.)

1976

The Super Bowl completes its first decade with the most entertaining and competitive rendition yet, as Pittsburgh's Terry Bradshaw fires a 64-yard touchdown pass to Lynn Swann, the final points of a 21-17 victory.

The Seattle Kingdome, located near the downtown area, opens in time for the expansion Seahawks to move in for their first NFL season. The Kingdome, built at a cost of $67 million, features the world's largest self-supporting concrete roof.

The expansion Tampa Bay Buccaneers begin play in Tampa Stadium, whose seating capacity is increased from the original 46,500 (in 1967) to 72,000. (The stadium now seats 74,315.)

In the stadiums themselves, 30-second clocks are installed at both ends of the field to indicate the amount of time remaining between the ready-to-play signal and the snap of the ball.

Many NFL teams feature new mesh-type jerseys as the older nylon styles are replaced. Wearing one of the new style jerseys, Buffalo Bills' running back O.J. Simpson reaches another milestone, setting an NFL

single-game record with 273 yards in a loss to Detroit.

The big draft gain of the year is defensive end Lee Roy Selmon, who goes to Tampa Bay in the first round.

1976								
AMERICAN CONFERENCE					**NATIONAL CONFERENCE**			
EASTERN DIVISION					**EASTERN DIVISION**			
	W	L	T	Pct.		W	L	T	Pct.
Baltimore	11	3	0	.786	Dallas	11	3	0	.786
New England*	11	3	0	.786	Washington*	10	4	0	.714
Miami	6	8	0	.429	St. Louis	10	4	0	.714
N.Y. Jets	3	11	0	.214	Philadelphia	4	10	0	.286
Buffalo	2	12	0	.143	N.Y. Giants	3	11	0	.214
CENTRAL DIVISION					**CENTRAL DIVISION**			
	W	L	T	Pct.		W	L	T	Pct.
Pittsburgh	10	4	0	.714	Minnesota	11	2	1	.821
Cincinnati	10	4	0	.714	Chicago	7	7	0	.500
Cleveland	9	5	0	.643	Detroit	6	8	0	.429
Houston	5	9	0	.357	Green Bay	5	9	0	.357
WESTERN DIVISION					**WESTERN DIVISION**			
	W	L	T	Pct.		W	L	T	Pct.
Oakland	13	1	0	.929	Los Angeles	10	3	1	.750
Denver	9	5	0	.643	San Francisco	8	6	0	.571
San Diego	6	8	0	.429	Atlanta	4	10	0	.286
Kansas City	5	9	0	.357	New Orleans	4	10	0	.286
Tampa Bay	0	14	0	.000	Seattle	2	12	0	.143

*Wild Card qualifier for playoffs

Baltimore won division title on the basis of a better division record than New England (7-1 to 6-2). Pittsburgh won division title because of a two-game sweep over Cincinnati. Washington won wild card berth over St. Louis because of a two-game sweep over Cardinals.

AFC divisional playoffs: OAKLAND 24, New England 21; Pittsburgh 40, BALTIMORE 14

AFC Championship: OAKLAND 24, Pittsburgh 7

NFC divisional playoffs: MINNESOTA 35, Washington 20; Los Angeles 14, DALLAS 12

NFC Championship: MINNESOTA 24, Los Angeles 13

Super Bowl XI: Oakland (AFC) 32, Minnesota (NFC) 14, at Rose Bowl, Pasadena, California

Pittsburgh's John Stallworth scores his second TD in Super Bowl III.

1. Running back Rocky Bleier (20) in Pittsburgh's Super Bowl IX clash with Minnesota.
2. Dallas' Robert Newhouse hits the deck in Super Bowl X.
3. The great O. J. Simpson was the game's star rusher of the '70s.
4. Super Bowl XI's MVP Fred Biletnikoff takes one of the key receptions that led to 32-14 win.

1977

It's the Oakland Raiders' day at the Rose Bowl in Pasadena, California, as they take a 16-0 halftime lead en route to a 32-14 victory over Minnesota in Super Bowl XI. The loss is the fourth in as many appearances for the Vikings.

Tampa Bay has the first choice of the draft again, and must decide between two running backs, USC's Ricky Bell and Tony Dorsett of Pittsburgh. They take Bell, leaving Dorsett for the Cowboys, who have moved up after a trade with Seattle.

Borrowing from baseball's batting gloves, many wide receivers and defensive backs wear gloves regardless of weather conditions. And on 4 December, the visiting Cincinnati Bengals defeat the Kansas City Chiefs 27-7 in the 5000th game in NFL history. On another happy note, the Tampa Bay Buccaneers defeat the New Orleans Saints 33-14 to end the longest streak in history of 26 games.

1977								
AMERICAN CONFERENCE					**NATIONAL CONFERENCE**			
EASTERN DIVISION					**EASTERN DIVISION**			
	W	L	T	Pct.		W	L	T	Pct.
Baltimore	10	4	0	.714	Dallas	12	2	0	.857
Miami	10	4	0	.714	Washington	9	5	0	.643
New England	9	5	0	.643	St. Louis	7	7	0	.500
N.Y. Jets	3	11	0	.214	Philadelphia	5	9	0	.357
Buffalo	3	11	0	.214	N.Y. Giants	5	9	0	.357
CENTRAL DIVISION					**CENTRAL DIVISION**			
	W	L	T	Pct.		W	L	T	Pct.
Pittsburgh	9	5	0	.643	Minnesota	9	5	0	.643
Houston	8	6	0	.571	Chicago*	9	5	0	.643
Cincinnati	8	6	0	.571	Detroit	6	8	0	.429
Cleveland	6	8	0	.429	Green Bay	4	10	0	.286
					Tampa Bay	2	12	0	.143
WESTERN DIVISION					**WESTERN DIVISION**			
	W	L	T	Pct.		W	L	T	Pct.
Denver	12	2	0	.857	Los Angeles	10	4	0	.714
Oakland*	11	3	0	.786	Atlanta	7	7	0	.500
San Diego	7	7	0	.500	San Francisco	5	9	0	.357
Seattle	5	9	0	.357	New Orleans	3	11	0	.214
Kansas City	2	12	0	.143					

*Wild-Card qualifier for playoffs

Baltimore won division title on the basis of a better conference record than Miami (9-3 to 8-4). Chicago won wild card berth over Washington on the basis of best net points in conference games (plus 48 net points to plus 4).

AFC divisional playoffs: DENVER 34, Pittsburgh 21; Oakland 37, BALTIMORE 31 (sudden-death overtime)

AFC Championship: DENVER 20, Oakland 17

NFC divisional playoffs: DALLAS 37, Chicago 7; Minnesota 14, LOS ANGELES 7

NFC Championship: DALLAS 23, Minnesota 6

Super Bowl XII: Dallas (NFC) 27, Denver (AFC) 10, at Louisiana Superdome, New Orleans, Louisiana

1978

The Super Bowl moves indoors, to the Louisiana Superdome in New Orleans, for game XII, as the Dallas Cowboys defeat the Denver Broncos 27-10.

The draft delights teams looking for wide receivers. New Orleans, choosing third, grabs Florida's Wes Chandler. Green Bay, with the sixth pick, takes Stanford's James Lofton. San Diego, eager to get some help for Dan Fouts, selects Arizona State's John Jefferson with the fourteenth choice.

On the field, Minnesota's Rickey Young sets an all-time record for receptions by a running back leading all NFL receivers with 88.

Quarterbacks Joe Namath and Fran Tarkenton retire from football.

1978

AMERICAN CONFERENCE EASTERN DIVISION	W	L	T	Pct.
New England	11	5	0	.688
Miami*	11	5	0	.688
N.Y. Jets	8	8	0	.500
Buffalo	5	11	0	.313
Baltimore	5	11	0	.313

CENTRAL DIVISION	W	L	T	Pct.
Pittsburgh	14	2	0	.875
Houston*	10	6	0	.625
Cleveland	8	8	0	.500
Cincinnati	4	12	0	.250

WESTERN DIVISION	W	L	T	Pct.
Denver	10	6	0	.625
Oakland*	9	7	0	.563
Seattle	9	7	0	.563
San Diego	9	7	0	.563
Kansas City	4	12	0	.250

NATIONAL CONFERENCE EASTERN DIVISION	W	L	T	Pct.
Dallas	12	4	0	.750
Philadelphia*	9	7	0	.563
Washington	8	8	0	.500
St. Louis	6	10	0	.375
N.Y. Giants	6	10	0	.375

CENTRAL DIVISION	W	L	T	Pct.
Minnesota	8	7	1	.531
Green Bay	8	7	1	.531
Detroit	7	9	0	.438
Chicago	7	9	0	.438
Tampa Bay	5	11	0	.313

WESTERN DIVISION	W	L	T	Pct.
Los Angeles	12	4	0	.750
Atlanta*	9	7	0	.563
New Orleans	7	9	0	.438
San Francisco	2	14	0	.125

*Wild Card qualifier for playoffs
New England won division title on the basis of a better division record than Miami (6-2 to 5-3). Minnesota won division title because of a better head-to-head record against Green Bay (1-0-1).
AFC first-round playoff: Houston 17, MIAMI 9
AFC divisional playoffs: Houston 31, NEW ENGLAND 14; PITTSBURGH 33, Denver 10
AFC Championship: PITTSBURGH 34, Houston 5
NFC first-round playoff: ATLANTA 14, Philadelphia 13
NFC divisional playoffs: DALLAS 27, Atlanta 20; LOS ANGELES 34, Minnesota 10
NFC Championship: Dallas 28, LOS ANGELES 0
Super Bowl XIII: Pittsburgh (AFC) 35, Dallas (NFC) 31, at Orange Bowl, Miami, Florida

1979

The Super Bowl gets its first re-match, as Dallas meets Pittsburgh at the Orange Bowl in Game XIII. The two teams play with the same competitive fire they showed in Game X (on 18 January 1976), and the same team wins. Quarterback Terry Bradshaw, the game's most valuable player, throws four touchdown passes in the Steelers' 35-31 victory.

In the draft, San Francisco has some luck. With the last pick of the third round, the 49ers choose a quarterback, Notre Dame's Joe Montana.

Tear-away jerseys are outlawed. Steelers' offensive linemen begin a trend toward tightly fitted jerseys offering opponents less opportunity to grab and use hands effectively.

San Diego quarterback Dan Fouts finishes the season with 4082 yards passing.

1979

AMERICAN CONFERENCE EASTERN DIVISION	W	L	T	Pct.
Miami	10	6	0	.625
New England	9	7	0	.563
N.Y. Jets	8	8	0	.500
Buffalo	7	9	0	.438
Baltimore	5	11	0	.313

CENTRAL DIVISION	W	L	T	Pct.
Pittsburgh	12	4	0	.750
Houston*	11	5	0	.688
Cleveland	9	7	0	.563
Cincinnati	4	12	0	.250

WESTERN DIVISION	W	L	T	Pct.
San Diego	12	4	0	.750
Denver*	10	6	0	.625
Seattle	9	7	0	.563
Oakland	9	7	0	.563
Kansas City	7	9	0	.438

NATIONAL CONFERENCE EASTERN DIVISION	W	L	T	Pct.
Dallas	11	5	0	.688
Philadelphia*	11	5	0	.688
Washington	10	6	0	.625
N.Y. Giants	6	10	0	.375
St. Louis	5	11	0	.313

CENTRAL DIVISION	W	L	T	Pct.
Tampa Bay	10	6	0	.625
Chicago*	10	6	0	.625
Minnesota	7	9	0	.438
Green Bay	5	11	0	.313
Detroit	2	14	0	.125

WESTERN DIVISION	W	L	T	Pct.
Los Angeles	9	7	0	.563
New Orleans	8	8	0	.500
Atlanta	6	10	0	.375
San Francisco	2	14	0	.125

*Wild Card qualifier for playoffs
Dallas won division title because of a better conference record than Philadelphia (10-2 to 9-3). Tampa Bay won division title because of a better division record than Chicago (6-2 to 5-3). Chicago won a wild card berth over Washington on the basis of best net points in all games (plus 57 net points to plus 53).
AFC first-round playoff: HOUSTON 13, Denver 7
AFC divisional playoffs: Houston 17, SAN DIEGO 14; PITTSBURGH 34, Miami 14
AFC Championship: PITTSBURGH 27, Houston 13
NFC first-round playoff: PHILADELPHIA 27, Chicago 17
NFC divisional playoffs: TAMPA BAY 24, Philadelphia 17; Los Angeles 21, DALLAS 19
NFC Championship: Los Angeles 9, TAMPA BAY 0
Super Bowl XIV: Pittsburgh (AFC) 31, Los Angeles (NFC) 19, at Rose Bowl, Pasadena, California.

1980

Pittsburgh becomes the first team to win four Super Bowls, spoiling the Los Angeles Rams' first Super Bowl appearance with a 31-19 victory in Game XIV, played at the Rose Bowl in Pasadena, California, before a live audience of 103,985 and a record number of television viewers, more than 35.3 million.

Seattle switches to white shoes, leaving only Minnesota wearing black, and Oakland Raiders' cornerback Lester Hayes is the NFL's leading interceptor with 13, the most since Dick Night Train Lane's NFL record 14 in 1951.

Dan Fouts breaks his one-year-old single-season passing yardage record, finishing 1980 with 4715 yards and leading the AFC west champion Chargers to the AFC Championship Game.

1980

AMERICAN CONFERENCE EASTERN DIVISION	W	L	T	Pct.
Buffalo	11	5	0	.688
New England	10	6	0	.625
Miami	8	8	0	.500
Baltimore	7	9	0	.438
N.Y. Jets	4	12	0	.250

CENTRAL DIVISION	W	L	T	Pct.
Cleveland	11	5	0	.688
Houston*	11	5	0	.688
Pittsburgh	9	7	0	.563
Cincinnati	6	10	0	.375

WESTERN DIVISION	W	L	T	Pct.
San Diego	11	5	0	.688
Oakland*	11	5	0	.688
Kansas City	8	8	0	.500
Denver	8	8	0	.500
Seattle	4	12	0	.250

NATIONAL CONFERENCE EASTERN DIVISION	W	L	T	Pct.
Philadelphia	12	4	0	.750
Dallas*	12	4	0	.750
Washington	6	10	0	.375
St. Louis	5	11	0	.313
N.Y. Giants	4	12	0	.250

CENTRAL DIVISION	W	L	T	Pct.
Minnesota	9	7	0	.563
Detroit	9	7	0	.563
Chicago	7	9	0	.438
Tampa Bay	5	10	1	.344
Green Bay	5	10	1	.344

WESTERN DIVISION	W	L	T	Pct.
Atlanta	12	4	0	.750
Los Angeles*	11	5	0	.688
San Francisco	6	10	0	.375
New Orleans	1	15	0	.063

*Wild-Card qualifier for playoffs
Philadelphia won division title over Dallas on the basis of best net points in division games (plus 84 net points to plus 50). Minnesota won division title because of a better conference record than Detroit (8-4 to 9-5). Cleveland won division title because of a better conference record than Houston (8-4 to 7-5). San Diego won division title over Oakland on the basis of best net points in division games (plus 60 net points to plus 37).
AFC first-round playoff: OAKLAND 27, Houston 7
AFC divisional playoffs: SAN DIEGO 20, Buffalo 14; Oakland 14, CLEVELAND 12
AFC Championship: Oakland 34, SAN DIEGO 27
NFC first-round playoff: DALLAS 34, Los Angeles 13
NFC divisional playoffs: PHILADELPHIA 31, Minnesota 16; Dallas 30, ATLANTA 27
NFC Championship: PHILADELPHIA 20, Dallas 7
Super Bowl XV: Oakland (AFC) 27, Philadelphia (NFC) 10, at Louisiana Superdome, New Orleans, Louisiana

1981

Oakland quarterback Jim Plunkett, cast off by New England and San Francisco in the late 1970s, completes a heroic comeback, throwing three touchdown passes to lead the Raiders to a 27-10 victory over Philadelphia in Super Bowl XV and is named most valuable player.

NFL rules-makers clean up the game by outlawing the use of 'stickum', a tacky glue-like substance used by receivers and defensive backs on their hands to help them catch the ball. Oakland Raiders' corner-back Lester Hayes was one such abuser.

Getting even stronger, Dan Fouts hikes his single-season passing record by approximately the length of the playing field, finishing the year with 4802 yards.

1981							

AMERICAN CONFERENCE EASTERN DIVISION

	W	L	T	Pct.
Miami	11	4	1	.719
N.Y. Jets*	10	5	1	.656
Buffalo	10	6	0	.625
Baltimore	2	14	0	.125
New England	2	14	0	.125

CENTRAL DIVISION

	W	L	T	Pct.
Cincinnati	12	4	0	.750
Pittsburgh	8	8	0	.500
Houston	7	9	0	.438
Cleveland	5	11	0	.313

WESTERN DIVISION

	W	L	T	Pct.
San Diego	10	6	0	.625
Denver	10	6	0	.625
Kansas City	9	7	0	.563
Oakland	7	9	0	.438
Seattle	6	10	0	.375

NATIONAL CONFERENCE EASTERN DIVISION

	W	L	T	Pct.
Dallas	12	4	0	.750
Philadelphia*	10	6	0	.625
N.Y. Giants	9	7	0	.563
Washington	8	8	0	.500
St. Louis	7	9	0	.438

CENTRAL DIVISION

	W	L	T	Pct.
Tampa Bay	9	7	0	.563
Detroit	8	8	0	.500
Green Bay	8	8	0	.500
Minnesota	7	9	0	.438
Chicago	6	10	1	.375

WESTERN DIVISION

	W	L	T	Pct.
San Francisco	13	3	0	.813
Atlanta	7	9	0	.438
Los Angeles	6	10	0	.375
New Orleans	4	12	0	.250

*Wild-Card qualifier for playoffs

San Diego won AFC Western title over Denver on the basis of a better division record (6-2 to 5-3). Buffalo won a Wild-Card playoff berth over Denver as the result of a 9-7 victory in head-to-head competition.

AFC first-round playoff: Buffalo 31, NEW YORK JETS 27

AFC divisional playoffs: San Diego 41, MIAMI 38 (sudden-death overtime); CINCINNATI 28, Buffalo 21

AFC Championship: CINCINNATI 27, San Diego 7

NFC first-round playoff: New York Giants 27, PHILADELPHIA 21

NFC divisional playoffs: DALLAS 28, Tampa Bay 0; SAN FRANCISCO 38, New York Giants 24

NFC Championship: SAN FRANCISCO 28, Dallas 27

Super Bowl XVI: San Francisco (NFC) 26, Cincinnati (AFC) 21, at the Silverdome, Pontiac, Michigan

1982

In the opening round of the AFC playoffs, Dan Fouts and his San Diego Chargers jump to a 24-0 lead before Miami makes it 24-24 in the third quarter. The Chargers win 41-38 in overtime, on a field goal by Rolf Benirschke. Speculation begins as to whether this is the greatest pro football game ever played.'

With just under a minute to play in the NFC Championship Game, San Francisco wide receiver Dwight Clark leaps high in the Dallas end zone. Joe Montana's pass, thrown under a heavy rush, hangs as if permanently suspended. Clark grabs it. The 49ers have a 28-27 victory and their first Super Bowl berth.

Arctic conditions in Detroit create a massive traffic jam outside Super Bowl XVI at

1. In 1979, Dan Fouts broke Joe Namath's record.

2. Joe Montana (16) in Super Bowl XVI.

3. Rickey Young on the way to setting a record of 88 receptions in '78.

4. Dallas QB Roger Staubach (12) hands off to Robert Newhouse (44) in Super Bowl XIII.

5. Steelers celebrate winning Super Bowl XV.

6. Oakland running back Mark van Eeghen.

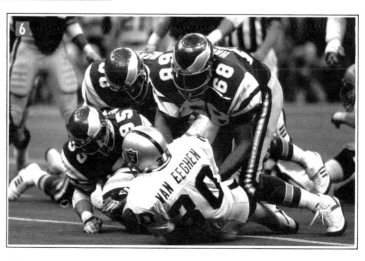

the Pontiac Silverdome. The San Francisco 49ers' team bus arrives a mere 45 minutes before kickoff. Joe Montana leads the 49ers to a 26-21 victory over the Cincinnati Bengals, passing for one touchdown and running for another to earn the most valuable player honours.

In one of the great draft choices of the decade, the Raiders pick Marcus Allen.

1982

AMERICAN CONFERENCE				NATIONAL CONFERENCE			
	W	L	T	Pct.		W	L	T	Pct.
L.A. Raiders	8	1	0	.889	Washington	8	1	0	.889
Miami	7	2	0	.778	Dallas	6	3	0	.667
Cincinnati	7	2	0	.778	Green Bay	5	3	1	.611
Pittsburgh	6	3	0	.667	Minnesota	5	4	0	.556
San Diego	6	3	0	.667	Atlanta	5	4	0	.556
N.Y. Jets	6	3	0	.667	St. Louis	5	4	0	.556
New England	5	4	0	.556	Tampa Bay	5	4	0	.556
Cleveland	4	5	0	.444	Detroit	4	5	0	.444
Buffalo	4	5	0	.444	New Orleans	4	5	0	.444
Seattle	4	5	0	.444	N.Y. Giants	4	5	0	.444
Kansas City	3	6	0	.333	San Francisco	3	6	0	.333
Denver	2	7	0	.222	Chicago	3	6	0	.333
Houston	1	8	0	.111	Philadelphia	3	6	0	.333
Baltimore	0	8	1	.056	L.A. Rams	2	7	0	.222

As a result of the players' 57-day strike, the 1982 NFL regular-season schedule was reduced from 16 weeks to 9. At the conclusion of the regular season, the NFL conducted a 16-team postseason Super Bowl Tournament. Eight teams from each conference were seeded 1-8 based on their records during the season.

Miami finished ahead of Cincinnati based on better conference record (6-1 to 6-2). Pittsburgh won common games tie-breaker with San Diego (3-1 to 2-1) after the Jets were eliminated from three-way tie based on conference record (Pittsburgh and San Diego 5-3 vs Jets 2-3). Cleveland finished ahead of Buffalo and Seattle based on better conference record (4-3 to 3-3 3-5). Minnesota (4-1), Atlanta (4-3), St. Louis (5-4) and Tampa Bay (3-3) seeds were determined by best won-lost record in conference games. Detroit finished ahead of New Orleans and the New York Giants based on better conference record (4-4 to 3-5 to 3-5).

AFC first-round playoff: MIAMI 28, New England 13
 LOS ANGELES RAIDERS 27, Cleveland 10
 New York Jets 44, CINCINNATI 17
 San Diego 31, PITTSBURGH 28
AFC second-round playoff: New York Jets 17, LOS ANGELES RAIDERS 14
 MIAMI 34, San Diego 13
AFC Championship: MIAMI 14, New York Jets 0
NFC first-round playoff: WASHINGTON 31, Detroit 7
 GREEN BAY 41, St. Louis 16
 MINNESOTA 30, Atlanta 24
 DALLAS 30, Tampa Bay 17
NFC second-round playoff: WASHINGTON 21, Minnesota 7
 DALLAS 37, Green Bay 26
NFC Championship: WASHINGTON 31, Dallas 17
Super Bowl XVII: Washington (NFC) 27, Miami (AFC) 17, at Rose Bowl, Pasadena, California

1983

John Riggins completes an amazing string of postseason rushing performances with a Super Bowl XVII showing that earns him most valuable player honours for his role in Washington's 27-17 victory over the Miami Dolphins.

Riggin's rushing yardage in the Redskins playoff sequence: 119 against Detroit in round one, 185 against Minnesota in round two, 140 against Dallas in the NFC Championship Game, and 166 yards in Super Bowl XVII. The Super Bowl total is a record, as are Riggins' 38 carries and his 43-yard scoring run.

A record six quarterbacks are taken on the first round as scouts hail this draft the best in more than a decade. The Dolphins,

picking twenty-seventh, can't get John Elway (Denver), Todd Blackledge (Kansas City), Jim Kelly (Buffalo), Tony Eason (New England), or Ken O'Brien (New York Jets), so they *settle* for Pittsburgh's Dan Marino. He leads Miami to a division title and is voted to the AFC-NFC Pro Bowl.

Rookie running backs chosen in the first round of the 1983 draft win the AFC and NFC rushing titles, and are instrumental in their clubs' reaching the playoffs: Eric Dickerson of the Rams is the league's leading ball carrier with 1808 yards. And Seattle's Curt Warner leads AFC rushers with 1449 yards, helping to lay the Seahawks' course to the AFC Championship Game.

In Washington, Riggins sets an all-time NFL record for touchdowns in one season, 24, breaking O.J. Simpson's 1975 mark by one. Meanwhile, most offensive linemen are wearing gloves to protect their hands.

1983

AMERICAN CONFERENCE EASTERN DIVISION					NATIONAL CONFERENCE EASTERN DIVISION				
	W	L	T	Pct.		W	L	T	Pct.
Miami	12	4	0	.750	Washington	14	2	0	.875
New England	8	8	0	.500	Dallas*	12	4	0	.750
Buffalo	8	8	0	.500	St. Louis	8	7	1	.531
Baltimore	7	9	0	.438	Philadelphia	5	11	0	.313
N.Y. Jets	7	9	0	.438	N.Y. Giants	3	12	1	.219
CENTRAL DIVISION					**CENTRAL DIVISION**				
	W	L	T	Pct.		W	L	T	Pct.
Pittsburgh	10	6	0	.625	Detroit	9	7	0	.563
Cleveland	9	7	0	.563	Green Bay	8	8	0	.500
Cincinnati	7	9	0	.438	Chicago	8	8	0	.500
Houston	2	14	0	.125	Minnesota	8	8	0	.500
					Tampa Bay	2	14	0	.125
WESTERN DIVISION					**WESTERN DIVISION**				
	W	L	T	Pct.		W	L	T	Pct.
L.A. Raiders	12	4	0	.750	San Francisco	10	6	0	.625
Seattle*	9	7	0	.563	L.A. Rams*	9	7	0	.563
Denver*	9	7	0	.563	New Orleans	8	8	0	.500
San Diego	6	10	0	.375	Atlanta	7	9	0	.438
Kansas City	6	10	0	.375					

*Wild Card qualifier for playoffs
Seattle and Denver gained Wild Card berths over Cleveland because of their victories over the Browns.
AFC first-round playoff: SEATTLE 31, Denver 7
AFC divisional playoffs: Seattle 27, MIAMI 20; L.A. RAIDERS 38, Pittsburgh 10
AFC Championship: L.A. RAIDERS 30, Seattle 14
NFC first-round playoff: Los Angeles Rams 24, DALLAS 17
NFC divisional playoffs: SAN FRANCISCO 24, Detroit 23; WASHINGTON 51, L.A. Rams 7
NFC Championship: WASHINGTON 24, San Francisco 21
Super Bowl XVIII: Los Angeles Raiders (AFC) 38, Washington (NFC) 9 at Tampa Stadium, Tampa, Florida.

1984

The Los Angeles Raiders defeat the Washington Redskins 38-9 in Super Bowl XVIII at Tampa Stadium on 22 January. Raiders running back Marcus Allen, voted the game's most valuable player, rushes for a Super Bowl record 191 yards on 20 carries, including the longest run from scrimmage in the game's history, a 74-yard touchdown carry.

Pittsburgh running back Franco Harris, needing only 363 yards to break Jim Brown's all-time NFL rushing record, is unable to come to terms in salary negotiations with the Steelers. The club waives him, clearing the way for Chicago's Walter Payton, only 325 yards behind Harris and 687 behind Brown, to set the new mark.

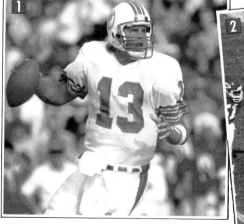

Harris is later picked up by Seattle after Curt Warner is injured.

In a season of superlative performances, Los Angeles Rams' running back Eric Dickerson breaks O.J. Simpson's single-season rushing record by totting up 2105 yards in only his second season – his 1808 in his rookie year also led the league. Dolphins' QB Dan Marino becomes the first passer to throw for over 5000 yards in a season, gaining 5084. He also set the record for most touchdowns thrown, at 48.

Meanwhile, Chicago's Walter Payton ran past Jim Brown's career rushing mark of 12,312 in week six, finishing 1984 with 13,309 yards. And San Diego's wide receiver Charlie Joiner overtook Charley Taylor for the all-time career receiving record, extending his total to 657.

1984

AMERICAN CONFERENCE EASTERN DIVISION				NATIONAL CONFERENCE EASTERN DIVISION			
	W	L	T	Pct.		W	L	T	Pct.
Miami	14	2	0	.875	Washington	11	5	0	.688
New England	9	7	0	.563	N.Y. Giants*	9	7	0	.563
N.Y. Jets	7	9	0	.438	St. Louis	9	7	0	.563
Indianapolis	4	12	0	.250	Dallas	9	7	0	.563
Buffalo	2	14	0	.125	Philadelphia	6	9	1	.407

CENTRAL DIVISION				CENTRAL DIVISION			
	W	L	T	Pct.		W	L	T	Pct.
Pittsburgh	9	7	0	.563	Chicago	10	6	0	.625
Cincinnati	8	8	0	.500	Green Bay	8	8	0	.500
Cleveland	5	11	0	.313	Tampa Bay	6	10	0	.375
Houston	3	13	0	.188	Detroit	4	11	1	.282
					Minnesota	3	13	0	.188

WESTERN DIVISION				WESTERN DIVISION			
	W	L	T	Pct.		W	L	T	Pct.
Denver	13	3	0	.813	San Francisco	15	1	0	.939
Seattle*	12	4	0	.750	L.A. Rams*	10	6	0	.625
L.A. Raiders*	11	5	0	.688	New Orleans	7	9	0	.438
Kansas City	8	8	0	.500	Atlanta	4	12	0	.250
San Diego	7	9	0	.438					

*Wild Card qualifier for playoffs

AFC first-round playoff: SEATTLE 13, Los Angeles Raiders 7
AFC divisional playoffs: MIAMI 31, Seattle 10; Pittsburgh 24, DENVER 17
AFC Championship: MIAMI 45, Pittsburgh 28
NFC first-round playoff: New York Giants 16, LOS ANGELES RAMS 13
NFC divisional playoffs: SAN FRANCISCO 21, New York Giants 10; Chicago 23, WASHINGTON 19
NFC Championship: SAN FRANCISCO 23, Chicago 0
Super Bowl XIX: San Francisco 38, Miami 16 at Stanford Stadium, Stanford, California.

1985

President Ronald Reagan took his second oath of office before tossing the coin for Super Bowl XIX on 20 January. Six million fans watch the game on television in the UK, with the game being won by San Francisco 38-16 over Miami.

NFL team owners adopt a resolution calling for a series of overseas preseason games, beginning in England in 1986. The Chicago Bears miss out on a perfect 16-0

1. Magic Marino – Miami's quarterback threw 5084 yards in '84 – an NFL record.
2. John Riggins (44) scores one of his record 24 TDs in '83 against Kansas City.
3. The key to Chicago's defense, Richard Dent was voted MVP of Super Bowl XX.
4. Marcus Allen's 191 rushing yards – set a Super Bowl record in '85.

regular season when they are beaten by the Miami Dolphins in week 13. And in the fiftieth NFL draft, defensive end Bruce Smith of Virginia Tech is taken by the Buffalo Bills first over all.

Despite their 11-5 regular-season record, the New England Patriots scramble through the playoffs to meet the Bears in Super Bowl XX. Leading the way was Pro Bowl running back Craig James.

1985

AMERICAN CONFERENCE EASTERN DIVISION				NATIONAL CONFERENCE EASTERN DIVISION			
	W	L	T	Pct.		W	L	T	Pct.
Miami	12	4	0	.750	Dallas	10	6	0	.625
N.Y. Jets*	11	5	0	.688	N.Y. Giants*	10	6	0	.625
New England*	11	5	0	.688	Washington	10	6	0	.625
Indianapolis	5	11	0	.313	Philadelphia	7	9	0	.438
Buffalo	2	14	0	.125	St. Louis	5	11	0	.313

CENTRAL DIVISION				CENTRAL DIVISION			
	W	L	T	Pct.		W	L	T	Pct.
Cleveland	8	8	0	.500	Chicago	15	1	0	.938
Cincinnati	7	9	0	.438	Green Bay	8	8	0	.500
Pittsburgh	7	9	0	.438	Minnesota	7	9	0	.438
Houston	5	11	0	.313	Detroit	7	9	0	.438
					Tampa Bay	2	14	0	.125

WESTERN DIVISION				WESTERN DIVISION			
	W	L	T	Pct.		W	L	T	Pct.
L.A. Raiders	12	4	0	.750	L.A. Rams	11	5	0	.688
Denver	11	5	0	.688	San Francisco*	10	6	0	.625
Seattle	8	8	0	.500	New Orleans	5	11	0	.313
San Diego	8	8	0	.500	Atlanta	4	12	0	.250
Kansas City	6	10	0	.375					

*Wild Card qualifier for playoffs

New York Jets gained first AFC Wild Card position on better conference record (9-3) over New England (8-4) and Denver (8-4). New England gained second AFC Wild Card position based on better record vs common opponents (4-2) than Denver (3-3). Dallas won NFC Eastern Division title based on better record (3-1) vs New York Giants (1-3) and Washington (1-3). New York Giants gained first NFC Wild Card position based on better conference record (8-4) over San Francisco (7-5) and Washington (6-6). San Francisco gained second NFC Wild Card position based on head-to-head victory over Washington.
AFC first-round playoff: New England 26, NEW YORK JETS 14
AFC divisional playoffs: MIAMI 24, Cleveland 21; New England 27, LOS ANGELES RAIDERS 20
AFC Championship: New England 31, MIAMI 14
NFC first-round playoff: NEW YORK GIANTS 17, San Francisco 3
NFC divisional playoffs: LOS ANGELES RAMS 20, Dallas 0; CHICAGO 21, New York Giants 0
NFC Championship: CHICAGO 24, Los Angeles Rams 0
Super Bowl XX: Chicago (NFC) 46, New England (AFC) 10, at Louisiana Superdome, New Orleans, Louisiana.

1986

Chicago annihilates New England 46-10 in Super Bowl XX in the Louisiana Superdome on 26 January. The game attracted 127 million TV fans in the U.S. alone. A tearful farewell for defensive co-ordinator Buddy Ryan who moves to Philadelphia as head coach. His '46' defense created the infamous 'Monsters of Midway II' a driving force in the Chicago Bears' unrivalled season.

Owners adopt the use of video replays as an officiating aid on controversial calls. This itself proves to be controversial, since on many occasions it was not used when it should have been. The New York Giants have nothing to complain about, however, as they power their way to the NFC title, and then destroy Denver 39-20 in Super Bowl XXI and snatch the game's ultimate accolade.

AIMING HIGH

A first-person insight into playing quarterback in the NFL by the man who has seen it all – from sacks to Super Bowl success

Joe Montana has personally led the San Francisco 49ers from the unwanted role of perennial also-rans into the brilliant sunlight reserved for champions in the 1980s. This feat is even more startling when you realize that many an NFL quarterback is stronger, faster, taller and has a better arm than the league's number one rated passer.

What separates Montana from his peers is acute 'game' intelligence – an absolutely uncanny ability to know what to do in every situation. There is simply no pro football player more magical under pressure. Montana's passes are perfectly timed and his running remains a constant threat.

Here, we 'sit in' on Joe Montana's observations on the game he plays so well.

ON FACING THE BIG GUYS

At a relatively normal height and weight (6 ft 2 in, 14 st 4 lb) the San Francisco 49ers' premier quarterback regularly faces the fierce onslaughts of the NFL's most physically awesome players.

Think of recent 49ers games against Chicago or Dallas, for example. Man-mountains like Dan Hampton (6 ft 5 in, 19 st 4 lb) and William 'the Refrigerator' Perry (6 ft 2 in, 22 st 7 lb) from the Bears and Randy White (6 ft 4 in, 18 st 11 lb) and Ed 'Too Tall' Jones (6 ft 9 in, 19 st 6 lb) from the Cowboys tend to attack quarterbacks like bulls go for matadors. A typically daunting prospect for Montana to contend with on succeeding Sunday afternoons.

'Some people make fun of my physique, being so thin. But sometimes I thank God I'm built the way I am because I'm a little bit lighter and have man-

Joe Montana is a leader in every respect. Although the NFL's top-rated passer is hardly the fastest, strongest, or longest throwing quarterback in the league, he does possess one of the game's best 'football minds'.

A PERSONAL VIEW BY

JOE MONTANA

Wide receiver Dwight Clark complements Montana's passing philosophy perfectly. A deceptively quick receiver with an incredible gift for finding holes in the secondary, Clark is also extremely sure-handed.

oeuvrability to get away from guys like this,' says the agile Montana.

'Even if I can't get away, at least I move enough so they don't get a solid hit. You have to depend on your linemen, and I think we have a great bunch of them up front. But every now and then somebody's going to get beat. I like our linemen to know that even if somebody does get through he's not always going to get me.'

ON COMMUNICATION WITH COACHES
While Montana is definitely the 49ers' 'field general', he accepts a lot of advice from the offensive co-ordinators high in a cordoned-off section of the press box at the very top of the stands.

Coach Sherman Lewis to Montana on the phone from upstairs: 'They're double-teaming Dwight [Clark, 49ers' wide receiver]. Let him go long and Russ [Francis, tight end] come in behind.' Montana to Lewis: 'They might not buy that, deep.' (Meaning Clark as a deep threat.) Lewis: 'Let Dwight clear out the middle, then, and send Russ into the gap.' Montana: 'Why not use that as a set-up [fake], then go to Dwight for the first [down]?'

Head coach Bill Walsh can arbitrate that and any decision as he deems fit, but he tends to let his quarterback defend his own choices. The watchwords here are mutual respect.

'Many things happen on the field that your coaches upstairs see somewhat differently than you do. When you get on the 'phone, one of the first things our coaches upstairs ask is, "What did you see?" When I go through and explain everything, being Italian I use my hands a little bit more than normal.

'It's just like any other conversation where there is a difference of opinion . . . But you can't get by without the help you

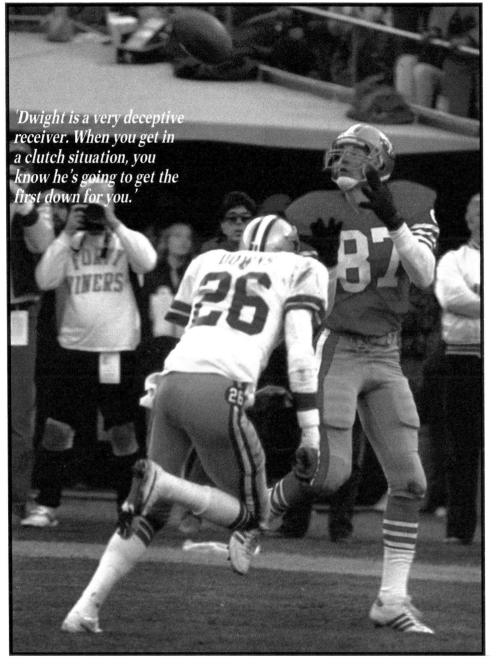

'Dwight is a very deceptive receiver. When you get in a clutch situation, you know he's going to get the first down for you.'

Consulting with coaches high up in the press box helps Montana to understand the defense better. 'Many things happen on the field that your coaches upstairs see somewhat differently than you do.'

get from upstairs. You might see part of the defense . . . you saw a key but you still don't know what the defense was. You come over and say, "What was the coverage here? I've seen this a couple of times, but I haven't been able to get the whole picture because of the rush."'

ON 49ERS RUNNING GAME
In 1985, Roger Craig set a San Francisco record for the number of single season receptions (92) and gained over 1000 yards (1016) doing it. This would've made for a great season, but Craig also happened to lead the 49ers in rushing (214 attempts for 1050 yards) at the same time. This is the stuff superstars are made of. His emergence means Joe Montana possesses a kind of

leverage and flexibility that any other quarterback in the league would envy.

'Our running game has helped our overall attack. The first few years I was here we really didn't have the quality of backs we have now. Guys like Roger Craig, who can run and catch the ball. Even though we feel Roger is a great runner inside, he's an exceptional open-field runner. It's good to finally get the chance to hand off the ball to

MAGNIFICENT SEVENTH
Although Montana is an automatic choice as number one quarterback for the 49ers, it wasn't always so. Even in college, as a student at Notre Dame University, South Bend, Indiana, Joe once calculated that he was only *seventh*-string quarterback!

guys like Roger or Joe Cribbs, and just stand back and watch them get through those holes and go after it. But it's tough going inside for a fullback and that's why we prefer to get him the ball on swing passes a lot.'

ON RAPPORT WITH DWIGHT CLARK

Superb wide receiver Dwight Clark's six-yard touchdown reception from Montana in the 1981 NFC Championship Game with only 51 seconds to play, not only defeated the Dallas Cowboys but sent San Francisco to its first Super Bowl, which it won. That catch drove out the demons that had haunted the 49ers since their infancy in 1946. The 49ers, finally, were no longer runners-up, and Clark was a decisive factor.

'Dwight is a very deceptive receiver. A lot of balls to him have been caught in medium range, but he can still get down the field. We don't use him down the field as much as we should. But when you get in a clutch situation, with him running a shallow pattern across the middle, you know he's going to get the first down for you. He's going to read it and he's going to find the hole.

'Some people say Dwight and I have a good rapport on and off the field and that helps. We both joined the 49ers together straight from university in 1979. Be that as it may, Dwight's main asset is his athletic ability and his ability to read defenses. Those would allow any quarterback to work well with him.'

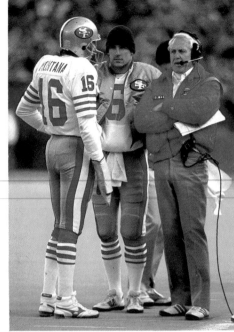
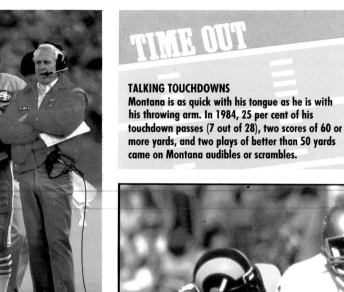

▲ With coach Bill Walsh and former back-up QB Matt Cavanaugh on the sideline, Montana must juggle opinions. 'Sometimes things get heated, but usually it's not between the three of us. It's usually on the phone.'

▼ Taking the defensive pressure off Montana is the double threat of Roger Craig. Catching 92 passes in 1985 plus running for 1050 yards, Craig gave defenses pause to think before rushing Montana.

TALKING TOUCHDOWNS
Montana is as quick with his tongue as he is with his throwing arm. In 1984, 25 per cent of his touchdown passes (7 out of 28), two scores of 60 or more yards, and two plays of better than 50 yards came on Montana audibles or scrambles.

'Our running game has helped our overall attack.' 'Roger [Craig] is a great runner inside, he's an exceptional open-field runner.'

Often lost in conversations about the San Francisco 49ers, in which the names of Montana, Craig and Clark dominate, running back Wendell Tyler was a force to be reckoned with. After an outstanding career with the Los Angeles Rams, Tyler was traded when a back named Eric Dickerson came along. Tyler quickly made his mark by setting a San Francisco season rushing record with 1262 in 1984, helping the team to Super Bowl XIX, it's first ever.

Tyler's presence in the San Francisco backfield means there is one more facet of Montana's game plan that can lead the 49ers to even further success.

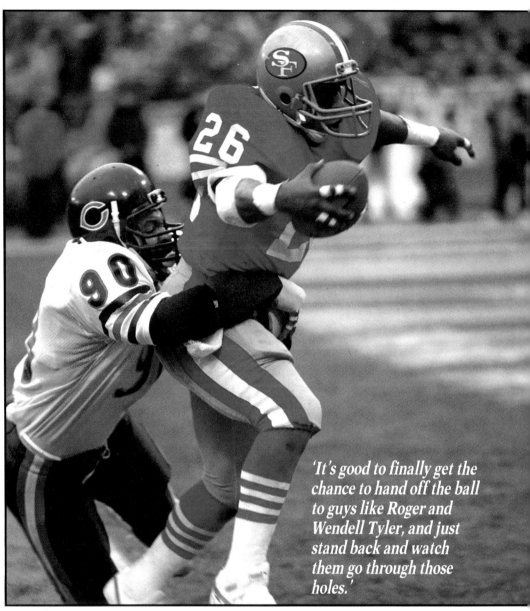

'It's good to finally get the chance to hand off the ball to guys like Roger and Wendell Tyler, and just stand back and watch them go through those holes.'

Any quarterback who is able to pass while on a *rollout* (moving across the backfield sideways) as well as when he drops back into the pocket has a great bargaining position at contract time.

ON ROLLING OUT

Montana's versatility as a passer-on-the-move and a runner when need be (five runs for 59 yards including a six-yard touchdown in Super Bowl XIX), makes opposing defenses wince whenever he chooses to roll out with the ball.

'We've gotten to the point where we are not just moving the pocket, but we are rolling out and throwing the ball. Something we need to do a little more of is throwing the ball to our left while rolling out. A lot of our rollouts have been to the right.

'Again, I think the ability to run the ball adds an extra something to our passing offense because when you get outside you really put a lot of pressure on the defense. They know that you not only can run, but you can throw the ball. We've thrown the ball quite a bit on the run, here and in college and I feel confident doing it.

'Any time you get a guy like Randy Cross or John Ayers or any one of our linemen out in front . . . it puts pressure on the defense to make a decision.'

ON THE SIDELINE CONFERENCE

With head coach Bill Walsh (one of the greatest offensive minds in NFL history) looking over Montana's shoulder, he could be forgiven if he was wary of disagreements. He isn't.

'With sideline conferences, Matt [Cavanaugh, former reserve quarterback] and I would get in a conservation about what they had been doing on defense, what Bill expects, what we should do, what we should be careful about if we are going to throw the ball.

'On the whole, these sideline meetings are pretty calm, but, as in anything else, the tighter the ball game, the more tense the situation. Sometimes things do get heated, but usually it's not between the three of us. It's usually on the phone.'

Mostly, though, Joe Montana does his talking on the field – where actions speak louder than words.

Fleet-footed Montana knows that no offensive line is impenetrable, and prides himself on the fact that he can scramble when he's in trouble. 'I like our linemen to know that even if somebody does get through he's not always going to get me.'

TAKING CH

An umpire signals a first down. Weighted yellow flags are thrown down to indicate a penalty.

ARGE

NFL officials must stand their ground in the vortex of violence that is pro football. Somehow they have to sort out the penalties from the permitted mayhem

O fficials are to professional football what traffic cops are to Manhattan the week before Christmas. It's their job to make order out of chaos.

Once the ball is snapped, each official's view suddenly becomes a five-second whirl of torsos, hands, arms, and legs as all hell breaks loose. At this moment, every man dressed in a shirt of vertical black and white stripes becomes an enforcer of the rules. He allows the assault (as long as it is legal) to flow around him, without intruding on its actions.

Considering there are over 60 separate penalties that can be called during the course of any game (from a five-yard infraction to the awarding of a touchdown), every NFL official has to be a complete master of his profession. Otherwise the game would turn into a free-for-all or simply grind to a screeching halt.

THE MAN WHO RUNS THE SHOW
Of the seven officials on the field (referee, umpire, head linesman, line judge, back judge, side judge and field judge), the *referee* is the final arbiter of any penalty given or rule disputed. In effect, the referee controls the game.

Taking a position in the backfield 10 to 12 yards behind the line of scrimmage, the referee's main task is to keep his eye on the quarterback during running and passing plays. He determines the legality of the snap, checks for any illegal motion and then stays with the QBs as long as the action surrounds them.

On passing plays, the referee drops back as the quarterback fades into the pocket, checking the legality of blocks by the offensive linemen, then directs his total concentration on the quarterback.

The referee has to do this. If he were to turn away for any reason while the defenders approached, he might well turn back

to the scene of the crime to find one dead quarterback, and a smiling 'Refrigerator'.

Anyone who witnessed the Chicago Bears' 1985 44-0 mauling of the Dallas Cowboys also saw Cowboys' quarterback Danny White knocked unconscious (and halfway out of Texas Stadium) then removed from the proceedings on a stretcher. If a quarterback's going to get concussed, the referee has to make sure it's all fair and square.

MIDDLE OF THE MAELSTROM
Watching over the giants in the trenches and that special breed called linebacker, the *umpire's* job is probably the most harrowing of any officiating position in pro football.

His domain is not for those of delicate temperament or who are fearful for their own safety. Indeed, there are some officials in the college and pro game who say they would never become umpires.

Lining up approximately four to five yards downfield, the umpire polices the line of scrimmage on every play, watching primarily for holding and illegal use of the hands by the offensive linemen, and for illegal head slaps by the defense.

Officials get together to confer over a decision. They may also be required to settle disputes between players on opposing teams.

It's a fine vantage point from which to view the explosion after the ball is snapped. It's also a great place to find yourself eating Astroturf and picking your teeth up off the ground.

Almost every NFL umpire incurs several moderate to severe injuries (everything from tearing cartilage to detached retinas) during his career. You can't make your living in the middle of a battlefield without getting hit by a stray linebacker sooner or later.

STERN STUFF
Retired umpire and former NFL fullback Pat Harder suffered only a chipped tooth in eight years as a player (when many players wore no facemasks), but got hit many times as an official. The worst came in San Diego, when a receiver coming across the middle struck him on the head.

Harder worked the following week, but on his way home from that game, he saw a flash of light in one eye. He knew immediately that it was the tipoff to an injury. The diagnosis: a detached retina. It cost him the final game of the 1981 season and playoff duty.

'In May after that year, I had open heart surgery for a four-way bypass,' Harder said. 'Three months later I worked my first preseason game. Early in the game I got

LADIES' MAN
Waiting to take the field before 80,000 fans at Tulane Stadium and a huge national television audience, referee Jim Tunney was on his first championship assignment – Super Bowl VI, 16 January 1972. He was asked by a young woman if he was refereeing the game. He told her he was and she asked if he was nervous. 'Me? No, I'm never nervous,' he told her. 'Really?' the woman said. 'Then what are you doing in the ladies' room?'

OFFICIALS' FIELD POSITIONS

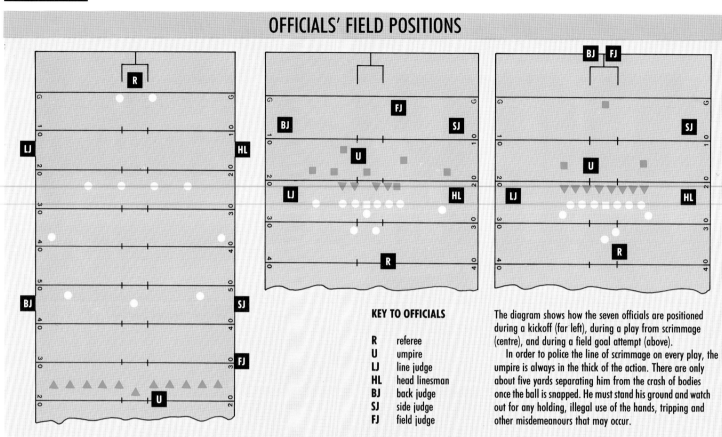

KEY TO OFFICIALS

R	referee
U	umpire
LJ	line judge
HL	head linesman
BJ	back judge
SJ	side judge
FJ	field judge

The diagram shows how the seven officials are positioned during a kickoff (far left), during a play from scrimmage (centre), and during a field goal attempt (above).

In order to police the line of scrimmage on every play, the umpire is always in the thick of the action. There are only about five yards separating him from the crash of bodies once the ball is snapped. He must stand his ground and watch out for any holding, illegal use of the hands, tripping and other misdemeanours that may occur.

The L.A. Raiders call vehemently for the decision and the official awards it to them, having untangled the truth from the jumble of players' bodies.

crunched, with a runner falling on my chest. To that point I was leery whether I could officiate all-out but when I got up everything, was okay.

JOB ON THE LINE

Compared to the bullets an umpire has to dodge 65 to 70 times a game, the *head lines-man* has it easy. He positions himself on the far side of the field right at the line of scrimmage and is responsible for ruling on offsides or any other kinds of encroachment prior to the snap.

On passing plays the head linesman is responsible for the receiver lined up closest to him. He will move with the receiver a limited way downfield (five to seven yards) and rule on any sideline plays in his area.

While he can't spread out a blanket and set down a picnic basket, the head linesman is not in the centre of traffic.

COURTING DANGER

It's a peculiar kind of court that's in session every autumn Sunday afternoon, but the offences commited are often of a brutal nature and so require swift and firm decisions. These are made by the four remaining officials on the field, the judges.

The *line judge* straddles the line of scrimmage on the other side of the field from the head linesman. He, too, is responsible for offside calls, but his primary responsibility is to rule whether or not the quarterback is behind or beyond the line of scrimmage when he throws a pass.

▲ The referee shows there's only inches to go for a first down. His remote controlled microphone ensures his verbal calls are heard by players and fans and the TV viewers watching coverage at home.
► A field judge raises his arms and calls a touchdown.

A safe and (relatively) secure 17 yards downfield, the *back judge* and *side judge* set up camp on opposite sides of the field.

The back judge concentrates on the wide receiver on his side. He is prepared to rule from a deep position on any actions taken against the receiver, or on holding or illegal use of hands by the receiver. He also rules on sideline plays in his area – if a pass receiver or runner is in or out of bounds.

The side judge mimics the back judge on his side of the field and also makes decisions involving catching, recovery, or illegal touching of a loose ball beyond the line of scrimmage. He is also responsible for making any clipping calls on punt returns.

The traffic is thinner, but faster where these two judges operate. They actually have to be able to move with world class sprinters in football gear (Willie Gault and James Lofton, for example) in order to render a valid decision.

On the other hand, they're far less likely to get hurt than the officials who arbitrate in the area around the trenches.

DISTANT VIEW

Last but not necessarily least, the *field judge* lines up a distant 25 yards downfield. Strange as it may seem binoculars are not part of his equipment. The action storms into his area fast and often.

The field judge concentrates on the movements of the tight end and observes the legality of the tight end's potential block(s) or of actions taken against him downfield. He also calls pass interference, fair catch infractions, and clipping by special team members on kick returns.

Whoever said, 'You can run, but you can't hide' did not have any NFL field judge in mind. While it may be true that a field judge would prefer wrestling with a man-eating shark rather than working one set of downs as an umpire, it's certainly not true that he is in any way cowardly. Pro football is a dangerous, exciting game. People get excited and people get hurt. Even field judges. During a game no place on an NFL football field is safe.

Nobody buys a ticket to watch the officials and that's the way it's supposed to be. The more invisible they are, the better they're doing their jobs. But no one should take them for granted either. The pressure to make *every* call a correct one is immense.

Bob Frederic, a referee in the NFL since 1968, sums it up this way.

'When I blow one I never admit it. I sure don't tell the team involved . . . although they know it and I know it. But then as officials, we're supposed to be perfect . . . So I guess I never made a mistake!'

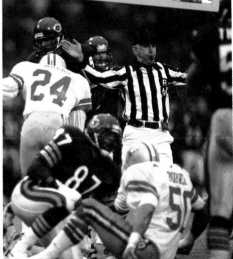

At the first 'American Bowl', between the Bears and the Cowboys at Wembley on 3 August 1986, referee Dick Jorgensen signals a touchdown.

THEATRES OF WAR

Set in the spectacular surroundings of Southern California, the Pasadena Rose Bowl has been a Super Bowl venue on three occasions. Seating well over 100,000, it was host for Super Bowl XXI.

INSIDE THE GAME

From the space-age scoreboard lighting up the sky to the perfect playing surface, many NFL stadiums are state-of-the-art results of the most advanced building technology available anywhere in the world

Pro football stadiums are the huge arenas where the modern gladiators of the gridiron game play out their struggles. But they are more than that. They are also factories that have turned football from a small-time college game into the biggest phenomena in the American entertainment industry.

Most NFL stadiums have seating capacities of between 50,000 and around 80,000. But it is the oldest stadium on the pro circuit – Soldier Field, home of the Chicago Bears – that holds football's attendance record. Though its normal seating capacity is 65,790, some 111,000 turned out on its dedication day on 27 November 1926 to watch the 29th Army-Navy game.

The latest batch of stadiums were completed during the 1970s. The Arrowhead stadium in Kansas City, home of the Chiefs, was completed in 1972 as part of the Harry S. Truman complex which comprises a 78,067-seat football stadium and a 42,500-seat baseball stadium. It cost $54 million, all raised by the sale of bonds.

The theatre-style seats have arm-rests and leg-room that is not bettered by any other stadium in pro football, but the massive structure is thought of as 'intimate' by spectators. There are no pillars to obstruct their view. From every seat, every fan can see every part of the field. And it is a 'true' bowl, with every seat facing the centre of the field.

MODERN COLISEUMS

The Giants' stadium in the New Jersey Meadowlands, just across the river from New York City, is a football-only stadium which is also now home to the New York Jets. But the Giants are proud not only of their new stadium, but also of the 24,000 capacity parking lot too. They reckon that all the fans should be out of the stadium and away from the stadium complex within half an hour of the final gun.

High living in Dallas means watching the game from one of the Texas Stadium's 178

circle suites. To buy a 40-year lease on one, the occupant has to buy $50,000 worth of stadium bonds, purchase their own furnishings and buy 12 season tickets a year.

Opened in 1971, the stadium is half-domed – the field is exposed to the elements but the spectators are under cover. This creates problems with the contrast between light and shade. But the architects thought that enclosing the stadium completely would create even more problems with heat and ventilation.

Dallas's neighbour Houston does have a domed stadium though – the Houston Astrodome. The home of the Oilers is named after the NASA Space Center in the City and

TIME OUT

PACKERS' TWIN PACK
Green Bay Packers are the only team in the NFL to have two domed stadiums. They are also the only team to be publicly owned, being kept in business by stock subscription.

But it means they have to do some travelling around. They have to play both in the small municipality of Green Bay – at Lambeau Field which they share with the local high school teams – and in the nearby city of Milwaukee, in Milwaukee County Stadium which they share with the small-time Milwaukee Brewers baseball team.

▲ Seating 80,638, the stupendous Pontiac Silverdome was the first stadium to be built with a Teflon-covered inflatable roof.
▶ Nicknamed 'The Gold Rush', the San Francisco cheerleaders entertain fans during Super Bowl XIX.

the Houston Astros baseball team.

The Louisiana Superdome, home of the New Orleans Saints, rises 273 ft – twice the height of the Capitol building in Washington. It has four scoreboards which show messages as well as the score, and its six giant TV screens show instant replays and commercials.

The Seattle Seahawks' Kingdome has the largest self-supporting concrete roof in the

world. And some of the stands are retractable and removeable so that different games can be played there. The Seahawks share their stadium with the Seattle Mariners baseball team, the Seattle Sounders soccer team and the Seattle Supersonics basketball team. At today's construction costs, sharing makes sense.

But perhaps the most unusual structure in the NFL is the Detroit Lions' Pontiac Silverdome. It has an inflatable roof made out

One of the most advanced of its kind in the world, the scoreboard at San Diego's Jack Murphy Stadium shows simultaneously:
1 The rushing and passing tally of both teams.
2 The scoreline, broken down into quarters.
3 Video replays of past plays.
4 A record of how other NFL teams are faring in games being played the same day. The 'F' indicates a final score and the '2' indicates the second quarter scoreline.

▼ The scoreboard can even applaud skilful play!

TIME OUT

DANCING CHIEF TO CHIEF
On a cold November day in 1962, Kansas City groundskeeper George Toma was patching a hole in the equipment shed when a complete stranger came strolling across the field. Toma jumped up and down, shouting, 'Get off the grass. What do you people think this is, a dance floor?' The stranger turned out to be Lamar Hunt, the owner of the Kansas City Chiefs.

Far right, In the early 1960s teams like the Houston Oilers pioneered domed stadiums. Named in conjunction with the NASA Space Center, the Houston Astrodome has an aluminium roof, seats 50,496 and has a massive scoreboard.

Above right, The 76,891-seat Giants Stadium is one of the 'true' bowls to be built in the mid '70s. Split into three main tiers, every seat faces the middle of the field. Unfortunately, the new stadium didn't signal any change in the Giants' fortunes – they lost the stadium's inaugural game on 10 October 1975 to Dallas and won only three games that season.

It's fitting that the top team in the NFL should have one of the most impressive stadiums. built in 1971, Chicago's Soldier Field boasts classical-style press boxes. During the 1985 season a total of 486,212 fans packed the stadium to see the Bears win every home game en route to winning Super Bowl XX – the highest attendance in Chicago's 65-year history.

The Star Spangled Banner! Every football game is preceded by a playing of the American National anthem. Rivalries are temporarily forgotten as fans and players stand to pay tribute to their country.

of Teflon-coated fibreglass fabric which is kept inflated by 25 blowers during a game, and just two at other times. The roof alone cost $4.5 million.

Only 11 of the 28 teams in the NFL still play on grass. The rest use some type of AstroTurf or artificial playing surface.

This has made the job of the groundsmen much easier. No longer do they have to stop visitors trampling the turf, or waste valuable time cutting and reseeding.

But AstroTurf does need fertilizer, in the northern stadiums at least. A kind of chemical 'fertilizer' is used to melt snow. This is important as snow is much harder to remove from AstroTurf than it is from grass.

AN EYE ON THE GROUND

Whatever the surface, the field is covered with tarpaulins to keep the snow off and, often, a system of hot-air blowers is used underneath the 'tarps' to warm the surface.

One of the legends of grass is George Toma, turf doctor extraordinaire for the Kansas City Chiefs. He got his first groundskeeping job in 1947, and is still talk-

ing about grounds and playing surfaces with enthusiasm.

'We had two guys, and we had to take care of the playing field, sweep the stands, and clean the toilets, offices, and dugouts every day. And when the game started, we had to keep score in the outfield by holding up traffic lights, green for a first down, red for a touchdown.

'Nowadays,' Toma says, 'the biggest chore we have is getting all the burn marks and shoe polish off the field after a game. We always can tell how hard the game was fought in the trenches by all the marks. We had a preseason game here against the Chicago Bears that took four men two days to get all the black marks out.'

'We've always painted our field and decorated our end zones,' says Toma proudly.

HIGHER GROUND

When the AFL and NFL began merging in 1966, Commissioner Pete Rozelle held a press conference in Kansas City. He said he didn't see much difference in the calibre of play between the two leagues but that the AFL Chiefs' playing field was the best he had ever seen and wished there were more fields like it in the NFL.

This comment made George Toma the most sought after head groundskeeper in

TIME OUT

CUSTOM-BUILT
Football stadiums can look as impressive from the outside as they do in the supercharged atmosphere within. Built in 1965, the Atlanta-Fulton County Stadium is unusual in being one of the few stadiums to be built at the very beginning of a team's franchise. Mayor Ivan Allen managed to raise the $18 million construction costs – and was rewarded by selling 45,000 season tickets in the first year.

American professional sports. Indeed Toma and company have been responsible for every Super Bowl and Pro Bowl since 1971.

The famous 1981 NFC Championship game between the San Francisco 49ers and the Dallas Cowboys was in danger of being literally washed out. Northern California had been hit by one solid week of torrential rain.

In desperation, the 49ers management brought George Toma in from Kansas City.

'We couldn't take the tarp off the field,' Toma said. 'We had to work on the field – seed it, and sod it, and aerate it – piece by piece, rolling the tarp off one section and then rolling it right back on.

'The tarp was on the field the whole week, and the newspapers made a big deal out of it. On the day of the game, we started taking the tarp off as the people were coming into the stadium, and it was like a matinee performance. The field was beautiful. As we took off the first piece of tarp, the crowd went, "Oooh". Then we took off another piece and the crowd went, "Aaah".

'You could see the pride in the 49ers' ground crew,' Toma said. 'They had been maligned all year. They were nicknamed, "The Sod Squad". But they did it. They showed 'em. I was happiest for them. Everyone was pleased.'

TIME OF THE SIGNS

There was a time when pro football score board operators were named 'Pops', wore long overcoats and carried hip flasks. These days they are young 'marketing directors' and 'producers' like 33-year-old Nancy Nichols at the Los Angeles Coliseum. On game days, she oversees 18 people and approximately $12 million worth of computers, signboards, video equipment and assorted software and programming. Together, all this expensive gear runs the stadium's huge 30 ft by 50 ft black and white 'matrix' board and 36 ft by 48 ft colour-video board.

Whether the playing surface is grass or AstroTurf, care of the field is a vital, 24-hour job.
Top right, A groundsman's nightmare – 49ers fans gather souvenir chunks of turf after an '83 playoff victory against the Detroit Lions.
Top left, Before each game the field has to be carefully painted with the names and logos of the home and rival teams.
Above, The ground crew must cover the field between games to stop it being waterlogged by rain, or frozen in winter conditions. Tarpaulins – like this one at Pasadena – provide the best protection.

What goes on, mainly, are graphics, animation, commercials, films, videos and replays. And the score? 'That's only a small part of what we do,' says Nichols. 'Really, it's mostly glitz and marketing – it's showbiz. It's balancing budgets, and making money, and giving people something to show for it.'

She works from a minute-by-minute schedule which includes introducing all the guests and sponsors the Raiders will 'welcome' on the matrix board and a list of prepackaged video tapes.

There are also standing instructions from Raiders' management: no distracting crowd shots on the video board during the fourth quarter, for instance. And there are special instructions: for instance, which 'DEE-FENSE!' graphic should be flashed on the board when the opposing team are going on third down.

'That's not for the fans,' Nichols says. 'That's to fire up the team on the sidelines.' Which raises the question, just who controls the scoreboard?

'That's tricky. Basically, we're performing a service for the Raiders,' she says.

GETTING IT RIGHT

The mood of the game can be set by what is on the video displays. They can drive the crowd crazy or prompt boos and cat calls. The operators have to be very, very careful. They don't show replays of illegal hits or bad calls by the officials. The coverage is slanted towards the home team. But they do show good plays by the other side, too.

Richard Zielinski, the Coliseum's video director feels that his contribution is very much part of the game.

'Five, ten years ago, the fans felt they were missing out on the TV's instant replay,' he says. 'Now people come out here and feel they have the best of both worlds. The Raiders give it to them live, then we give them the Raiders 30 feet high a couple of seconds later.' That's hi-tech for you.

Being a world class wide receiver takes a lot of mental, as well as physical, discipline. Steve Largent talks at first hand about the brain work behind the team work

'Having great hands,' says Seattle wide receiver Steve Largent, 'is a cliché that doesn't go very far when you try to describe what catching a football is all about.' Largent should know. By the time he retires, his status as the greatest receiver ever will shine like a neon light across the NFL record book. Right now, everyone just *knows* it.

Check the facts. Charlie Joiner, the leading lifetime receiver to the end of 1985, had taken 716 receptions against Largent's 624. But Joiner has been playing *seven* years

ALL IN THE MIND

A PERSONAL VIEW BY

STEVE LARGENT

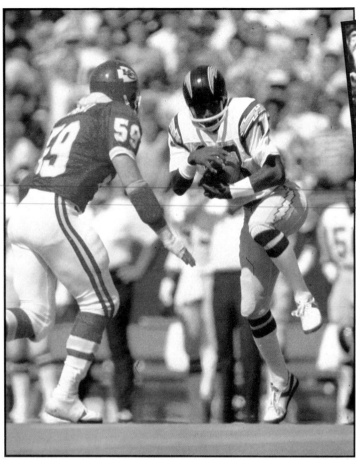

▲ San Diego wide receiver Charlie Joiner (18) holds most of the NFL receiving records – but Largent is quickly catching him up. Fred Biletnikoff (25), *top right*, Oakland's star of the '60s and '70s, is one of Largent's model receivers.

longer and is now nearing the end of his career. Seattle's No. 1 asset has a lot more playing life in him yet and has still managed to make his way to more touchdowns than Joiner.

So if you want to find out what it takes to catch a football – whatever the pressure and whatever the direction – Steve Largent is the man to ask.

MIND GAMES

What he *won't* tell you is that it is all about physique. 'Look at Howard Twilley [ex-receiver for Miami],' argues Largent. 'His hands were small. He was slower than most

'You can develop better concentration, although some of it is innate . . . Again, it takes practice. You've got to prepare yourself for a variety of situations.'

wide receivers, too. But one thing he had was great concentration.'

And it's concentration that Largent sees as 'the key to the whole thing'. Of Fred Biletnikoff, famed receiver for the Los Angeles Raiders in the '60s and '70s, Largent says, 'He would spend hours working on just one aspect of the game.

It's an example he has followed closely himself. 'You *can* develop better concentration, although some of it is innate. Some people can't concentrate when there are no distractions; some people can't concentrate when there are distractions. Again, it

> '*A lot of running a successful pattern against good defensive backs is being able to pick up quickly how a defensive back is playing and the coverages being used.*'

takes practice. You've got to prepare yourself for a variety of situations.'

Taking 79 receptions for an average gain of 16.3 yards in '85, Largent proves that practice, in his case, makes perfect.

DEFENSIVE DEVILMENT

Concentration is needed in trying to outwit, outplay and outrun the defense. One thing's for sure – when Steve Largent walks out to play, defensive backs are going to be out to get him. To counter this, you've got to think quick. Says Largent, 'A lot of running a successful pattern against good defensive backs is being able to pick up quickly how a

▲ Outpacing L.A. Raiders' cornerback Lester Hayes (37) is no easy task – but Largent manages it during a 1985 clash.

◄ Largent puts his head down to bulldoze his way past Green Bay cornerback Mike McLeod (28).

defensive back is playing, and the coverages being used.

'It's almost like a chess match. You just have to have the right play on at the right time. The same is true of the defense, which

TIME OUT

SLOW START

Few players have ever improved so radically in their pro football years as Steve Largent. He was first picked as a fourth round draft choice for the Houston Oilers in 1976. 'There were a dozen receivers drafted before me,' admits Largent. 'They were rated right.'

is trying to get the right coverage at the right moment.'

Successful passing plays can't, of course, be developed on the spur of the moment. The co-ordination between quarterback and receiver has to be precise – right down to

> '*After you play football for some 20 years, some things become a little more natural. You reach a certain comfort zone . . . you don't get uptight.*'

the last split second. A receiver has to adapt to a defensive challenge, but his running route must be carefully plotted in advance.

'My philosophy of running routes is to be real disciplined,' says Largent. 'The key for me has been to give the quarterback the exact picture in practice the week before a game that he'll see in the game itself, so when it happens in a game situation he'll

▲ Seattle's No. 1 offensive weapon takes time out.

► Sometimes, even the best must fall. Largent is brought down by cornerback Louis Wright (20) of the Broncos on one of the 79 receptions he took in '85 for a total gain of 1287 yards. But his 16.3-yard average proves he's one of the hardest receivers to tackle.

already have seen that route, that particular move several times already.

'After you play football for some 20 years, some things become a little more natural. You reach a certain comfort zone. You feel comfortable because you've been in it so many times before, you don't get uptight or feel you're going to choke. You've been there.'

ALWAYS PREPARED

During the early 1980's when Jim Zorn was quarterback with Seattle, many considered that the Seahawks took a runnin' and gunnin' approach on offense. But to Largent, Zorn's scrambling and passing tactic was less spontaneous than it seemed. Comment-

> *'I get a lot of personal satisfaction from catching 12 passes – when we win. But when we lose it takes the edge off any personal accomplishments.'*

ing at the time, he said, 'A lot of times it may look as if we're making things up on the spur of the moment. But the difference between what we do and pure improvization is tied into Jack Patera's coaching philosophy. We prepare for every situation.

'There are basic rules for handling emergencies. The receiver's responsibility,

when a play breaks down, is to work his way back to the quarterback. If the play turns out to be only a three- or four-yard gain, that's better than a minus-10-yard sack, obviously.

'Because we're so well-schooled, sometimes it may look as though all the receivers are on their own. But when Jim [Zorn] is reading a secondary, he knows from the pre-game preparation how we'll react to certain situations.

TIME OUT

PRO BOWL PRO
Largent has been to the Pro Bowl five times since 1979 – and for good reasons. He had taken more Pro Bowl receptions (15) than any other player in history, and holds the record for the most receptions (8) ever gained in a game.

'We never have what you would call a "primary receiver", for example. We're seeing the entire range of possibilities. The possibilities may change from week to week, as much as sixty per cent depending on the opponent, but basically the rules are the same.'

GOLDEN MOMENT

Steve Largent's principles have never been better put into practice than on 25 November, 1984. It was then that he piloted the Seahawks to the playoffs with a massive 12 catches for 191 yards in an end of season clash with Denver. In a career already studded with superlatives, it was Largent's finest hour.

But what did it feel like for the man himself? Says Largent: 'This was a fun game to play in, particularly for me because I was catching a lot of balls and we were successful. I get a lot of personal satisfaction out of catching 12 passes – when we win. But when we lose it takes the edge off any per-

'I don't think I've thrown three passes in my career and I don't think I've completed one. I always like to think I'd be a good quarterback, but the truth is, I don't think I would.'

sonal accomplishments.

'The Broncos are the type of team where you don't go in feeling like you're overwhelmed by their physical ability, although they have excellent players and have improved the last three years [1981-83]. But they always find a way to win.

'I'm aware of what our defense is doing, the field position, the time. I'm also aware of many more subtle things: how well we're controlling the ball, how long our defense is staying on the field, how long we're staying on the field on offense.'

Those are the type of teams that scare you the most. They never give up; they never feel like they're out of any game and those are the games you never feel comfortable about until it's over, no matter what the score is.'

It was a neck-and-neck battle, but at the final whistle Largent had a lot to feel com-

Largent sees discipline and a carefully rehearsed co-ordination between quarterback and receiver as the key to running successful passing routes. Here he puts theory into practice in a race for the ball in a game against the Cincinnati Bengals.

fortable about – Seattle won 27-24.

When he's on the field Largent never gives less than 100 per cent. But when he's on the bench he doesn't relax his attention for a minute. 'I may be sitting, but I'm into the game,' he says. 'I'm aware of what our defense is doing, the field position, the time. I'm also aware of many more subtle things: how well we're controlling the ball, how long our defense is staying on the field, how long we're staying on the field on offense.

'I'm also trying to concentrate on areas where we can attack at some point during the game and noting if they're developing a pattern in their coverages. I don't talk to the coaches at all unless I feel I've got a handle on what's going on.'

But then it's not often that Largent doesn't know what's going on. Giving total commitment and total concentration on and off the field is what makes him No. 1.

DUEL IN THE SUN

New York Jets' record rusher Freeman McNeil, *second from top*, finds open ground for the AFC in the 1986 Pro Bowl in one of ten attempts for 30 yards. A parachutist, *above*, joins the opening ceremonies. Fans celebrate, *right*, for the TV cameras at the start of the game.

When the superstars of the AFC line up opposite their counterparts in the NFC in Hawaii, the heat is on. No mere exhibition match, the Pro Bowl pits the best against the best

It's played among the swaying palm trees of Hawaii, against a background of tropical scenery, and in temperatures which never drop below 21°C (70°F). But any rumours that the Pro Bowl is just one long beach party are completely unfounded. Sure, the players certainly don't mind spending a week in Honolulu on the Hawaiian island of Oahu. In fact, the Pro Bowl, which some players even used to consider a nuisance, has never been more popular among the participants. But it's still an NFL game. It may be played after the playoffs and the Super Bowl, but it's the icing on the cake of the season rather than an anti-climax.

WORTH WINNING
Former Raiders' head coach John Madden, who coached four AFC Pro Bowl squads, claims the experience he gained at the Pro Bowl helped the Raiders win Super

The Aloha Stadium in Honolulu, *below*, has been the home of the Pro Bowl since 1980. Phil Simms, *above*, was the NFC QB in '86, throwing 3 touchdowns. Dan Fouts, *right*, passed for the opposition.

Bowl XI against the Minnesota Vikings.

'At those Pro Bowl camps,' said Madden in 1977, 'we took every position and went down the list looking for anything they had in common. Defensive linemen, for instance, might all have big feet, or quick feet, big bones, long arms, big hands – we made that kind of study, checked out everything we could think of. Much of our information on how to win the Super Bowl came from things we did at the Pro Bowl.

'The hottest people at a Pro Bowl camp, of course, are the Super Bowl players, and there are a lot of things to talk with them about – especially if they win. I talked with all of them about what they did during the week ahead of the game, and how to approach the Super Bowl, those kinds of things.'

STAR WARS
The 1971 Pro Bowl, the first Madden coached in, was more meaningful than

PRO BOWL FACTS

SELECTION OF SQUADS

The AFC-NFC Pro Bowl teams are selected by ballot of the head coaches and players in each conference. Each team has two equal votes: the head coach's and a consensus of the players' selections.

Coaches and players vote only for players in their conference, but may not vote for players from their own teams.

The following positions make up the 41-man rosters of each conference:

- four wide receivers
- two tight ends
- three offensive tackles
- three guards
- two centers
- two quarterbacks
- four running backs
- three defensive ends
- two nose tackles
- three outside linebackers
- three inside linebackers
- three cornerbacks
- three safeties
- one punter
- one kicker
- one kick-return specialist
- one special teamer.

A forty-second player, called a 'need player', will be named to the AFC and NFC squads by each head coach.

COACHING STAFFS

The coaching staffs for the Pro Bowl in each conference will be the head coach and staff of the teams that are eliminated in the AFC and NFC Championship Games.

In 1985, Mike Ditka had the unenviable task of having less than one week to coach 43 players to work together on the NFC squad.

PLAYING RULES

A standard 3-4-4 defense must be employed and either the strong or weakside linebacker must blitz. Pass coverage is limited to man-to-man with a free safety, and a three-deep zone with a strongside rotation by the cornerback; the middle man of the three remaining linebackers must go weakside in zone coverage.

SUDDEN-DEATH OVERTIME

If the score is tied at the end of regulation play, the team scoring first during sudden-death overtime will be the winner. The game is automatically ended upon any score.

▲ AFC linebacker Randy Gradishaw leaps into the air to stop AFC centre Jeff Van Note in 1980.
▶ Right guard Russ Grimm of the Redskins was a key part of the NFC's powerful '86 offense.

most. The pregame atmosphere was highly charged. It was the first contest pitting all-stars from the NFL (which had been re-named the NFC) against stars from the old American Football League (now the AFC).

There were still scars left over from the sometimes bitter war between the two leagues. (The AFL-NFL conflict had lasted from 1960, when Lamar Hunt founded the AFL, through 1966, when the two leagues hammered out a merger agreement. The two leagues retained their separate iden-tities until 1970, then realigned to create the current AFC and NFC structure.)

Five Super Bowls had been played before the first AFC-NFC Pro Bowl. The Green Bay Packers preserved the honour of the old NFL by winning the first two world cham-pionship games against the AFL's Kansas City Chiefs and Oakland Raiders. But in January, 1969, Joe Namath and the upstart New York Jets startled the football world by upsetting the mighty Baltimore Colts in Super Bowl III. The following year the Chiefs added salt to the NFL's wounded pride by disposing of the Minnesota Vik-ings in Super Bowl IV. Then in January of 1971, Baltimore, an NFL team which had been shifted to the AFC, defeated Dallas in Super Bowl V.

MATTER OF PRIDE

So when it came time to play the first AFC-NFC Pro Bowl at the Los Angeles Coliseum in 1971, emotions were running higher than in previous all-star games.

'In other years, I would use three big bottles of Alka-Seltzer,' said former Los Angeles Rams' trainer George Menefee, who worked with the Pro Bowl teams for many years, just prior to the 1971 game. 'I'd hand out about five hundred aspirin tablets, too. They needed help before they could work out. This year I've used up only about a third of a bottle of Alka-Seltzer and 50 aspirin tablets.'

Fran Tarkenton, then playing for the New York Giants, summed up the NFC's attitude before the game. 'You can feel the excitement,' said Tarkenton, who shared NFC quarterbacking duties with San Francisco's John Brodie. 'It's a matter of pride and I think we're all aware that we represent the league this year.'

The AFC squad treated the game with equal solemnity. 'We've had exceptional concentration at practice,' Madden said just prior to the game. 'The players worked really hard.'

RETRIBUTION
Apparently no one worked harder than Dallas Cowboys' cornerback Mel Renfro. In addition to tipping a pass by Oakland quarterback Daryle Lamonica into the hands of Green Bay linebacker Fred Carr, which set up an early NFC field goal, Renfro personally took care of the AFC with two fourth-quarter punt returns for touchdowns of 82 and 56 yards. The NFC won the 1971 Pro Bowl 27-6.

UNSUNG HEROES
The game of NFL superstars has regularly had its own stars, even if they weren't the players one would expect. For example, in 1975, quarterback James Harris of the Los Angeles Rams, who was a pregame replacement for the injured Fran Tarkenton, took

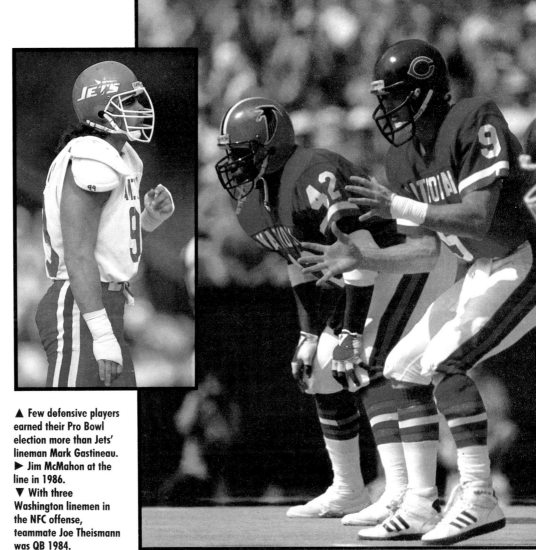

▲ Few defensive players earned their Pro Bowl election more than Jets' lineman Mark Gastineau.
▶ Jim McMahon at the line in 1986.
▼ With three Washington linemen in the NFC offense, teammate Joe Theismann was QB 1984.

over from Jim Hart in the second quarter. Within a minute and a half of the fourth quarter, Harris threw two eight-yard touchdown passes, one to Mel Gray and one to Charley Taylor, as the NFC came from behind to win 17-10. Harris was named the player of the game.

In 1976, the hero was even more unexpected. Mike Boryla of Philadelphia, who only made the roster because several other quarterbacks couldn't play, entered the game with 5:39 remaining and the NFC trailing 20-9. Boryla threw a 14-yard touchdown pass to Terry Metcalf and then an eight-yarder to Mel Gray for a 23-20 NFC victory.

Despite Boryla's late heroics, the player of the game was Billy 'White Shoes' Johnson of Houston, who not only returned a punt a record 90 yards for a touchdown but he also set records for punt return yards in a game and a career.

BEFORE HAWAII
Johnson is one of surprisingly few players to hold AFC-NFC Pro Bowl records from before 1980, when the game was moved to Hawaii. Each year since then, Aloha Stadium has seen a number of new marks generated by offenses led by men such as Phil Simms or Dan Fouts, or defenses spurred by strong men such as Richard Dent or Mark Gastineau.

Running back O. J. Simpson still holds one of the most impressive records from the pre-Hawaii Pro Bowls. In 1973, at Texas

▲ The star-studded bench of the NFC squad prepare to celebrate their 1986 victory, by 28-24, in the closing two minutes of the 1986 Pro Bowl. It gave the NFC a 10-6 winning record.

▶ In a dramatic moment of the 1960 Pro Bowl, Pittsburgh QB Bobby Layne (22) jets a pass over the heads of Doug Atkins (81) and Big Daddy Lipscombe (76).

Stadium, he became the first back in the Pro Bowl to gain 100 yards rushing, as he carried 16 times for 112 yards and one touchdown in a 33-28 AFC victory. Simpson also caught three passes for 58 yards and was selected the player of the game.

That same year, John Brockington of the Packers set a mark by scoring three touchdowns, two rushing and one on a three-yard pass from Billy Kilmer. Not only is that still a game record, but it also keeps Brockington tied for the most touchdowns scored in a career in the Pro Bowl.

BUILDING BRIDGES

Three of the men primarily responsible for bringing the Pro Bowl to Hawaii were Mackay Yanagisawa, the former manager of Aloha Stadium who first came up with the idea for the Hula Bowl in 1947; Frank Valenti, a former sportscaster for the Honolulu CBS affiliate; and Herman Clark, a Hawaii native and former Chicago Bears player whose position was guard.

After receiving encouragement from George Halas, the late Bears owner (and Clark's former NFL coach), the trio made a pitch to the NFL owners in 1977 to host a Pro Bowl in Aloha Stadium.

'We were obviously very pleased when the NFL agreed to bring the Pro Bowl to Aloha Stadium,' says Valenti, 'but none of us dreamed it would catch on as it has. One thing we proposed, which we hoped the league might go for, was to host the game every *other* year, since we felt the league probably would want to play the game in NFL cities at least some of the time.'

But the game hasn't moved from Hawaii since 1980, when a sell-out crowd of 48,060 witnessed the highest scoring game in AFC-NFC Pro Bowl history (a 37-27 NFC victory). Pro Bowl, Hawaiian-style, has been a smash success story in the 50th state, and looks set to remain a happy marriage.

In the Pro Bowl game held in Hawaii on 2 February 1986, New York Giants quarterback Phil Simms brought the NFC back from a 24-7 halftime deficit to a 28-24 win over the AFC. Simms, who completed 15 of

27 passes for 212 yards and 3 touchdowns, was named the MVP of the game. The win gave the NFC a 10-6 Pro Bowl record versus the AFC since 1970.

HAWAIIAN ALL-STARS

The Pro Bowl has won the hearts of Hawaiians, and the love affair shows no signs of diminishing. 'Enthusiasm continues to run very high for the Pro Bowl here,' says Bill Kwon, sports editor on the *Honolulu Star-Bulletin*. 'People in Hawaii are very sophisticated football fans. They've also grown up on all-star games, such as the Hula Bowl. But with the Hula Bowl, you're not always sure you're going to get the top college players to compete. Also, the festive atmosphere of the Pro Bowl seems to work perfectly in Hawaii.'

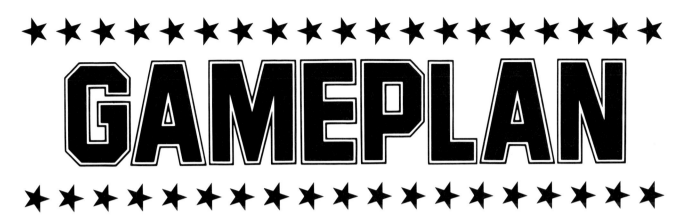

GAMEPLAN

When the offensive team huddles before each play, each player must be fully conversant with over 200 plays and variations in the team's playbook. Fortunately, from the fan's point of view, nowhere near that number needs to be understood to appreciate the game. But there are basics that should be learned before you can enjoy the game properly.

If you've only recently become interested in American Football, this chapter will outline for you, in logical steps, the fundamentals of the game. For those of you already hooked and to a degree well-versed in the technical aspects, this chapter also includes those nuances and variations that make the game plan so multifaceted. With ample illustration and instructively captioned photographs, the often-confused looking scramble on the field will become much clearer.

Starting with the basic rules of the game, the opening section looks at the dimensions of the field, the markings on it, the official size of the ball, the number of players allowed to appear on a roster, the official timing of the game and so on. We then move on to the basics of the running game, the basis of nearly every team's attack, and the way in which the great teams have consistently won over the past 60-odd years. Although to many fans, the running game can't compare in excitement to the passing attack, the fact of the matter is no coach would last more than a year if he excluded running from the playbook. And as for excitement, you need only look at the likes of Joe Morris of the Giants, Freeman McNeil of the Jets and Eric Dickerson of the Rams to remind you that running is alive and well in the NFL.

For big yardage in a hurry, though, there is no easier way to get it than passing. And from the blocking of the offensive linemen to the patterns run by the wide receivers, tight ends and running backs, there must be a precise understanding from each of what is happening at any given moment. Because, while passes can be successful for big gains, their very nature means that they can be just as easily intercepted by the defence – hence the excitement whenever the quarterback drops back ready to make a pass.

As for the defence, they must be prepared to react in a split second to the moves of the offense, and determine just as quickly whether or not they are defending a run or a pass. Two separate sections deal with these topics on a subject rejuvenated with the appearance of first the awesome Chicago defense that led them to Super Bowl XX, and then the amazing New York Giants squad led by all-universe linebacker Lawrence Taylor.

Finally, something slightly out of the ordinary. A fictional game in which the rules and penalties are laid out clearly in the context they are most understandable. Just about every possible penalty is listed in this game, and there is even an over-time time period that makes use of recently introduced (and to some controversial) instant replay ruling.

BATTLE FIELD

Get to grips with the basics of the gridiron game, where brawn and brains meet. Here are the facts from type of turf to the role of the referee. Check out how much you know – or have forgotten

D uring a Green Bay Packers' offensive slump in the 1960s, head coach Vince Lombardi called a team meeting. 'We're going back to basics,' he said. 'Back to fundamentals. Now this,' he said, holding up a ball, 'is a football.' 'Hold on, coach,' interrupted split end Max McGee. 'You're going too fast.'

It doesn't do any harm to go on a refresher course now and then whether you're playing or just watching! In fact, watching American Football for the first time on TV, the game can seem a complex and confusing jumble of players.

But it's really very simple – it's all about territory and possession. The aim of the game is for one team to score more points than the other by running and passing the ball across the opponents' goal line, or by kicking it through the opponent's goal posts.

THE BALL

A good place to begin, then, is with a look at the football itself.

Lombardi was right when he stressed to his team that the football is the most funda-

mental feature of the game. It not only gives the sport its name, but its unusual shape also makes the action of the game unique.

The official football used in the National Football League is a rubber bladder inflated to 12.5 to 13.5 psi, enclosed in a pebble-grained casing of natural tan coloured leather (not pigskin), weighing 14 to 15 oz.

THE FIELD

The types of playing surfaces vary from stadium to stadium in the NFL, and are almost evenly divided between natural grass and artificial turf. But one thing remains constant throughout the league – the size, shape and markings of the field.

An NFL field is a rectangle measuring 120 yards long by 53⅓ yards wide. The actual field of play is 100 yards long, with two 10-yard deep sections called *end zones* extending from each goal line. The width of the field is bounded by the *side-lines*, and the length by the *end lines*, which mark the back of the end zone. The end lines also mark the position of the goal posts, through which the ball is kicked to score field goals and extra points after touchdowns.

Parallel to the goal lines, the field is sectioned off every five yards with the *yard lines*. These are numbered every 10 yards up to the 50-yard line, or *midfield stripe*, and give the field its 'gridiron' look.

The pair of parallel dotted lines, called *hashmarks*, running from goal line to goal line define the area within which the ball has to be played on any down. The marks are one yard apart, and the two lines are 18½ feet apart. This is the same as the space between the up-

rights on the goal posts.

One line you'll never see marked, though, is the *line of scrimmage*. This is an imaginary line parallel to the goal line determined by wherever the ball is placed, or *spotted*, after a play has ended. On each play, the offensive and defensive teams line up on either side of it. Between the two teams is a *neutral zone* measuring the length of the ball. Neither team may enter it before the ball is snapped.

TIMING

American Football games are divided into four 15-minute *quarters*, separated by a 15-minute half-time break; there are also two-minute breaks after the first and third quarters because the teams change ends after every 15 minutes of play. Changing ends in this way prevents either team from gaining any advantage from a weather condition such as sun glare or wind direction.

In addition to these breaks, each team is permitted to call three 90-second *time outs* during each half. The game clock is stopped during time outs and they are usually called on the field by a team's offensive and defensive captains.

Also, the officials can call time outs to assess penalties, measure yardage gained, replace equipment, tend to injured players, and to inform the benches that two minutes remain in the second and fourth

quarters of the game, called *two-minute warnings*.

The offensive team must deal with an additional time limit: the *30-second clock*. Unless each offensive play begins within 30 seconds of the referee's whistle indicating the ball is ready to be played, the offense will be penalized by a 5-yard loss of yardage.

THE PLAYERS

On the day of a match each NFL team is allowed 45 players and these make up the roster. From the roster, 11-man units are organized into the offensive, defensive and special team squads. The special teams come into play on kickoffs, punts, field goals and extra points. Only 11 of the 45 can be

PLAYER NUMBERS

All NFL players are numbered according to their positions*:

1 -19	Quarterbacks and kickers
20-49	Running backs and defensive backs
50-59	Centers and linebackers
60-79	Defensive linemen and interior offensive linemen
80-89	Wide receivers and tight ends
90-99	Defensive linemen

* All players who had been in the National Football League prior to 1972 may use their old numbers.

TIME OUT

WHY 11?
American Football teams might today be fielding 15 men a side had there not been a game played on 15 May 1876 between McGill University from Montreal and Harvard University in Cambridge Massachussetts. Four of the McGill team fell ill so both teams agreed to play 11-a-side.

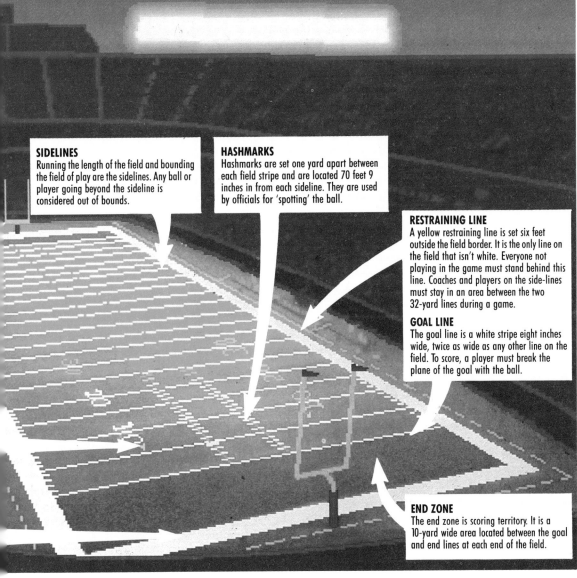

SIDELINES
Running the length of the field and bounding the field of play are the sidelines. Any ball or player going beyond the sideline is considered out of bounds.

HASHMARKS
Hashmarks are set one yard apart between each field stripe and are located 70 feet 9 inches in from each sideline. They are used by officials for 'spotting' the ball.

RESTRAINING LINE
A yellow restraining line is set six feet outside the field border. It is the only line on the field that isn't white. Everyone not playing in the game must stand behind this line. Coaches and players on the side-lines must stay in an area between the two 32-yard lines during a game.

GOAL LINE
The goal line is a white stripe eight inches wide, twice as wide as any other line on the field. To score, a player must break the plane of the goal with the ball.

END ZONE
The end zone is scoring territory. It is a 10-yard wide area located between the goal and end lines at each end of the field.

TIME OUT

An NFL field measures 53⅓ yards wide. This unusual size was established by football pioneer Walter Camp in the late 1880s. Under pressure to reduce injuries by opening up the game with a larger field, Camp settled for 53⅓ yards, the largest space that would fit in the new stadium at Harvard.

Good blocking by the offensive line on passing plays is crucial to their success. Here, the line forms an excellent protective pocket around quarterback Terry Bradshaw (12), helped out by running back Franco Harris (32). Bradshaw has three main options on this play. He can fake a handoff to running back Rocky Bleier (20) and then get set to throw to one of his receivers downfield. If they're all covered, he can throw to his 'safety valve' Harris. His last option is to make the handoff to Bleier on a draw play, fooling the defense who have left big gaps. Whichever he chooses, Pittsburgh's Bradshaw is keeping the Dallas defense honest because they have to be wary of so many options: for instance, a draw play, a play action pass or a screen pass might be attempted.

on the field at any one time.

The starting offensive team contains:

• Linemen (blockers), consisting of the center, two tackles and two guards.

• Receivers, usually two wide receivers and a tight end.

• The backfield, which includes the quarterback and his running backs, who are also eligible to receive the ball.

The defense contains three

NUMBERS IN POSITIONS

Here's how an average 45-man NFL roster breaks down in terms of number of players per position:

Offensive linemen	8
Receivers	6
Running backs	5
Quarterbacks	3
Defensive linemen	6
Linebackers	8
Defensive backs	7
Kicker	1
Punter	1
Total	45

groups of players as well:

• The line, which is known as a front four (or three depending on the situation).

• Linebackers, of whom there are three or four (again, depending on the situation).

• The secondary, consisting of two cornerbacks and two safeties, who are primarily pass defenders.

Besides the head coach, each team also has a staff of assistant coaches. Their numbers vary with each team and each specializes in working with certain positions – such as receivers, the offensive line, linebackers – or areas of strategy, such as coordinating offensive and defensive plays.

FORWARD OR BACK

Progress in a football game is measured in yards. Any time a team is on offense, it is given four chances, or *downs*, to gain 10 yards. If it advances the ball this distance or more, the team makes a first down, retaining the ball and wins the right to

Denver Broncos' quarterback John Elway (7) receives up-to-the-minute information on the sideline.

four more downs.

A team that fails to make a first down in three tries usually *punts* (kicks) the ball downfield on fourth down and the other side gets its chance to go on offense.

If a team tries to make a first down and fails on fourth down,

the other team gets the ball and a first down where the play was stopped.

The offensive team's situation is described as the down and the distance to go to make a first down. For example, a team on second down with seven yards to go for a first down is said to be 'second and seven'.

Downs are carefully measured by two men officially known as linesmen (unofficially, 'the chain gang') who are stationed along the sidelines. They carry two rods attached to a chain that is exactly 10 yards long. The chain is stretched its full length from the first down line of scrimmage. If any portion of the ball is advanced beyond the chain during the four plays allowed, it's classed as a first down.

The linesmen are accompanied by another official who carries a pole with large flip-cards on top. These cards are numbered 1, 2, 3 and 4, and simply indicate which down is being played.

HOW THE TEAMS LINE UP BEFORE THE BALL IS SNAPPED

FULLBACK
Very powerful runner who lines up behind tight end (on the strongside). He carries the ball in short yardage situations and is expected to block well and be a good receiver. In most modern offenses, fullbacks and halfbacks are known simply as running backs.

WIDE RECEIVER
Usually the team's fastest receiver, he is stationed before the snap several yards from the offensive linemen.

TACKLES AND ENDS
Usually called the front four (in a 4-3 formation), they are the largest men in the defense; their main objectives are to stop running plays at the line of scrimmage and rush the quarterback. In a 3-4 set, there is a nose tackle plus two ends; the fourth lineman is replaced by an additional linebacker.

TIGHT END
A big, strong receiver who lines up next to the offensive line to add blocking power.

TACKLE

GUARD

CORNERBACKS AND SAFETIES
Collectively known as defensive backs, they work in the defense area known as the secondary. They are required to tackle even the biggest runners yet they need the speed to catch the fastest receivers. They are occasionally required to blitz.

LINEBACKERS
The defensive team's handymen. Linebackers must pursue running plays, drop back and defend passes, and make all out pass rushes (called blitzes).

END

HALFBACK
This is the team's handyman, who runs, blocks, receives and sometimes throws on option plays.

QUARTERBACK
This is the man in charge. He calls the plays, is the primary passer and ball handler and occasionally runs with the ball.

WIDE RECEIVER

CENTER, GUARDS AND TACKLES
These five men make up the offensive line, or interior linemen. The right and left guards line up on either side of the center, and the right and left tackles line up to the outside of the guards. They block for running backs and create a pocket to protect the quarterback on passing plays.

CORNERBACK

On each down, the offense attempts a *play*: a set plan of action in which each player has certain responsibilities. The play is indicated, or 'called', in the huddle by the quarterback, seven yards behind the line of scrimmage.

The play is usually decided, however, by the coaches either on the sidelines or up in the press box, where they are

TOUCHDOWN

To score a touchdown, a player must break the plane of this 8-in thick goal line and enter the end zone while he is in possession of the ball.

equipped with headsets that enable instant communication with the rest of the coaching staff. Plays are relayed to the quarterback via hand signals from the sideline or else by a player being sent in with them.

MOVING THE BALL
Once a team is in possession of the ball, they have several options for gaining yardage to advance the ball to the opponent's goal line. The obvious place to begin is with the running game.

Technically, any offensive player can run with the ball, but it's almost always the running backs who take on this role. Quarterbacks, wide receivers and tight ends occasionally carry the ball. But quarterbacks usually only run with it on short yardage situations or when forced to by defenders on a pass rush.

The most basic running play is the *handoff*, in which the quarterback receives the snap from the center, turns around and places the ball into the hands of the running back moving towards the line of scrim-

mage. On many plays, the quarterback will fake a handoff to one runner and then handoff to another.

A variation of the handoff is the *pitchout*. Here, the quarterback turns from the center and makes an underhand toss to a back sweeping wide to one side of the field.

Often, one of the backs will begin to run towards a sideline before the ball is snapped. This action is legal if only one offensive player is in *motion* before the ball is snapped, and as long as he runs parallel to or away from – not towards – the line of scrimmage.

However, all offensive players must be completely still for a full second before the snap. Defensive players can shift and move as they please as long as they are not in the neutral zone or touching a member of the offensive team.

AERIAL ATTACK
Although a team's quarterback does most of the passing, legally, any offensive player can do so. After taking the snap, the quarterback drops back, or re-

Quarterback Dieter Brock (5) of the Los Angeles Rams calling signals at the line of scrimmage.

treats, into the *pocket*, a semi-circle of protection provided by his blockers (usually the offensive line plus a running back or two). The quarterback then scans the field for a receiver who's free of defenders.

But one of the problems with passing is that as soon as the defense spots a passing play, their front line (and sometimes linebackers and secondary men) charge the offense and attempt to penetrate it, so as to get to the quarterback before he can throw the ball. If this *pass rush*, forces the quarterback out of the pocket, he'll have to run from the pressure, or *scramble*. If the defense tackles the quarterback behind the line of scrimmage, they are said to have made a *sack*.

ELIGIBLE RECEIVERS
The only offensive players who are ineligible to catch passes are the five interior linemen (center, tackles and guards), and the quarterback if he has

THE OFFICIALS

There are seven officials on the field for an NFL game. They are:

REFEREE Has general control and final authority. He observes the snap and the motion of the backs, as well as checking the legality of line blocking, quarterbacks and rushers, and defenders' contact with punter.

UMPIRE Primarily rules on equipment and player's conduct on line, including legality of blocking and possible false starts. He watches defensive linemen, and offensive linemen downfield on pass plays.

HEAD LINESMAN Rules on offside, encroachment and action on the line before the snap. He has full responsibility for ruling plays to his sideline, and is in charge of the chain crew. He helps keep track of the down, determining runners' forward progress and signals the forward point of ball.

LINE JUDGE Keeps time, backing up clock operator; rules direction of passes, and whether or not passer is behind the line of scrimmage. Watches action at line before and after snap, and watches the wide receiver on his side.

BACK JUDGE Watches tight end or near back if end is on opposite side, and watches for legality of blocks and actions. Calls clipping (blocking from behind) on punt returns, rules on legality of catches and calls pass interference. He lines up on same side as line judge, 15-17 yards deep.

FIELD JUDGE He's 22-25 yards downfield on head linesman's side, keying on tight end or near back, watching for legality of their blocks and actions against them. Times 30-second clock between plays and

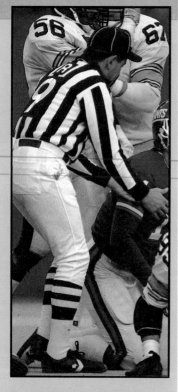

The referee heads the team of seven officials; he has ultimate control.

intervals between quarters, calls pass interference, fair catch penalties and clipping on kick returns.

SIDE JUDGE Stands on same side as head linesman, 17 yards deep. Assists referee in decision involving catches, fumble recoveries, marking where balls or players went out of bounds, and illegal touching of loose ball.

already taken a direct snap from the center.

Passes can be caught anywhere within the field's boundaries, and for a pass to be ruled *complete*, or legal, the receiver must have the ball clearly in his possession and have both feet inside the boundaries (sideline and end lines).

There are 11 more eligible receivers the quarterback does his best not to pass to – the defense. Defenders have as much right to catch a thrown ball as the receivers, and because of this neither may impede the other physically from catching a pass. If one does, the officials will rule a *pass interference* penalty. When a pass is caught by the defense, it is said to be *intercepted*.

QUICK YARDAGE

The forward pass is self-explanatory; if it is not caught, *incompletion*, the game clock stops, play resumes at the previous line of scrimmage and the down is increased by one. Only one forward pass is allowed in each down.

When a runner sees that he is about to be stopped by the defense, he can *lateral* the ball to a teammate who is either alongside or behind him, in order to keep the play going.

TURNOVERS

Fumbles (a loss of the ball by the ball carrier) and *interceptions* – known collectively as

turnovers – can be advanced by the defense at any time. Similar to a fumble is a *muff*, which occurs when a player makes an unsuccessful attempt to get a free ball. It is illegal to try to advance the ball by muffing, batting or kicking it forward.

SCORING

In the NFL, there are four ways in which teams can score. A *touchdown*, worth six points, is awarded when a runner with the ball crosses or touches his opponent's goal line, or when a player catches a pass or recovers a fumble in his opponent's end zone.

After a touchdown, the scoring team is allowed to try for an extra point, which follows the same format as a field goal, except that the ball is placed on the two-yard line. The kick must then pass over the crossbar and between the uprights. The team will also be awarded a single point if instead of kicking it they run or pass the ball into the end zone, in the same manner as a touchdown. Though rarely seen, teams can dropkick the ball for a score. The third way to score is with a field goal which is worth three points if successful.

The final, and least common way of scoring is the *safety* (not to be confused with the player position). Two points are awarded to a team whose defensive unit tackles an offensive ball carrier behind his own goal line. A safety can also be scored when an offensive player is called for an infraction, or penalty, behind the goal line (such as holding) or if the ball is snapped, carried or fumbled over the end line. A play in which a snapped ball hits a goal post is also ruled a safety.

Although Lombardi's remarks to his players may have been a joke, they illustrate a vital fundamental: football is a simple game – it is the tactics that make it endlessly fascinating.

KICKING THE BALL FOR POINTS OR TERRITORY

PUNT
Used on fourth downs when too many yards needed for a first down and the distance is too great for a field goal.

KICKOFF
To start each half, and following scores, the ball is kicked from a tee on kicking team's 35-yard line.

PLACEKICK
For field goal and extra point attempts, the ball is held for the kicker after receiving the snap.

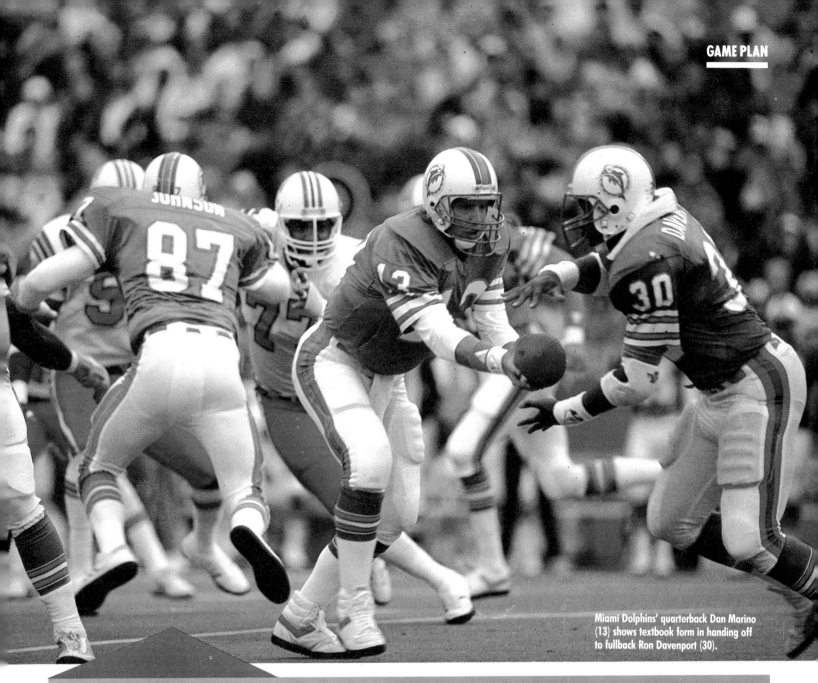

Miami Dolphins' quarterback Dan Marino (13) shows textbook form in handing off to fullback Ron Davenport (30).

THREE WAYS OF GETTING THE BALL TO THE BACKS

HANDOFF
This is a very common type of running play in which the quarterback places the ball directly into the running back's hands.

FLARE PASS
This is a quick pass to the running back who is moving towards the sideline of the field in the area that is called the 'flat'.

PITCHOUT
This is a lateral toss to a running back who is sweeping behind the line of scrimmage towards the sideline of the field.

O N T H

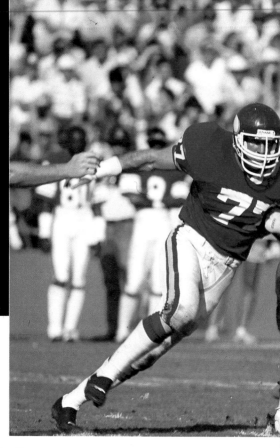

Watch the offensive line. Players in the glamour positions – quarterback, running back, wide receiver – cannot gain yardage without some ferocious teamwork from the men in the trenches

Watching a great runner like Tony Dorsett or Walter Payton pick his way through the defense for a long gain is one of the most exciting sights in football. But while players like these grab the limelight for their obviously exciting skills, they couldn't possibly gain the yardage they do without help from the rest of the team. What a running back needs most of all is an excellent offensive line in front of him, to clear paths and alleys through the defense.

What the offensive line does is *block* – that is, they move defensive players out of the way of the running back, and stop them from getting near him. They can do so with bent arms, shoulders, and backs, but cannot grasp or trip the defender in any way.

Every player on the offense, even the quarterback at times, blocks. The linemen have the primary responsibility but running backs and tight ends also contribute. There are no comparative statistics, like yards gained or tackles made, to single out exceptional blockers (one reason for the relative anonymity of offensive linemen).

The only way a blocker's performance can be assessed is by pouring over game films, which is something coaches spend a lot of time doing.

A block does not have to be good to look at, or come out of the textbook to grade out well.

All that matters is that the blocker gets the job done – which is to make room for the runner or prevent a defender from getting to him. That way, runners win games, stay healthy and, perhaps, earn the

HOLE NUMBERS

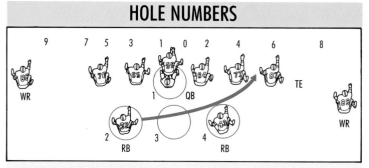

Each hole (space) next to the lineman is numbered – odd: left, even: right. Backfield player spaces are also numbered: the quarterback 1, with 2 on his left, 3 behind, 4 on his right. If the quarterback calls a

'26' play it means the running back (2) would run through the off-tackle hole (6) – verbal shorthand on this scale has been developed to a fine art form, to meet the demands of a fast-moving game.

most valuable player award. Runners love really good offensive linemen, and they make or break a team.

BLOCKING PATTERNS

The most basic type of line blocking is the traditional power, drive or straight-ahead block. In this method, an offensive lineman blocks the defender lined up directly across from him at the line of scrimmage.

But there are two reasons why this type of blocking can't always be used. Defensive linemen don't always line up nose-to-nose with their offensive counterparts; they have too much size, speed and explosive strength for one man to handle alone. They are, after all, the biggest, strongest, meanest players on the field.

Consequently, offenses use *blocking combinations*, which

The Dolphins demonstrate how to block effectively and clear a path through the defenders out to nail their man with the ball. As No. 37 starts his run, his offensive line takes out the opposition and blocks the pursuing 77.

are precisely timed variations of *single-* and *double-team* assaults (double-teaming is two men teaming up to block on one defender).

THE POWER GAME

Running plays directed up the middle in the area between the two offensive guards generally come under the heading *inside running*. Offenses who control the ball well are particularly good at this. They are usually characterized by short quick bursts either by huge fullbacks who can plough through the line, or nimble, lighter backs, such as Marcus Allen, who can leap over it. Inside running

PULLING LINEMEN

Interior linemen must be big, strong and very quick. These skills come together when a lineman *pulls*. He leaves his position at the snap and runs parallel to the line of scrimmage in the running lane, either to make a trap block or lead block for a running back. Whichever he is doing, the move must be carefully timed and executed. He will have to be in the right place at the right time.

running lane

means short yardage and first downs made the hard way.

Strategically, running inside has a number of advantages, not least of which is when the offense can employ what are known as *quick hitters*. In the

huddle the play is decided. Then after breaking out of the huddle and lining up, the center snaps the ball to the quarterback on the first sound he hears. A quick handoff is then given to a running back, hoping to catch the

BLOCKING

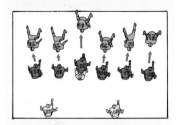

Power Straight-ahead blocking; linemen against linemen.

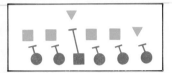

Angle Linemen slant and block the first man to the right or left.

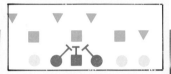

Wedge Three blockers against one defender, often the nose tackle.

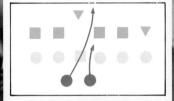

Lead One running back leads the other through the hole in the line.

Double-team Two linemen team up to take out one defender.

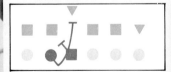

Cross Block Two linemen exchange blocking assignments.

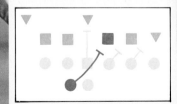

Isolation A defender is left and the linemen hit by an RB.

defense asleep on its feet.

More importantly, if the defense has been putting on a heavy pass rush, these quick hitters will slow them down a bit, or 'keep them honest', on future passing plays.

RUNNING OUTSIDE

Two of the most fundamental running plays in American Football are the *off-tackle slant* and the *sweep*. The off-tackle play was considered a staple for many years in the NFL, and to some coaches it still is.

The play itself is a simple handoff to a running back who angles his run just to the outside of either the left or right offensive tackle, the outermost player of the interior linemen, and inside the tight end.

Because of the extra blocking potential of the tight end, defenses are compelled to put an extra linebacker on the tight end's side (which is known as the *strongside*). If the offense can consistently find holes on these off-tackle plays, the defense will have to bolster up the strongside, so weakening the middle and *weakside*, which the defense will try to exploit.

SWEEPING UP

The sweep takes the off-tackle play a little farther outside. It's aimed outside the tight end and the strongside linebacker, and towards the defensive back on that side. While sweeps are still a common sight, the now predominant 3-4 defense (three

As New Orleans Saints' fullback bursts through L.A. Rams' line, he finds there's nowhere to go and is about to lose ball to the opposition.

linemen instead of four and four linebackers instead of three, as in the traditional 4-3) has made the play more difficult to run.

Offensive linemen have to be particularly quick on sweep plays. They have to step back from the line of scrimmage and then lead block the running back around the end (this is known as *pulling*). Running backs need enough speed to get round to the outside, turn the corner and head upfield before the defense can fully react.

There are three main types of sweeps. The *power sweep* has both offensive guards pulling and leading the running back around the end. The *fullback sweep* converts the smaller halfback into a lead blocker. And the *option sweep* gives the running back the option of continuing his run, or throwing a pass from behind the line of scrimmage if he spots an open receiver downfield.

DECEPTIVE MOVES

For American Football coaches, the game is one of strategy. Moves and countermoves, fakes and deception, surprisingly obvious moves – are all employed to gain advantage over the opposing team. Three running play strategies in particular – *draws, misdirections and traps* – depend on deception to make them work.

The draw play is about as simple as you can get. Each member of the offense acts as

DECEPTIONS

Draw Play On this quick-hitting draw, the left guard and the tackle indicate that a pass is to be made, then split the rushing defensive end and tackle to create a running lane instead.

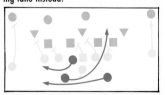

Misdirection The halfback and the left guard start from right to left, but the fullback takes the ball inside instead of attempting a yardage gain.

though a pass play is in progress – the quarterback drops back to look for receivers, the offensive line stands up to make a protective blocking pocket, and the running backs stay back to block anyone who gets through.

When the defense sees this apparent pass play developing, they will naturally put on a big rush. But once they've been lured into the backfield and pushed to the outside, the quarter-back hands off to a running back who will hopefully find acres of room up the middle.

Heavy responsibility falls on the offensive linemen here, since they have to convince the defense that they are indeed pass blocking. If the defense catches on too soon, however, the quarterback or the running back could be tackled for a big loss.

Coaches love to use the draw play after a succession of passing plays. And it, too, will keep the defense honest if it is used successfully enough, since they'll be wary the next time they see a pass coming.

Similar in idea to the draw play is the *misdirection*. Simply, the direction of the running appears to be one way but then suddenly and unexpectedly shifts to another.

In this case, the offense is trying to confuse the defensive linemen and fool the linebackers into moving out of position. Once the linebackers commit themselves to pursuing the initial action of the running backs (who usually take the handoff going one way after faking a run in the other) it's usually too late for them to get back in position to attempt to tackle the runner.

SETTING THE TRAP

Draw plays depend on the deceptive actions of the offensive line, while misdirection plays depend on the running backs to fool the defense. The onus shifts

A successful running attack depends on co-ordinated lead blocking up front. Here, the center (52) and fullback (32) make room for their running back (28).

once again to the offensive line with the employment of trap plays, often seen in the NFL.

After the ball is snapped, an offensive lineman pulls back from the line in a similar fashion to that on a sweep play. The defensive lineman opposite, seeing the newly created hole, rushes through, only to be blocked by another offensive lineman waiting for him – and

TIME OUT

BIG GUNS
The standard NFL running game doesn't change much until the offense get inside the opponent's five-yard line. The defense always make changes in their own end, such as bringing in extra linemen. Offenses respond to this by bringing in more heavy artillery of their own, usually an extra tight end and their most powerful running backs.

OFF TACKLE SLANT

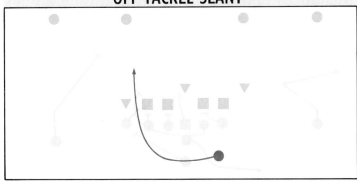

One of pro-football's most frequently used plays, it can be run to the strong or weakside. The quarterback fakes to the fullback, then hands off to the running back. The running back then hits the hole made by the fullback blocking the defensive tackle and runs for daylight in the backfield, guarded by the tight end who is accompanying him ready to block if necessary.

MEN IN MOTION BEFORE THE SNAP

The use of motion before the snap can achieve a number of things. Above all, motion is used to force the defense to make adjustments and to keep them on the hop. The defense adjustments can open up a weak spot that the offense can then exploit.

But there are other things that it can do. First, it can place a running back closer to the outside before the play begins – from there he can take a quick pitchout or flare pass, or can even serve as a lead blocker. Second, it can bring a receiver into the backfield in time to make him a potential ball carrier on end around plays or reverses. Third, it can put a receiver, particularly the tight end, in position behind the offensive line to be a lead blocker for a running back. Finally, it can bring a second, third or fourth player to one side of the formation to serve as blockers or to help flood that side of the field with potential pass receivers.

Whatever the move, though, it is sure to put the defense off balance and make them more prone to making a mistake.

Motion can also be effective against defenses using man-to-man coverage. The offense tries to make the defense shift with the motion man, thereby leaving the defense open in the area of the shift (right).

The man in motion is only allowed to move forward by one step. But he can run from side to side parallel to the line of scrimmage, as long as he stops moving before the snap.

the trap is then sprung.

Although the guards are most often called upon to execute the trap block, centers and tackles are also used. When the play is run against defensive ends or linebackers, it's said to be a long trap, while short traps are run against defensive tackles. In each case, however, the aim is to shift the defender to make room for the running back with the ball.

If traps can be used successfully enough, teams will attempt the *false trap*. Here, the defensive lineman follows the offensive lineman instead of rushing through the hole, wary not to be duped again. But instead of carrying the ball to the outside as before, the running back shoots straight up the middle into the empty hole.

Running strategy in American Football is based on outwitting the defense. If the offense can show enough

THE SWEEP IN ACTION

After the ball is handed off to the running back by the quarterback the running back must try and follow his interference blockers around the end of the defensive line. An interference blocker runs ahead of the man with the ball, not necessarily hitting (blocking) defenders, but generally getting in their way. If the running back overruns his blockers, he has very little room to manoeuvre as he is in danger of getting too close to the side line. But if he stays with his blockers into the secondary – the deepest territory of the defense – he can burst through from behind them into the open and, with any luck, straight for the end zone and go for a touchdown.

draws, traps and mis-directions, the defense will become an easy target for ordinary straight-ahead blocking.

RAZZLE DAZZLE 'EM
All offenses have trick plays up their sleeves, designed to work against specific teams, personnel or alignments. Usually called *gadget plays*, they come under the general heading of *razzle dazzle* because of the speed, timing and distances covered. Teams practise them and enter them in the playbook, but they are used sparingly, if at all, during a season.

Most gadget plays involve passing of one sort or another, but the most common is a running play – the reverse. Here, the quarterback gets the snap and runs (sprints out) towards a sideline, handing off the ball to a running back or receiver sprinting in the opposite direction. A double reverse adds another handoff and a triple reverse adds yet another.

A play such as this, especially if there is more than one

handoff, illustrates why teams shy away from them. Gadget plays can be slow to develop, giving the defense time to recover from their initial confusion and surprise. And if the defense diagnose a gadget correctly, it can result in a huge loss of yardage for the offense, since most of the planned action takes place well behind the line of scrimmage. Finally, all the ball handling significantly increases the chance of fumbling especially in the net.

Razzle-dazzling provides some spectacular moments in NFL games. But, whatever the arena, when gadget plays work, they work big.

PLAY CALLING
Each hole, or space, between or beside the interior linemen is designated by a number – odd numbers to the left and even to the right. The spaces the running backs *stand* in are also numbered – 2 to the left, 3 directly behind the quarterback, and 4 to the right. The backs are designated by the number

Washington Redskins' fullback John Riggins finds a gaping hole in the Miami Dolphins' defense. Without his offensive linemen creating gaps for him he won't gain much yardage.

of the space they are set in before the snap, regardless of whether they're halfbacks or fullbacks. The quarterback, however, is always the number 1 back.

This numbering system for backs and holes in the offensive line and for backs enables play calling to become a kind of verbal short hand. Supposing the quarterback in the huddle called for the halfback who was in the *number 2* space to take a handoff and then run through the *number 6* hole in the line (just to the outside of the right side offensive tackle). Then the quarterback would call for a '26' and his teammates would all know what he meant.

While this is a simple example of calling plays using the whole and back numbering system, it forms the basis of every team's playbook – sometimes

known as 'the Bible', since players have to completely memorize over 200 plays.

Many of the plays, though, can get very complicated. And despite how the team likes to abbreviate and jargonize its players, formations and motions, there are long lists of excellent college players who never made the grade because they couldn't memorize the playbook.

ATTACK FROM THE AIR

*The play that brings the crowd alive is
the long pass down the field. But the
long bomb is just one type of the most
exciting play in the game*

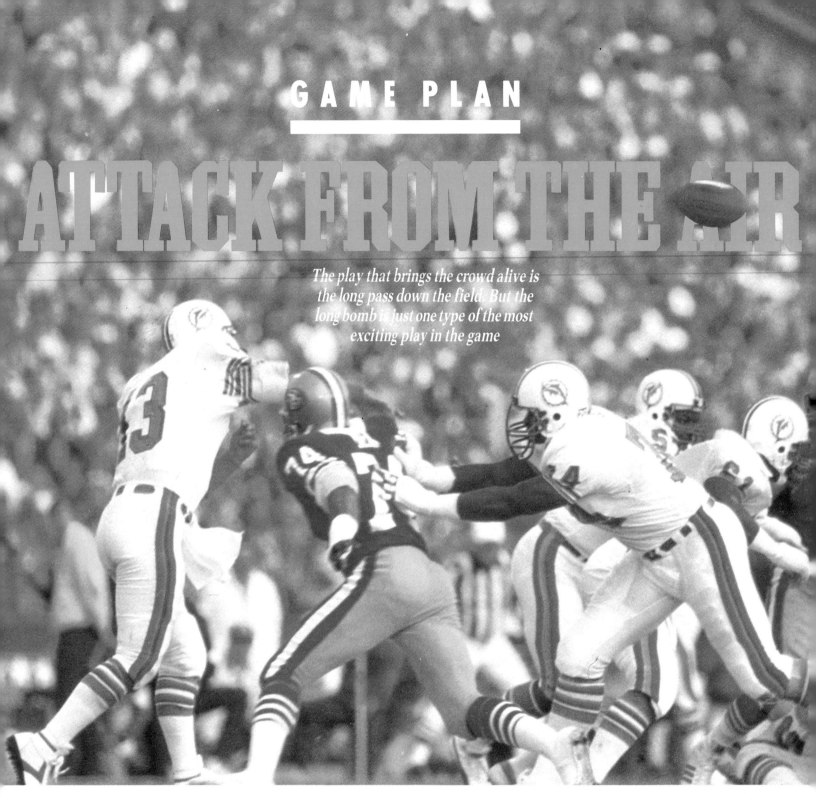

Running, or rushing, is one way to gain ground. Potentially much more spectacular is the passing game.

In recent years coaches have been concentrating more and more on this side of offensive play. Plays have become more complicated and the game has been opened up to aerial attack.

Pass blocking by the offense is vital to give the QB room to manoeuvre. Without it, both the short and the long pass would have little chance of success. The time given by this form of blocking is essential if the receivers are to be able to

run their pass patterns.

And the special plays involving motion of players before the snap and tactics such as the *play action pass, the shotgun formation, screen passing* and *flea-flicking* would not work.

As usual it is around the QB that the action takes place.

QUARTERBACKS

It is virtually impossible for a team to achieve any consistent success without an outstanding quarterback. The entire offense revolves around his performance; he establishes the rhythm and sets the tempo.

Playing quarterback in the

NFL can mean a quick ride to glory, but it is also a complex, demanding position, filled with pressures, that requires a uniquely skilled athlete. A quarterback must have a strong arm and a quick release; he has to be able to unload the ball rapidly, with precision, to a very small (but often crowded) point on the field. Overall quickness and durability are important. It also helps to be relatively big and strong in order to withstand punishing hits, and be tall enough to see over huge linemen.

An effective quarterback must possess other important

qualities as well: he must be an outstanding leader, he must be intelligent, and he needs an ordered disciplined mind. Also, he needs a sense of timing and patience. The quarterback has to sit back in the passing pocket and wait for the play to develop. But every fraction of a second that a quarterback 'buys' for his receivers increases his own chances of being sacked by the defense. It all takes enormous concentration (not to mention courage).

Quarterbacks are generally classed as either scramblers or pocket passers, depending on their style of play and their

TREES, BRANCHES AND ROUTES

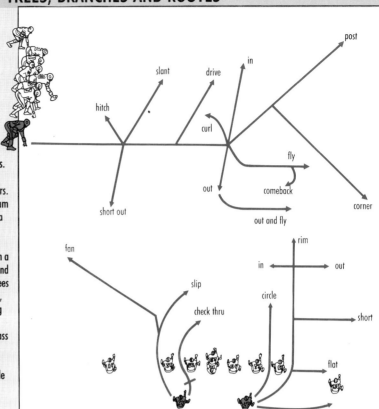

Every pass pattern in a team's offense is part of a larger series, which, when drawn on a blackboard, can resemble a leafless tree, with every branch a pass route. In a game there would be even more turns and angles on each pattern to reflect the 'moves' a receiver employs to elude pass defenders.

The chart displays some of the most frequently used pass patterns for receivers. (the names of the patterns differ from team to team, but usually the designation of a pass pattern describes the route.)

Some of the more common patterns include the *hitch*, or *buttonhook*, in which a tight end runs about seven yards, stops and turns towards the QB; the *zig-in*, which sees the wide receiver cut sharply in, then out, then in again; and *posts*, which are long runs towards the goal posts.

Because running backs begin their pass routes several steps behind the line of scrimmage, their range of pass patterns tends to differ slightly from those of wide receivers and tight ends.

Just one pass completion is all it takes to break a game wide open anywhere on the field. But with receivers running patterns such as hitches, posts, zig-ins and down-and-outs, the quarterback needs a deadly and accurate arm and great sense of timing if he is to find the hands of his catcher.

mobility. Scrambling and pocket quarterbacks must both be outstanding passers. But the scramblers often run with the ball – particularly when their original plays break down – and are adept at passing when they are on the run.

The passing game in the NFL today, however, is based around pocket passing, in which the quarterback will retreat into the pocket established by his offensive line plus perhaps, a back or two, set up, and quickly study his options. Mobility is still an asset of course; it helps a quarterback to be an escape artist when a defensive lineman is breathing down his neck. Many quarterbacks who were scramblers and runners early in their careers become pocket passers as age and injuries finally take their toll.

Ultimately, the success or failure of a passing game hinges on a quarterback's ability to read the defensive coverage. If a quarterback senses before the snap that the play called in the huddle won't work against the defensive alignment he sees at the line of scrimmage, it is up to him to call an audible, to switch to a play that has a better chance of success against that particular type of coverage.

There are 11 men on an offensive unit, each with an important role. But it is the quarterback who is relied upon to have the instincts and the intelligence to outwit the defense.

PASS BLOCKING

Quarterback may be the spotlight position in the NFL, but a quarterback will be in little position for glamour if his pass protection fails.

Good blocking is probably even more important to the success of the passing attack than it is to the running game.

But there is one basic distinction between run blocking and pass blocking. Instead of firing across the line of scrimmage to clear defenders out of the path of a ball carrier, pass blocking usually requires offensive linemen to retreat one-to-three steps from the line when the ball is snapped. Then they set up and brace for impact, and ward off the hard-charging defensive players.

Until recently, the blocker operated at a disadvantage. Under NFL rules, his hands had to be cupped or closed, and his arms had to be flexed inward – they could not be extended forward to create a push.

NEW RULES

But in the 1977 season, the rules were relaxed, allowing the blocker to extend his arms and open his hands – an amendment that swung the advantage full circle to the offense.

Now, after breaking a pass rusher's momentum with an initial strike, a blocker can fend him off with open hands, keeping him at bay with open arms.

The key to pass blocking is always one's positioning. The

BUYING TIME FOR THE QUARTERBACK

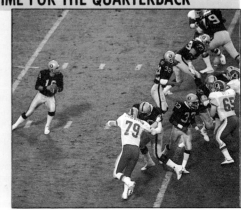

The key to successful passing is protection. The offensive linemen must step back and straighten up, ready to take on the largest and meanest defensive players, intent on sacking the quarterback. The toughest assignments fall to the centre and two guards, who must prevent their counterparts from getting past them.

blocker has to face his man, with his shoulders square and his head up, never taking his eye off his target.

Size and strength are the raw materials for an offensive lineman, and so are feet. The best linemen all have 'quick feet,' meaning they can dance agilely, like a boxer. This allows them to slide from side to side, pedal back and forth, or swivel from angle to angle while maintaining unshakeable balance.

In addition to the offensive linemen, running backs are also called upon to pass block. The general rule for blocking assignments is to try to keep the offensive linemen matched against the defensive linemen, and the running backs matched against any charging linebackers or defensive backs.

The pass protectors know they have done their job well if they have kept the pass rush away from the quarterback for at least two and a half seconds, because that is usually all the time a quarterback needs to get his pass away.

PASS RECEIVERS

Offensive formations are primarily dictated by the positioning of the wide receivers, tight ends, and running backs, all of whom are eligible to catch passes on every play.

Wide receivers are so called because they are usually split away from the interior linemen. In most normal formations, there will be two wide receivers, one to the left and one to the right.

Wide receivers are part sprinter and part acrobat; they must have the speed to beat a defender and the ability to catch the ball in a crowd. Since they usually have slighter builds than the rest of the offensive personnel, they aren't called upon to block as much as the linemen and running backs. Wide receivers who are not the primary targets in a passing play are used as decoys.

The tight end lines up close to one of the two offensive tackles. Because tight ends (on the average) are much more physically imposing than wide receivers, they present a different set of problems for the defense. The tight end is constantly used to block on running and passing plays, and has also become an increasingly attractive passing target.

Running backs are also being used more frequently as receivers. They have always been integrated into pass blocking schemes, and have always been available for pass catching duty. But more than ever there is a demand for running backs who can catch the ball.

In addition to speed, quickness, and good hands, a receiver must have the ability to concentrate totally on the ball, to 'look' the ball into his hands – even with tacklers descending upon him.

PASS PATTERNS

All receivers run patterns, or routes, to break free from defenders and get open. Receivers spend hours perfecting their fakes, cuts, and timing so that their patterns become disciplined and sharp. Receivers also synchronize their routes with the quarterback so he will know instinctively where the receiver is throughout the pass pattern and how to time his release. This is because there are different distance options that can be used on nearly every pass route.

Obviously, different pass patterns are required for backs, wide receivers, and tight ends.

Receivers also play an important part on running plays: they usually try to run convincing pass patterns to draw attention – and defenders – away from the direction of the run.

Through their flare action (the co-ordinated movement of the running backs as they block or go out for passes), running backs often hold the keys to passing plays.

It is impossible to run a perfect pattern every time. Poor field conditions, bad weather, congestion caused by the defense, and even a slip can play havoc with a receiver's pattern. When a pattern is irrevocably broken, the receiver will try to improvise a new route in an attempt to get open.

SHORT PASSING GAME

For a team that does not have a great running back, an offense structured around a short passing game can be the surest way to control the ball.

The short, ball control passing game requires patience above all. It also demands more discipline and even tighter execution than the running game (because of the more intricate timing involved).

The success of the short passing game is based largely on an ability to quickly scatter the linebackers (especially against a 3-4 defense). One way offenses try to do this is to vary greatly their formations with motion and shifts before the snap to confuse the coverage.

It is crucial for receivers to get off the line of scrimmage quickly. Although defenders can no longer jostle receivers all over the field before the ball is thrown, they can still 'chuck' (bump) the receiver once as long as it's done within five

What makes the tight end so important is his combination of size, speed and agility. When put in motion, he adds to one side of the formation awesome blocking potential plus a great target for his own team's quarterback.

yards of the line of scrimmage.

The receiver, therefore, must have outstanding release technique so he can maintain his pattern and break loose despite any initial contact from a linebacker or defensive back.

There are many methods of establishing a short passing game. They include the use of delay patterns, screen passes, quick passes over the middle to the tight end, pick plays (where a receiver actually sets a screen for another receiver downfield), and pass routes that attack the spots underneath the deep coverage area of a team's zone defense.

LONG PASSING GAME

The most exciting play in pro football is the long pass – 'the bomb'. It is the quickest way to put six points on the scoreboard.

The bomb is also probably the hardest play to execute consistently. This is because of the many defenses designed to stop it and the timing that is required – from the quarterback getting the time to set, find his receiver, and throw; to the receiver beating the initial chuck, getting open, and making the catch.

The objective of the long passing game is to isolate one or more receivers deep downfield against just one defender. That means the rest of the play must

be designed to attract the attention of the defense away from the deep receivers(s).

Wide receivers always have been the most frequent targets for long passes because of their great speed and elusive moves. But as the passing game has opened up, running backs and tight ends also are increasingly being called on to run long pass routes.

There are some obvious downs and situations that call for a long pass. If a team is faced with a third-and-30 situation, it's a safe bet it isn't going to run up the middle very often.

But because defenses adjust to such situations with extra men in the secondary (or extra pass rushers), the bomb is an even more effective weapon when it is tried under less obvious circumstances, such as third-and-inches, or even first-and-10.

It a team can establish early success at throwing long during a game, it can soften up the defense, and make it even more vulnerable to the other two major prongs in its offensive attack – the short pass and the running game.

PLAY ACTION PASS

One of the most popular methods of keeping linebackers off balance is the play action pass.

Essentially, the play action pass is a pass off a fake run. Like its opposite the draw play (a run off a fake pass), in order for it to work the play fake has to be pulled off expertly; it has to be believable. The offensive linemen must appear to be blocking for a running play, by pulling and giving the appearance of leading a sweep, for instance, while the quarterback fakes a handoff to a running back who

SHORT YARDAGE THROUGH THE AIR

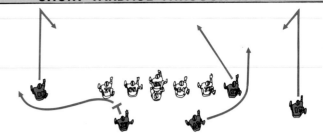

Both wide receivers turn in on hitches after a quick burst off the line, and the tight end slants in across the middle. The running backs first act as pass blockers and then as safety valve receivers, for loops or screens.

LONG PASSING – AERIAL CIRCUS

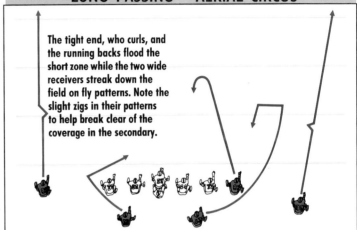

The tight end, who curls, and the running backs flood the short zone while the two wide receivers streak down the field on fly patterns. Note the slight zigs in their patterns to help break clear of the coverage in the secondary.

MULTIPLE RECEIVER FORMATION

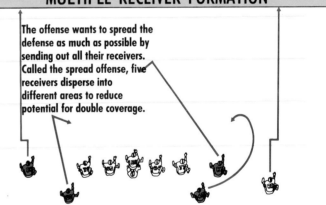

The offense wants to spread the defense as much as possible by sending out all their receivers. Called the spread offense, five receivers disperse into different areas to reduce potential for double coverage.

FOOLING THE DEFENSE – THE PLAY ACTION PASS

At the snap, the quarterback spins around towards the running back for an apparent handoff or pitchout before he passes.

As the linemen initiate their blocks to create holes, the quarterback makes his fake to the running back, which must be convincing.

The back hits the hole (without the ball), and continues through drawing defenders to him. The quarterback rolls out in search of a receiver.

continues through the line.

If the linebackers have been properly fooled by this deception, and are pulled into the line of scrimmage area expecting a run, some of the short zones will be vacant. And that is where the quarterback throws, often to a running back who has delayed a moment in the backfield before slipping out on his pass route.

Play action is a strategy that is largely dictated by down and distance. It seldom works on obvious passing downs because the linebackers won't go for the run fake as readily. But it is a play that can work beautifully on third-and-inches or first-and-10. It is also a common ploy in goal line situations, when the defense is constantly watching for the run.

SCREEN PASSES

An effective strategy against a defense mounting a heavy pass rush is the screen pass.

On a typical screen, as the quarterback drops into position to throw, the offensive linemen relax their blocks slightly to allow a little penetration by the defense into the

backfield. As the defensive rush charges by, the offensive linemen slide off in the direction of the intended pass.

Meanwhile, a wide receiver steps back off the line of scrimmage, or a running back swings into the flat, the area of the backfield behind the line of scrimmage and towards the sideline. The quarterback, sometimes after a fake arm pump to enhance the impression that the play is going to be a downfield pass, will then loop

On most passing plays, the quarterback must drop back into his pocket before finding an open receiver. Here, the classic drop back motion, left, is contrasted with the more modern sprint back action.

a pass over the oncoming rushers to the waiting receiver behind the line, who by then has a wall of blockers in front of him comprising all of the regrouped offensive linemen. (Screens are one of the few occasions when a center will pull from his original position

to lead the blocking.)

One of the advantages of the screen pass is that it can create additional running room for quick backs who may have had trouble breaking loose on ordinary runs from scrimmage.

But in order to make screens more effective, a team usually has to establish a successful passing game, which in turn inspires a hard pass rush by the defense–including blitzes, which can leave a defense particularly vulnerable to screens.

THE SHOTGUN FORMATION

One way to reduce the initiative of special defenses that are designed to sabotage the passing game – even if the offense still has to pass – is to use the shotgun formation. In the shotgun, the quarterback lines up five or six yards behind the center, or drops back to a similar spot before the snap.

Probably the biggest advantage of the shotgun is that it enhances the quarterback's ability to read the defensive coverage. Because he is already in position to pass, with the field in front of him, the quarterback has a panoramic view.

The shotgun has gained in popularity during the past few years, partly as an answer to defenses featuring extra pass defenders. But not every team uses the shotgun, due to its inherent disadvantages. The center has to make his long snap 'blind' (without looking between his legs), because he has to handle his blocking assignment (the nose tackle in the 3-4, or a dogging middle linebacker in the 4-3). That increases the chance of a miscue on the exchange – particularly in bad weather. Also, crowd noise can interfere with the quarterback's signal call. And, finally, though there are running plays from the shotgun formation, they are used infrequently.

Also, when a team goes into a shotgun any of the surprise factor is lost. The defense can be almost certain of a pass.

GAME PLAN

COUNTER ATTACK

Defensive play is tough, but it's also very fast – lightning-quick reflexes and split-second timing are needed in a constant struggle to outguess the opposing offense – and destroy it

Defensive tactics can be complicated. But it all boils down to one basic idea summed up by Buddy Ryan, former defensive coach for the Chicago Bears. He says, 'I like a defense that gets after people'.

Getting after people – for the Bears or any other football team – means being not only alert to the swiftest changes in offensive play but also being in a position to pounce.

If the quarterback's main weapon is surprise, the defense has to be sure to cover every possibility and read – or *key* into – the offensive play.

THE 3-4 DEFENSE

The 3-4 has become the most prevalent defense in the NFL.

It features a three-man front line made up of a *nose tackle* flanked by two *defensive ends*. The nose tackle positions himself directly across from the center. The ends play straight across or slightly to either side of the offensive tackles.

In the 3-4 every moment counts. The ends must determine in a split second from the offensive tackles' initial thrusts whether the play is going to be a run or a pass. Generally, a tackle attacks the end if the play is a run; he will drop back to

A hard-hitting defense is at the core of every successful team – and crushing the quarterback for big losses will always lift defenders' spirits.

THE DEFENSE PLUGS THE LINE . . .

. . . LEAVING THE RUNNING BACK ALONE . . .

. . . WITH NOWHERE TO GO . . .

. . . BUT DOWN

Defenses must react in a split second to the actions of the individual offensive blockers as soon as the ball is snapped. Here, the Minnesota Vikings' defense have read their keys correctly, filling in the holes and stacking the offense enough to prevent Andra Franklin (37) from gaining even a single yard for Miami. A moment's hesitation by the defense can be fatal.

block if it's a pass. If the play is a run the defensive end will move toward the play's flow. On a pass he'll attempt to tackle the quarterback, trying to prevent him from throwing the ball or scrambling for a big gain.

The three *down* linemen are so called down because they set up close to the ground in three-point stances – both feet and one hand on the ground – before the snap. They are supported by four linebackers. The inside linebackers roam the area directly between the two defensive ends. The two outside linebackers set up outside the defensive ends.

The linebackers playing inside are bigger and stronger than the outside men, who rely more on quickness and agility to play their positions. Linebackers in the 3-4 must also have the speed to cover receivers. On runs, the inside linebackers are responsible for cutting off ball carriers who get past the down linemen. The linebackers outside must stop running plays, or force them inside.

In the 3-4, two cornerbacks and two safeties (free and strong) are set in the secondary. All provide pass coverage, with the cornerbacks also defending the run.

4-3 DEFENSE
An alternative to the standard 3-4 is the 4-3 defense, which replaces a linebacker with a defensive lineman, and brings a heavier presence to the line.

The primary defense used in the NFL in the 1950s, '60s, and early '70s, the 4-3's popularity has now declined, but virtually every team still uses it in certain game situations, such as on definite passing downs.

The 4-3, with its extra defensive lineman, is good against the run because there are more tacklers waiting for the running back at the line of scrimmage; and because four defensive front men can better neutralize the blocks of four or five offensive interior linemen.

For the same reason – one more lineman – defenses using the 4-3 can generate a much greater pass rush, making it harder for offensive lines to ward off by double – and triple – teaming the individual rush men.

Three linebackers (one middle and two outside) position themselves behind the defensive linemen in the 4-3. The middle linebacker places himself anywhere between the two defensive tackles, similar to the

THE NOSE TACKLE

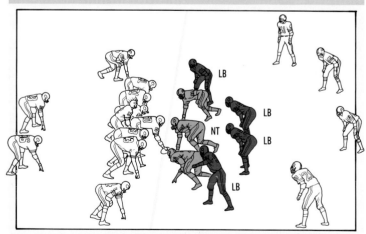

The success of the 3-4 defense can hinge on the play of the nose tackle, who lines up directly across from the center. An excellent nose tackle controls the center and two guards. He has an advantage over these three players because he knows which way he's going to attack the offensive line; the center and guards must react to his move. Strength, quickness, and agility are required of the nose tackle, representing a difficult and rare blend of athletic skills.

DEFENSIVE OPTIONS AT THE LINE

4-3   FLEX   SHORT YARDAGE

There are only a handful of basic defensive formations, but hundreds of permutations. The 4-3 is the classic set, featuring four down linemen and three linebackers. Though widely replaced by the 3-4 the 4-3 is still used on definite passing downs.

The Flex is based more on reading, rather than rushing the quarterback. It deploys linemen off the line, giving them room to react to whatever comes.

Made famous by Tom Landry's Dallas Cowboys, the Flex is run from a 4-3 formation; this puts extra emphasis on the defensive linemen.

For short yardage plays, the strategy is simple: put as many big men on the line as possible.

SUBMARINE

On short yardage plays, defensive linemen assume low stances to 'submarine' a blocker's surge. This is an attempt by the defenders to hit hard at the blockers legs, knocking him over like a skittle pin.

alignment of inside linebackers in the 3-4. The deployment of the outside linebackers is more flexible in the 4-3.

All three linebackers must be very mobile because they are responsible for covering more area than any of the linebackers in the 3-4. To compensate for their large territories, and to confuse the quarterback, the three players will not start each play from the same position. They constantly move around into new areas behind the defensive linemen to support the down linemen and fill the running lanes if a run develops out of the play.

The *flex* defense (so named because it is a 'flexible' 4-3) is designed primarily to stop the run. It stalls an option running attack by closing all gaps in the line.

But the flex is relatively weak against the pass because defensive linemen must read run 'keys' first: if they are looking for where the play is going, they are less able to rush the passer. In the typical flex align-

ment, there are seven men near the line of scrimmage (four down linemen and three linebackers). Two defensive linemen (in any combination) set up two to three yards off the line of scrimmage. The other two linemen position themselves normally and attack the offense. The players off the line

are passive, making no penetration. They wait and read, then react to the play.

SHORT YARDAGE DEFENSE
If the offense has a few vital yards to make, for another first down or for a score, the defense must be ready. Usually they will bring in three or four extra

Defenses show their muscle when faced with short yardage situations. They'll put as many as 10 of their biggest men on the line, replacing the pass coverage with sheer brute force.

KEEP THEM GUESSING

DE AND DT STUNT

LB STACK

Keeping an offense off-balance and confused is vital for a successful defense.

NFL defenses use a variety of different tactics throughout a game to keep the offense guessing. Very rarely will an offense see the same positioning of all defensive players twice in one game. They are constantly moving around, setting up in different positions, and always experimenting – trying to expose weaknesses.

No matter how effective a defense is at stopping the running game, failure to prevent pass completions will kill a team. This responsibility falls on the secondary – the cornerbacks and safeties.

These players must be exceedingly fast but they must also be very hard hitters. Here, although the pass has just been completed to the tight end, the safety's crunching tackle was so hard that he knocked the ball loose.

STACK In a stack, any linebacker (outside or inside) sets up directly behind a defensive lineman. The offense then doesn't know from which direction the linebacker will come. He can go right, left, or straight ahead – following the defensive lineman and causing considerable offensive blocking problems.

STUNTS On a stunt, defenders exchange their rushing routes, by looping around each other after the ball has been snapped. Stunts can involve defensive players in any combination – linemen with each other, linemen with linebackers, and so on. The objective of a stunt is to take advantage of, or create, gaps in the offensive line.

SLANTS A slant is a planned charge by a defensive lineman to the left or right instead of straight ahead. The advantage lies with the defensive lineman, because he knows where he is going from the time he positions himself.

PINCH In the pinch tactic, the defensive linemen position themselves in the gaps between offensive blockers and 'pinch' against one offensive lineman. The charge by the linemen who are pinching renders that blocker helpless.

Stacks, stunts, slants and pinches can be used in combinations as well; their effectiveness depends heavily on execution.

linemen, replacing the outside linebackers and one or both safeties. The defensive linemen will set up in the gaps between each offensive player, crouching as low to the ground as possible. Their job is to penetrate, undermine the surge of the offense, fill in the holes in the line, and stack the play up.

The middle linebacker will often be the only man set off the line of scrimmage. When the ball is snapped, he instantly tries to recognize where the play is going and propels himself to that point, hopefully meeting the ball carrier head-on and driving him back.

The drawback to bringing in extra defensive linemen is that the defense becomes vulnerable to a play action fake or a pass. Because they are playing without much pass defense support, the cornerbacks and the safeties (if they're in the game), have to be alert to running backs coming out of the backfield as receivers, or receivers slipping off the line into the end zone unnoticed.

Just as on offense, the strong-side and weakside of a defense are determined by the positioning of the tight end. Whatever side of the offensive line the tight end positions himself also becomes the strongside of the defense. If the tight end goes in motion or shifts sides, the strongside goes with him.

ALIGNMENT OPTIONS

The defense, whether in a 3-4 or 4-3 alignment, has one outside linebacker who always positions himself at the tight end's side of the field. This is the strongside linebacker. The opposite linebacker is designated as the weakside.

In the defensive secondary, the way both safeties line up is also determined by the positioning of the tight end. The strong safety goes to the strongside of the defense, while the free (or weak) safety plays on the other side and is allowed to roam, following the quarterback's movements.

When the offense sends a man in motion, the defense has to

PINCH

SLANT

DT DT DE DE

DEFENSIVE SHIFTS

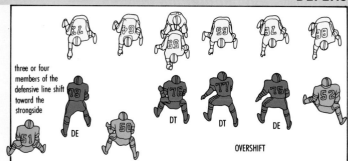

three or four members of the defensive line shift toward the strongside

OVERSHIFT

DE DT DT DE

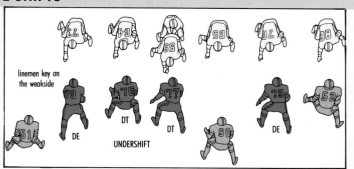

linemen key on the weakside

UNDERSHIFT

DE DE DT DT

In the 1950s and early 1960s, defenses usually lined up in a straight or 'even' 4-3, where the defensive linemen play directly across from the offensive linemen.

But offensive teams soon learned how to exploit it. Then came the *overshift* and *undershift*.

In a true overshift, all four members

of the defensive line shift toward the strongside. An undershift is exactly the opposite; the defensive line shifts *away* from the strongside.

Defenses use overshifts and undershifts in various ways to gain an advantage at the point where they feel the offensive team is going to attack.

On a running play, the name of the game for the defense is pursuit. Reaction time has to be extra fast to read the play, and rapid acceleration is needed to catch the running backs, many of whom are world-class sprinters.

Sometimes, the defense are helped out by poor offensive blocking, leaving the running back to face as many as six defenders entirely alone.

THE MAN IN CHARGE

A middle (or inside) linebacker is the quarterback of the defense on most NFL teams, and is responsible for calling the defensive front and coverage formation. He's given this job because he has the best position on the field to see what the offense is doing.

Like his counterpart on offense, the linebacker does not usually select the formations himself. He often gets the defensive play call by looking to a coach on the sidelines for his decision. These are made by hand signals.

Once the defensive play is chosen, the middle linebacker turns to his teammates in the huddle and relays the information the coach has given him. He will first call out the defensive front, 4-3 or 3-4, and any over or under shifts. He then calls the pass coverage, stating whether the secondary should drop back into zones, or play man-to-man.

adjust, because motion can change the strength of the offensive formation from one side to the other. The adjustments a team makes depend entirely on its defensive personnel.

Teams that have a strong man-to-man coverage react quickly to changes in strength. They send a defensive player across the field following the motion man. The defense then compensates to the side away from the motion, to guard against being left open in the area vacated by the man follow-ing the motion.

The defense can also rotate to or away from the motion. These adjustments occur when the defense is playing a zone coverage. In this case, defensive players rotate at the snap of the ball to their predetermined positions, instead of following the offensive player.

PREDICTING THE PLAY

The middle linebacker (in a 3-4, the two inside linebackers) keys – or assesses – the centre and two guards. He watches their

Despite their immense size, many defensive ends have the agility to fend off two blockers, dodge running backs coming out of the backfield, and put a heavy pass rush on the quarterback.

THE FORCE

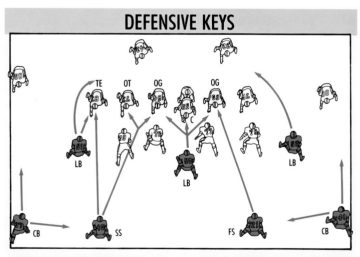

There are certain areas of the field that a defense must protect at all costs. One of the most crucial of these is the outside on a running play.

A safety or cornerback (depending on which way an outside play is being run) must not let a ball carrier get outside him, because he could be the last defender between a runner and the goal line. Either player has to force the run back towards the middle of the field (or formation) where his teammates are pursuing the play.

Determining who is going to force the ball carrier depends on the wide receiver. If a receiver sets up, or *splits*, less than 10 yards outside his nearest teammate, the cornerback will usually be the force man; more than 10 yards, and the safety usually has the responsibility.

first movements off the line of scrimmage to determine his own action.

The strongside linebacker's first key is the tight end. If the tight end stays in and blocks, the linebacker assumes the play is going to be a run; if the tight end releases, it's most likely a pass. The linebacker then checks the running lane (the lane behind, and parallel to, the line of scrimmage) where guards run when pulling on a rushing play. If there is a guard moving through the lane, the strongside linebacker will step up to disrupt the play. If not he will look for the first running back coming into his area.

The weakside linebacker has the same keys as the strong-side linebacker except that he first has to check the running lane because there is no tight end on his side.

Predicting upcoming plays isn't always easy, but then neither are any of the defense's jobs. In the end though it all comes down to Buddy Ryan's 'getting after people'.

DEFENSIVE KEYS

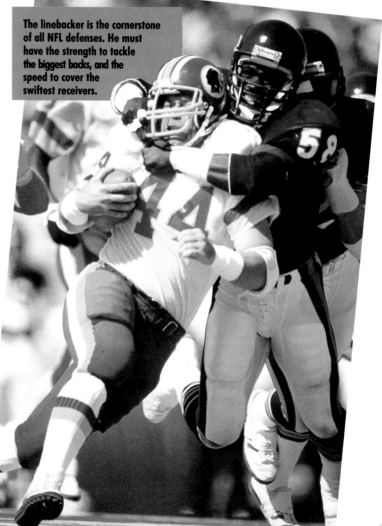

The linebacker is the cornerstone of all NFL defenses. He must have the strength to tackle the biggest backs, and the speed to cover the swiftest receivers.

Keys help defensive players anticipate what type of play the offensive team is going to run. Each player on defense has a mental checklist to go through before each play. He must key (scrutinize) areas of the field and certain offensive players immediately before and after the ball is snapped. In a split second, by reading his keys, he has to determine whether the play is a run or pass. He then instinctively reacts to his keys and assumes his defensive role given the front or formation his team is in at the commencement of any given play.

Keys aren't always reliable, though. Many times an offense will show false keys to deceive the defense. Or else the offensive linemen can make quick fakes to make the defense move the wrong way. So as on most plays, the defense must counter strategy with strategy of their own.

FOOTBALL RULES OK

Presented as a list, the rules of American Football make heavy reading. Seen in an actual game, their purpose is clear. The game report that follows is fiction – the rules are fact

All NFL games begin with the *coin toss* to determine who receives the opening kickoff and what ends the teams will take for the first quarter. As is the custom, the visiting team gets to call – let's call them the Blues. Fortunately for them, they guess right and choose to receive first, which can be psychologically important.

The Reds chose to defend the half of the field that has the sun behind them. The referee instructs the team captains to stand on their respective sides of midfield, and then signals to the crowd what has taken place.

The game opens with the Reds kicking off from their own 35-yard line, but the *kickoff goes out of bounds* before being touched by anyone. That's a five-yard penalty, so they must re-kick from their own 30.

This time the kick stays in play and the Blues return it all the way to the Reds' 47. There's a flag on the field, though, and it turns out that *clipping* (blocking from behind) was called on one of the Blues' blockers at their own 39-yard line. The penalty is 15 yards from that point, so the Blues start the game with a first down at their own 24.

The Blues open up with a 30-yard pass completion to wide receiver Jimmy Bell, giving

OFFSIDE AND ENCROACHMENT – FIVE YARDS

forgetting the snap count can cost five yards

LT

LB

blitzing linebackers often jump the gun

One of the most common penalties in American Football is offside, illustrated *left* and signalled by the referee, *below*. It's called when either an offensive or defensive player crosses the neutral zone at the snap. If a defensive player jumps across the line and touches an opponent, it's called *encroachment*, which carries the same five-yard penalty and is signalled exactly the same way.

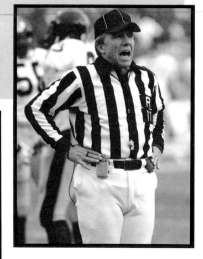

To begin each game, and overtime if necessary, there is a coin toss, *left*, to determine who kicks off and what ends the teams will take. The custom is that the visiting team's captain calls the toss.

Blocking is as important to a team's success as any other skill, but it can injure a player if it's done illegally, *below*. Clipping, blocking from behind (as illustrated to the right of the picture), incurs a 10-yard penalty.

them a first down at the Reds' 46. On the next play, an off-tackle run to the weakside, running back Bert Smith picks up eight yards, but offensive guard Stan White is called for *offside* – he jumped across the line of scrimmage before the ball was snapped. They still have first down, but with 15 yards to go from their own 49.

The five yards are quickly made up when the Reds' nose tackle, Reggie Kline, is called for *encroachment*, similar to offside but he touched an offensive lineman. So it's first down and 10 from the Reds' 46 again.

With three successive passes, Blues' quarterback Kenny Merrill leads his team to the Reds' three-yard line, where bruising fullback George Murphy pounds his way across the Reds' goal for a touchdown. The PAT is good and the Blues lead 7-0.

After receiving the kickoff, the Reds have little luck moving the ball and are forced to punt from their own 39. With the kick still in the air, returner Calvin Spiller waves his arm to signal a *fair catch*, which means that the ball will be dead once he catches it, and that the Blues will take over from that spot. If he drops it, it's considered a *free ball* and both teams are eligible to recover it. But Spiller catches it and the Blues have a first down at their own 26.

DEFENSIVE HOLDING

Despite a sputtering drive, the Blues manage to score another touchdown, making the score 14-0. They were helped by a *defensive holding* call against Reds' linebacker Terry McNeil, who grabbed Blues' tight end Tony Warren as he came off the line and attemp-

PASS INTERFERENCE

Once a pass is in the air, neither the receiver nor the defender can interfere with each other's attempt to catch it. If the defender is called, the offense gets a first down from the point that the infringement took place; it's a 10-yard penalty if the offense is called.

ted to get free for a pass. It was a 10-yard penalty.

Quarterback David Marler finally gets his team playing up to their potential and leads them to an error-free drive all the way for a touchdown, cutting the Blues' lead in half to 14-7. Excellent coverage on the ensuing kickoff means the Blues have to start on their own 23. Things go from bad to worse as Blues' quarterback Merrill gets no help from his blocking and must scramble on three successive plays, ending up with a

fourth down and two from his own 31. Out comes the punter.

Blues' punter Walter James has a heavy rush to contend with but still manages a good kick. As he gets it off, a Reds' defender brushes just past him, and James figures that's good enough to have a *roughing the kicker* penalty called. He tumbles in a very dramatic way. But the officials don't buy it and penalize James 15 yards for *simulating being roughed up by a defender* and make him punt again.

As a result, the Reds end up

Some of the most exciting finishes to games have come about because of pass interference calls on the defense. In effect, the offense is awarded a completion at the spot the penalty took place, so defenders, especially late in the game when their team is winning by a touchdown or less, must take extra care not to interfere when trying to intercept or bat away the ball.

Just as importantly, timing plays a crucial part. Defensive backs are taught to hit the receiver just as he catches the ball if they see that going for the ball is impractical. But hitting the receiver only a fraction of a second before the ball arrives is illegal, and can spell disaster, especially on long passes.

with excellent field position, at the Blues' 42. But on their first play, they are called for having *too many men on the field* at the snap (someone got his assignment wrong and came out when he shouldn't have). Now it's first down and 15. Despite the slow start to the drive, Reds' quarterback Marler finds running back Phil Biggs on a long pass for a touchdown. The PAT is good and the score is tied at 14 as the first quarter ends.

PILING IT ON

On the kickoff, the Reds manage to hold the Blues for a short return, but after the initial tackle, linebacker Craig Jolie tries getting in on the act, though just a little too late. The Reds give up 15 yards for the *piling on* penalty.

The Blues come out flying on the next series of downs. Trying to surprise the Reds, Kenny Merrill throws long to wide receiver Alfred Skaggs. The pass is overthrown and Reds' safety Ricky Jordan moves into position to intercept. Skaggs grabs him and is called for *offensive pass interference*. Once the ball is in the air, both players have an equal right to it, and therefore cannot interfere with the other. The Blues replay the down but 10 yards back.

In seven plays, the Blues move down to the Reds' four-yard line. Because there's less than 10 yards to the end zone, the Blues have a 'first and goal' from the four. When running back Smith is prevented from getting over the goal line, tight end Curt Thompson tries helping out by pushing him over. That's a 10-yard penalty for *helping the runner*, so it's still first and goal, but from the 14.

An *incomplete pass* leaves a second down, so another pass looks inevitable. Unfortunately, offensive guard Bill Brandon is called for being *illegally downfield* when the ball was thrown (he thought the play was a short pass to a running back, so he left the line to help). Another 10 yards and the Blues find themselves with a first and goal from the 24.

The next two pass attempts are batted down, so the Blues send on the field goal squad. Things look pretty dismal when the

Not only has the QB been sacked, *right*, but the referee signals 'illegal man downfield', after spotting a lineman crossing the line of scrimmage.

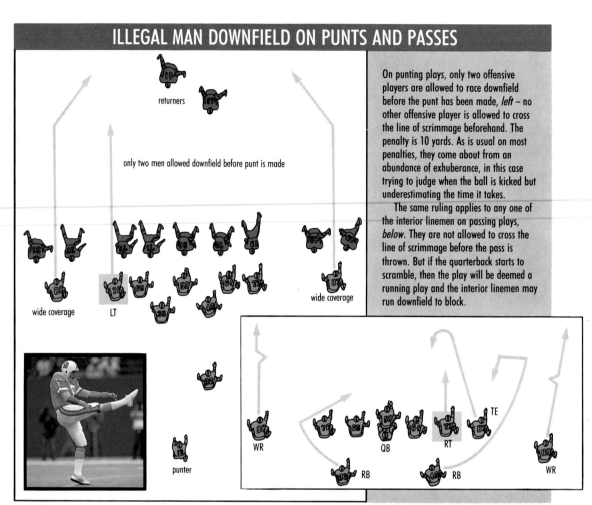

ILLEGAL MAN DOWNFIELD ON PUNTS AND PASSES

returners

only two men allowed downfield before punt is made

wide coverage   LT   wide coverage

punter

On punting plays, only two offensive players are allowed to race downfield before the punt has been made, *left* – no other offensive player is allowed to cross the line of scrimmage beforehand. The penalty is 10 yards. As is usual on most penalties, they come about from an abundance of exhuberance, in this case trying to judge when the ball is kicked but underestimating the time it takes.

The same ruling applies to any one of the interior linemen on passing plays, *below*. They are not allowed to cross the line of scrimmage before the pass is thrown. But if the quarterback starts to scramble, then the play will be deemed a running play and the interior linemen may run downfield to block.

WR   QB   RT   TE
RB   RB   WR

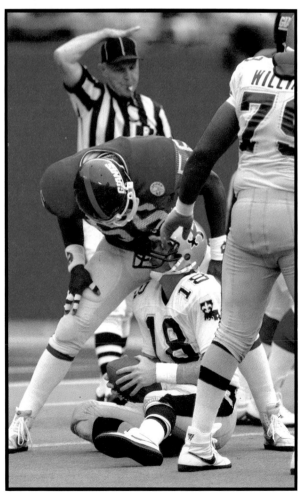

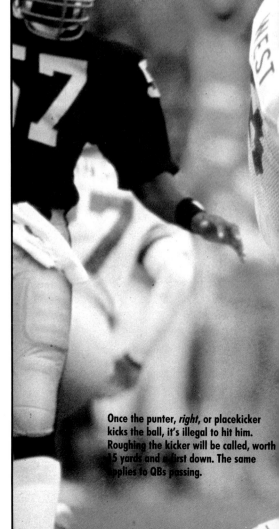

Once the punter, *right*, or placekicker kicks the ball, it's illegal to hit him. Roughing the kicker will be called, worth 15 yards and a first down. The same applies to QBs passing.

kick is blocked, but they perk up again after the referee rules that Reds' safety Paul Stringer *began his run up to block the kick before the snap* – that's a 15-yard penalty. The Blues line up again to try for the field goal, but this time it's a fake, and holder Todd Blackmore scampers unhampered for a touchdown. The extra point is good and the score is 21-14 for the Blues.

On the following kickoff, one of the Blues' coverage *touches the face guard* of Reds' returner John Toomay, adding five yards to the return.

Later on in the drive Reds' offensive tackle Fred Sully is called for *holding* a defensive end while blocking on a pass play – he is legally allowed to use an open hand, but he's not allowed to clutch his opponent in any way. And it's a 10-yard penalty.

Quarterback Marler leads his team down the field with time running out in the first half, but there's a setback when the Reds are called for an illegal *crackback block*. A receiver who is split more than five yards from the nearest offensive linemen is not allowed to run to the inside of the field to block a linebacker or secondary man

below the legs on a running play. It's a 15-yard penalty but the Reds manage to score a field goal before the half ends.

SECOND HALF SENTENCE

With the score at 21-17 for the Blues, the Reds are first to receive. An excellent runback to the Blues' 48 is added to when one of the coverage team is called for *unsportsmanlike conduct*. He claimed the returner had stepped out of bounds much earlier and argued with the referee – 15 yards.

Not wanting to waste this great oportunity, Reds' QB Marler takes his time to make sure the play takes best advantage of the defense. But the 30-second clock runs out before the snap and the Reds are penalized five yards for *delay of game*. It doesn't stop their momentum and they end up scoring a touchdown from a long run by Phil Biggs, making the score 24-21 for the Reds.

After exchanging punts, there is a spate of penalties. On the second punt, the Reds are called for *fair catch interference* – they are not allowed to touch the punt returner once he has made his fair catch signal. The

FLAG WAVING

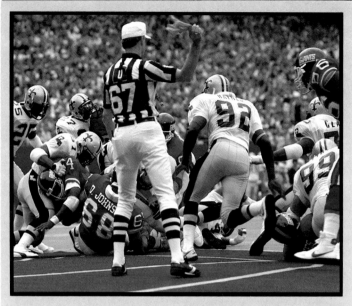

It is the job of the officials to keep track of the game and to call penalties when necessary. When a penalty is spotted, the official pulls out one of the two yellow flags he carries and throws it on the ground towards the spot at which the infringement took place.

Once the play has ended, the official consults with the referee (and possibly other officials), instructing him as to what happened and who was in the wrong.

Once the referee is happy that everything is in order, he moves to the centre of the field to let the crowd and both teams hear his decision. This he does both with his hand signals and by using his remote microphone that's linked to the public address system. The whole procedure is so smooth that only a few seconds are needed from the flag being thrown to the public announcement being made – a fact all fans greatly appreciate.

Blues gain 15 yards.

On the second play after the punt return, Blues' tight end Pete Malone is put in motion but the officials rules he was *moving toward the line of scrimmage at the snap* – and penalized five yards. Quarterback Merrill manages to lead his team to the Reds' 27-yard line, but they are penalized 10 yards when running back Davis fumbles and tries *batting the ball* forward towards the end zone. With a fourth down, the Blues send in their kicker.

The Blues attempt a fake field goal with the holder throwing a short down and out pass to tight end Malone, who's slipped off the line and moved towards the end zone. He has to come back for the pass at the three, is tackled, and a defender butts him with his helmet as he tackles him. It's a 15-yard penalty for *butting with the helmet*, but because there is less than that to the end zone, the ruling is that the ball is moved 'half the distance to the goal line'. In two plays the Blues score a touchdown and it's 28-24 for the Blues.

On the PAT, a Reds' player *runs into the kicker*, but it's un-

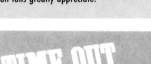

RETURN TO SENDER
St Louis Cardinals' Roy 'Jet Stream' Green appeared to set an NFL record on 21 October 1979 when he returned a kickoff for 108 yards against the Dallas Cowboys. But after the officials had consulted over the matter, they decided that Green was only six yards deep in the end zone when he began his return – not eight. So now Green shares the record for the longest kickoff return with Al Carmichael of the Green Bay Packers and Noland 'Super Gnat' Smith of the Kansas City Chiefs – all three players with 106-yard returns.

intentional. The kick is good, so the five-yard penalty is tacked onto the kickoff – the Blues will kickoff from their own 40, instead of the 35.

The long kickoff sails through the Reds' end zone and they are awarded a *touchback* – they start play on their own 20.

After moving down the field, Reds' quarterback Marler gets hit well after throwing the ball.

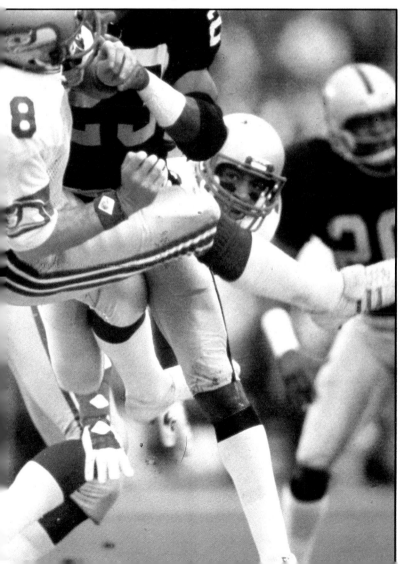

FACE MASK PENALTIES – ACCIDENTAL AND INTENTIONAL

In the interests of players' safety, the stiff penalty of 15 yards is assessed against a team whose player twists, turns or grabs a player by his face mask, *left* and *below*. The dramatic photograph was taken in Super Bowl XVI, as Cincinnati's Cris Collinsworth managed to catch a long pass with San Francisco's Eric Wright doing everything to stop him. A player may accidentally touch a face mask, *far left*, which incurs a five-yard penalty.

It's a 15-yard penalty for *roughing the passer* and a first down – at the Blues' 27. The Reds' defense holds and the Blues are forced to try a field goal. This time a Blues' defender is called for *unnecessary roughness* on an offensive lineman (taking a pot-shot out of frustration). This moves the ball to the Blues' 12 (it was a 15-yard penalty) as the third quarter ends.

ILLEGAL BATTING
On the first play of the fourth quarter, quarterback Marler rolls left on a play action pass and looks for his tight end in the end zone. On the rollout, he's sacked and *fumbles* the ball. One of Marler's lineman tries *batting* it out of bounds for safety's sake. It's called and penalized 10 yards, leaving first down and 20 from the Blues' 22.

After a couple of ineffectual running plays, the Reds line up for their third-down play. The play is called so that the ball will be snapped on Marler's third 'Hut!', but one of the linemen stutters on the second one, luring Blues' nose tackle Marty Lorimar across the line. The

Reds are penalized five yards for a *false start* and have a third and 23 from the 25-yard line.

The Reds' field goal attempt is good, putting the score at 28-27 for the Blues.

THE LIFE OF A PUNTER
The Blues get nowhere on offense and are forced to punt the ball. Just after getting the ball off, punter James is belted by an onrushing cornerback, who's called for *roughing the kicker* – 15 yards and an automatic first down. Another dismal effort forces the Blues into another punting situation.

This time, they are called for having an ineligible man downfield before the ball is kicked – only two men are allowed to leave the line of scrimmage beforehand. It's a 10-yard penalty and the Blues are forced to punt again. Walter gets off an incredible punt, sailing over the return man and going out of bounds at the Reds'

When an offensive lineman has his elbows out and hands in, it's difficult to detect holding, *below*. NFL officials are trained to spot such penalties.

three-yard line. That's where the Reds will take over with less than five minutes left in the fourth quarter.

On their second play from scrimmage, Reds' quarterback Marler mishandles the snap from center and the ball rolls into the end zone. Marler pounces on it but the defense pounces on him, scoring a safety – two points. The score is now 30-27 for the Blues.

Because the safety was scored against the Reds, they have to kickoff, from their own 20. It's called a *free kick*, and must be either punted or drop-kicked: in both cases, there is no snap, and the team lines up as though it were a normal kickoff situation – the rules are the same.

Luckily for the Reds, the Blues are unable to generate any offense and are forced to punt. The Reds get the ball back and are given a break when Blues' defensive end Ken Robertson *twists the face mask* of Reds' running back Biggs. The 15-yard penalty takes the ball to midfield.

On the next play, a defender is called for *tripping* Reds' center Cliff Cowley. That's a 10-yard penalty which takes the ball to the Blues' 40.

Things look grim for the Reds as Marler fires a pass and wide receiver Billy Owens fumbles

HOLDING ON PASSING AND RUNNING PLAYS

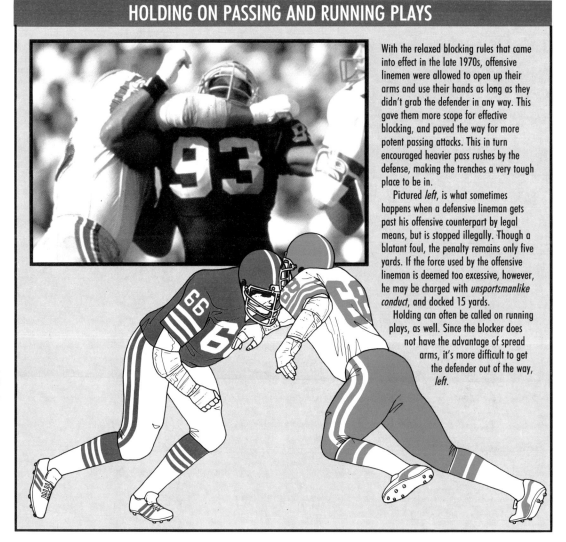

With the relaxed blocking rules that came into effect in the late 1970s, offensive linemen were allowed to open up their arms and use their hands as long as they didn't grab the defender in any way. This gave them more scope for effective blocking, and paved the way for more potent passing attacks. This in turn encouraged heavier pass rushes by the defense, making the trenches a very tough place to be in.

Pictured *left*, is what sometimes happens when a defensive lineman gets past his offensive counterpart by legal means, but is stopped illegally. Though a blatant foul, the penalty remains only five yards. If the force used by the offensive lineman is deemed too excessive, however, he may be charged with *unsportsmanlike conduct*, and docked 15 yards.

Holding can often be called on running plays, as well. Since the blocker does not have the advantage of spread arms, it's more difficult to get the defender out of the way, *left*.

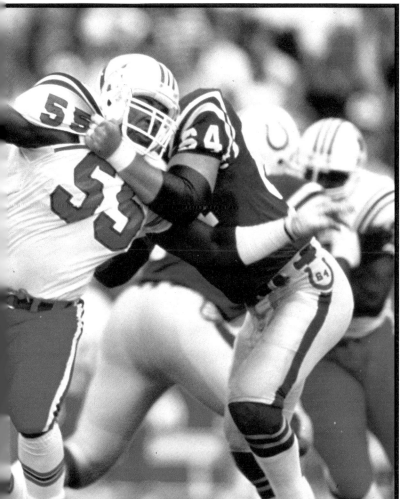

Indianapolis Colts' Benn Utt grabs New England Patriots' Don Blackmon after being beaten on a blitz, *left*. The penalty is five yards but the sack could mean a lot more yards lost to the offense.

the ball, which bounces about until Blues linebacker Fredricks kicks it out of bounds with 15 seconds left in the game. The 10-yard penalty *for illegally kicking the ball* takes the Reds to the Blues' 30.

Trying to surprise the Blues, Marler calls a draw play up the middle – it works and takes the ball to the Blues' 12. With their last time out, the Reds set up for a field goal. As the clock runs out, the kick is good and ties the game at 30, forcing *overtime*.

OVERTIME
With the home team Reds' fans screaming wildly, the officials meet at midfield for the coin toss. The Reds win and decide to return the kick. There is little wind and it's twilight, so neither end is worse than the other. The Reds' fans erupt. Whoever scores first wins.

With a deep kickoff, the Reds return to their own 32-yard line. Two quick passes take the ball to midfield and it looks as though the Reds are going for the kill. In seven more plays, the Reds get down to the Blues' 17 with a third down and one, and they attempt a pass.

The Reds take up a short-yardage alignment and the defense puts nine men at the line and has two cornerbacks. But the Reds have decided to go for a play action and receiver Owens sprints down the sideline. The pass is overthrown and he catches it just disappearing out of the end zone. The field judge rules it out. But the fans think it's good and the Reds' team think it's good. It's up to the *Replay Official*.

Equipped with two monitors and a high-speed video cassette recorder (VCR), it takes the *Replay Official* only one look to make his decision. He informs the referee who goes to midfield to make his announcement. The TD is declared good and the Reds win 36-30 in overtime.

79

GAME PLAN

The special teams squads are as important as both the offense and the defense – a missed field goal could mean the difference between finishing out of the playoffs or winning the Super Bowl

Modern American Football strategy relies heavily on the special teams. Every NFL club has special 11-man groups that take care of punts, punt returns, kickoffs, kickoff returns, field goal and extra point attempts. The reason they are so important is that in every kicking situation there is the possibility of a touchdown.

A certain kind of player is needed on special teams, summed up by Walt Michaels, former head coach of the New York Jets: 'Everyone has some fear. A man who has no fear belongs in a mental institution. Or on special teams.'

KICKOFFS

On a kickoff, the ball is spotted on the kicking team's 35-yard line. Their aim will be to kick the ball as deep as possible while limiting the returner to as short a return as possible. The kicking team will put their fastest players near the sideline to contain the runner (to keep him to the inside of the field), and their hardest hitters toward the middle.

So, members of the kicking team are assigned positions to the left or right of the kicker. They are given numbers in the team playbook from 1 to 5. Those players on the left are numbered L1 to L5 and on the right R1 to R5.

In order to avoid kicking to a dangerous return man, and to foil returns in general, a kicker can *squib kick* the ball. When a squib kick (a low, hard drive)

hits the field, it usually starts bouncing crazily, which makes it very difficult to handle. The effectiveness of the squib kick was never more apparent than in Super Bowl XVI, when San Francisco's Ray Wersching took advantage of the hard artificial surface in the Pontiac Silverdome, in Michigan, to continually blunt the returns of Cincinnati.

KICKOFF RETURNS

There are three separate groups of players to be found on a kick-off return team.

The first wave consists of five blockers, who line up on the opponent's 45- or 50-yard line. Their first assignment is to guard against a possible *onside kick*, a short 10-yarder that can be legally retrieved by the kicking team. Once the ball is kicked off, they retreat to a predetermined spot to block for the kick returner. The five players included in this group are usually quick offensive or defensive linemen, or linebackers who are also excellent blockers.

The second group comprises a four-man *wedge* of blockers, who position themselves about their 25-yard line. The wedge men have the most critical blocking assignments, since they are the ones who clear the path for the return man by shaping themselves into a 'V' pattern, knocking down the first wave of tacklers.

The last group consists of the two return men, who set up near the goal line to receive the kickoff. Kick returners are usually running backs, wide receivers, or defensive backs – players who are used to handling the ball. There are three essentials for kick returners: good hands, speed, and courage, since there are at least 10 men barrelling down the field at full speed to stop them.

ONSIDE KICKS

A kickoff becomes a *free ball* (anyone can recover it) once it has travelled at least 10 yards. An *onside kick* takes advantage of this rule; the kicking team's objective is to recover the ball before the receiving team can get to it, instead of conceding possession by kicking it far downfield. Consequently, the

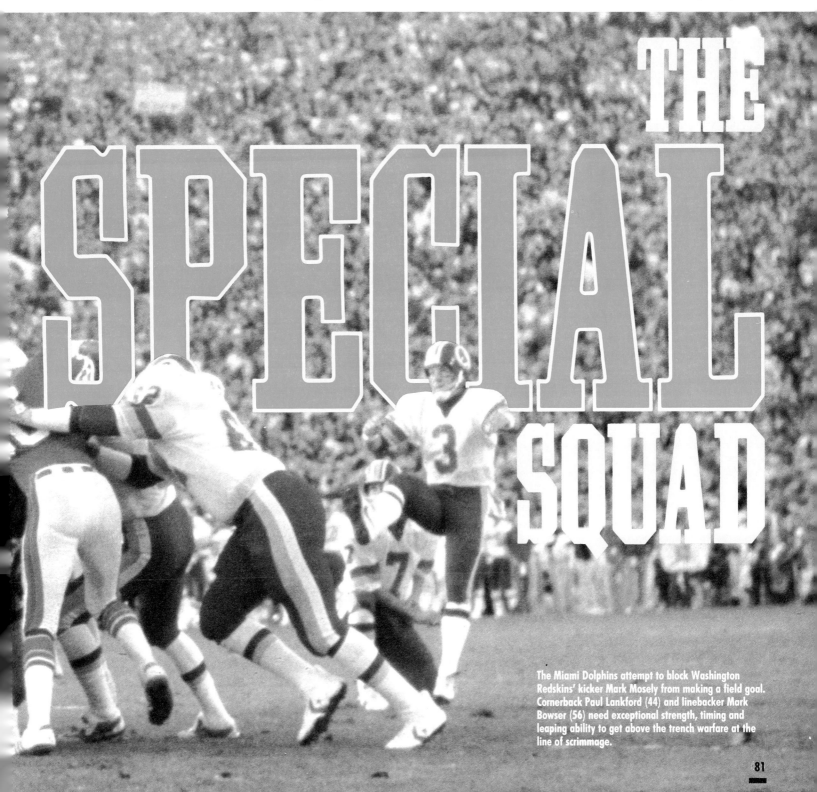

THE SPECIAL SQUAD

The Miami Dolphins attempt to block Washington Redskins' kicker Mark Mosely from making a field goal. Cornerback Paul Lankford (44) and linebacker Mark Bowser (56) need exceptional strength, timing and leaping ability to get above the trench warfare at the line of scrimmage.

CONTAINING THE RETURN

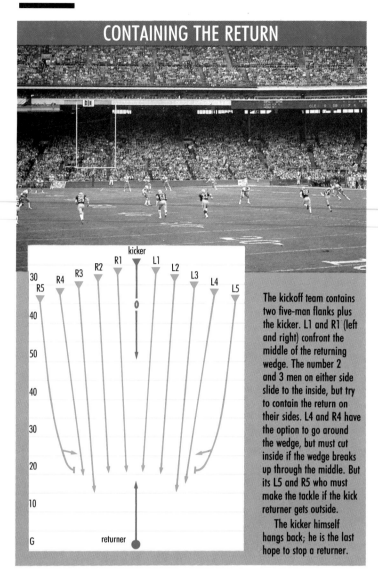

kicker

30 R5 R4 R3 R2 R1 L1 L2 L3 L4 L5
40
50
40
30
20
10
G   returner

The kickoff team contains two five-man flanks plus the kicker. L1 and R1 (left and right) confront the middle of the returning wedge. The number 2 and 3 men on either side slide to the inside, but try to contain the return on their sides. L4 and R4 have the option to go around the wedge, but must cut inside if the wedge breaks up through the middle. But its L5 and R5 who must make the tackle if the kick returner gets outside.

The kicker himself hangs back; he is the last hope to stop a returner.

THE 10-YARD ONSIDE KICK

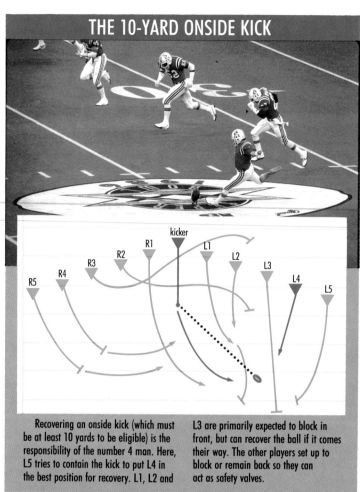

kicker
R1 R2 R3 R4 R5 L1 L2 L3 L4 L5

Recovering an onside kick (which must be at least 10 yards to be eligible) is the responsibility of the number 4 man. Here, L5 tries to contain the kick to put L4 in the best position for recovery. L1, L2 and L3 are primarily expected to block in front, but can recover the ball if it comes their way. The other players set up to block or remain back so they can act as safety valves.

SETTING UP RETURN BLOCKING

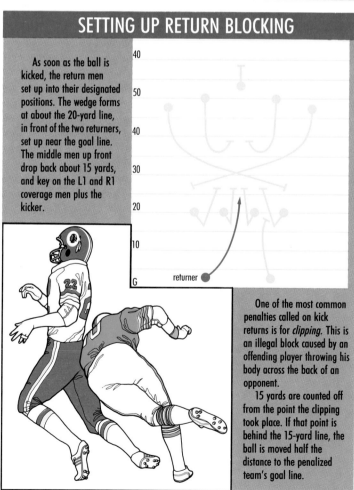

As soon as the ball is kicked, the return men set up into their designated positions. The wedge forms at about the 20-yard line, in front of the two returners, set up near the goal line. The middle men up front drop back about 15 yards, and key on the L1 and R1 coverage men plus the kicker.

40 50 40 30 20 10 G   returner

One of the most common penalties called on kick returns is for *clipping*. This is an illegal block caused by an offending player throwing his body across the back of an opponent.

15 yards are counted off from the point the clipping took place. If that point is behind the 15-yard line, the ball is moved half the distance to the penalized team's goal line.

---

players required for executing an onside kick must be quick and have good hands.

Onside kicks are most frequently used late in a game by a team that's behind and in need of at least one more possession to attempt a score. They aren't often tried at other times because if the receiving team does recover the ball (as it will most of the time), it will have much better field position – usually near the 50-yard line.

An onside kick can either be kicked softly in a short arc or as

a hard, low drive – much like a squib kick. The kicker tries to aim the ball at a predetermined area, 10 yards away, so that the kicking team can make a legal recovery.

However, despite the type of kick, deception is the kicking team's greatest ally.

When the receiving team suspects an onside kick is coming, especially late in the game, it will insert its own onside specialists. Like the players on the kicking team, they have good hands and are accustomed to handling the ball; they are often wide receivers, tight ends, running backs, and defensive backs. These players are positioned 10 yards from where the ball is being kicked, usually near the 45-yard line.

FIELD GOALS AND 'PATS'

There are two ways a team can score by kicking the ball: *points after touchdowns* (also called PATs, extra points, or conversions) and *field goals*.

In both cases the ball must be

kicked from the ground. It is positioned vertically, at a slight angle, by a holder and it must pass between the uprights and over the crossbar of the goal post for it to be successful.

Extra points are worth one point and are only kicked after a touchdown has been scored. The ball is initially placed on the three-yard line, is snapped to the holder and kicked from about the 10-yard line. Since the goal post is set 10 yards deep in the end zone, extra point attempts are approximately 20-yard kicks.

Field goals, which are executed in the same basic manner as conversions, are worth three points and can be kicked from any spot on the field, though they are rarely attempted beyond the 40-yard line.

Soccer-style kickers (also known as *sidewinders*) have become predominant in the NFL. But the straight-on kicker was the only type of kicker in the NFL before the mid-1960s. They'd approach the ball facing forward and kick it with their toes, using a special shoe with a metal cap. Shoes aren't necessary for kickers and recently there have been several barefoot kickers in the NFL, most notably the New England Patriots' Tony Franklin.

There is actually a third way to score on a kick – the drop kick – which hasn't been used for years, though it's a legal way to kick field goals. A drop kick starts off like a punt, but the kicker allows the ball to hit the ground before kicking it after the bounce.

BLOCKING KICKS

Field goals and extra points (as well as punts) can be blocked by the defensive team. But when it happens, it's usually the result

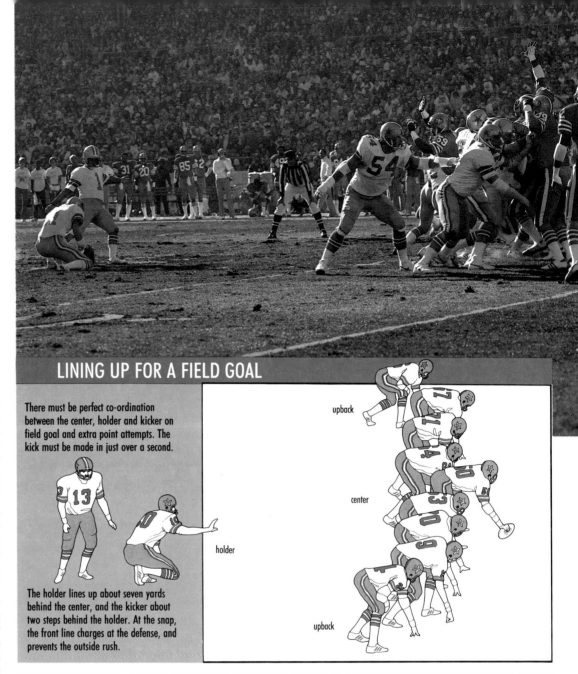

LINING UP FOR A FIELD GOAL

There must be perfect co-ordination between the center, holder and kicker on field goal and extra point attempts. The kick must be made in just over a second.

The holder lines up about seven yards behind the center, and the kicker about two steps behind the holder. At the snap, the front line charges at the defense, and prevents the outside rush.

upback

center

holder

upback

PUTTING PRESSURE ON THE FIELD GOAL SQUAD

The best chance a defense has of blocking a field goal or extra point is to overload one side of the line with a heavy rush. This isolates the tight end and upback on three or more defenders, at least one of whom should get free to attack the kicker.

kicker

holder

upback

upback

overload

safety
(in case of short kick)

SPREADING OUT THE COVERAGE ON PUNTING PLAYS

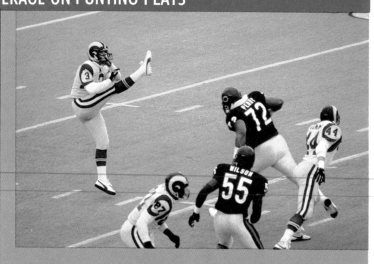

upback   upback

fullback

punter

The priority on all punt coverage plays is to get downfield as quickly as possible, to stifle any chance of a good return. At the snap, everyone up front on the line blocks until the ball has been kicked. The two men lined up on either end sprint down the field immediately, trying to keep the returner to the inside. Once the ball has been kicked, however, everyone, including the punter himself, runs downfield to prevent the returner from making good yardage. Their aim is to tackle the returner before he's gone too far.

The sign of a good punt coverage team is to hold the returners to five yards or less on each kick, while punting an average of at least 43 yards, giving a net gain of about 38 yards.

of a mistake by the kicking team. Because of the short time involved in making a kick, if there is a good snap, a good hold, and the line blocking is reasonably competent, it's difficult for any defensive men to penetrate before the ball is in the air.

The longer the time taken for the kick, however, the more chance there is for a block. Most kickers take at least a tenth of a second longer to hit the ball from beyond 40 yards. There is also a lower trajectory, due to the increased distance. As a result, more long field goal attempts are blocked than short ones.

Most members of the field goal/extra point blocking teams are tall defensive linemen and linebackers who are excellent pass rushers. These players fill in the middle areas along the line of scrimmage and either try to break through the offensive line to block the kick or leap high in the air to bat down a low kick. The players on the outside of the defensive line (chosen for their quickness) are actually the players with the best chance of blocking an attempt, because

For special teams, one of the most important things they can do is block a kick. Usually attempted by linebackers and cornerbacks, blocked punts can put a team in scoring position.

of their direct, and sometimes unimpeded line to the backfield. Two or three players are usually set deep (on long field goal attempts) to guard against gadget plays or to return a kick that falls short of the end zone.

THE PUNTING GAME

Except for the punter, the punt coverage team is comprised primarily of defensive players.

NOBODY'S PERFECT
In his 11-year career with the San Francisco 49ers, kicker Tommy Davis missed only two of his 350 extra point attempts. This is still the best record in NFL history – an incredible 99.43 per cent!

Linebackers are ideal punt coverage men, since they are usually the surest, quickest, and most aggressive tacklers.

The players who man the two outside positions for the punting team race down the field at the snap before the ball is punted. They must be able to manoeuvre around blocks by members of the return team and have the speed to get downfield quickly – sometimes

before the return man even has a chance to catch the ball. This job usually belongs to quick cornerbacks and safeties.

The center, as on field goals and extra points, has a crucial assignment on punts. He must snap the ball – very accurately – approximately 15 yards, which is the distance the punter stands back from the line of scrimmage.

The fullback, who stands between the center and punter (at a slight angle, so he won't interfere with the snap), must be a very reliable blocker, able to pick up any rusher who breaks through the line. There are also two other blockers in the backfield, called *upbacks*, who stand just behind the linemen to either side of the center. They reinforce the middle of the line, which receives the most pressure from the defense.

BLOCKING PUNTS

The most common way of blocking a punt is to mass an unexpected number of players against one part of the offensive line (this is known as *overloading*). In an all-out effort to get to the punter and block the punt, all 10 members of the blocking team (excluding the returner) can be assigned to rush.

The offensive center is a prime candidate to be attacked by a punt-blocking team, as he has the difficult assignment of making the snap to the punter and will be off balance for a split second afterwards.

When a team decides to return a punt (instead of trying to block it), every player on the return team knows which direction the ball will be run back and must stick to the plan. Punt returners rarely run the ball back haphazardly, though it often looks as if they do!

Returning punts is one of the most dangerous jobs in the game. When a punt is in the air, the returner must concentrate totally on the flight of the ball, and must make one of several choices. He can catch the ball and run with it through a swarming maze of tacklers; he can wave his arm in the air (while the punt is in flight) and call for a *fair catch*; or, if the punt appears too difficult to handle, he can let it bounce and roll dead.

The fair catch rule stops the play as soon as the ball is caught, and play will start at that point.

RAZZLE DAZZLE ON FIELD GOALS AND PUNTS

Just as on passing and running plays, there are gadgets designed to work on special teams plays. Onside kicks are an example of gadgets for kickoffs. Mostly, though, gadgets are used on punts and field goal attempts.

FAKING A FIELD GOAL
The quarterback is used as ball holder on field goals because of his ball handling abilities. And his expertise in running plays also comes in handy.

The holder's first assignment, before he calls the snap signals, is to examine the defense to determine if there is an overload to one side of the line (which may signify an all-out block attempt).

For example, if the holder sees a defensive overload to the right side of the line (six men to the right of the center), he may call an audible for a gadget play, because he knows the defense will be vulnerable on the side away from the overload. In that case, instead of placing the ball for a kick when he receives the snap, the holder will stand up and roll out to the left side of the line with three options. He can continue to run the ball himself. He can pass to the left upback, who, after hearing the audible, will run downfield as a receiver, or he can pitch the ball back to the kicker, who has trailed the holder down the line on a parallel course, anticipating a lateral.

If this play is executed properly, it is almost impossible for an overloaded defense to stop it.

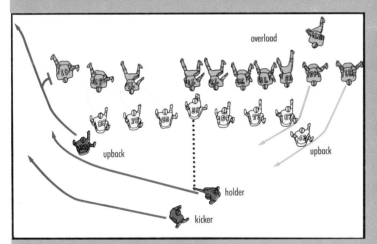

FAKING A PUNT
The most common planned gadget play from a punt formation calls for the fullback (or the player who lines up between the center and punter) to receive the snap directly from the center. After catching the snap, the fullback then runs to a designated hole, or gap, in the offensive line. He'll often have blocking help from one or both of the *upbacks* (lined up just behind the line on either side of the center), who lead him through the hole or to the outside. This gadget is used when the punting team has only a few yards (rarely more than five) to go for a first down.

The most common unplanned gadget play from punt formation involves the spontaneous actions of the punter. If he sees an opening in the defense and feels he can pick up the necessary yardage for his team to maintain possession, the punter may try to run the ball. This move is often unknown to any other person on the field (or even the coach on the sideline). It can be very successful if the punter catches the defense napping but it can turn into a costly blunder if it fails.

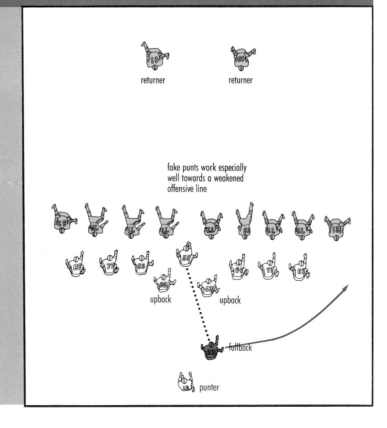

fake punts work especially well towards a weakened offensive line

BLUEPRINT VICTORY

The coach's preparation for each game relies heavily on poring over game films and past performances. The result is the game plan itself, a complex strategy of innovation and attack

American Football is chock-full of jargon, some of which is based on mistaken notions of what the original term or phrase meant. Other terms and phrases are exaggerated by the press to such an extent that the average fan is left with a very different idea from what NFL players and coaches actually mean.

One of the best examples of this is the *game plan*, which is commonly thought of as being on a par with the most tightly guarded state secrets, or as being some mysterious formula for assured victory.

A game plan is really a list of plays that a team has practised and intends to use at some point during a game. The plan breaks down that list into runs and passes – against different defensive fronts, for short yardage situations, at the goal line, for the two-minute offense, against zone defenses, and so on.

In simple terms, the game plan is a list of runs and passes broken down into what one team wants to do against another. It stems from one or two philosophies: either studying the other team's defense and building a plan of attack to exploit its weaknesses; or else taking what the offense does best while hoping to find some favourable matchups.

Once a team has put together its game plan, it then has to put it into practise. It has to decide how to use it in the actual game, and how to call the plays in the various situations that come up against the opposition.

GAME PLAN IN ACTION

To begin with, the offense starts out with the knowledge that it has one sure advantage over the defense: it knows the play and the snap count. From there, it wants to keep the advantage, trying to ensure that the defense must guess where the play is going and when.

So when a coach or player states that his team will try to establish a running or passing game, it's not quite the truth. In that case the defense would know what was coming the majority of the time. A good game plan aims to present a mixture of plays. The secret of offensive success comes from being both a running and a passing team in some kind of unpredictable mixture.

Despite the inherent logic in this, teams often do things like throw long bombs out of desperation, or resort to gadget plays if things aren't going so well for them.

What a mixture of plays does, more than anything else, is force the opposition to cover the entire field – and keep them guessing their player positions.

So on running plays, the offense wants the defense to think that they are as likely to run sweeps to the outside as they are to run inside. On passes, the aim is to mix patterns to the outside with patterns to the inside and up the middle. As for depth, the offense wants to show the defensive secondary that they're willing to throw as far as the goal line, and any-

FOR

After a week's intense preparation, Landry's game plan is complete and ready to guide Dallas from the kickoff to the end of the game. A good game plan — and Landry does some of the best — can greatly influence the outcome.

POSSESSION-TYPE FOOTBALL FROM THE OFFENSE'S FIVE-YARD LINE

The golden rule for offenses between their own goal line and their five-yard line is simple – don't create any turnovers. A fumble here will surely result in the opposition taking advantage and scoring easily.

For plays from this area of the field, the playbook will include mostly straight handoffs and the most basic runs, usually up the middle. You won't see many pitchouts, passes into coverage, or swoops that are likely to lose yards. A loss of yardage here would leave the offense in a very dangerous position which could well result in a safety for the defense.

A tight end will often replace a wide receiver, providing extra blocking power where it's needed – and big running backs sometimes replace quicker but lighter backs. This size is necessary for plays where brute force replaces subtlety.

If nothing else, the offense must get to at least the five-yard line, to give its punter the required 15-yard distance to punt from the line of scrimmage – anything less and the punt is liable to be blocked.

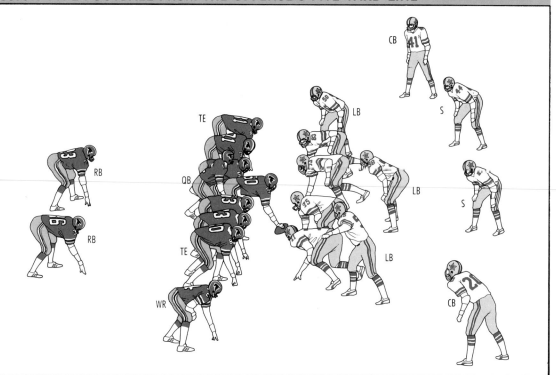

where in between.

Naturally, since the defense has no idea what the offense is going to do, but knows that it could go anywhere, it has to lay off coverage slightly, so giving the offense that much more room to manoeuvre.

SELECTING PLAYS

All good teams strive for variety in their play selection. They coach it, they draft players to achieve it, and they build their entire teams on that vital basis.

A good example of a team having a limited offense and then turning it around with excellent play selection is the New York Giants. For years, they were purely a fullback-orientated team, running Rob Carpenter and Butch Woolfolk up the middle, between both tackles.

This allowed the defense to tighten up their coverage, since they didn't have to play the entire width of the field.

The Giants' passing attack was as uninspired, throwing possession-type passes to slow receivers. The Giants just weren't stretching the defense either way.

Today's Giants are a different story. With Phil Simms quickly maturing as one of the league's top quarterbacks, his arsenal of players has improved dramatically. Running back Joe Morris has the speed and moves to go either inside or outside, while wide receivers Lionel Manuel, Bob Johnson and Stacy Robinson provide the deep threat. Tight ends Zeke Mowatt and Mark Bavaro give the Giants

the power and strength for the short passing game.

Because Simms is taking advantage of his personnel, and mixing the plays effectively, the Giants have become, within only a few years, one of the NFL's offensive powerhouses.

MIXING PLAYS

Just because a team doesn't have an exceptional group of players, it needn't abandon the idea of mixing plays. The San Francisco 49ers went to Super Bowl XVI without great running talent – in short, without Wendell Tyler and Roger Craig.

But the 49ers succeeded by passing when their opponents thought they were going to run, and vice versa. And instead of running outside, they would throw flares and swing passes to the running backs, which accomplished the same thing. In fact, it worked so well that the 49ers went home from the Super Bowl as winners.

PREPARING FOR A GAME

Under the rules for the NFL video exchange, each team is entitled to videos of its upcoming opponent's previous three games. If the opponent is a team they've played recently – say, a divisional rival – then they'll also have videos of their previous meetings.

The offensive coaches extract

COMING FROM ALL SIDES

The Pittsburgh Steelers' four Super Bowl teams had arguably the best mix of talent ever seen in the NFL. Quarterback Terry Bradshaw was blessed with running backs Franco Harris, a powerful inside runner who could also sweep with equal effectiveness, and Rocky Bleier, a great all-round runner and receiver. Wide receivers Lynn Swann and John Stallworth were perhaps the best one-two combination in history, being equalled of late only by the Miami Dolphins' 'Marks' brothers – Mark Clayton and Mark 'Super' Duper.

Rounding out the receiving corps were tight ends Randy Crossman and Bennie Cunningham – a tight end in the classical mould, a big powerful blocker as well as a sure-handed, swift receiver who could run impeccable patterns. With that talent, Bradshaw's play selection and mixture had a scope unlikely to be matched.

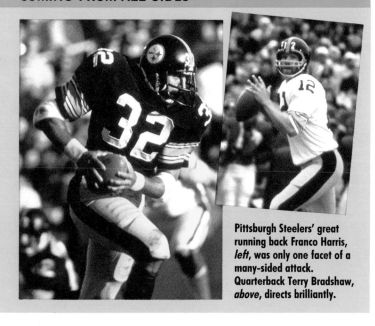

Pittsburgh Steelers' great running back Franco Harris, *left*, was only one facet of a many-sided attack. Quarterback Terry Bradshaw, *above*, directs brilliantly.

defensive information from the video and feed it into a computer, which then informs them, on a statistical and average basis, what the defense is likely to do in every situation.

Given that knowledge, the offensive coaches build up their game plan, deciding which of their plays and players would work best against those situations. Then they break down the plays further by down situation and position on the field.

FIELD POSITION

In order to have an effective game plan, the usefulness of each play has to be assessed among other factors, for its effectiveness at different positions on the field. In coaching terms, the field is divided into *plus* and *minus* areas – the territory in the offense's half is minus, and in the defense's half it's plus.

The first area to consider is the offense's goal line up to the minus-5. The only thing to consider here is how to get out of trouble, with the five-yard line being the imperative. Why the five-yard line? Because from there, their punter will have the proper amount of room to kick; otherwise he'll be cramped and the chances of being blocked will increase. What's more, a blocked punt in that area of the field almost guarantees the opposition some points.

Suppose a kickoff return was fumbled and the team had to start at its two-yard line. The set of plays for that part of the field would include direct no-nonsense runs, straight hand-offs, no pitchouts, no passes thrown into coverage or sweeps that could lose yardage. The latter would certainly end up giving the defense a safety, scoring two points.

Once past the five, the offense uses plays drawn for the area from the minus-5 to the minus-20. The priority here is to avoid a turnover. Gaining yards helps of course – and the punter will have plenty of room to manoeuvre – but a turnover could be disastrous.

OPENING UP

Once past the 20-yard line, the offense can reach into its basic playbook. From here, things get a bit more interesting.

On first down, the defense is most likely to show run prevention. So the offense wants some first-down runs that have a

chance against that alignment. But it also wants some first-down passes that can exploit the defense's commitment to the run.

Besides these first-down plays, the offense then needs a set for second and short (three yards or less) and second and long (seven or more). The offense also needs a similar group for third down situations.

In this area of the field, from the minus-20 to midfield, the offense wants runs and passes that work against normal defenses (a 4-3-4 or 3-4-4), plus runs and passes for every one of the combination defenses that the coaches saw on the videos.

On third downs, for instance, the offense needs several categories of plans. It would work up a short-yardage game plan for situations when it needs a yard or two to keep a drive going; for when it needs between three and six yards and expects to see a normal defense; and a plan for third and long that would be geared to beat the defenses with five, or more, defensive backs.

PULLING OUT THE STOPS

In the area between midfield and plus-20, the offense wants to show the defense everything it's got. It wants to force the defense to cover sideline to sideline, and from the line of scrimmage to the end line at the back of the end zone. When a de-

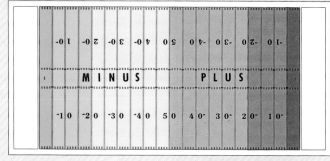

A coach's view of the football field turns it into a game of plus and minus

offense's priority is to reach the 5 safe play area – avoid turnovers

minus-20 to midfield and midfield to plus-20 is where teams can open up a tight, pressing defense to contend with the toughest yardage to gain.

From a coaching standpoint, deciding what plays to use in any given situation can best be seen diagrammatically. For example, a shotgun formation from midfield, *top right*, clearly shows how the space on the field is taken advantage of. The short yardage set, *right*, with its three tight ends and closely grouped backfield, looks like it can't fail. This formation has a twist built in – because tight ends are also eligible pass receivers, they can slip out on play action passes.

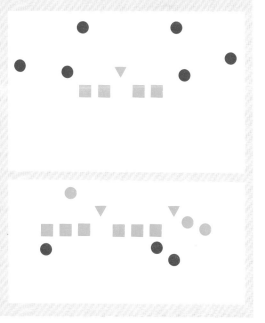

A common problem with game plans that deal with goal line situations is that they become too conservative, using only straight-ahead power drives. In Super Bowl XVI, against a stubborn San Francisco 49ers defense, the Cincinnati Bengals failed in four attempts to cross the goal line from inside the five.

REACHING INTO THE PLAYBOOK – MOVING THE BALL FROM MIDFIELD

When a team reaches this area of the field, they can reach into their playbook and really be creative. There is nothing preventing them from using any play in the book, so you'll quite often see long bombs, deep 'in' patterns, and passes going to anywhere on the field. The offense is at its greatest advantage here, with a huge range of possibilities to exploit.

The key here is that the offense has the entire width of the field to work with, as well as at least 50 yards deep. This spreads out the defense, which in turn leaves gaping holes in the coverage. But this has to be taken advantage of by using the plays in an unpredictable mixture. If the defense doesn't know what's coming, they will obviously have to defend as much territory as possible.

The defense will most likely show a run defense on first downs, so the offense wants some effective running plays against the formation, plus some passing plays that will exploit it. After that, the offense wants to make opportunities for itself with good play selection.

fense is forced to cover the field like that, huge holes are likely to open up for the offense.

Once inside the 20-yard line, things change once again. The offense can't afford to be reckless because a score is at stake. Also, the field has effectively shrunk to 30 yards or less, so the defense can concentrate its coverage a lot more easily.

In these close quarters, the defense will be playing man-to-man coverage, and probably blitzing a good deal – since it will be pressuring the offense anyway, it may as well send in a linebacker. But blitzing is also a good idea – if it succeeds, it can push the offense right out of field goal range.

GOAL LINE STRATEGY
The area inside the 20-yard line (plus-20) is broken down further towards the goal line. Instances arise, for example, when a team has a first-and-10 from, say, the 11-yard line. First down isn't the problem here because the defense must still be wary of everything. But second-and-six from the seven yard line or third-and-five from the six give coaches nightmares.

On those plays, the offense *has* to pass. The defense knows the offense has to pass. And there are only 15 or 16 yards to work with.

If the offense does end up with a first down inside the 10-yard

line, that calls for still another set of plays. Some power runs up the middle behind two tight ends are a matter of course, as are play action passes and roll-outs after faking up the inside. In short, something that keeps the defense off balance enough to take best advantage of the small area.

Offenses also need a set of plans for the end of a half when they're behind and need to catch up in a hurry, and another for when they're ahead and want to run out the clock.

The advantages of building up a game plan before a game are easily understood, yet for a

number of reasons, teams may not stick to them throughout a game. One reason is that a team may play a whole game and never find itself in many of the situations it has prepared itself for when making its game plan. Another, and usually more apt, reason is that the offense's plays just don't work.

STRATEGIC PHOTOGRAPHY
To test the last reason, teams station a photographer high up in the stands, in the coach's booth. He shoots pictures of the defensive formations for every play – before, during, and after the snap. He then organizes the

photos according to the categories in the game plan, and during the halftime intermission coaches can see if their game plan is working.

Because the game plan is based on information taken from game videos, which show what the opponent has done in the past, the plays used *should* work against whatever defenses are used. If they don't, it's for one of two reasons.

The first is that although the defense looks the same as it did on film, it's doing something quite different. The second reason is simply that the offense just isn't executing their plays

The L.A. Raiders – one of the last teams to allow QBs to call their own plays.

IN BODY AND SPIRIT

The game of football may be in the hands of the quarterback, but it's in the minds of the coaches. Mentally, most quarterbacks have become passengers in an offensive vehicle usually steered through headsets worn by the coaches.

Not long ago, all quarterbacks called their own plays in the huddle. It was up to them to determine which of the plays in the playbook would work best in any given situation. But defensive specialization has now smothered old-fashioned innovation.

Of the 28 teams in the NFL, the Saints and the Raiders were the last to allow their quarterbacks to call their own plays. Even at college level, quarterbacks are sent in plays from the sidelines. This happens to

such an extent that not one of the major universities have quarterbacks calling their own plays.

Jim Plunkett, the Raiders' QB, says: 'Enough of the game is being taken away from the players. A lot of the game should be played by the guys out there. I feel the quarterback should call the plays.'

But Plunkett, and many of the older QBs, like Richard Todd, once of the Saints, grew up calling their own plays. Players like Dan Marino of the Dolphins grew up playing football in high school and college where plays were sent in, so when he moved to Miami he fitted in very well. And no one is likely to complain at what Marino has achieved since playing in the pros. Especially his coaches.

properly. If so, a good talking to at halftime might work, but if it's the first reason, changes in the game plan are needed.

Suppose the game plan called for a pass play in the midfield to plus-20 area of the field, to a tight end running a medium length 'in' pattern. At halftime, however, the photographs taken from the coach's booth show that the safety is reacting to the play, leaving the quarterback no option but to avoid the tight end because he's so well covered.

The head coach will note the situation and inform the quarterback to change the play next time it's needed. So instead of having the tight end run an 'in' pattern, he'll have him run a 'cross' beneath the safety and behind the linebackers.

WINNING ATTITUDE

The toughest parts of the game plan for most coaches are the short yardage and goal line situations. That's the area that so often separates the winners from the losers.

Coaches know that if their plays are better than their opponents', they're probably going to win. But in an evenly matched game, teams will either sink or swim depending on how well their game plan takes them across the goal line when the going gets tough.

Coaches must constantly update their game plans in an effort to out-guess their opponent throughout the game.

THE OFFENSE AT THE PLUS-5 – THE GOAL LINE SITUATION

From this position on the field, the offense doesn't want to give the ball away because a score is at stake – in coaches' eyes, not being able to score from here is as bad as giving up the ball on your own goal line.

The effective playing area has shrunk considerably by now, so the offense wants to keep the defense as off balance as possible. Power runs up the middle are staples, but play action passes and rollouts are also needed to keep the defense honest.

The situation that desperately has to be avoided are third downs inside the 10-yard line with five or more yards needed for a first down or a touchdown. They are forced to pass, but the problem is that the defense knows they have to pass as well, and position players accordingly.

In these situations, heavy rushes will be seen, but only in conjunction with exceptionally tight man-to-man coverage. Above all, the onus here is to score – an ability that separates the great teams from the also-rans.

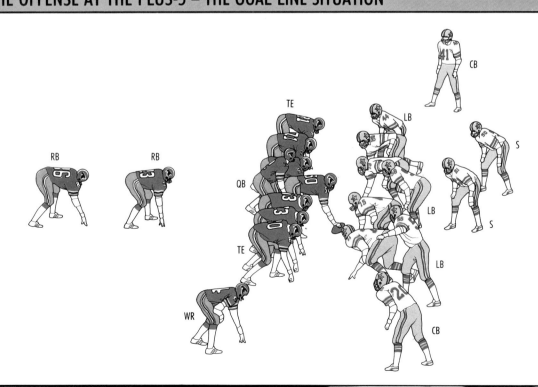

COI

GOT IT AREED

The passing game in the NFL proves it's better to give than receive. The offense has all the options and unless the defensive pass coverage is spot on, the offensive receivers will have a field day. Good defenses, though, have a few tricks of their own

I t's the play the crowd loves: the long bomb to a wide receiver who soars into the air to catch it, usually being hit by one or two defensive players the moment the ball is caught. Or the short pass tossed over the heads of the rampaging defensive linemen, bearing down on the quarterback with mayhem in their hearts.

For however much running backs like Jim Brown, O. J. Simpson, Larry Csonka, Franco Harris, Walter Payton or Eric Dickerson appear to have dominated the game, pro football is still about the forward pass. It is, after all, the quickest – and most spectacular – way of gaining yardage. Naturally teams concentrate heavily on defending it.

THE FORWARD PASS
The forward pass, however, is difficult to defend against because the offense will always try to pit man against man: the receiver has the advantage. He knows where the ball is going to and when it will arrive, and however many men may smack into him after he's caught it, the receiver should be in contention with only one defensive back or linebacker.

Over the past few years, led by teams like San Diego, the passing attacks in the NFL have become more and more sophisticated. Decoy pass receivers now flood the secondary, and the evolution of the tight end position has opened up a whole range of possibilities for the offensive teams.

Before, quarterbacks mostly threw either short passes (under 10 yards), or long, going deep for the bomb. Now with tight ends like Kellen Winslow (San Diego) and Dave Casper (L.A. Raiders), the quarterback can throw medium length passes to men fast enough and big enough to pick up fifteen or so yards in a one-on-one situation against the opposing team's linebackers.

Defensive backs do more than just tackle when a receiver they're covering catches the ball. Their aim is to knock the receiver as hard as they can while trying also to bat the ball away.

Running backs are also expected to be able to receive. Some, like the great Walter Payton, can also throw a pretty good forward pass on option play. So the defense can never really know where the pass is coming from and who it's going to. All they can do is cover possible receivers so as to give the quarterback few or no options – and then try and hustle him into making a mistake.

MULTIPLE DEFENSIVE BACKS
Normally, the defense fields three linemen, four linebackers and four defensive backs (in a 3-4 set), or four linemen and three linebackers (in a 4-3). But sometimes, one or two extra backs are added, usually at the expense of one or two linebackers.

A formation with five defensive backs is known as a *nickel* defense, and six with a *dime* defense. The justification for this is that some offenses are sending up to five receivers into the secondary – too many for the linebackers to help cover. So if the defense packs the secondary themselves, it's that much harder for the quarterback to find an open receiver – and no quarterback is going to throw a pass deliberately that's going to be intercepted. Nor can he throw the ball away, since he'll be penalized.

The problem is that a defense with extra defensive backs who replace one or more linebackers is vulnerable to scrambling quarterbacks. Players like Jim McMahon of the Chicago Bears or John Elway of the Denver Broncos are adept at running for a

TIME OUT

RIPPING TIME
The tear-away jersey, which was popular in the NFL throughout the 1970s, used to give defensive backs problems – as they got a hand on the receiver, the jersey would fall off. Now illegal, the first tear-away jersey was worn by All-American halfback Tom Harmon at the University of Michigan in 1939.

MULTIPLE VS MULTIPLE

CB

WR

FS

RB

nickel back

RB

MLB

SS

WR

TE

OLB

CB

In sure passing situations, the offense will put in as many receivers as possible. The defense counters this by putting in extra | defensive backs. Here, an extra back has been put in, known as a nickel back; one more would be a dime back.

first down when they see the defensive coverage back into the secondary to protect against the expected pass.

MAN-TO-MAN

Fans love man-to-man pass coverage, since it sets up a classic confrontation between two individuals. But safety-conscious defensive coaches don't like it at all and few teams use it regularly – an exception being the L. A. Raiders. Their two famous cornerbacks, Lester Hayes and Mike Haynes, play crunching man-to-man pass coverage on even the best wide receivers in the NFL.

But to play man-to-man, a defensive back needs exceptional intelligence coupled with a natural ability – and few players are taught the necessary skills in college, where coaches are often even more cautious than in the NFL.

In a straight man-to-man, the linebackers cover the running backs; the cornerbacks cover the wide receivers; the strong safety covers the tight end; and the free safety 'roams'.

The free safety may also help double-team an opponent's most dangerous receiver. But cornerbacks have the toughest job on man-to-man coverage. They must keep the receiver between themselves and the quarterback. Backpedalling off the line, a cornerback mirrors every move the receiver makes until the ball is thrown; then he moves in, timing his hit to the ball's arrival, or cutting in front of the receiver to intercept or bat down the pass.

BUMP AND RUN

The *bump and run* is a trailing technique used by defensive backs (most often cornerbacks) when they are matched one-on-

one against a wide receiver.

In the typical bump and run situation, a defensive back will position himself directly opposite the receiver. As the receiver comes off the line of scrimmage, the defensive back's first move is to make contact (a *bump*). The defensive back can only hit the receiver within five yards of the line; beyond that it is considered illegal contact.

After the initial bump, the defensive back will trail right behind the receiver. The back must never take an inside fake; if he does the receiver can run right past him. He can take an outside fake and let the receiver run to the middle, because

Zones are designed to be filled by one player, who converges on any receiver entering it. But when a team's players have great pursuit skills, there is often an overlap with effective results.

that's where his defensive help will converge.

The defensive back must concentrate totally on the receiver. He cannot worry when the pass is going to be thrown; he does not even look back for the ball until the receiver does. All he is trying to accomplish in the bump and run is to break up the pass play. The only time he should have a chance at an interception is when the ball is poorly thrown.

ZONE DEFENSE

The basic idea of a *zone defense* is deceptively simple. So much

ROTATING ZONES TO STRONG AND WEAKSIDES

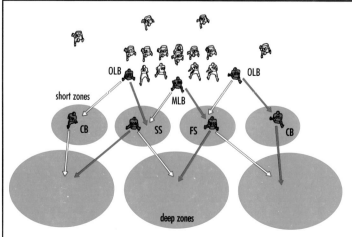

OLB

OLB

short zones

MLB

CB

SS

FS

CB

deep zones

The defense divides the passing area into four short zones and three deep zones. In a 4-3 alignment, the three linebackers and one defensive back (usually a cornerback) take the short zones. The two safeties and the other cornerback take the long zones. Because the linebackers retreat at the snap in one direction and the defensive backs in another, the effect is one of rotation.

The assignments in the weak zone are the opposite of the strong zone. There's still the same rotation effect, but it goes counter-clockwise away from the strongside. From a 3-4 defense, the rotating zone positions can stay the same (and have a rushing linebacker), or juggle the number of deep and short zones.

BACK TO FRONT
Drafted by the St. Louis Cardinals in 1979 as a defensive back, Roy Green has become one of the best wide receivers in the NFL. His speed and ball-catching abilities so impressed St. Louis coach Jim Hanifan, that they were thought to have better use on offense. Few can make the conversion to receiver with such success.

so that it often confuses the defense itself.

The brainchild of the legendary coach Vince Lombardi of the Green Bay Packers, a zone defense involves seven or eight defensive players dropping back to cover a pre-arranged area of the field, called a *zone*. They stay in the effective centres of their zones, alert to but not reacting to where the receivers go, until the ball is thrown. Once the ball is in the air, they converge on the receiver.

In any zone defense, there are two areas covered: *short* zones and *deep* zones.

A defensive player assigned to a short zone is responsible for an area 10 to 20 yards downfield. Someone assigned to a deep zone has a much larger area of responsibility, covering all the way back to the goal line if necessary.

Obviously, a player defending a deep zone often finds himself playing man-to-man defense against a speedy receiver.

The key to a good pass defense is communication between the defenders – they

MAN-TO-MAN COVERAGE

The offense has the advantage on passing plays because it knows exactly where the play is going. Defenses are put at a further disadvantage when they play man-to-man coverage, and so most coaches use it only rarely. Also, colleges hardly use it.

The responsibilities of the defense, however, are simple. The linebackers cover the running backs, the free safety roams or helps on double coverage, the strong safety covers the tight end, and the cornerbacks cover the wide receivers.

DOGS AND BLITZES – STOPPING THE PASS AT THE SOURCE

Rather than wait for the quarterback to throw the ball before attempting to block a pass, defenses can go straight for him – before he can throw. There are two basic ways of doing this, but the strategies are similar. Sacking the quarterback is their aim.

In what's known as a *dog*, the linebackers all rush the quarterback, through any available holes in the offense, just as the snap is made. Because linebackers usually wait and then pursue, the offense is caught off-guard, with their front line being completely outnumbered.

The same thinking applies to a blitz, in which the cornerbacks and safeties mount the rush (often with linebackers as well).

DOUBLE ZONES

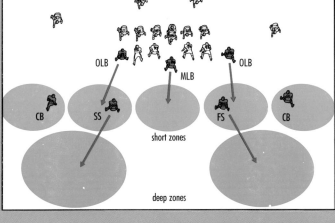

In this alignment, which concentrates its coverage 10 to 15 yards from the line of scrimmage, there are five short zones and two deep zones. Defenses have to be wary, though, of tight ends finding the huge gap between the two safeties.

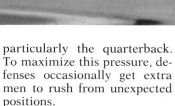

must make sure that their teammates are aware of all the potential receivers moving into the secondary, and the type of patterns being run.

The zone defense is vulnerable to the short pass dropped into the area behind the linebackers and in front of the defensive secondary. For this reason, a zone defense is mostly useful in third-and-long situations (such as third down and 20 yards or more needed for a first down gain). The defense in this instance are happy to give the offense five or 10 yards, knowing that the offense will still have to punt or try a field goal on the next play.

DOGS AND BLITZES
The purpose of a pass rush is to increase pressure on an offense, particularly the quarterback. To maximize this pressure, defenses occasionally get extra men to rush from unexpected positions.

In a *dog*, a linebacker (or any combination of linebackers) leaves his regular area of coverage and streaks past the line of scrimmage into the backfield through available holes in the offensive line.

In a *blitz*, secondary men – alone, together, or in combination with linebackers – try to get to the quarterback. Whereas a dog can be played to stop the run as well as the pass, the blitz is used primarily to stop only the pass (though it leaves the defense vulnerable to the run).

Cornerbacks blitz from their outside positions and safeties come from their deep areas straight upfield. Safeties must time their blitzes perfectly; they must be careful not to show their blitz or commit themselves too early.

When a defensive player dogs or blitzes, he has the element of surprise in his favour. A player must disguise the fact he is coming, especially from the quarterback. If a quarterback at the line can sense that a blitz is coming, he can call an audible to take advantage of the situation. Of course, sometimes defenders tip-off a blitz intentionally – and falsely – to make the quarterback change his play.

The best example of blitzing is seen with Chicago's famous '46' defense, which constantly shows one thing but executes another.

Lester Hayes of the Los Angeles Raiders is one of the most successful cornerbacks in the league, and an almost certain Hall of Famer. One of the few men who still play man-to-man, Hayes' success is based on dogged pursuit and an uncanny ability to recover in a split second from the receiver's fakes.

THE BIG TIME

Where were you when the New York Giants beat Denver in Super Bowl XXI, or when the Chicago Bears thrashed New England in Super Bowl XX? Chances are you were watching the television with some friends, refreshing yourself with drinks and food as varied as the teams that comprise the NFL. For millions of fans, both in the US and worldwide, the Super Bowl has come to represent the pinnacle of sporting entertainment. Only the World Cup and the Olympics can hope to generate the same interest – and that only every four years. So what is it about the Super Bowl, and indeed American Football in general, that commands such interest?

For starters, the sport produces some of the most memorable sporting spectaculars. It's just that kind of game – bodies hurling into each other, graceful sprinters leaping high to snare 60-yard passes, running backs like dynamos breaking through seemingly impenetrable walls of massive defensive linemen for long gains, linebackers blitzing through the offensive line with lightning speed to sack the quarterback with crushing ferocity. In short, there isn't much that American Football doesn't offer, and what it offers it does so with unstinting abundance and consummate skill.

It would be a grave mistake to think that exciting football only started with the inception of the Super Bowl. But for those of us who have only recently taken up the sport, or are under, say, 40 years of age, the Super Bowl is perhaps the main contributor to the most exciting moments. Of the many pre-Super Bowl battles, perhaps one stands out from the rest because of its excitement and also because of it

being the first televised championship to be seen by a national audience. It was between the New York Giants and the Baltimore Colts for the NFL Championship of 1958.

Much more recently, in the third week of the 1986 campaign, the New York Jets met the Miami Dolphins in a game that turned out to be a high flying battle between quarterbacks Dan Marino and Ken O'Brien. After the final score in overtime and when all the statistics were totalled, O'Brien and Marino had combined for the highest ever combined passing total in NFL history – some 927 yards! All that plus last-minute heroics and a close-call final score of 51-45.

During the 1970s, there was one team that was almost unbeatable. From 1973 to 1980, the Pittsburgh Steelers dominated the NFL like no other team had done before or since. They were one of those magical teams whose depth at every position was awesome, from quarterback Terry Bradshaw to running backs Franco Harris and Rocky Bleier, from wide receivers Lynn Swann and John Stallworth to defensive linemen Mean Joe Greene and L C Greenwold, and from linebackers Jack Lambert and Jack Ham to cornerback Mel Blount. The list goes on. In all, the Steelers finished off the decade with four Super Bowl wins and a unique place in NFL history.

This chapter also includes the phenomenal Dolphins team of 1972 who became the first and only unbeaten team over a season, as well as the first and one of the best ever Super Bowls – Green Bay against Kansas City.

Dolphins' quarterback Dan Marino (13), who led the NFL in passing yards in 1985 with 4137 yards and 30 touchdown passes, completed 60 per cent of his passes in the 51-45 loss to the Jets in Week 3 of the '86 season.

A score of 51-45, a game that went into overtime, a tying touchdown on the last play of regulation time, and a record combined passing yardage. The New York Jets/Miami Dolphins contest in Week 3 of the 1986 season was one of the greatest gridiron clashes ever seen

I n front of 71,025 New York Jets' fans in Meadowlands Stadium New Jersey, on 21 September 1986, the Miami Dolphins stretched the home team to their limits in one of the most exciting games in NFL history. Although it was only the third week of the 1986 schedule, the Jets' fans were already thinking Super Bowl – but they couldn't in their wildest dreams, have imagined what was going to happen on that sunny Sunday afternoon.

From the opening couple of drives, it became evident that quarterbacks Dan

THE PASS

Ken O'Brien, the Jets' quarterback, completed 67.4 per cent of his passes during New York's victory. In 1985 he completed 297 of 488 passes, with 25 touchdown passes, and his 3888 passing yards was the second-highest in the team's history.

QUARTERBACK STATISTICS

This is how the greatest combined passing yardage in a single game was achieved.

	Pass Att.	Comp.	Yds	TD	Pct.	Int.	Rush	Sacks
Dan Marino	50	30	448	6	60	2		2-13
Ken O'Brien	43	29	479	4	67.4	1	1-8	3-30

Marino of the Dolphins and Ken O'Brien of the Jets were going to pass. Neither team had a breakaway runner and both had excellent receiving corps.

After exchanging punts, the Jets got a break when backup wide receiver Curt Sohn returned a Miami punt 27 yards to the Dolphins' 23. But the Jets failed to score a touchdown, and settled for a 32-yard field goal with less than five minutes left in the first quarter.

Miami came right back, though, spearheaded by Marino's deadly accurate passing. They marched 67 yards after the kickoff to score a touchdown on a six-yard pass to wide receiver James Pruitt, putting the score at 7-3 for Miami.

JET PROPULSION
The second quarter started with a bang and maintained the momentum until the first half ended. In all, 42 points were scored, 28 of those going to the Jets. And of those four touchdowns, two were scored on long passing plays from O'Brien to wide receiver Wesley Walker.

MASTERS

STARTING LINEUPS

MIAMI	Offense	NEW YORK
Mark Duper	WR	Wesley Walker
Cleveland Green	LT	Jim Sweeney
Roy Foster	LG	Ted Banker
Dwight Stephenson	C	Joe Fields
Ronnie Lee	RG	Dan Alexander
Greg Koch	RT	Reggie McElroy
Bruce Hardy	TE	Mickey Shuler
Mark Clayton	WR	Al Toon
Dan Marino	QB	Ken O'Brien
Lorenzo Hampton	RB	Johnny Hector
Woody Bennett	RB	Tony Paige
	Defense	
Barry Bennett	LE	T. J. Turner
Bob Baumhower	NT	Joe Klecko
George Little	RE	Mark Gastineau
Bob Brudzinski	LOLB	Charles Jackson
Jackie Shipp	LILB	Kyle Clifton
John Offerdahl	RILB	Lance Mehl
Hugh Green	ROLB	Bob Crable
Paul Lankford	LCB	Jerry Holmes
William Judson	RCB	Russell Carter
Lyle Blackwood	SS	Lester Lyles
Johnny Lynn	FS	Bud Brown

Dolphins' quarterback Dan Marino is sacked by Jets' defensive end Mark Gastineau (99). Gastineau, in his eighth year, made one solo tackle during the Jets' victory, and assisted in another two tackles.

The barrage began with a 10-play, 83-yard drive that culminated in a one-yard run by running back Johnny Hector, slashing up the middle and finding a huge hole. But the play was set up when Miami linebacker Bob Kozlawski interfered with Jets' tight end Rocky Klever at the one.

With the Jets leading 10-7, they kicked to Miami, who were awarded a touchback at their own 20 after Pat Leahy's kickoff sailed into the end zone and the Dolphins' Pruitt declined to return it.

MIAMI MAGIC

On first down, Marino dropped back to pass. He had enough time, and his receivers were running their pattern well, despite close coverage. But as the big rush came, Marino took his chances with Mark Clayton, drilling a pass to the near sideline. Uncharacteristically for Marino, the pass was low, and it was scooped up by Jets' safety Lester Lyles who rambled to Miami's 10. After a quick pass inside to Klever, the Jets scored again on an eight-yard run by Johnny Hector, finding bags of room up the middle, making it Jets 17, Miami 7.

Miami came back with two touchdowns in just two and a half minutes, after New York's two in just over two minutes.

Marino went to work. Quick passes to Clayton and Mark Duper, plus two penalties by the Jets, took the ball to New York's one-yard line. From there it was a play action pass to tight end Dan Johnson at 7:34.

Ken O'Brien faltered, throwing a high pass on the ensuing possession that tipped off wide receiver JoJo Townsell's fingers

right into the hands of Miami cornerback Don McNeal. That took the ball to the Jets' 30, and it took only two plays for Marino to find Mark Duper in the far corner of the end zone. With five minutes left in the first half it was 21-17 for the Dolphins.

MORE TO COME

Time meant nothing to the Jets though, as they came storming back with two more touchdowns in two and a half minutes.

The first touchdown followed a magnificent 65-yard pass and run play from O'Brien to 10-year veteran wide receiver Wesley Walker, who was 15 yards in the clear of any Miami player because of a mixup in the Dolphins' coverage. After the play, coach Shula could be seen explaining, in no uncertain terms, to linebacker Bud Brown precisely why Walker was left so alone.

New York's second touchdown was almost a gift. After the Walker touchdown,

TIME OUT

DYNAMIC DOUBLE ACT
The Jets/Dolphins clash was one for the record books. Dan Marino's 448 yards plus Ken O'Brien's 479 combined to set a new single-game NFL record of 927. Marino's six touchdown passes equalled Bob Griese's old team mark set in 1977, while O'Brien missed out on Joe Namath's club record for a single game by only 17 yards.

Miami failed to move the ball and had to punt. The Jets couldn't get things moving, so they too punted. As Dave Jennings' kick soared high in the air, Dolphins' returner Reyna Thompson called for a fair catch at midfield. With defenders barrelling down and less than a minute to play, it was the wisest decision to take.

James Pruitt bumped into Thompson just as the ball was about to be caught. Quick-acting Jets' linebacker Matt Monger grabbed the ball and ran to Miami's two. But the officials ruled that because a fair catch was called, the ball couldn't be advanced beyond the point of fumble.

With a first down on Miami's 49, O'Brien wasted no time. With plenty of blocking in front of him, he found Wesley Walker sprinting down the sideline between two defenders, taking the score to 31-21. Miami had time for only a couple of plays before the first half ended.

BREATHLESS

Jets' fans hardly had time to catch their breath when, with 4:16 gone in the third quarter, Dan Marino found Mark 'Super' Duper on a 46-yard bomb to close to within three points of New York. It was, in fact, the first of three unanswered Dolphins' scores of the period. Less than three minutes later, Miami's placekicker Fuad Reveiz connected on a 44-yard field goal that evened the score at 31-31.

Miami now had the momentum, and the Jets looked like falling apart. On the kickoff following the Dolphins' field goal, New York's offense spluttered. And when run-

Finding himself on the wrong side of a charge by Dolphins' defensive tackle George Little (99), *above*, Jets' running back Dennis Biglen (23) is unable to keep hold of the ball. *Top*, Jets' running back Johnny Hector (34), who carried the ball 22 times for a gain of 82 yards, is tackled by Dolphins' linebacker Bob Brudzinski (59). Brudzinski made six solo tackles during the game and assisted on four more. Al Toon, Jets' wide receiver, catches the ball on the sideline, *right*. Toon went on to make seven receptions for 111 yards.

ning back Dennis Bligen fumbled on his own 26, giving the Dolphins possession, things looked grim for the Jets. They looked even worse, when, after six plays, Marino found tight end Bruce Hardy on a one-yard pass into the end zone. That put Miami ahead 38-31, two thirds of the way through the third quarter.

GATHERING HIS TROOPS
For a while, it seemed as though things had settled down a bit, without a point being scored for 15 minutes. But then Ken O'Brien gathered his troops and put together an impressive 80-yard drive, including a 36-yard pass to wide receiver Al Toon, and a one-yard run by Tony Paige on a fourth-and-one that kept the drive alive. Finally, from the Dolphins' seven, O'Brien pitched left to Bligen who danced his way for six points. Leahy's extra point tied the score at 38.

But Miami weren't finished yet. With less than three minutes left in regulation time, Wesley Walker fumbled the ball after catching the pass from O'Brien. Miami linebacker Jackie Shipp pounced on it and the Jets' hopes sank. In three plays, Marino justified those fears by finding Mark Clayton right in the middle of the end zone. Miami 45, New York 38.

This time, O'Brien couldn't find the magic and the Jets were forced to punt with only 1:57 left. Yet with poor usage of time, runners going out of bounds to stop the clock, and New York taking their second of three allotted time outs, they forced Miami to punt. Because Reggie Roby's punt rolled through the end zone, the Jets managed to get possession on their own 20-yard line with just 1:18 to play.

What New York faced was 80 yards, a bit more than a minute to play, and they were armed with only one time out. A quick sideline pass to tight end Mickey Shuler gained five yards before he stepped out of bounds and stopped the clock with :58 left. Then O'Brien scrambled to the sideline on the next play, stopping the clock at :42.

Next play O'Brien dropped back to pass and found Shuler up the middle for seven yards. As the Miami defense converged, he lateralled to Johnny Hector trailing behind, who managed to gain another 21. Unfortunately, Hector didn't manage to get out of bounds, so the ball was spotted on Miami's 39 with the clock still running. O'Brien called the Jets' last time out with only 35 seconds left.

With a first and 10, O'Brien found Shuler again, this time to the opposite side, and again he tried to pitch out to a trailing back, this time Bligen. When he saw it wouldn't work, Shuler turned upfield, broke several tackles, and managed to get out of bounds at the 35 with :26 showing on the clock. Yet another pass to Shuler took the ball to the 21, but this time he was unable to reach the sideline. With a quick count, though, O'Brien was able to throw the ball out of bounds and stop the clock with five seconds left. There was time for only one more play – which running back Tony Paige brought in.

Miami knew the Jets had to pass, and the fans knew they had to pass. The only questions were: where and to whom? The answers were: on the goal line in the middle of the field; and to Wesley Walker. Surrounded by five Dolphins' defensive backs Walker took the catch. For nearly a minute the stands rocked until Pat Leahy came on to try the tying extra point.

The score was tied at 45 on the last play of regulation time; the game was now going into sudden-death overtime!

GOING FOR THE KILL
The fans had even more to cheer about when the Jets won the toss and elected to receive the kickoff to start the extra time.

Reveiz's kick found its way into the arms of Jets' kick returner Mike Harper. As he was being tackled at his own 22, the ball appeared to pop loose before he was down, and half the Miami squad jumped on it. So sure were the Dolphins that it had been a legitimate fumble that their offense, led by Marino, came trotting onto the field. But they only got half way before the officials ruled that Harper had been tackled before the ball came loose.

That was all O'Brien and his Jets needed. On their fifth play in overtime, O'Brien found Wesley Walker streaking down the right sideline form an incredible 43-yard touchdown catch.

After a three hour, 49 minute marathon, the Jets came away with a startling 51-45 triumph. The 1986 season had well and truly arrived.

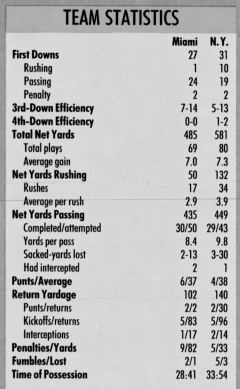

TEAM STATISTICS

	Miami	N.Y.
First Downs	27	31
Rushing	1	10
Passing	24	19
Penalty	2	2
3rd-Down Efficiency	7-14	5-13
4th-Down Efficiency	0-0	1-2
Total Net Yards	485	581
Total plays	69	80
Average gain	7.0	7.3
Net Yards Rushing	50	132
Rushes	17	34
Average per rush	2.9	3.9
Net Yards Passing	435	449
Completed/attempted	30/50	29/43
Yards per pass	8.4	9.8
Sacked-yards lost	2-13	3-30
Had intercepted	2	1
Punts/Average	6/37	4/38
Return Yardage	102	140
Punts/returns	2/2	2/30
Kickoffs/returns	5/83	5/96
Interceptions	1/17	2/14
Penalties/Yards	9/82	5/33
Fumbles/Lost	2/1	5/3
Time of Possession	28:41	33:54

A field judge signals a touchdown as Jets' wide receiver Wesley Walker (85) takes another successful pass. The 10-year veteran from California made six receptions for 194 yards.

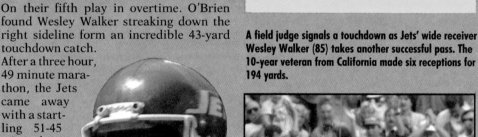

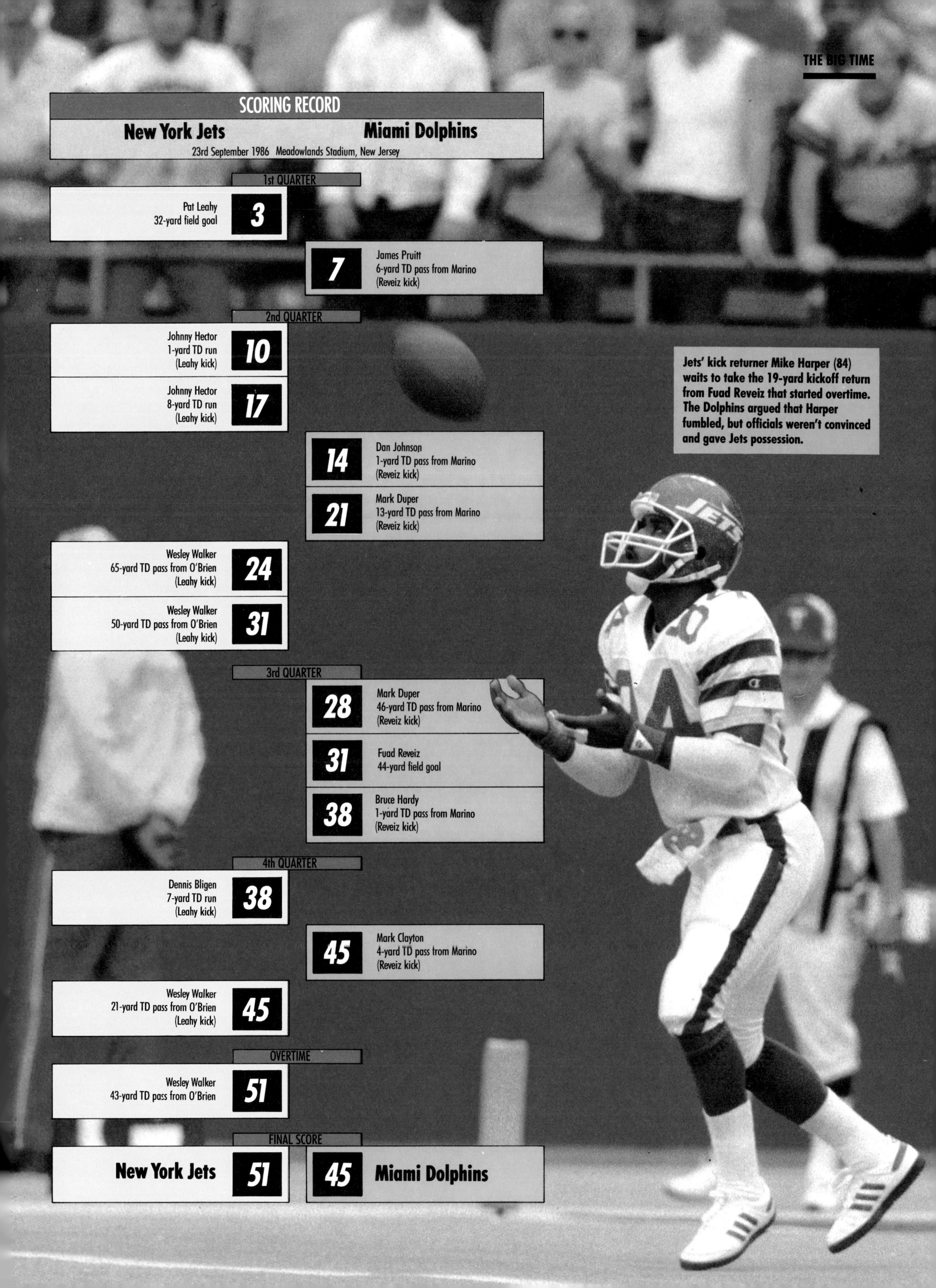

SCORING RECORD

New York Jets   Miami Dolphins

23rd September 1986 Meadowlands Stadium, New Jersey

1st QUARTER

Pat Leahy
32-yard field goal
3

7
James Pruitt
6-yard TD pass from Marino
(Reveiz kick)

2nd QUARTER

Johnny Hector
1-yard TD run
(Leahy kick)
10

Johnny Hector
8-yard TD run
(Leahy kick)
17

14
Dan Johnson
1-yard TD pass from Marino
(Reveiz kick)

21
Mark Duper
13-yard TD pass from Marino
(Reveiz kick)

Wesley Walker
65-yard TD pass from O'Brien
(Leahy kick)
24

Wesley Walker
50-yard TD pass from O'Brien
(Leahy kick)
31

3rd QUARTER

28
Mark Duper
46-yard TD pass from Marino
(Reveiz kick)

31
Fuad Reveiz
44-yard field goal

38
Bruce Hardy
1-yard TD pass from Marino
(Reveiz kick)

4th QUARTER

Dennis Bligen
7-yard TD run
(Leahy kick)
38

45
Mark Clayton
4-yard TD pass from Marino
(Reveiz kick)

Wesley Walker
21-yard TD pass from O'Brien
(Leahy kick)
45

OVERTIME

Wesley Walker
43-yard TD pass from O'Brien
51

FINAL SCORE

New York Jets **51**   **45** Miami Dolphins

Jets' kick returner Mike Harper (84) waits to take the 19-yard kickoff return from Fuad Reveiz that started overtime. The Dolphins argued that Harper fumbled, but officials weren't convinced and gave Jets possession.

THE BREAKTHROUGH GAME

THE 1958 NFL CHAMPIONSHIP
BALTIMORE COLTS 23 NEW YORK GIANTS 17

THE BIG TIME

ROUGH

On one day in 1958 pro football became a major world sport. The great Colts/Giants clash is still remembered as one of the most exciting championships ever played

Pro football really arrived on 28 December 1958. On that winter day, the New York Giants hosted the Baltimore Colts in the NFL Championship game. It wasn't just another game; it turned out to be The Game, an electrifying sudden-death thriller that through TV coverage impressed the NFL indelibly on the sporting consciousness of America.

In '58 there were no domed stadiums, no artificial playing surfaces, and no TV breaks. But there was the New York Giants. Four-time winners of the NFL Championship, and runners-up on eight other occasions, the Giants were by far the better known of the two teams. Their hallmark was a magnificent defense — the first defense to have a glamorous image.

It was built round the powerful linemen named Jim Katcavage, Rosey Grier, Andy Robustelli and Dick Modzelewski. Next came a barbed wire secondary, featuring safety Jim Patton, who led the NFL with 11 interceptions in 1958, and Emlen Tunnel, who Giants' head coach Jim Lee Powell called 'the greatest safety of all time'. Their main target on the Colts offense was quarterback Johnny Unitas. Just three years earlier, Unitas, then a skinny crewcut lad of 22, had been cut by the Steelers, who had drafted him in the ninth round from the University of Louisville. He was playing semi-pro ball on the sandlots of Pittsburgh for $6 a game when the Colts called to offer him a tryout. The rest is history.

The team was well stocked at the other skill positions, with clutch split end Raymond Berry, mercurial halfback Lenny Moore, and aptly nicknamed fullback Alan (The Horse) Ameche. There was also a dependable offensive line, anchored by massive (6 ft 3 in, 19 st 4 lb) left tackle Jim Parker.

The sellout crowd of 64,185 fans — including some 15,000 from Baltimore — were treated to delightful weather. But the game itself actually got off to an uninspired start. Neither team could move the ball early, and there were three quick turnovers.

BOLTING AHEAD

A 36-yard field goal gave the Giants a 3-0 lead at the end of the first quarter. But it was in the second quarter that the game began to heat up. Baltimore tight end, Big Daddy Lipscomb, recovered a fumble by Giants halfback Frank Gifford on New York's 20-yard line. It was the Colts first play from within striking distance of the end zone and they made swift work of it. Covered by a devastating block from tight end Joe Parker, Colts fullback Ameche blasted into the end zone to put Baltimore on top 7-3.

It was the break the Colts had been waiting for. Two plays later QB Johnny Unitas lashed back with a perfect drive. With halfback Lenny Moore running wide on sweeps, and Ameche sprinting up the middle, Unitas kept confusing the Giants with short passes to offensive end Raymond Berry. The last play of the drive was a 15-yard touchdown bullet to Berry after a fake to Ameche, which sent the Colts into the dressing room at halftime with a 14-3 lead.

FIGHTING BACK

Despite its stumbling start, Baltimore had gained nearly 200 yards in the first half, while the Giants had managed just 86. In the New York locker room at halftime, offensive coach Lombardi suggested a new strategy. Since the Colts had been dogging Giants' halfback Frank Gifford so intensely throughout the first half, why not use him more as a decoy for the rest of the game?

Early in the second half, the Colts pushed the Giants' defense all the way to the New York three-yard line, where Baltimore had a first down with four cracks to get into the end zone and break the game open.

But the Giants threw out their chests and began snorting fire.

Ameche drove into the line on first down for a yard, no more. Unitas tried a sneak, and gained a foot. Ameche hit the line again . . . no gain.

On fourth-and-goal from the one-yard line, Unitas called for a pitch to Ameche, who was then supposed to pass to tight end Jim Mutscheller in the end zone. Mutscheller was open, but Giants linebacker Cliff Livingston read the play all the way and nailed Ameche before he could throw.

'There was just no way they were going to score,' said Huff. 'We were like wild animals out there. They weren't gonna get a damn thing.'

Leaping high, the Colts' star offensive end Raymond Berry, catches a pass from Unitas to bring Baltimore to the Giants' eight-yard line. Unitas' favourite receiving target, Berry set a championship record with 12 receptions for 178 yards.

The New York fans began to rock Yankee Stadium. And the Giants' offense, infused with momentum from the stirring goal-line stand, picked up the beat.

On third-and-two from his own 13, QB Conerly faked to Gifford and flipped the ball to Rote at the 40. Rote shed several tacklers before he was finally scissored by two Colts at the Baltimore 25, where he also shed the ball. But it turned into an Immaculate Fumble. The ball bounced into the arms of Giants' halfback Alex Webster, who had been trailing the play in convoy, and he reached the Colts' one-yard line before being stopped.

The Giants had matched their entire offensive output in the first half on one crazy, providential stroke. They cashed in two plays later when fullback Mel Triplett powered for a touchdown.

Suddenly, it was 14-10 and all hell was breaking loose in the stands. The Giants' defense, back on the field, was throwing its weight around. Dick Modzelewski twice infiltrated the Colts' backfield, sacking Unitas once and driving him out of the pocket another time. Baltimore had to punt.

The baton was once again handed back to the New York offense, and Conerly spirited the Giants down the field, netting a big 46-yard gain on one pass to Bob Schnelker off a fake double reverse.

In the first minute of the fourth quarter, Conerly isolated Gifford on a linebacker in the right corner of the end zone and pinpointed a touchdown pass to make it 17-14.

SNAP ATTACK

As the minutes ticked away in the fourth quarter, things looked bleak for Baltimore. A 46-yard field goal attempt by Bert Rechichar, who handled the Colts' long attempts, was no good. In the Colts' next series, Giants' defensive heavies Robustelli and Modzelewski took turns blowing past Unitas's protection, sacking him on successive plays, and forcing a punt.

'At that point,' said Webster, 'we just had to keep the ball, run out the clock, and they'd never get another chance. We were so hot . . . everything was working so well . . . it sure looked like our game.'

The Giants took over on their own 19, and wound the clock down to 2:30. On third-and-four at the Giants' 40, Gifford took a hand-off on a power sweep. A first down would all but assure a Giants victory, but the Colts defense held them inches short. Coach Howell was forced to order a punt, and Chandler booted the ball cleanly downfield all the way to the Baltimore 14. There, New York lined up in the 1950s version of the Prevent defense, covering the sidelines and the deep zones.

There was 1:56 left on the clock, and the air was electric. A cold, grey mist was settling into the floodlit stadium, creating an eerie backdrop for the events to follow.

Unitas quickly threw two incompletions.

Jumping over the line, fullback Mel Triplett scores the Giants' first touchdown – bringing them back into a fighting position in the third quarter.

Suddenly, it was third-and-10. The Colts were 86 yards from the end zone with just 79 seconds left. The Giants looked invincible. But football magic was in the making.

'We had the game locked up in the third period,' said Unitas, 'and it looked like we had blown it. We were so damn disgusted with ourselves that we struck back at the Giants in a sort of blind fury the last time we got the ball.'

Unitas hit halfback Lenny Moore on the crucial third-down play for 11 yards and a

STARTING LINEUPS

Colts Offense		Giants Offense
82 Raymond Berry	E	Kyle Rote 44
77 Jim Parker	T	Roosevelt Brown 79
63 Art Spinney	G	Al Barry 68
50 Madison Nutter	C	Ray Wietecha 55
68 Alex Sandusky	G	Bob Mischak 62
60 George Preas	T	Frank Youso 76
84 Jim Mutscheller	E	Bob Schnelker 85
19 Johnny Unitas	QB	Don Heinrich 11
45 L. G. Dupre	HB	Frank Gifford 16
24 Lenny Moore	HB	Alex Webster 29
35 Alan Ameche	FB	Mel Triplett 33

Colts Defense		Giants Defense
89 Gino Marchetti	E	Jim Katcavage 75
70 Art Donovan	T	Roosevelt Grier 76
76 Gene Lipscomb	T	Dick Modzelewski 77
83 Don Joyce	E	Andy Robustelli 81
66 Don Shinnick	LB	Cliff Livingston 89
36 Bill Pellington	LB	Sam Huff 70
55 Leo Sanford	LB	Harland Svare 84
20 Milt Davis	DHB	Carl Karilivacz 21
23 Carl Taseff	DHB	Lindon Crow 41
17 Ray Brown	S	Jim Patton 20
80 Andy Nelson	S	Emlen Tunnel 45

first down. Then he began tearing into the Giants' defense with passes to Berry, ripping off gains of 25, 16 and 21 yards.

With the Unitas-to-Berry combo clicking, the Colts moved all the way to the New York 13 with 19 seconds left. But they were out of time outs. The field goal unit ran onto the field and, without benefit of a huddle Steve Myhra kicked a 20-yard field goal with seven seconds left to force the first sudden-death overtime in the history of pro-football.

WINNING DRIVE

Two plays into overtime the uncanny Unitas proceeded to choreograph 13 plays that made football history, and assured his place in the archives.

'We all got our confidence from Johnny,' said Berry, who set a championship game record with 12 receptions for 178 yards. 'I can't explain it, but I absolutely knew we were going to score on that drive.'

After moving to the Baltimore 43 on two runs by L. G. Dupre and a swing pass to Ameche, Unitas was slammed by Giants' tight end Dick Modzelewski for an eight-yard loss to create a tense third-and-15 call.

The Colts lined up in a new formation, with both ends split wide and Moore, the primary receiver, stationed in the right slot. Moore was heavily covered, so Unitas instead fired to old faithful, Berry, for a 21-yard gain and a first down.

The irrepressible Modzelewski had been charging into the backfield too fast to suit Unitas, so next he set up the sting. He called a trap for Ameche up the middle. When big Mo tore in as Unitas expected, and Huff

The winning touchdown – taking a short pass from Unitas, fullback Alan Ameche blasts through the right side of the line while halfback Lenny Moore (24) and teammates take care of the opposition ... 'They couldn't have stopped him if we'd needed ten yards,' said Unitas after Ameche's score made it 23-17 to the Colts in overtime.

second-guessed by almost everyone. 'There is no gamble when you know where you're throwing,' Unitas said. 'And if there had been any danger of an interception, I would have thrown it away.'

So it was third-and-goal from the one. No need for subtlety here. But even now, Unitas fooled the Giants, sending Ameche on a play called '16 Power' through the right side of the line, instead of going behind Parker, the Colts' meal ticket, on the left.

As Unitas handed off to Ameche, Baltimore linemen Alex Sandusky and George Preas ripped open a gigantic hole in the line, and Ameche barrelled into the end

HOW THEY SCORED

BALTIMORE	0	14	0	3	6	–23
N.Y. GIANTS	3	0	7	7	0	–17

NYG – Pat Summerall, 49-yard field goal	3-0
BC – Alan Ameche, 2-yard TD run (Myhra kick)	3-7
BC – Raymond Berry, 15-yard TD pass from Unitas (Myhra kick)	3-14
NYG – Mel Triplett, 1-yard TD run (Summerall kick)	10-14
NYG – Frank Gifford, 15-yard TD pass from Conerly (Summerall kick)	17-14
BC – Steve Myhra, 20-yard field goal	17-17
BC – Alan Ameche, 1-yard TD run (no kick)	17-23

cheated toward the sideline to help with the pass coverage, Ameche fired up the middle for an impressive and useful 23-yard gain to the Giants' 20.

THROWING SURPRISE

On first down, Ameche gained a yard off right tackle. On second-and-goal from the 7, Unitas stunned everyone – especially Ewbank – by floating an audacious pass to offensive end Jim Mutscheller, who took it to the one-yard line.

Even though it worked, the call was later

zone, literally falling from his own momentum. The Colts had won 23-17. There was no need for the extra point.

It was Unitas' day; he had won with his head. 'The man was a genius,' said linebacker Sam Huff. 'I never saw a quarterback that good on those two drives.' Neither had most of the spectators and Unitas was an inevitable winner of the game's most valuable player award.

GREATEST IMPACT

But one player could never take the credit for a game of such energy and excitement that it was – and still is – called 'the greatest game ever played'. Says Tom Landry, the Giants' defensive co-ordinator who went on to coach the Dallas Cowboys to five Super Bowls, 'There were some other forces at work for that game. The way everything blended together – the television, where the game was played, and the fact that pro football was ripe for expansion – was the key. I consider it the greatest because of its impact.'

Giants offensive lineman Kyle Rote put it more simply: 'Everything came together then for the greatness of pro football.'

TIME OUT

CABLE CUT

During Unitas' game-winning overtime drive, excited fans accidentally disconnected a television power cable. Some 50 million TV screens suddenly went blank and commentator Chuck Thompson was forced to do a radio play-by-play through the most vital moments of the game. Thankfully the picture came back in time for Ameche's touchdown dive.

Drafted in 1967, Bob Griese was a champion quarterback just waiting for a break at the big time. In '72, he led Miami to glory in Super Bowl VII.

THE PERFECT SEASON

The Miami Dolphins finished 1969 with a dismal 3-10-1 record – the worst in the entire league.

The Dolphins had just finished their fourth year as an expansion team and, like a typical expansion team, they had yet to come even close to a winning season.

In 1970 the AFL and NFL finally got married (taking the latter's name) after a ten-year love-hate affair, and Miami became a member of the AFC's Eastern Division.

To inaugurate their first season in the NFL, Dolphins' owner Joe Robbie offered Baltimore Colts' head coach Don Shula a percentage ownership of Miami if he would leave the state of Maryland for the humid shores of southern Florida. This was an offer Shula couldn't refuse. Colts' owner Carroll Rosenbloom protested that Robbie had stolen Shula from him and NFL Commissioner Pete Rozelle agreed. Robbie was charged with tampering, and lost Miami's first-round turn in the next player draft to Baltimore. Robbie didn't mind too much as he considered having Shula as his new head coach a prize worth the punishment.

BEST IN THE BUSINESS

In seven years as the head coach of Baltimore (1963–69), Don Shula had fashioned the finest won-lost record in professional football (73-26-4). Whereas the Miami Dolphins didn't know what a winning season looked like, Don Shula considered any position lower than first as a losing season.

Joe Robbie would surely have given a man with Shula's proven track record a number of years to turn around the Dolphins' fortunes. Well, if Rome wasn't built in a day, Miami sure was. With Shula in control, the Dolphins went from the 1969 doormat of the AFL to a 10-4 record and a wild card berth in the playoffs in 1970.

Robbie's taking in Shula as a minority partner looked like the move of a genius. The Dolphins, who drew a paltry 34,000 attendance per game in 1969, rocketed to 78,000 (capacity) in 1970. The people of Miami had obviously been waiting for a winner to whom they could give their undying allegiance.

In Shula's second Miami season, the Dolphins made it all the way to the Super Bowl with a 1971 record of 10-3-1. They edged Kansas City 27-24 in the divisional playoffs

In 1972 the Miami Dolphins won all 14 regular season games, the American Conference playoff and championship games, and Super Bowl VII. The Dolphins achieved the single finest year in the NFL history – an absolutely perfect season. This is how the Dolphins' dream came true

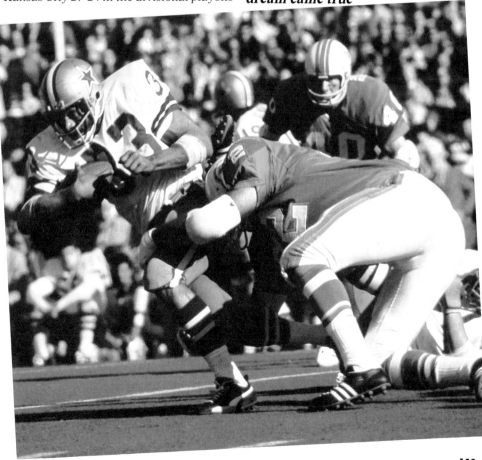

Dallas running back Duane Thomas (33) fights for yardage in Super Bowl VI. Miami lost the game but gained vital experience.

and shut out Shula's former squad Baltimore 21-0 in the AFC Championship.

Their opponent in Super Bowl VI was a Dallas Cowboys team that had dominated their division every season since 1966 and contested the previous Super Bowl.

Experience won out over youthful enthusiasm that day as Dallas defeated the Dolphins 24-3. Shula and the Dolphins gained valuable information on how to handle the tremendous pressure of being in a Super Bowl. They learned from their loss. The future was all Miami's.

Don Shula is the type of coach who wants to have control of all aspects of his team's play on the field. In Baltimore he used to have difficulties with the legendary Johnny Unitas, who definitely had his own thoughts on how best to move the ball. But upon moving to Miami and meeting the Dolphins' quarterback, Shula changed his tune.

'Bob Griese understands perfectly what we are trying to do,' Shula said. 'He likes to work within the system and gets a kick out of calling the right play at the right time.'

Bob Griese was a Rose Bowl-winning quarterback out of Purdue University who obtained a $200,000 contract from Joe Robbie to sign with the (then) not-so-hot Miami Dolphins in 1967. While Griese couldn't turn the Dolphins into winners, he did manage to complete over 55 per cent of his passes in every season he played. This meant Griese was of championship calibre, just waiting for the chance to prove it.

STAR SUPPORT

Already established as a top receiver with the Cleveland Browns, Paul Warfield came to Miami in 1970 and proceeded to become something of a ghostly legend – gliding effortlessly around the secondary, throwing subliminal fakes and catching the ball with a relaxed grace that made him seem in a different dimension to the other players labouring heavily across the field.

Running backs Larry Csonka and Mercury Morris made a dramatic contribution to the 1972 team. Where Csonka was a brutal runner who delighted in overpowering defenders who tried to tackle him, Morris was more like a whippet or an Olympic 400 metre man taking the corners. As a one-two punch they were to prove devastating.

In the offensive line, the big name was all-pro guard Larry Little who could pull and blast as well as anyone in the game.

TIME OUT

A HUNDRED IN A HURRY
When Don Shula's Dolphins won game number nine in 1972 by ripping the Patriots 52-0, Shula became the first coach in NFL history to win 100 league games inside of ten seasons – a record not even Hall of Fame coaches George Halas, Curly Lambeau, Paul Brown, Sid Gillman, Weeb Ewbank or Steve Owen could match.

Paul Warfield (42) was Miami's leading pass receiver in '72, with 29 receptions for 606 yards and a 20.9 yard average.

The winning touchdown. In the final minutes of the '72 AFC divisional playoff, the Dolphins were trailing 13-14 to Cleveland and their perfect season seemed in jeopardy, Jim Kiick (21) made an eight-yard run to save the day.

Primed for attack – bulldozing offensive guard Bob Kuechenberg was a key figure in the Dolphins' success.

And on the defense, the one man with an established reputation was middle linebacker Nick Buoniconti, who overcame his lack of linebacker size with agility, ball sense and a brilliant flair for blitzing.

BOUND FOR GLORY

The Dolphins' 1972 season opened in Kansas City. In the 1971 Divisional playoffs, the Chiefs had taken Miami into sudden-death overtime before being beaten 27-24. The Chiefs were also inaugurating their brand-new Arrowhead Stadium and the fans were screaming for revenge in plush surroundings. Some 79,829 midwesterners went home glum that afternoon as Bob Griese threw a 14-yard touchdown strike to tight end Marlin Briscoe, Larry Csonka bulled over from the two-yard line and the Dolphins cruised to a 20-10 victory.

In game two, Miami had another breeze, rolling over the hapless Houston Oilers 34-13. Csonka scored from the four-yard line, Mercury Morris tiptoed in from the two and Morris' alternate Jim Kiick scored twice, from a one-yard run and on a six-yard pass

from Griese.

Game three was to prove the toughest of all Miami's regular season games. The Minnesota Vikings had won their central division every year since 1968 and had a fierce defense known as 'The Purple People Eaters'. The Vikings led 14-6 with less than five minutes to go in the game when the Dolphins' placekicker Garo Yepremian struck for a clutch 51-yard field goal, and Griese hit second-string tight end Jim Mandich for a

Nick Buoniconti was a middle linebacker with speed agility and a will to blitz.

▲ Quarterback Bob Griese spins around to hand off in Super Bowl VII.
◀ Invincible running back Larry Csonka proves that it takes two defenders to ground him.

3-yard touchdown pass. After this game (played in Minnesota), the Dolphins began to believe they could beat anyone.

'Broadway Joe' Namath and the New York Jets entertained Miami in game four and received a 27-17 beating for their hospitality. The Dolphins were on their way home with a commanding 4-0 record and were already the only undefeated team in the NFL.

Game five found Bob Griese being carried off the field on a stretcher and 38-year-old reserve quarterback Earl Morrall coming on to take his place. Griese's ankle injury finished him off for the remainder of the regular season and Don Shula would have been excused for thinking that the Dolphins' successful season was over.

It didn't turn out that way. Earl Morrall dusted off his throwing arm and proceeded to take charge of a championship team. Against San Diego, he threw one 18-yard touchdown pass to slow but sure-handed Howard Twilley and another 19-yarder to the brilliant Paul Warfield. The Dolphins beat the Chargers 24-10.

BUFFALO SURPRISE
Miami encountered its last really tough regular season battle against the Buffalo Bills. With one minute gone in the fourth quarter of game six, the Bills were only down by one point, 17-16. The Dolphins had been playing slipshod football, but then Mercury Morris made one of his patented 15-yard clutch runs into Buffalo's end zone and saved the game (and Miami's perfect record) which ended 24-23.

With a 6-0 record, the Dolphins looked like world-beaters. In their final eight games of the regular season they proved it by shutting out the Baltimore Colts 23-0 (game seven), repaying the Bills for the earlier scare 30-16 (game eight), hammering the Patriots 52-0 (game nine), again stopping Namath and the Jets 28-24 (game ten), showing no mercy to the Cardinals 31-10 (game 11), beating the Patriots a second time 37-21 (game 12), defeating the New

Wide receiver Howard Twilley (81) made Miami's first score in Super Bowl VII with a massive 28-yard touchdown pass from Griese. It was a fitting end to a season he finished with an impressive 18.2 yard receiving average.

York Giants after a hard-fought game 23-13 (game 13), and ending their regular season on a flawless note by again shutting out Baltimore 16-0.

No NFL team had completed their season without defeat since the fabled Chicago Bears of 1942, when only 11 games led to the championship contest.

The Dolphins had clinched their division title with four games yet to play. This meant Shula was able to rest any player with a nagging injury for an entire month. Miami entered the playoffs poised, single-minded and healthy.

THE FINAL ASSAULT

Earl Morrall remained the Dolphins' quarterback in their AFC playoff game against the Cleveland Browns. Miami held the lead until only eight minutes were left in the game. A 27-yard touchdown pass from Cleveland quarterback Mike Phipps to wide receiver Fair Hooker put the Browns briefly in the lead 14-13. But reliable running back Jim Kiick went for eight yards at 10:06 in the fourth quarter, and his touchdown secured the game for the Dolphins 20-14.

The AFC Championship game found Miami against a Pittsburgh Steelers gang only two seasons away from the beginning of their dynasty the rest of the '70s.

Morrall had trouble igniting the Dolphins so Griese returned at last to the wars in the second half of the game. The Steelers forged ahead briefly 10-7 on a Roy Gerela 14-yard field goal, but then Griese took

charge, Jim Kiick scored two touchdowns on runs of two and three-yards and the Dolphins prevailed 21-17.

REDSKINS REPULSED

Miami had climbed the mountain to Super Bowl VII and meeting them at the peak were the Washington Redskins.

In game films Shula and Griese found the Redskins' defensive variations surprisingly simple to deal with and in the game itself Griese was easily able to employ what he had learned.

Miami made sure everyone knew exactly who deserved to be world champion by coasting past a befuddled Washington team 14-7. The Redskins saved themselves from an embarrassing whitewash by picking up a Dolphin fumble at midfield and going in for the touchdown with only three minutes left to play.

The game was over and safety Jake Scott was voted MVP – in tribute to his role in Miami's stunning defense. But the real star was the man who had powered them to the top, the 'perfect coach' – Don Shula.

► The man who made the Dolphins. In one of football's greatest success stories, Don Shula coached Miami from obscurity to championship glory in just two years.
▼ Star running back Jim Kiick was Miami's versatile offensive weapon with 137 rushing attempts and 21 receptions.

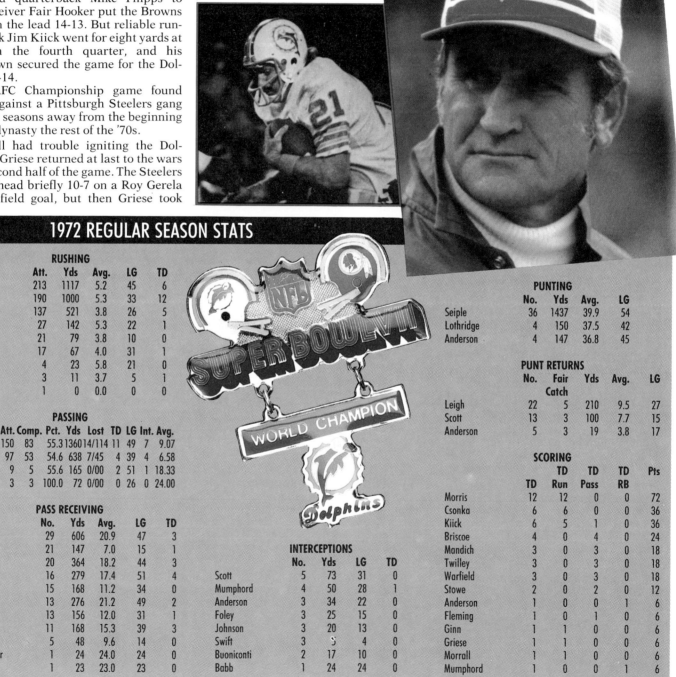

1972 REGULAR SEASON STATS

RUSHING

	Att.	Yds	Avg.	LG	TD
Csonka	213	1117	5.2	45	6
Morris	190	1000	5.3	33	12
Kiick	137	521	3.8	26	5
Ginn	27	142	5.3	22	1
Leigh	21	79	3.8	10	0
Morrall	17	67	4.0	31	1
Warfield	4	23	5.8	21	0
Griese	3	11	3.7	5	1
Del Gaizo	1	0	0.0	0	0

PASSING

	Att.	Comp.	Pct.	Yds	Lost	TD	LG	Int.	Avg.
Morrall	150	83	55.3	1360	14/114	11	49	7	9.07
Griese	97	53	54.6	638	7/45	4	39	4	6.58
Del Gaizo	9	5	55.6	165	0/00	2	51	1	18.33
Briscoe	3	3	100.0	72	0/00	0	26	0	24.00

PASS RECEIVING

	No.	Yds	Avg.	LG	TD
Warfield	29	606	20.9	47	3
Kiick	21	147	7.0	15	1
Twilley	20	364	18.2	44	3
Briscoe	16	279	17.4	51	4
Morris	15	168	11.2	34	0
Stowe	13	276	21.2	49	2
Fleming	13	156	12.0	31	1
Mandich	11	168	15.3	39	3
Csonka	5	48	9.6	14	0
Den Herder	1	24	24.0	24	0
Ginn	1	23	23.0	23	0

INTERCEPTIONS

	No.	Yds	LG	TD
Scott	5	73	31	0
Mumphord	4	50	28	1
Anderson	3	34	22	0
Foley	3	25	15	0
Johnson	3	20	13	0
Swift	3	9	4	0
Buoniconti	2	17	10	0
Babb	1	24	24	0

PUNTING

	No.	Yds	Avg.	LG
Seiple	36	1437	39.9	54
Lothridge	4	150	37.5	42
Anderson	4	147	36.8	45

PUNT RETURNS

	No.	Fair Catch	Yds	Avg.	LG
Leigh	22	5	210	9.5	27
Scott	13	3	100	7.7	15
Anderson	5	3	19	3.8	17

SCORING

	TD	TD Run	TD Pass	TD RB	Pts
Morris	12	12	0	0	72
Csonka	6	6	0	0	36
Kiick	6	5	1	0	36
Briscoe	4	0	4	0	24
Mandich	3	0	3	0	18
Twilley	3	0	3	0	18
Warfield	3	0	3	0	18
Stowe	2	0	2	0	12
Anderson	1	0	0	1	6
Fleming	1	0	1	0	6
Ginn	1	1	0	0	6
Griese	1	1	0	0	6
Morrall	1	1	0	0	6
Mumphord	1	0	0	1	6

THE PERFECT MATCH

When the San Francisco 49ers and Miami Dolphins entered Super Bowl XIX with the best combined won-lost record in history, the fans looked forward to a truly great Battle of Champions. They were not going to be disappointed

The 1984 season found two teams standing shoulder to shoulder like twin Everests at the end of game 18. The San Francisco 49ers had gone 15-1 in the regular season, an NFL record, and had soundly beaten the New York Giants and the Chicago Bears, in the NFC eliminations.

The Miami Dolphins had annihilated all AFC pretenders, winning their first 11 games before losing to San Diego and the Los Angeles Raiders at the season's end. Miami finished 14-2 and crushed Seattle and Pittsburgh in the AFC tournament.

The Dolphins and 49ers had buried their opponents. The funerals had taken place. They alone remained standing on the battlefield that would go down in football history as Super Bowl XIX.

BIGGEST AND BEST

No two teams entered a Super Bowl with finer records or bigger reputations. The 49ers, under head coach Bill Walsh, were Super Bowl XVI champions. They missed a third Super Bowl appearance in Super Bowl XVIII by an eyelash, losing 24-21 to Washington in the NFC Championship game after several very controversial plays.

The Dolphins, led by the imperial Don Shula, were two-time Super Bowl winners and finalists more times (5) than any other team, save the Dallas Cowboys.

Kim Bokamper (58) piles into the action as Miami's defense collapses around San Francisco's Roger Craig (33).

★ ★ ★ STANFORD STADIUM ★ STANFORD ★ CALIFORNIA ★ 20 JANUARY 1985 ★ ★ ★

The more balanced 49ers entered the game as favourites, but the 6 ft 4 in shadow of record-breaking Dan Marino (55 touchdown passes in 1984) rendered the bookmakers' opinion irrelevant, if not ridiculous. Coach Walsh's succinct opinion of Miami's QB? 'The man is awesome.'

At the Dolphins' press conference the Thursday before Super Bowl XIX, Marino squinted at TV lights and the hordes of reporters and awkwardly fielded the barrage of questions. When asked, 'Are you concerned with all that's expected of you?' He replied, 'What's expected of me?'

'To be the greatest quarterback this side of the Second Coming,' was the answer. There was laughter and Marino modestly replied, 'Aw . . . to do the best I can. That's what I expect of me.'

The 49ers' quarterback, Joe Montana, earnestly answered questions at his press conference in front of a slightly smaller and less attentive audience. Before Super Bowl XIX, Montana had thrown an excellent, but relatively mortal (relative to Marino, that is) 32 touchdown passes in 1984.

'Most of my preparation is mental,' said Montana. 'Quarterback is the least physical and most mental position on the team.'

HOWITZERS AND TIME BOMBS

On Super Sunday, the 49ers ignored the euphoria that had surrounded Miami's record-studded ascent, and chose instead to concentrate on their own, intricate weave of offensive and defensive plays. True, Miami possessed the long-range howitzer in Dan Marino's gifted right arm, and the Dolphins' offense was undeniably explosive and rapid-fire. So San Francisco chose to attack Miami with subtlety: more sleight of hand than hand grenade, more time bomb than mortar round, and ultimately more devastating.

For Dan Marino, Super Bowl XIX began as if it was just another day at the office. He completed nine out of his first 10 passes as expected for 103 yards.

The first quarter finished with Miami leading 10-7 and Marino looking unstoppable. He called his plays sequentially, without a huddle, and his short scoring pass to tight end Dan Johnson reflected the bewilderment of San Francisco's defense.

Then suddenly, with only 60 seconds gone from the second quarter, the Marino avalanche was stopped dead and Joe Montana took complete charge. For the next 11 minutes 55 seconds, the 49ers cut like buzz-saws through the Dolphins' bedraggled defense.

TIME OUT

HOME ADVANTAGE
For only the second time in Super Bowl history, the venue for the championship game – chosen at least one year in advance – was in one of the participating team's back yards. California's Stanford Stadium is just outside San Francisco. The only time this happened before was for the Rams, when Pasadena was the site for Super Bowl XIV. The Rams, though on home ground, lost 31-19 to Pittsburgh.

They drove for three quick touchdowns. Montana threw eight yards to running back Roger Craig for a 14-10 lead and never looked back. Montana ran six yards for the second TD and then sent Craig churning two yards through the porous Dolphin line to make the score 28-10.

Montana was holding an offensive clinic while his buddies on the 49ers defense turned Dan Marino's atom-bomb arm into a pop-gun. The Dolphins managed three possessions (after each 49ers TD), ran nine plays from scrimmage and gained the grand total of one yard. Three rushes netted minus-three yards, while Marino completed one of six passes for four yards. To add insult to injury, Miami's Reggie Roby punted three times for a net average of only 26 yards.

STORM WARNINGS

Four days before the game, Miami defensive end Doug Betters had sounded storm warnings that shouldn't have been ignored by his teammates. 'There's gonna come a time when our offense runs into a brick wall,' he had said. 'We don't want it to happen, but it could. If it does, then we'll have to do it with defense.'

Betters was right about the 'brick wall', but his side-kicks on the Dolphins defense couldn't even begin to hold the fort. They

STARTING LINEUPS

MIAMI	Offense	SAN FRANCISCO
85 Mark Duper	WR	87 Dwight Clark
79 Jon Giesler	LT	77 Bubba Paris
61 Roy Foster	LG	68 John Ayers
57 Dwight Stephenson	C	56 Fred Quillan
64 Ed Newman	RG	51 Randy Cross
74 Cleveland Green	RT	71 Keith Fahnhorst
84 Bruce Hardy	TE	81 Russ Francis
83 Mark Clayton	WR	88 Freddie Solomon
13 Dan Marino	QB	16 Joe Montana
22 Tony Nathan	RB	26 Wendell Tyler
34 Woody Bennet	RB	33 Roger Craig
	Defense	
75 Doug Betters	LE	65 Lawrence Pillers
73 Bob Baumhower	NT	78 Manu Tuiasosopo
58 Kim Bokamper	RE	76 Dwaine Board
59 Bob Brudzinski	LOLB	57 Dan Bunz
53 Jay Brophy	LILB	50 Riki Ellison
51 Mark Brown	RILB	64 Jack Reynolds
56 Charles Bowser	ROLB	58 Keena Turner
28 Don McNeal	LCB	42 Ronnie Lott
49 William Judson	RCB	21 Eric Wright
47 Glenn Blackwood	SS	27 Carlton Williamson
42 Lyle Blackwood	FS	22 Dwight Hicks

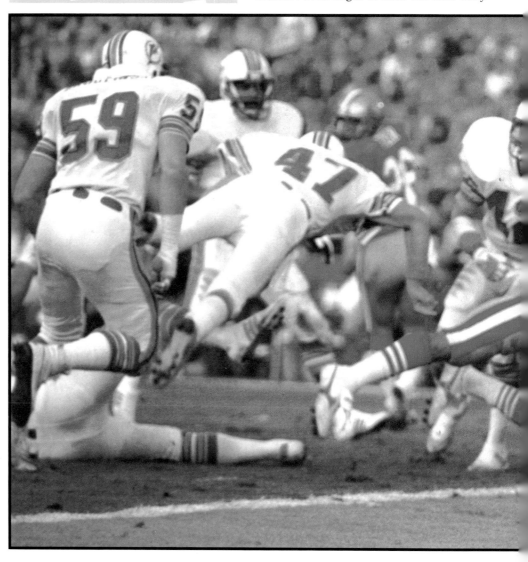

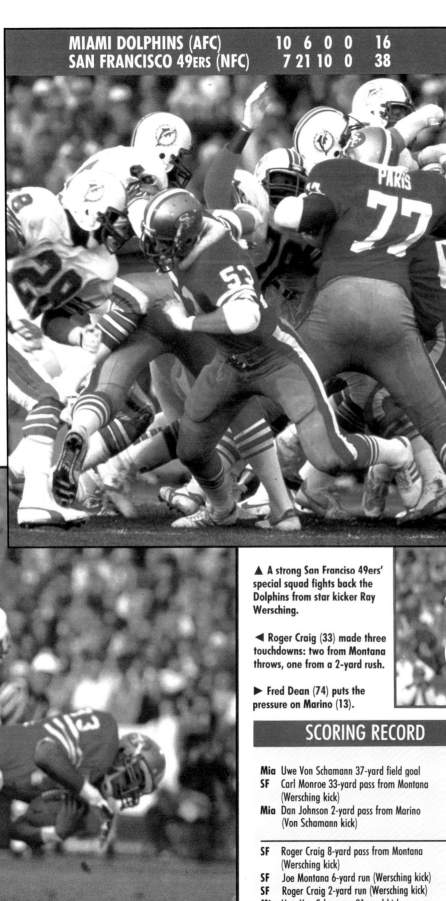

| MIAMI DOLPHINS (AFC) | 10 6 0 0 | 16 |
| SAN FRANCISCO 49ERS (NFC) | 7 21 10 0 | 38 |

played a three-man defensive front line and tried to focus mainly on tight pass-coverage against Joe Montana's assorted arsenal of receivers.

With only a three-man line facing him, Montana had no pass-rush pressure. Subsequently, he hit on 24 of 35 pass attempts for 331 yards and three touchdowns. For the sake of variety, Montana personally rushed for 59 yards and one touchdown. In effect, the San Francisco QB was treating the AFC Champion's defense as if it were a stationary object.

The Dolphins' defenders were so absorbed with the 49ers' long-receivers that they totally neglected Montana's ad-lib dashes. 'One-time,' Montana said, 'I was running right behind one of their linebackers, who was chasing one of our receivers. He never did see me.'

This kind of defensive tunnel-vision was mitigated somewhat by two Miami field-goals that were achieved inside a frenetic 11 seconds! This made the score a more respectable 28-16. As the half-time gun sounded, the Dolphins were somehow only two touchdowns in arrears.

The Miami Dolphins stormed on to the field for the second half of Super Bowl XIX and promptly ground to *minus*-ten yards on their first possession. This ominous beginning led immediately to yet another 49ers' score. Ray Wersching kicked a comfortable 27-yard field goal for a 31-16 lead,

▲ A strong San Franciso 49ers' special squad fights back the Dolphins from star kicker Ray Wersching.

◀ Roger Craig (33) made three touchdowns: two from Montana throws, one from a 2-yard rush.

▶ Fred Dean (74) puts the pressure on Marino (13).

SCORING RECORD

Mia	Uwe Von Schamann 37-yard field goal	0-3
SF	Carl Monroe 33-yard pass from Montana (Wersching kick)	7-3
Mia	Dan Johnson 2-yard pass from Marino (Von Schamann kick)	7-10
SF	Roger Craig 8-yard pass from Montana (Wersching kick)	14-10
SF	Joe Montana 6-yard run (Wersching kick)	21-10
SF	Roger Craig 2-yard run (Wersching kick)	28-10
Mia	Uwe Von Schamann 31-yard kick	28-13
Mia	Uwe Von Schamann 30-yard kick	28-16
SF	Ray Wersching 27-yard field goal	31-16
SF	Roger Craig 16-yard pass from Montana (Wersching kick)	38-16

and a 16-yard TD pass from Montana to Craig found the third quarter ending with San Francisco in a commanding 38-16 lead. This turn of events made even taciturn Bill Walsh 'comfortable'. It also turned out to be the final score.

ELEPHANTS AND BUFFALOS

Exactly how did Bill Walsh and his 49ers arrive at this 'comfortable' position? How did they manage to anaesthetize the single most powerful offensive force (Dan Marino) after only one quarter of play?

San Francisco opened defensively in its customary three-man front with four linebackers. Throughout the practice week, however, Walsh and defensive co-ordinator George Seifert had emphasized a four-man front with variations in coverage behind it.

'We knew we'd need it to win,' said Walsh. 'We wanted to avoid going into the

TEAM STATISTICS

	Miami	San Francisco
Total First Downs	19	31
First Downs Rushing	2	16
First Downs Passing	17	15
First Downs Penalty	0	0
Total Net Yardage	314	537
Total Offensive Plays	63	76
Average Gain per Offensive Play	5.0	7.1
Rushes	9	40
Yards Gained Rushing (net)	25	211
Average Yards per Rush	2.8	5.3
Passes Attempted	50	35
Passes Completed	29	24
Had Intercepted	2	0
Times Tackled Attempting to Pass	4	1
Yards Lost Attempting to Pass	29	5
Yards Gained Passing (net)	289	326
Punts	6	3
Average Distance	39.3	32.7
Punt Returns	2	5
Punt Return Yardage	15	51
Kickoff Returns	7	4
Kickoff Return Yardage	140	40
Interception Return Yardage	0	0
Total Return Yardage	155	91
Fumbles	1	2
Own Fumbles Recovered	1	0
Opponent' Fumbles Recovered	2	0
Penalties	1	2
Yards Penalized	10	10
Total Points Scored	16	38
Touchdowns	1	5
Touchdowns Rushing	0	2
Touchdowns Passing	1	3
Touchdown Returns	0	0
Extra Points	1	5
Field Goals	3	1
Field Goals Attempted	3	1
Third Down Efficiency	4/12	6/11
Fourth Down Efficiency	0/0	0/1
Time of Possession	22:49	37:11

SUPER BOWL RECORDS

Individual
Most points – 18, Roger Craig (3-TD)
Most touchdowns – 3, Roger Craig (1-r, 2-p)
Most PATs – 5, Ray Wersching (5 att.)
Most passes attempted – 50, Dan Marino
Most passes completed – 29, Dan Marino
Most yards gained – 331, Joe Montana
Most touchdown attempts without interception – 35, Joe Montana

Team
Most games – 5, Miami (1972, '73, '74, '83, '85)
Most consecutive games – 3, Miami (1972, '73, '74)
Most points scored – 38, SF
Most points each half – 28, (1st), SF
Most points, each half, both teams – 44, (SF 28, Mia 16) (1st)
Most points, each quarter, both teams – 17, (Mia 10, SF 7) (1st)
Most touchdowns – 5, SF
Most PATs – 5, SF
Most field goals, both teams – 4, (Mia 3, SF1)
Most first downs – 31, SF
Most first downs, both teams – 50, (SF31 Mia 19)
Most first downs, rushing – 16, SF
Fewest first downs, rushing – 2, Miami
Most first downs, passing – 17, Miami
Most first downs, passing, both teams – 32, (Mia 17, SF 15)
Most yards gained – 537, SF
Most yards gained, both teams – 851, (SF 537, Mia 314)
Fewest rushing attempts – 9, Miami
Fewest rushing attempts, both teams – 49, Mia 9, SF 40)
Most passes attempted – 50, Miami
Most passes attempted, both teams – 85, (Mia 50, SF 35)
Most passes completed – 29, Miami
Most passes completed, both teams – 53, (Mia 29, SF 24)
Most yards gained – 326, SF
Most yards gained, both teams – 615, (SF 326, Mia 289)
Most kickoff returns – 7, Miami
Most kickoff returns, both teams – 11, (Mia 7, SF 4)

Super Bowl touchdown record-breaker Roger Craig (33)

fourth quarter with tired defensive linemen. 'We needed better pressure on Marino. Going to four, we also shut down their running and forced them to pass.'

Seifert said a variation of coverages were used to support the 'Elephants' (the 49ers' description of their four-man front). 'We were in a Nickel most of the time, but we also used what we call "Buffalo".'

The leading characteristic of the 49ers Buffalo was that it freed defensive end Fred Dean (traded prior to the '86 season) to act as a 'rover'. He pulls off the line of scrimmage, creating a 3-3 look. The line becomes a combination of Dwaine Board, Gary (Big Hands) Johnson, and either Jeff Stover or Michael Carter. Dean joins linebacker Keena Turner and defensive back Jeff Fuller, positioned as a third linebacker. The starting defensive backs are joined by reserve Tom Holmoe in a configuration that is five deep.

ALL-OUT ASSAULT
The Elephants applied pressure, and the variations gave Marino recognition problems downfield, where 49ers' defensive backs swarmed.

'The big thing, to me, was that Marino didn't have time to look off his primary receiver, once we started getting pressure up front,' said 49ers' safety Dwight Hicks. 'It made a big difference in the secondary.'

'The Dolphins throw the ball 70 per cent

of the time,' said Bill Walsh. 'That made our ability to mount a rush – an all-out assault – very important.'

Midway through the third quarter, the rush got there. 'We were getting closer, working down in front of him [Marino],' Walsh said. 'Our coverage may have been somewhat tighter than what he was used to seeing.' Walsh's modesty could be compared to Sitting Bull commenting that there were a few more arrows flying at the Little Bighorn than General Custer was used to.

'It was important to hit him [Marino],' Johnson explained. 'To let him know we were there. In a lot of the films, it looked like people got to him, and then stopped. I think it may have been kind of new to him.'

Take Marino's statistics out of the context of the game and they seem more suited for victory than one-sided defeat (289 net yards on a Super Bowl record 50 attempts). But the bulk of his plus-stats were achieved during the first 15-minutes of play. Over the last three quarters, Marino averaged a skimpy five yards per attempt.

A THOROUGH BUTT-KICKING

Nat Moore, the Dolphins' veteran receiver, defused suggestions that Marino was the reason Miami lost Super Bowl XIX. 'It would be ludicrous to say one person was off,' Moore said. 'It was a thorough butt-kicking, and the entire offense has to own

JOE MONTANA MVP

Joe Montana won the most valuable player award for his exceptional play throughout the game. His 6-yard touchdown run took the 49ers to a 21-10 lead in the second quarter. He threw three touchdown passes, completing 24 of 35 attempts for 331 yards.

► Eric Wright (21) intercepts Dan Marino's third quarter pass to Mark Clayton (83).

▼ Mike Walter (99) stops Miami's Woody Bennett.

up to it, as well as the entire team.'

Randy Cross, Keith Fahnhorst, and Fred Quillan led the 49ers' offensive line that was the genesis of a Super Bowl-record 537-yard day. Running backs Wendell Tyler and Roger Craig had 28 rushes and 12 receptions between them, and Craig set a Super Bowl record with three touchdowns.

The defense put together key plays by Johnson, Board, and Turner, and finally an interception by Eric Wright, who leaped in front of Dolphins' wide receiver Mark Clayton at the 49ers' one-yard line with 3:27 left in the third quarter. Marino's deep game, reduced here to a highly readable 27-yard attempt, was finished for the day.

In the last quarter, Carlton Williamson intercepted Marino in the end zone. Miami's defense later saved face with a goal-line stand at its own two yard line. Academic gestures, both. Wright's inter-

ception had sealed the coffin.

On Monday, after the game, Walsh was asked to assess the impact of his strategy.

He spoke, instead, of the energies and skills of the 49ers players. 'Their play resulted from a backlog of development. It would be awfully hard to isolate the impact of coaching in a game like this.'

OUT OF OBSCURITY

Bill Walsh's typical self-effacement is not borne out by the facts. It took him a scant two seasons to raise his team from habitual obscurity to the heights as Super Bowl XVI champs. His brilliant offensive tactics were emulated around the league (imitation is indeed, the sincerest form of flattery). Surrounded by copy-cats, Walsh still managed to bring his 49ers back to the Super Bowl in 1985 and a second victory.

What had happened in San Francisco – from acquisition of talent by whatever means were available, to development and nurturing of the optimum winning climate – happened in the most part because of Bill Walsh. Super Bowl XIX's end result is the ultimate vindication and celebration of a great coach's greatest victory.

THE BIG TIME

SUPER BOWL

When the Chicago Bears mauled the New England Patriots 46-10, the Super Bowl record book was re-written – largest margin of victory, most points in a game, most rushing touchdowns, longest punt. It was the most one-sided Super Bowl in history. On 26 January 1986, the Chicago Bears showed the world what great American Football was really all about.

CHICAGO BEARS (NFC)	13	10	21	2	46
NEW ENGLAND PATRIOTS (AFC)	3	0	0	7	10

The Chicago Bears' astonishing performance in Super Bowl XX was the icing on the cake of an already astonishing season. The offensive weaponry of Jim McMahon, Walter Payton and even William Perry provided the points, while the unflinching '46 defense' lead by MVP (most valuable player) sack specialist Richard Dent and bruising safety Gary Fencik stopped the hopeful Patriots dead.

The Bears regular season was the kind that legends are made of. Chicago made few mistakes in a 17-win course to the championship game. New England was a rival whose success – moving from 'Wild Card' outsiders to Super Bowl contenders – was equally astonishing.

But no one wins a Super Bowl without a season's dedicated training to that end. Under coach Mike Ditka the Bears roared through their first 12 games with a defense that allowed only 12.5 points per match,

☆☆☆☆☆ **Louisiana Superdome** ★ **New Orleans**

holding a fine Dallas Cowboys side to a nil score on the way.

'We've been working hard the last two years to be the best ever,' said MVP Richard Dent, the Bears' defensive end. 'I believe we're in the running, and if we're not, I'd like to see who's better.'

WILD CARD CHAMPIONS

While Bears euphoria was building to a deafening pitch, their Super Bowl XX opponents were quietly going about their business. The New England Patriots had always been regarded as the team that *nearly* made it. In their 25-year history, they built a reputation for having some superb players on their rosters, but were never able to make them into a title-chasing team.

THE BIG GAME

On the afternoon of 26 January 1986, the space-age style Louisiana Superdome was packed to capacity. For the 73,818 fans inside, the atmosphere was one of euphoria – neither team had played in a Super Bowl before. The Bears were firm favourites to win. But there was hope in the Patriots' camp too.

Coach Raymond Berry opted to establish a passing game early on. This would, he hoped, unsettle the famed 46 defense of the Bears and open up a path for their ground game. Young Tony Eason had kept the starting job at quarterback after the injury of veteran Steve Grogan. Eason's hope was to take full advantage of the all-round skills of running back Craig James.

Chicago, meanwhile, held all the aces. Their defense was their strength – no one had figured it out all season. More often there were seven or eight defenders blitzing a confused opposition. On offense, they

Loyal Bears fans reveal their true colours and Chicago's Honey Bears – the name for their glamorous band of cheerleaders – hoist their legs high in the carnival-style build-up to Super Bowl XX.

TIME OUT

SUPER TITLE
The title of the world championship comes not from the trophy or the stadium but from . . . a little rubber ball! Lamar Hunt, owner of the Kansas City Chiefs, remembered his daughter's toy, her 'Super Ball', when a title was being sought in 1967.

were equally threatening.

After kickoff, the Bears began the game nervously. On only the second play, running back Walter Payton fumbled and the Patriots big-play defense recovered.

New England even took an early 3-0 lead, when Tony Franklin converted Payton's fumble into a 37-yard field goal. It was the quickest score in Super Bowl history, coming just 1:19 after the game had started. The points were the first scored against Chicago in the playoffs after back-to-back

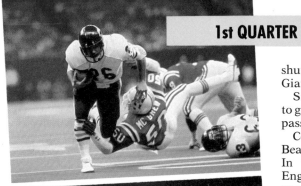

shutouts (no scores) on the New York Giants and Los Angeles Rams.

Significantly, the Patriots were unable to gain even one yard in the three plays – all passes – that preceded the field goal.

Coach Berry was hoping to catch the Bears off guard early by throwing the ball. In three previous playoff games New England had thrown a *total* of only 42 passes. Now each of their first six plays from scrimmage was a pass. The change in play had not worked. Six passes resulted in five incompletions and a sack.

'I didn't think we could just run the ball and cram it down the Bears' throats,' said Berry. 'I thought it was really important to get some balance back into our offense.'

COMMANDING LEAD

Before the first quarter was over, the Bears were in complete command, thanks to two of New England's six turnovers (4 fumbles and 2 interceptions). After Jim McMahon's 43-yard pass to Willie Gault set up rookie Kevin Butler's tying 28-yard field goal, Dent forced fumbles on successive plays. The Bears recovered both on the New England 12-yard line.

Butler's second field goal gave Chicago the lead for good. When running back Matt Suhey scored on an 11-yard run a minute later, the Bears led 13-3. A 10-point lead never seemed so secure.

McMahon, who had been the centre of attention during an eventful pregame week in New Orleans, scored the first of his two touchdowns on a nifty two-yard run midway through the second quarter. As time ran out, Butler's third short field goal of the half, from 24 yards, gave the Bears a 23-3 lead.

In a vain attempt to stem the tide, Berry replaced Eason – who was 0 for 6 passing and had been sacked three times already by the powerful Chicago defense

◀ Just 23 seconds from the end of the first quarter and a sequence of key blocks by the Bears offense enables Matt Suhey (26) to complete an 11-yard touchdown run. Fred Marion's (31) desperate charge fails to stop him and the Bears have a 10-point lead.

– with veteran quarterback Steve Grogan. Grogan went on to complete 17 of 30 passes for 177 yards, though most of those came long after the game was decided.

CHICAGO BEAR-HUG

If the 23-3 halftime score was not enough to discourage the Patriots, the statistics certainly were. New England had minus-5

STARTING LINEUPS

CHICAGO	Offense	NEW ENGLAND	CHICAGO	Defense	NEW ENGLAND
83 Willie Gault	WR	86 Stanley Morgan	99 Dan Hampton	LE	60 Garin Veris
74 Jim Covert	LT	76 Brian Holloway	76 Steve McMichael	LT-NT	72 Lester Williams
62 Mark Bortz	LG	73 John Hannah	72 William Perry	RT-RE	85 Julius Adams
63 Jay Hilgenberg	C	58 Pete Brock	95 Richard Dent	RE-LOLB	56 Andre Tippett
57 Tom Thayer	RG	61 Ron Wooten	55 Otis Wilson	LLB-LILB	57 Steve Nelson
78 Keith Van Horne	RT	67 Steve Moore	50 Mike Singletary	MLB-RILB	50 Larry McGrew
87 Emery Moorehead	TE	87 Lin Dawson	58 Wilber Marshall	RLB-ROLB	55 Don Blackmon
85 Dennis McKinnon	WR	81 Stephen Starring	27 Mike Richardson	LCB	42 Ronnie Lippett
9 Jim McMahon	QB	11 Tony Eason	21 Leslie Frazier	RCB	26 Ray Clayborn
34 Walter Payton	RB	33 Tony Collins	22 Dave Duerson	SS	38 Roland James
26 Matt Suhey	RB	32 Craig James	45 Gary Fencik	FS	31 Fred Marion

TEAM STATISTICS

	Chicago	New England
First downs	23	12
Rushes-yards	49-167	11-7
Passes	12-24	17-36
Net yards passing	241	116
Plays-total yards	76-408	54-123
Sacks-yards lost	3-15	7-61
Return yards	69	175
Punts-average	4-43.3	6-43.8
Fumbles-lost	3-2	4-4
Penalties-yards	6-35	5-35
Time of possession	39:15	20:45

◀ Chicago turns the game upside-down. *Inset* New England's back-up quarterback Steve Grogan (14) is well and truly sacked by Bears' defenders Richard Dent (95) and Dan Hampton (99), a pair of men that any quarterback should fear and with a combined weight of over 35 stone.

A flying tackle by New England's wide receiver Greg Hawthorne (27) stops cornerback Leslie Frazier (21) firmly in his tracks, after intercepting Eason's pass.

yards rushing, minus-14 yards passing, minus-19 yards in total offense and just one first down.

Chicago had New England in a Bear-hug from which they could not break free.

The Bears erased any hopes the Patriots might have had on their first offensive play of the second half.

Rich Camarillo's 62-yard punt forced Chicago to begin play on its own 4-yard line, McMahon faked handoffs to both Suhey and Payton and retreated into his end zone. He spotted wide receiver Willie Gault heading toward the right sideline far downfield, and hit him with a 60-yard pass at the New England 36. McMahon took the ball in himself with a one-yard dive eight plays later.

Even William 'The Refrigerator' Perry got in on the fun. Making his

Bears quarterback Jim McMahon (9) had all the luck in the passing game, completing 12 out of 20 passes for 256 yards. New England's Tony Eason (11) failed all six of his attempted passes.

SUPER BOWL RECORDS

INDIVIDUAL

Set
Longest punt – 62 yards, Rich Camarillo, New England
Most kickoff returns – 7, Stephen Starring, New England

Tied
Most PATs – 5, Kevin Butler, Chicago
Most safeties – 1, Henry Waechter, Chicago
Most touchdowns rushing – 2, Jim McMahon, Chicago
Most touchdowns by interception return – 1, Reggie Phillips, Chicago
Most fumbles recovered – 2, Mike Singlotary, Chicago

TEAM

Set
Most points – 46, Chicago
Widest margin of victory – 36, Chicago
Most points, second half – 23, Chicago
Most points, third quarter – 21, Chicago
Most points, third quarter, both teams – 21, Chicago (21), New England (0)
Fewest first downs rushing – 1, New England
Fewest yards gained rushing – 7, New England
Lowest average yards per rush – 0.6, New England
Most touchdowns rushing – 4, Chicago
Most times sacked, both teams – 10, New England (7), Chicago (3)
Quickest score, start of game – 1:19, New England

FINAL SCORE   BEARS 46   PATRIOTS 10

RICHARD DENT MVP

Defensive end Richard Dent won the most valuable player award for his outstanding play in leading the Bears' awesome defense against the New England Patriots in Super Bowl XX.

Dent contributed two of the Bears' seven sacks, and his pass rush was influential in causing two interceptions.

Celebration time in the Bears' camp. And what a victory – the largest winning margin in Super Bowl history. The Bears' defensive squad are doubly jubilant as defensive end Richard Dent (95) is named MVP for his part in the destruction of the Patriots.

first appearance on offense since week 10, Perry was sacked by Dennis Owens in the first quarter as he was rolling (running) right, looking to throw into the end zone after taking a pitch from McMahon. But in the third period, to the delight of the crowd, Perry scored on a one-yard 'run' to take the Bears into a 41-point lead.

Grogan led the Patriots to their only touchdown early in the fourth quarter. He completed seven passes for 65 yards on the drive, which ended with an eight-yard scoring pass to Irving Fryar.

RECORD BREAKERS

The Bears' defense was magnificent. They had set the tone of the match in the opening few plays and they never let up on the pressure. The Patriots had nowhere to go. And the statistics proved it. The Bears scored more points and won by more points than any team in Super Bowl history.

New England finished with a net total of only 7 yards rushing, a Super Bowl record, and 123 yards in total offense. Eason and Grogan were sacked seven times.

Later, Chicago's quarterback Jim McMahon had only one regret. 'I'm sorry we couldn't get number thirty-four (Walter Payton) in the end zone,' he said.

Payton, the NFL's all-time career rushing leader, was the game's top ground

SCORING RECORD

NE	-Tony Franklin 36-yard field goal	0-3
Chi	-Kevin Butler 28-yard field goal	3-3
Chi	-Kevin Butler 24-yard field goal	6-3
Chi	-Matt Suhey 11-yard run (Butler kick)	13-3
Chi	-Jim McMahon 2-yard run (Butler kick)	20-3
Chi	-Kevin Butler 24-yard field goal	23-3
Chi	-Jim McMahon 1-yard run (Butler kick)	30-3
Chi	-Reggie Phillips 28-yard pass interception (Butler kick)	37-3
Chi	-William Perry 1-yard run (Butler kick)	44-3
NE	-Irving Fryar 8-yard pass from Grogan (Franklin kick)	44-10
Chi	-Safety, Waechter tackled Grogan in end zone	46-10

gainer with 61 yards on 22 carries.

Such record breaking made sad reading for New England fans. Their only consolation in the matter was that they got the quickest score in history (1:19) and punter Rich Camarillo hit a best-ever punt of 62 yards. A small consolation, perhaps, for their defeat by a side which even Patriots' coach Berry described as 'one of the greatest teams in the history of the game'.

Back in Chicago, where more than 1000 fans had filled Daley Center Plaza and braved a wind-chill factor of 36 degrees below zero to watch the game on a giant TV screen, the celebration was in full force almost as soon as the final gun had sounded.

PITTSBURGH
DYNASTY

*In a 1972 playoff, the Steelers'
looked set for another defeat. Then
came a pass that was to announce
their arrival as the most dominant
team in history*

C an one play put a whole team on the
road to greatness? Can one lucky
break turn around years of bad fortune? It seemed to be the case for the
Pittsburgh Steelers in 1972.

After almost 40 years in football they had
nothing to show for it except the largest
collection of wooden spoons in the gridiron
game. Then, in a playoff against the
Oakland Raiders (now the Los Angeles
Raiders), the tide turned. Not with an over-
whelming victory or a dazzling individual
performance, but on one moment of magic.

One incredible pass, caught by rookie
running back Franco Harris won that game
for Pittsburgh. Dubbed 'The Immaculate
Reception', it was the springboard for the
Steelers to dominate the NFL for the better
part of the following decade.

A COACHING CHALLENGE

The whole story began three years earlier.
The Steelers had always been a graveyard
for head coaches. Sixteen had come and
gone in just 35 years with an average
career-span of just over two seasons.

When Chuck Noll was appointed in 1969,
there seemed no reason why he should be
any different. He'd been dubbed a defensive genius as an assistant at the Baltimore
Colts, and immediately decided to use the
draft to build Pittsburgh into a championship team.

Aged just 36, Noll faced a mammoth
task. The Steelers had never won any kind
of title. Since they were formed in 1933 as
the Pittsburgh Pirates, they'd had just
eight winning seasons.

How quickly it all changed. Noll, a low-
profile, hard-working coach, began brilliantly with his very first draft. He picked
'Mean' Joe Greene, an All-American defens-

'When Franco came, we turned
the corner,' said Pittsburgh coach
Chuck Noll of the arrival of running
back Franco Harris in '72.

ive tackle from North Texas State. He was a surprise choice, met with indifference by Steelers fans. But Noll remained confident.

Greene, he declared, would be the cornerstone of Pittsburgh's championship team. Time proved him right.

That first season ended with a typical Steeler record of 1-13 and Noll looked like failing – just as every other Steeler coach had done. But the pool of talent soon expanded. In 1970, Noll chose quarterback Terry Bradshaw as his offensive leader. Five games were won that season.

A year later, the draft included defensive linemen Dwight White and Ernie Holmes – players who, with Greene, were to form a defense so tough it was called 'The Steel Curtain'. Pittsburgh finished 6-8 only just missing a .500 season (equal numbers of games won and lost).

A CRUCIAL YEAR

But it was 1972 that proved pivotal. That year, running back Franco Harris was drafted from Penn. State University.

The rookie started just two of the first seven games that year, but then took off in pursuit of team records and glory. Ending his first season with 1056 rushing yards, and a six game streak of 100-yard performances, Harris was the ingredient the Steelers had badly missed. He was voted Rookie of the Year and took Pittsburgh to the AFC Central title with an 11-3 record. It

was the Steelers' first title in their 40-year history and by far their best showing of any season up till then.

Pittsburgh entered completely new territory with the playoffs – they'd never reached such an important game before.

They were matched against an Oakland Raiders team who, having won their fifth divisional title in six years, were old hands at the playoff business.

The game turned into a defensive slog. Neither team wanted to make a crucial mistake and the punters were just about the busiest men on the two squads.

The first-half ended scoreless and without a hint of the drama to come. In the third quarter, the Steelers edged ahead

THE IMMACULATE RECEPTION

The miracle pass – Pittsburgh's John Fuqua (33) tussles with Oakland safety Jack Tatum (31) in the final seconds of the '72 playoff. Failing to take the catch, Fuqua fell to the ground. Incredibly, the ball bounced off Tatum's shoulder and into the eager arms of Steelers' rookie running back Franco Harris. To the amazement of the 50,000 Pittsburgh crowd, Harris sped to the end zone for the most famous touchdown in football history. It was christened the 'Immaculate Reception' and the name has stuck.

'Bradshaw, running out of the pocket...
...looking for somebody to throw to...
...fires it downfield...
...and there's a collision...'

SUPER BOWL IX

12 January 1975

PITTSBURGH STEELERS   16
MINNESOTA VIKINGS   6

An 80,997 crowd gathered at the New Orleans Tulane Stadium for the Steelers' first ever Super Bowl appearance. Although they had reached the contest with a 10-3-1 regular season against Minnesota's 10-4, Pittsburgh were firm favourites.

On the day, it was the combined power of running back Franco Harris and the Steel Curtain defense that justified Pittsburgh's new found reputation. The Steelers outrushed the Vikings by the vast margin of 249-17. Setting two Super Bowl records, the fleety Franco Harris rushed 34 times for 158 yards.

And it was Harris who scored the first touchdown, increasing Pittsburgh's lead to 9-0 after 1:35 of the third quarter. But in the fourth the Vikings bounced back with a blocked punt that safety Terry Brown recovered in the end zone.

With the scores at 9-6 and about ten minutes remaining, Super Bowl IX was coming to an exciting finish. But Bradshaw repeatedly confused the Vikings defense with misdirection running plays. From the Steelers 42, a 30-yard pass to tight end Larry Brown brought the offense back into an attacking position. After Harris and Rocky Bleier carried the ball from the Vikings 28 to the four-yard line, Bradshaw again passed to Larry Brown. This time it was for the conclusive touchdown, ensuring Pittsburgh's victory at 16-6.

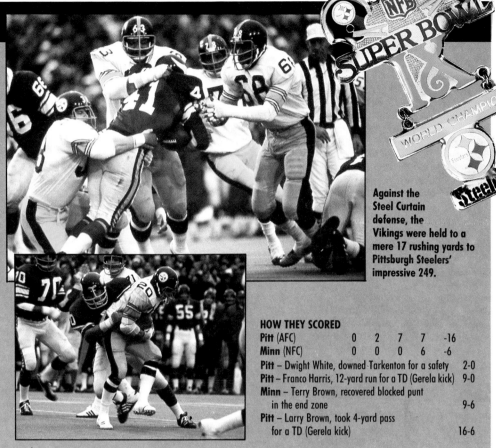

Against the Steel Curtain defense, the Vikings were held to a mere 17 rushing yards to Pittsburgh Steelers' impressive 249.

HOW THEY SCORED

Pitt (AFC)	0	2	7	7	-16
Minn (NFC)	0	0	0	6	-6

Pitt – Dwight White, downed Tarkenton for a safety	2-0
Pitt – Franco Harris, 12-yard run for a TD (Gerela kick)	9-0
Minn – Terry Brown, recovered blocked punt in the end zone	9-6
Pitt – Larry Brown, took 4-yard pass for a TD (Gerela kick)	16-6

with two field goals. Noll's policy of mistake-free football seemed to be paying off. Pittsburgh kept things tight and the Raiders were being squeezed out.

But in the final two minutes of the game, Oakland began a drive. Kenny 'The Snake' Stabler guided them down to the Steelers' 30-yard line. From there he suddenly broke loose on a scramble. Wide open spaces had been left by the anxious Pittsburgh secondary as they hunted down the receivers.

Stabler saw the gap and went from the line. He made it after an amazing 30-yard chase. George Blanda kicked the extra point and the Raiders were in front for the first time.

Only 1:13 remained and the Steelers' hopes sank. Bradshaw tried to start a quick drive, but it soon failed on his own 40-yard line. There were just 22 seconds remaining when Bradshaw tried one last time. It was fourth and 10. If nothing came of this obvious plan for another pass, then the game would be over and Oakland would be through to the AFC Championship game.

THE MIRACLE PASS

Quarterback Bradshaw stepped back into the pocket and looked for his primary target, wide receiver Barry Pearson, but there was too much coverage.

Bradshaw began to scramble and decided to aim long for running back John 'Frenchy' Fuqua who came blasting out of the backfield. Fuqua dived for the ball on the Raiders' 36 with Oakland's hard-hitting safety Jack Tatum right with him.

The ball hit Fuqua's hands, but he couldn't hold on. It then deflected off Tatum's shoulder and, finally, came to rest with Harris. The rookie rusher scooped the ball almost off his toes in full stride and sped untouched into the end zone for the miracle touchdown.

Few people who saw it happen could believe it at first. Harris had been trailing the play as a mere bystander and seemed to come from nowhere. Never a team to accept defeat easily, the Raiders protested long and loud to the officials who'd given the score immediately.

The rules at the time stated that two offensive players could not touch the ball

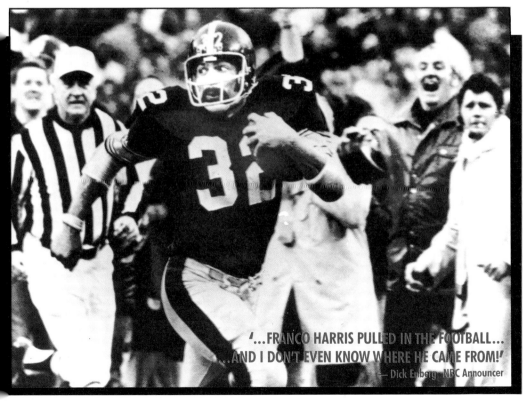

'...FRANCO HARRIS PULLED IN THE FOOTBALL... AND I DON'T EVEN KNOW WHERE HE CAME FROM!'
— Dick Enberg, NBC Announcer

SUPER BOWL X

18 January 1976

PITTSBURGH STEELERS   **21**
DALLAS COWBOYS   **17**

Cold weather greeted the Dallas and Pittsburgh teams as they ran onfield at the Miami Orange Bowl. But for the players, temperatures ran high – this was one of the truly great Super Bowls.

The game got off to a thrilling start. Cowboys' linebacker Thomas Henderson caught the kickoff and sprinted 53 yards upfield, and was only saved from scoring by a tackle from kicker Roy Gerela.

But the Cowboys soon had another chance. After a failed punt by Pittsburgh's Bobby Walden, Dallas were on the Steelers' 29. A lightning pass by quarterback Roger Staubach to Drew Pearson took them to a 7-0 lead.

Pittsburgh's Terry Bradshaw wasted no time in replying. After cunningly alternating a ground game with quick passes to receiver Lynn Swann, he finally found tight end Randy Grossman in the end zone for the tying score.

Dallas opened the second quarter with a 36-yard field goal by Toni Fritsch, giving them a three point lead they maintained until the fourth quarter.

It was then the battle really begun. With a safety and two field goals, Pittsburgh came back to a winning position. With only 3:02 left on the clock, Bradshaw was caught with a third and four on his 36. Instead of going for a first down, Bradshaw went – incredibly – for a massive 64-yard pass which was caught by Swann for the Steelers' second touchdown.

Never one to accept defeat, Staubach instantly struck back with an 80-yard drive lasting just over a minute. A 34-yard scoring pass to rookie receiver Percy Howard cut the deficit to 21-17. It was a brave last attempt, but too late to change the outcome of the game. Pittsburgh had won their second successive Super Bowl.

When Franco Harris (32) has got the ball, one defender is never enough – here three Cowboys collide to block his run *above*.
A 6 ft 9 in tall, Dallas' defensive end Ed Jones (72) proved a fierce opponent *inset*.

HOW THEY SCORED

Dall (NFC)	7	3	0	7	–17
Pitt (AFC)	7	0	0	14	–21

Dall – Drew Pearson, 29-yard TD pass (Fritsch kick)	7-0
Pitt – Randy Grossman, 7-yard TD pass (Gerela Kick)	7-7
Dall – Toni Fritsch, field goal	10-7
Pitt – Reggie Harrison, blocked Hoopes' punt for a safety	10-9
Pitt – Roy Gerela, 36-yard field goal	10-12
Pitt – Roy Gerela, 18-yard field goal	10-15
Pitt – Lynn Swann, 64-yard TD pass	10-21
Dall – Percy Howard, 34-yard TD pass (Fritsch kick)	17-21

consecutively on a pass play but the officials maintained the ball careered off Tatum's shoulder, making Harris' catch perfectly legal. The score stood. Roy Gerela kicked the extra point and the Steelers' miracle was complete.

The Steelers/Raiders game was stopped for several minutes while the officials listened to the Oakland protests and, after it was all over, Raider quarterback Ken Stabler attempted a miracle of his own. In the remaining seconds, he fired a few final bullets and actually overthrew to an open Cliff Branch on the final play of this historic, exciting game.

But the Steelers weren't going to be denied, and their 13-7 victory was saved by the clock.

THE TEAM OF THE '70s

Pittsburgh had overcome all the years of hardship and avoided a near-certain defeat with one of the greatest magic moments in football's 50-year history. The Steelers had broken the ice. They were up with the con-

TIME OUT

CHANGING TIME RULES
So controversial was the 'Immaculate Reception', that it caused a change in the NFL's rules. After 1972, receivers were allowed to touch the ball even if their own teammate was the last man to touch it. Only if the teammate had deliberately batted the ball would the play be called illegal. Such a ruling would have made Franco Harris' game-winning catch indisputably legal – whether it had touched an opposing player's fingers or not.

SUPER BOWL XIII

2 January 1979

PITTSBURGH STEELERS   **35**
DALLAS COWBOYS   **31**

After the last minute thrills of Super Bowl X, sportswriters predicted a stirring sequel when Dallas and Pittsburgh met again for Super bowl XIII. They were not disappointed.

Dallas leaped off with the first drive of the game, but a fumble by Drew Pearson allowed Steelers' quarterback Bradshaw to begin his revenge. Zig-zagging back to the Cowboys' 28, a pass to John Stallworth gave Pittsburgh a 7-0 lead early in the game.

Staubach knew he could waste no time in fighting back. Following a fumble recovery by Ed 'Too Tall' Jones, Staubach sent a 39-yard scoring pass into the hands of wide receiver Tony Hill. A kick by Rafael Septien repeated Super Bowl X's exciting first quarter score of 7-7. But the thrills kept on coming. Dallas went ahead 14-7 when linebacker Thomas Henderson slammed into Bradshaw – leaving the ball for fellow linebacker Mike Hegman to race for a 37-yard TD.

Less than two minutes later, Bradshaw caught Stallworth in full stride on a short first down pass. Stallworth accelerated for a record tying 75-yard touchdown play. An acrobatic touchdown by Steelers' running back Rocky Bleier took Pittsburgh to 21-14.

A tragically bungled touchdown pass by veteran tight end Jackie Smith denied Dallas the chance to equalize in the third quarter. Pittsburgh's Franco Harris wasted no such opportunities when he rushed 22 yards to increase the Steelers' lead to 28-17. Then a high pass from Bradshaw to Swann, took the Steelers' lead to 18 points.

A four-minute drive gave Staubach the chance for a seven-yard TD pass to tight end Billy Joe DuPree. Scarcely two minutes later and Staubach was back again – this time spinning a four yard scoring pass to Butch Johnson.

HOW THEY SCORED

Pitt (AFC)	7	14	0	14	-35
Dall (NFC)	7	7	3	14	-31

Pitt – John Stallworth, 28-yard TD pass (Gerela kick)	7-0
Dall – Toni Hill, 39-yard TD pass (Septien kick)	7-7
Dall – Mike Hegman, 37 yard TD fumble return (Septien kick)	14-7
Pitt – John Stallworth, 75-yard TD pass (Gerela kick)	14-14
Pitt – Rocky Bleier, 7-yard TD pass (Gerela kick)	14-21
Dall – Ralph Septien, 27-yard field goal	17-21
Pitt – Franco Harris, 22-yard TD run (Gerela kick)	17-28
Pitt – Lynn Swann, 18-yard pass (Gerela kick)	17-35
Dall – Billy Joe DuPree, 7-yard pass (Septien kick)	24-35
Dall – Butch Johnson, 4-yard pass (Septien kick)	31-35

There was no stopping Steelers' wide receiver John Stallworth in Super Bowl XIII. After a short pass in the second quarter, he made an incredible 75-yard touchdown run.

Pittsburgh's star QB Terry Bradshaw, hoists another game-winning pass against the Dallas Cowboys in Super Bowl XIII on 2 Jan 1979.

tenders now. All they needed was more of that winning experience.

The Pittsburgh reign continued with the 1974 regular season after Bradshaw was reinstated as starter. By then his team were used to success, and began to put their experience to full use. Another AFC Central title was won and, again, the Oakland Raiders were beaten in the playoffs.

It set up a Super Bowl IX meeting with the Minnesota Vikings. The Steel Curtain defense held the Vikings to a mere 17 yards on rushing offense. Harris ran for a Super Bowl record of 158 yards on his own. After scoring a nine yard touchdown, he carried off the most valuable player award, and led his team to a 16-6 win.

The franchise which had once been certain to lead the list of losers was now among the certs for honours each season.

SUPER BOWL SEQUEL

Pittsburgh repeated their Super Bowl victory in 1975. That campaign followed a similar pattern to the last. A second straight AFC title and a second straight conference championship win over Oakland brought them face-to-face with the Dallas Cowboys in Super Bowl X.

Swann was the MVP this time as a 21-17

win was recorded. Pittsburgh was only the third team to repeat a Super Bowl victory since the event started.

Bradshaw had his best-ever season in 1978 and there was no stopping the Steeler steam roller to Super Bowl XIII where they beat Dallas 35-31 in one of the closest title games for years.

It was Stallworth's turn in 1979. He totted up a then-record 70 receptions to lead the team to a fourth Super Bowl, this time a match-up against west coasters the Los Angeles Rams. Stallworth grabbed two bombs and Bradshaw again took the MVP honours in a brilliant 31-19 win.

The Steelers were now undoubtedly the team of the decade, and it was all down to the Noll building programme which didn't leave a weak link.

Future Hall of Famers seemed to appear in every area: the Steel Curtain defense with its fiery front four led by Joe Greene; the linebackers held together by madcap Jack Lambert; a secondary with Mel Blount at its heart; a ground game revolving around the tireless Franco Harris; an offensive line to open holes and protect the QB with centre Mike Webster at the helm; a squad of receivers with the speed and safe hands of Lynn Swann and John Stallworth; and finally the strong-arm, keen-brained quarterbacking of on-field general Terry Bradshaw.

Any of these men would have stood out as a star on any one team. Put them all together and the opposition never stood a chance.

The Steelers dominated the '70s in the same way that the Green Bay Packers stood head and shoulders above the rest in the early 60s. And when something like that happens, people look back for the turning point, the moment when the magic started. For Pittsburgh, that moment came with 22 seconds remaining in the divisional play-off game of 1972 against Oakland.

In one split second 40 years of bad fortune were forgotten, when a deflected pass fell into the hands of a rookie running back who ran in for a game-winning touchdown. It came with The Immaculate Reception.

SUPER BOWL XIV

The Steelers stand ready to make history (top).
Stallworth takes the catch that insures victory (above).
Steelers celebrate (above left).

20 January 1980

| PITTSBURGH STEELERS | 31 |
| LOS ANGELES | 19 |

Although the prospect of winning four Super Bowls in only six years seemed too much to ask, the Steelers entered California's Rose Bowl as 11½ point favourites over the L.A. Rams. And as Super Bowl XIV kicked off, Pittsburgh looked set to achieve the impossible. The first time they had the ball, they drove 55 yards to set up a field goal by rookie Matt Bahr.

But straight from the second kickoff, the Rams came back. Gaining 59 yards on eight plays, they looked blocked by the Steelers defense, when a one-yard run by fullback Cullen Bryant took them into the lead.

A 47-yard kickoff return by Larry Anderson brought the Steelers instantly back into the game. Snappy passing play by Bradshaw took Franco Harris dangerously close to the Dallas end zone. From one yard he was unstoppable and walked over for his first touchdown.

But again the Rams hit back – this time with a 31-yard Frank Corral field goal that tied the scores at 10-10.

A second field goal by Corral, gave the Rams a half time lead, but the Steelers spirits remained high. At the start of the second half, Anderson again proved his value with a

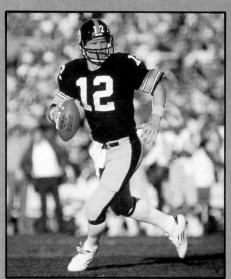

Playing in his fourth championship game, Terry Bradshaw was on his finest form in Super Bowl XIV.

stunning kickoff return. From his own 39, it took Bradshaw a mere five plays to hoist a 47-yard pass to Swann.

But each kickoff brought its own surprises and this time it was the Rams turn. A 50-yard pass from quarterback Vince Ferragamo to Billy Waddy sent them up to the Steelers' 24. Ferragamo then went for a rushing play, handing off to halfback Lawrence McCutcheon who stopped to throw a staggering 24-yard touchdown pass to Ron Smith.

With the Rams leading 19-17, the game still flowed back and forth like a yo-yo. But it was Bradshaw who fired the winning shots – first with an immaculate 73-yard touchdown pass to Stallworth, then with a 43 yarder, again caught by Stallworth to set up Franco Harris' insurance score. With substantially the same team who had fought for the Steelers' first Super Bowl victory in 1975, Pittsburgh proved they didn't know the meaning of 'impossible'.

HOW THEY SCORED

Los Angeles (NFC)	7	6	6	0	-19
Pittsburgh (AFC)	3	7	7	14	-31
Pitt – Matt Bahr, 41-yard field goal					3-0
LA – Cullen Bryant, 1-yard TD run (Corral kick)					3-7
Pitt – Franco Harris, 1-yard TD run (Bahr kick)					10-7
LA – Frank Corral, 31-yard field goal					10-10
LA – Frank Corral, 45-yard field goal					10-13
Pitt – Lynn Swann, 47-yard TD pass (Bahr kick)					17-13
LA – Ron Smith, 24-yard pass					17-19
Pitt – John Stallworth, 73-yard TD pass (Bahr kick)					24-19
Pitt – Franco Harris, 1-yard TD run (Bahr kick)					

TEAM CHECK

The New York Giants, after winning Super Bowl XXI, became the twelfth team to win the coveted trophy since the game began in 1967. Denver, who played for the championship in 1978, became the second team to lose in their first two appearances. The first team to do so was the Minnesota Vikings, who went on to claim the undisputed, and dubious, distinction of losing in all four of their Super Bowl games, the last three of which came in a four-year span. Contrast that with the Pittsburgh Steelers, who won in all four of their appearances, while becoming the only team to win that many. The Miami Dolphins and Dallas Cowboys share the record for most appearances at five, and each has won the trophy twice.

Some teams, such as the Philadelphia Eagles, Cleveland Browns and the Detroit Lions, have never won a Super Bowl, although their histories are dotted with NFL Championships, which were competed for before the Super Bowl came into existence. Two teams from the old AFL, the Houston Oilers and Buffalo Bills, each won two AFL Championships in succession, although their histories since joining the NFL have not been so bright.

In the chapter that follows, the Giants and Broncos are highlighted in depth with coverage of their recent years as well as the background from when they began playing. This is followed by a page each of statistics and records, they provided the American

Football enthusiast with an unbeatable reference guide.

The remaining 26 teams, however, have not been neglected, as one full page is devoted to each in the form of record and fact boxes, similar to those included for the Giants and Broncos. Through them, the history of each team – from past coaches to game, season and career records – is comprehensively outlined. What might be lacking in terms of interesting anecdotes and the flavour of some past squads is more than made up for in the sheer volume of statistics.

Certain teams, such as the Chicago Bears, Washington Redskins and the Green Bay Packers, mirror both the development of the NFL since its beginning, and also the changing fortunes of the United States since the turn of the century. National economics, war, and times of prosperity all contribute to the multilayered story of the NFL. Obviously, newer teams such as the Seattle Seahawks and Tampa Bay Buccaneers, who came into existence in 1976, and those whose beginnings date back to 1960 with the formation of the AFL, can't hope to offer the same scope. But those teams do offer something else – tangible landmarks which offer the fan easy access to the great eras and players of the past.

The teams following on from the Giants and Broncos features are listed in alphabetical order based on the city in which they are based.

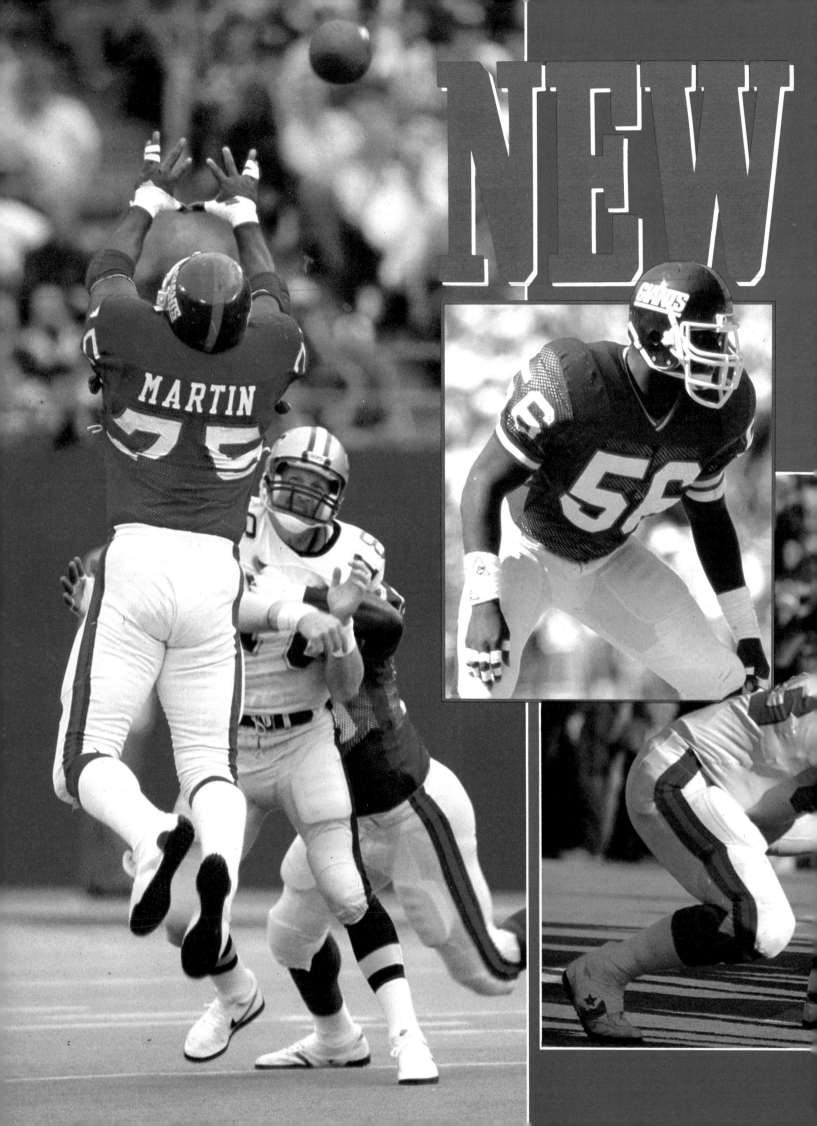

NEW

NEW YORK GIANTS

After decades lurking in the shadows of the Jets, the Giants are back in the limelight, with one of the youngest and most exciting teams New York has seen in years

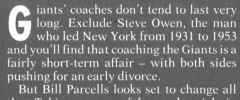

Giants' coaches don't tend to last very long. Exclude Steve Owen, the man who led New York from 1931 to 1953 and you'll find that coaching the Giants is a fairly short-term affair – with both sides pushing for an early divorce.

But Bill Parcells looks set to change all that. Taking over one of the toughest jobs in football in 1983, he managed to make league losers into wild card contestants in just a year. By 1985 they were within a breath of winning their division, and in 1987, they went on to defeat the Denver Broncos in Super Bowl XXI. Not bad for four years' work.

THE YOUNG ONES

It's a feat Parcells has achieved by opting for the promise of youth rather than the certainty of experience. No less than 25 members of the '85 squad had three or fewer years playing experience. In spite of this, an amazing 11 club records were broken as the Giants recorded their first two consecutive winning seasons in no less than 22 years.

Opportunities knocked at every door in '85. New York's six regular-season losses were by an average of just over three points per game. In a 30-29 loss to Dallas at Giants Stadium, quarterback Phil Simms fumbled as he retreated from center. At Texas Stadium, when the Giants lost 28-21, a pass by Simms was deflected by Ed 'Too Tall' Jones and returned 65 yards for a touchdown by defensive end Jim Jeffcoat.

'It was frustrating to watch when you really consider how well we played,' general manager George Young said. 'Sometimes there was just no excuse for defeat. When you've got victory well in hand, you should be able to do something about it. We didn't. You just hope that you get another chance to do it next time.'

Defensive end George Martin, *far left*, leaps high to intercept a pass by QB Marc Wilson of the Raiders. *Inset*, Lawrence Taylor, the Giants' great linebacker. The offensive line, *left*, ready to make a snap.

GIANTS

CONFERENCE: NFC

DIVISION: EASTERN

TEAM COLOURS: BLUE,

RED AND WHITE

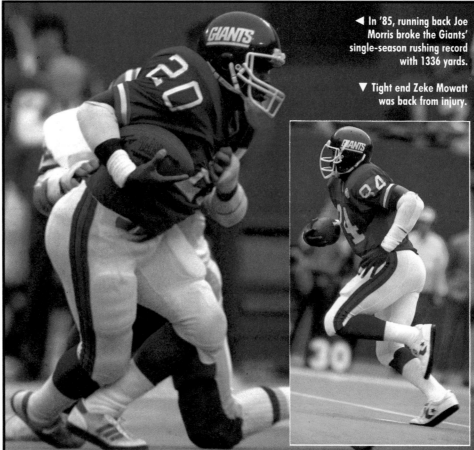

◄ In '85, running back Joe Morris broke the Giants' single-season rushing record with 1336 yards.

▼ Tight end Zeke Mowatt was back from injury.

The 1985 season ended on a down note with a 21-0 whitewash at the hands of Chicago in the divisional playoffs. In nine of the Giants' first 11 possessions they were forced to punt after only three plays. In the second quarter, New York ran 11 plays and netted minus-11 yards.

It was a sad end to an otherwise successful season, and, as might be expected, it created some doubts about the Giants' future. But they could find solace in the fact that Chicago flattened the Rams 24-0 the following week before routing New England 46-10 in Super Bowl XX.

PARCELLS OF TALENT

General manager George Young has been happy with Parcells and his staff.

'Success breeds confidence and maturity in a coaching staff,' Young said. 'They are starting to understand how to use players and Bill is using his assistants to his best advantage. A coach doesn't come in his first season and become a Hall of Fame coach. Chuck Knox is one of the best coaches in the business, but he's never been to a Super Bowl. And Chuck Noll, who is one of the best ever, went 1-13, 5-9 and 6-8 in his first three seasons.

Quarterback Phil Simms, who was voted MVP at the 1986 Pro Bowl, proved what he could do by avoiding injuries for the second straight year. He set an NFL record for consecutive-games yardage gained with 432 against Dallas and 513 the next week against Cincinnati. He finished the season with 275 completions in 495 attempts for 3829 yards. That followed his record-busting season of 1984 when he set Giants' marks for completions (286), attempts (533), and yardage (4004).

Simms also continued to gain the confidence of his teammates. 'We've been doing a lot of things right, and a lot of things wrong,' Simms said. 'Mostly, though, I think we're finally doing things right. I

HONOURS

NFL Eastern Conference Champions 1958, 1959, 1961, 1962, 1963
NFC Wild Card Qualifier for Playoffs 1981, 1984, 1985
NFL Champions 1927, 1934, 1938, 1956
NFL Eastern Division Champions 1933, 1935, 1939, 1941, 1944, 1946
Super Bowl Winner 1987

HALL OF FAME

Morris (Red) Badgro, Roosevelt Brown, Ray Flaherty, Frank Gifford, Joe Guyon, Mel Hein, Wilber (Pete) Henry, Arnie Herber, Cal Hubbard, Sam Huff, Alphonse (Tuffy) Leemans, Vince Lombardi, Tim Mara, Hugh McElhenny, Steve Owen, Andy Robustelli, Ken Strong, Fran Tarkenton, Jim Thorpe, Y. A. Tittle, Emlen Tunnell, Arnie Weinmeister

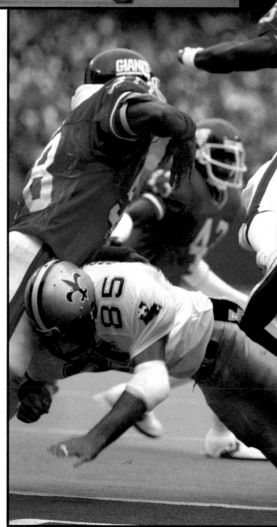

think that Bill Parcells has the right amount of confidence in our offense.'

But Simms finished the '85 season with 20 interceptions, finishing second in the NFC to Minnesota's Tommy Kramer, who threw 26. Parcells must hope that Simms throws fewer interceptions in future.

If the Giants' running game continues to improve, Simms may feel less pressure, causing his rate of interception to drop. Joe Morris, who at 5 ft 7 in is one of the NFL's smallest players, proved that size doesn't matter.

Morris was the NFC's number-three rusher in 1985 with a club record 1336 yards. Remarkably, he became only the second Giants rusher to surpass 1000 yards (Ron Johnson gained 1182 yards in 1972 and 1027 in 1970).

Morris has quickness and excellent moves, but he is also a determined inside runner who plays and acts like a tough guy. He had a nose-to-nose shouting match with Dallas's Randy White during the first Cowboys-Giants game in 1985.

'Joe is going to be a 1000-yard runner for a long time,' Simms said. 'He's got that dedication to the game that just makes him tough to stop. It's hard to believe that a guy with that kind of size can be so effective in tough-yardage situations.'

Morris had six 100-yard games in 1985 and gained 202 against Pittsburgh in the regular-season finale when he also scored three touchdowns

BAVARO'S BRAVADO

Rookie George Adams, who played behind Morris, lived up to his billing as a first-round draft choice by gaining 498 yards despite some injuries. After proving to be a strong blocker and runner at fullback for the USFL's New Jersey Generals' backfield with Herschel Walker, Maurice Carthon

► Raul Allegre emerged as the Giants' premier kicker mid-way through the '86 season.
▼ The Giants defense tries to block a score by New Orleans.

gained only 70 yards in limited playing time with New York in '85.

Tight end Zeke Mowatt returned to the Giants in '86 after being out all of '85 with a knee injury. His return was welcomed, but he had a tough time trying to win back his position from the excellent 1985 rookie Mark Bavaro, who graded super well as a blocker and receiver. Bavaro, the club's second-leading receiver with 37 receptions, had a noticeable penchant for making the tough catch.

Remarkably, the Giants' leading receiver – Lionel Manuel – had only 49 receptions. But he turned those catches into 859 yards for an average gain of 17.5 yards. He also took one 51 yards for a touchdown. Simms managed to spread his passes among several receivers, and eight players had 20 or more receptions.

IN THE TRENCHES

Center Bart Oates, another former USFL player, had an outstanding season in place of the injured Kevin Belcher, who was recovering from an offseason automobile accident. Oates gained a reputation as one of the NFL's best run-blocking centers.

Guard Billy Ard and tackle Brad Benson have transformed the left side of the line from the weakest to the strongest part of the offense. In fact, Benson, the nine-year veteran, is now considered one of the best left tackles in the entire NFL.

No one would have guessed that the Giants would be the number-two defense in the league in 1985 without Mark Haynes, who missed the first half of the season in a contract dispute and the second half with a groin injury.

But the New York Giants survived at cornerback with Elvis Patterson, who led the team in interceptions with six. Patterson also got burned a few times, too. The Giants still managed to finish fourth in pass defense, which was attributable largely to defensive end Leonard Marshall's 15.5

| STADIUM: GIANTS STADIUM |
| CAPACITY: 76,891 |
| PLAYING SURFACE: ASTROTURF |
| HEAD COACH: BILL PARCELLS |

sacks, second in the NFC. He was selected to the Pro Bowl.

Chicago was the unchallenged champion of defense in the NFL in '85, allowing only 258 yards per game. But the Giants were the best of the rest and not far behind the Monsters of Midway, permitting an average of just 270 yards.

The linebackers continue to improve as Gary Reasons, Andy Headen, Carl Banks, and Byron Hunt complemented Taylor and Harry Carson, both of whom played in the Pro Bowl. This is still the best overall group of linebackers in the league. Taylor had 13 sacks in 1985, but it was considered a below average year by his Superman standards.

Marshall, who had a weight problem for two years, was the team's most improved player. But coaches are now saying that he could become the best pass-rushing end in the league.

No doubt, the Giants have the defensive unit to reach a Super Bowl. The future

▲ A winning combination – QB Phil Simms and center Bart Oates prepare to take the snap. In '85, Simms threw for 3829 yards and 22 TDs, finishing with a rating of 78.6.

◄ With the Bengals' defensive line taken care of, running back George Adams breaks free.

COACH – BILL PARCELLS

Bill Parcells began his fourth campaign in 1986 as head coach of the Giants and is the 12th head coach in Giants' history. After beginning in truly disastrous fashion, Parcells has turned his team into a consistent winner.

Parcells managed to change a last-place club in 1983 into a Wild Card qualifier in 1984, with a 9-7 record. Not satisfied with this, Parcells guided the 1985 edition of the Giants to a 10-6 record, a Wild Card entry, and a victory over the then defending Super Bowl champions San Francisco 49ers 17-3, in the first round of the playoffs. And, of course, he coached the squad to victory in Super Bowl XXI.

Parcells was picked for the top spot after seeing two seasons' duty as the Giants' defensive co-ordinator and linebacker coach. Born 22 August 1941, Parcells started his pro coaching career in 1980 as linebacker coach for the New England Patriots. His career record as head coach is 38-29-1 following the 1986 season.

may hinge on the return to form by Lawrence Taylor. Marshall must also prove that the 1985 season was not a fluke.

Seeing the Giants on winning form may be something of a novelty for football's young fans, but for Channel 4 commentator and former Giants' running back Frank Gifford it's a return to past glory.

Gifford's heyday was in the '50s and early '60s when he accumulated no less than 3609 rushing yards and 367 receptions for 5434 yards more on the way to securing his immortal place in the Hall of Fame. With the added bonus of fullback Mel Triplett and linebacker Sam Huff, it was a boost that helped the Giants fight through to their third-ever NFL Championship in 1956.

TOP GIANTS

After a slow season in 1957, they returned to league-leading form in '58 with the best defense in the league, and a tough running game led by Gifford, Triplett, running back Alex Webster and rookie Phil King. The team was in the running with the Browns all season, and on 9 November defeated Baltimore 24-21 before a record Yankee stadium crowd of 71,163.

In one of the most exciting games in football history, they went on to face Baltimore

again for the NFL Championship. A Giants victory looked certain until the final seconds of the game when the Colts tied the game 17-17 with a field goal. The Giants started with the ball in sudden-death overtime, but a drive fell inches short of midfield. Led by QB Johnny Unitas, the Colts moved to the winning touchdown on a one-yard run by Alan Ameche after 8:15 of overtime.

The Giants won the Eastern Conference Championship in 1961 and '62 and were in contention again in 1963. The Giants had 10 starters who were aged 30 or older. New York had won eight of its final nine games. A 33-17 victory over Pittsburgh in the final game of the season enabled the Giants to win their third consecutive Eastern Conference title. Quarterback Y. A. Tittle led the league in passing with 3145 yards and 36 touchdown passes. Wide receiver Del Shofner had 64 receptions for 1181 yards and nine touchdowns.

The Giants had to play in another championship game on a freezing winter day, this time in Chicago with the temperature well below zero, 29 December 1963. Tittle was injured in the second quarter. He later returned to play, but the Bears' fierce defense throttled the Giants' movement.

Chicago won the contest 14-10.

The following year, 1964, everything fell apart. Gary Wood was given the quarterback's spot but the rookie could not reverse the Giants' slide. New York closed with a 2-10-2 record and finished in last place for the first time since 1947. Gifford and Webster retired after the season. Not until 1984 were they to see their team on comparable form again. Twenty years in the wilderness was a long time, and many fans as well as former players are glad to see the Giants back in the big time.

THE GIANTS STATISTICS

RECORD HOLDERS

Individual Records – Career

Category	Name	Performance
Rushing (Yds)	Alex Webster, 1955-1964	4638
Passing (Yds)	Charlie Conerly, 1948-1961	19,488
Passing (TDs)	Charlie Conerly, 1948-1961	173
Receiving (No.)	Joe Morrison, 1959-1972	395
Receiving (Yds)	Frank Gifford, 1952-1960, 1962-64	5434
Interceptions	Emlen Tunnell, 1948-1958	74
Punting (Avg.)	Don Chandler, 1956-1964	43.8
Punt Return (Avg.)	Bob Hammond, 1976-78	9.1
Kickoff Return (Avg.)	Rocky Thompson, 1971-72	27.2
Field Goals	Pete Gogolak, 1966-1974	126
Touchdowns (Tot.)	Frank Gifford, 1952-1960, 1962-64	78
Points	Pete Gogolak, 1966-1974	646

Individual Records – Single Season

Category	Name	Performance
Rushing (Yds)	Joe Morris, 1985	1336
Passing (Yds)	Phil Simms, 1984	4044
Passing (TDs)	Y. A. Tittle, 1963	36
Receiving (No.)	Earnest Gray, 1983	78
Receiving (Yds)	Homer Jones, 1967	1209
Interceptions	Otto Schnellbacher, 1951	11
	Jim Patton, 1958	11
Punting (Avg.)	Don Chandler, 1959	46.6
Punt Return (Avg.)	Merle Hapes, 1942	15.5
Kickoff Return (Avg.)	John Salscheider, 1949	31.6
Field Goals	Ali Haji-Sheikh, 1983	35
Touchdowns (Tot.)	Joe Morris, 1985	21
Points	Ali Haji-Sheikh, 1983	127

Individual Records – Single Game

Category	Name	Performance
Rushing (Yds)	Gene Roberts, 12-11-50	218
Passing (Yds)	Phil Simms, 13-10-85	513
Passing (TDs)	Y. A. Tittle, 28-10-62	7
Receiving (No.)	Mark Bavaro, 13-10-85	12
Receiving (Yds)	Del Shofner, 28-10-62	269
Interceptions	Many times	3
	Last time by Carl Lockhart, 4-12-66	
Field Goals	Joe Danelo, 18-10-81	6
Touchdowns (Tot.)	Ron Johnson, 2-10-72	4
	Earnest Gray, 7-9-80	4
Points	Ron Johnson, 2-10-72	24
	Earnest Gray, 7-9-80	24

REGULAR SEASONS

Year	W	L	T	Pct.	Pts	Opp.
1960	6	4	2	.600	271	261
1961‡	10	3	1	.769	368	220
1962‡	12	2	0	.857	398	283
1963‡	11	3	0	.786	448	280
1964	2	10	2	.167	241	399
1965	7	7	0	.500	270	338
1966	1	12	1	.077	263	501
1967	7	7	0	.500	369	379
1968	7	7	0	.500	294	325
1969	6	8	0	.429	264	298
1970	9	5	0	.643	301	270
1971	4	10	0	.286	228	362
1972	8	6	0	.571	331	247
1973	2	11	1	.179	226	362
1974	2	12	0	.143	195	299
1975	5	9	0	.357	216	306
1976	3	11	0	.214	170	250
1977	5	9	0	.357	181	265
1978	6	10	0	.375	264	298
1979	6	10	0	.375	237	323
1980	4	12	0	.250	249	425
1981§	9	7	0	.563	295	257
1982	4	5	0	.444	164	160
1983	3	12	1	.219	267	347
1984§	9	7	0	.563	299	301
1985§	10	6	0	.625	399	283
1986*	14	2	0	.875	371	236
27 Years	172	207	0	.454	7579	8125

‡NFL Eastern Conference Champion
§NFC Wild Card Qualifier for Playoffs
* Super Bowl Champion

1986 SEASON

	Off.	Def.
Total First Downs	324	284
Rushing	127	78
Passing	171	177
Penalty	26	29
Third Down Efficiency	37.3	35.4
Total Net Yards	5378	4757
Avg. Per Game	336.1	297.3
Total Plays	1076	996
Avg. Per Play	5.0	4.8
Net Yards Rushing	2245	1284
Avg. Per Game	140.3	80.3
Total Rushes	558	350
Net Yards Passing	3133	3473
Avg. Per Game	195.8	217.1
Tackled/Yards Lost	46/367	59/414
Gross Yards	3500	3887
Att./Completions	472/260	587/334
Completion Pct.	55.1	56.9
Had Intercepted	22	24
Punts/Avg.	79/44.8	89/39.3
Punting Yds.	3539	3499
Penalties/Yards Lost	96/738	119/988
Fumbles/Ball Lost	31/10	36/19
Touchdowns	42	26
Rushing	18	10
Passing	22	15
Returns	2	1

Avg. Time of Possession	31:50	28:10
W	**L**	**T**
14	2	0

Emlen Tunnell HB/DB

Y. A. Tittle QB

COACHING HISTORY

434-367-32

1925	Bob Folwell	8-4-0
1926	Joe Alexander	8-4-1
1927-28	Earl Potteiger	15-8-3
1929-30	LeRoy Andrews	26-5-1
1931-53	Steve Owen	154-108-17
1954-60	Jim Lee Howell	54-29-4
1961-68	Allie Sherman	57-54-4
1969-73	Alex Webster	29-40-1
1974-76	Bill Arnsparger*	7-28-0
1976-78	John McVay	14-23-0
1979-82	Ray Perkins	24-35-0
1983-86	Bill Parcells	38-29-1

*Released after seven games in 1976

ALL-TIME GREATS

One of the best all-round backs in NFL history was Frank Gifford. As an equally gifted rusher and receiver, Gifford played a big part in the Giants' winning six conference titles in the late '50s and early '60s. Gifford's contribution was much larger than the number of times his name appears in the team record book would indicate. But Gifford does hold two important, career records – most yards receiving (5434 in 1952-1960, 1962-64), and most total touchdowns (78). Gifford was inducted into the Pro Football Hall of Fame in 1977.

The Giants have had a host of all-pro quarterbacks in their 61-year history, but the man who holds the most important records is Charlie Conerly, a grizzled ex-Marine from Mississippi. After a steady 14-year career with the Giants, Conerly holds the records for most yards passing, career (19,488 in 1948-1961), and most touchdowns passing, career (173).

The most gifted foot in Giants' annals belonged to Pete Gogolak, a very solid player on a series of uninspired Giants teams.

Gogolak owns the all-time marks for most field goals, career (126 in 1966-1974), and most points, career (646).

Frank Gifford HB

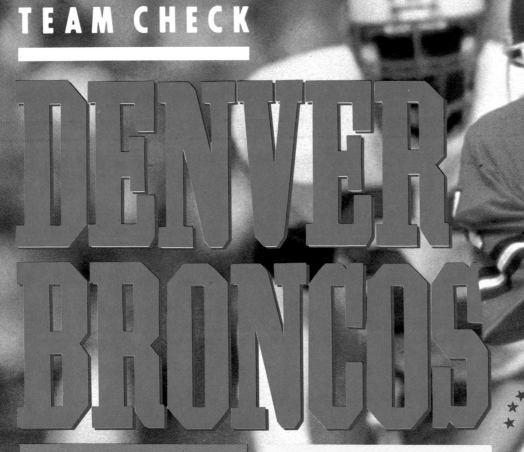

DENVER BRONCOS

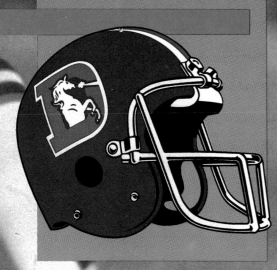

CONFERENCE: AFC

DIVISION: WESTERN

TEAM COLOURS: ORANGE, ROYAL BLUE, AND WHITE

HEAD COACH: DAN REEVES

The team from The Mile High City need to get their running game together before they can hope to take off on a flight to sky high Super Bowl success

The Denver Broncos play their home games at Mile High Stadium in the middle of the Colorado Rockies. The Broncos have been climbing Super Bowl Mountain since 1967.

Named as a charter member of the American Football League in 1959, the Broncos went their first 13 seasons without achieving a winning record. Then, in 1973, Denver fought to a 7-5-2 record and since that time have remained Super Bowl contenders.

The Broncos made the play-offs for three consecutive seasons in 1977, '78 and '79. Their two Super Bowl appearances were in Super Bowl XII when they lost to the Cowboys, 27-10 and in Super Bowl XXI when they were trounced by the Giants. The Broncos have yet to

reach their full potential in the league.

Denver's victories and defeats come in bunches. They have gone 24-8 over the 1984 and 1985 seasons, won ten or more games six times since 1976, and own the fourth-best record in the NFL over that period. Winning isn't the problem in the Mile High City. The problem is winning when it really counts.

Despite going 11-5 in 1985, tying them for the third-best winning percentage in the league, the Broncos failed to make the playoffs – the first 11-game winner ever to do so. A year earlier, after finishing with a 13-3 record, they lost their divisional playoff game against Pittsburgh, 24-17.

KNOWING HOW TO WIN

'In 1985, we were better as a football team,' said head coach Dan Reeves, 'but we were unfortunate in that we did not make the playoffs. We learned a lesson from it – you must control your division to make the playoffs. You can't depend on someone else.'

For the past three years the story of the Denver Broncos has been the story of John Elway. The record shows that Elway knows how to win, but with no heavy-duty run-

In an '85 contest with the Houston Oilers, quarterback John Elway gives the ball to Sammy Winder, on the way to securing Denver a convincing 31-20 win.

ning back to split opposing defenses' point of focus, the Denver QB spends a lot of each Sunday afternoon scrambling from sideline to sideline.

Coach Reeves is well aware of the unbalanced nature of his team's offense. 'The thing we have to do is get back on the track, as far as our running game is concerned,' he says. 'We can't rely strictly on the pass.'

Fortunately for the Broncos' head coach, John Elway is one of the best (and most heralded) quarterbacks in the league. When he first arrived his press clippings were even more impressive than his 70-yard spirals. He was supposed to be the sport's new golden boy, the new Namath or Montana.

If he hasn't quite reached that exalted level, he is surely on the way. In 1985, Elway set Denver single-season records for pass attempts (605) completions (327), and passing yards (3891). He threw 22 touchdown passes and was voted the Broncos' most valuable offensive player by his Denver teammates.

More important, perhaps, he was learning how to win. In Elway's last 34 starts before the end of the '85 season, he was a winner in 25. Considering that Denver had no fewer than 11 games decided in the final few minutes during the 1985 season, he showed that he was performing well under the pressure of clutch games.

HONOURS

AFC Champion 1977, 1986
AFC Western Division Champion 1978, 1984
AFC Wild Card Qualifier for Playoffs 1979, 1983

HALL OF FAME Willie Brown

STADIUM: DENVER MILE

HIGH STADIUM

CAPACITY: 75,100

PLAYING SURFACE: GRASS

DAN REEVES – BRONCOS' BEST

After spending his entire pro career as both player and coach with the Dallas Cowboys, Dan Reeves became the ninth head coach in Denver Broncos' history on 28 February 1981. They went from 8-8 to 10-6 in his first year.

Reeves led the Broncos to an 11-5 record in 1985, barely missing a playoff berth. He guided them to the AFC Western Championship in 1984, with a sparkling 13-3 record, plus a 9-7 mark and a playoff berth in 1983. He is now the winningest coach in Denver history with a five-season record of 45-28.

Reeves joined the Cowboys as a free agent running back in 1965 and in eight seasons with them, rushed for 1990 yards and caught 129 passes for 1693 yards.

His astute knowledge of the game led him to become a player-coach for two years (1970 and 1971), before moving on to offensive backfield coach (1972, 1974-76). He became offensive co-ordinator in 1977, and his widely acknowledged success at that position made Reeves a natural for a head coaching job when the Broncos came calling.

Running backs Sammy Winder (23, above) and Gerald Willhite (47, right) are both capable of big plays, but the Broncos need extra rushing talent to make it to the playoffs.

Denver needs a 1000-yard runner to line up alongside Elway in the backfield. If they find one or if someone already on the team turns to gold, the Broncos could go all the way to the top.

Sammy Winder, the Broncos' most consistent back, missed two games in '85 and was unable to start in three others. Yet he still led the team in rushing with 718 yards and scored eight touchdowns.

RECEIVING HOPE

Gerald Willhite, who is as adept catching passes as he is doing backflips, will return as a swing man. And Gene Lang, who ran for a surprising 318 yards before a broken hand sidelined him, should provide some added depth. But if there is to be a home-run threat in the backfield with Elway, it is more likely to be Steve Sewell, who gave hints in his rookie season of developing into a big-play runner and receiver.

'Sewell got better as the season went along,' Reeves said of the number-one draft choice from Oklahoma. 'We're expecting great things from Steve.'

If the runners aren't quite there yet, the receivers certainly are. Steve Watson and Vance Johnson complement each other as well as any pair in the division. Watson runs the medium pass routes to perfection, – while Johnson, the speed merchant from Arizona, is the target for Elway's long-range rockets. Watson had 61 catches for 915 yards, Johnson 51 for 721 in 1985.

Tight end is more of a blocking position in the Broncos' scheme, and Clarence Kay and James Wright combined for 57 catches and 585 yards in '85. Mike Barber is in reserve.

A WEALTH OF TALENT

Up front, Denver does not present many star names. But they make up in ability what they lack in notoriety.

Center Billy Bryan, who has started 62 consecutive games, was an AFC-NFC Pro Bowl alternative last season. Tackle Dave Studdard has appeared in 105 consecutive games, while Ken Lanier, the other tackle, didn't miss a start in 1985.

The guards are Paul Howard, the Broncos' 13-year veteran, and Keith Bishop, who also doubles as one of the game's best long snappers on punts.

On the bench young Mark Cooper and Winford Hood have both demonstrated they are reliable offensive linemen. And tackle Dean Miraldi, who joined the club early in the season, proved to be a capable reserve player.

'Our offensive line is a good group,' Reeves says. 'I think we have young players who can challenge and possibly move into starting roles, but if they don't, our starting

TIME OUT

BIG DEAL

Broncos' coach Dan Reeves was so keen to acquire quarterback John Elway, that he was prepared to make a major trading deal in NFL history. To win him from the Baltimore Colts, who had first round choice in the draft, he exchanged their own 1983 number one pick, their 1984 first-round pick, and backup quarterback Mark Hermann.

unit certainly is solid already.'

The main reason the Broncos have stayed near the top of the NFL comes down to one word – defense. Assistant head coach Joe Collier has molded a solid unit who don't make big plays, they just prevent them.

But, for head coach Reeves it isn't quite enough. He wants more aggressiveness. He wants more blitzing. What he really wants in fact, is a little less Denver and a lot more Chicago Bears.

'We want to dominate games defensively a little more than we did last year,' Reeves said. 'But first, we've got to determine if we have the personnel for that style of play.

This indicates that the defensive line-up may change as a new philosophy is put into effect. The key word is 'attack'.

The pivotal new addition may well be Ricky Hunley, a talented young player for whom the club forfeited a first and third-round draft choice in 1986 and a fifth-round pick in 1987.

Hunley will become something of a free-lancer, a 'position' Karl Mecklenburg proved can be very effective. After two years of relative obscurity, Mecklenburg emerged as a Pro Bowl starter. He led the Broncos with 13 sacks. He's joined by 14-year veteran Tom Jackson and Jim Ryan outside. It's Jackson that Ricky Hunley may replace.

Louis Wright, who has played in five Pro Bowls, is at left cornerback. Mike Harden, a fine player, starts on the right side, but may be pressed by currently injured Mark Haynes, obtained in a draft-day trade with the New York Giants. Another Pro Bowl choice, Dennis Smith, is at strong safety, and Steve Foley at free.

'We have a solid secondary,' says Reeves. 'We're as good as anybody in the league when our top guys are in there.'

ORANGE CRUSH

Denver's defenders have enjoyed a fine reputation in the NFL ever since 1977, when they had the stingiest defense in the AFC and were nicknamed the 'Orange Crush'. That year the Broncos swept to the best record in football, 12-2. Since that time, their only losing season was in strike-shortened 1982, when they were 2-7.

The Broncos defensive strength is not, however, shared by the special teams who had a poor season in every category in 1985. Rich Karlis converted on just 23 of 38 field-goal attempts, the lowest percentage (.605) of his four-year NFL career. Chris Norman, the punter, was even less consistent, averaging only 40.9 yards-per-attempt. Obviously, considerable improvement is necessary in both categories.

The Broncos began to live up to their name as early as 1962 when head coach Jack Faulkner led his team to a shocking 30-21 victory over the San Diego Chargers (a team they had never beaten previously). Denver finished the season at a respectable 7-7. Faulkner was named AFL coach of the year and home attendance was up more than 100 per cent over the previous year.

In 1967, future all-pro, Floyd Little, the Syracuse All-American running back, became the first number-one draft choice ever to sign with the Broncos. And as a sign of the times, Denver defeated the Detroit Lions 13-7 in a preseason game. It was the first time an AFL team won a game over an NFL team.

RUNNING ATTACK REQUIRED

Most teams would be more than satisfied with the Denver Broncos' won-lost percentage over the past few years and their prospects for the immediate future. But Dan Reeves knows 11 victories aren't worth much if they don't lead to the playoffs.

Reeves wants enough regular season victories to *assure* the Broncos a place in the playoffs and a giant step forward towards the Super Bowl again. Without a first class running attack, however, Denver's chances of January action are pretty thin.

The Broncos' defence is the main reason for the team's consistency over the years. The 6 ft 4 in, 16 st 3 lb figure of linebacker Steve Busick (now traded to the Rams) leads his team to battle. *Inset* Houston running back Mike Rozier (33) discovers the squeeze of the 'Orange Crush' the hard way. Linebacker Jim Ryan moves in for the kill.

THE **BRONCOS** STATISTICS

COACHING HISTORY

180-207-9

Year	Coach	Record
1960-61	Frank Filchock	7-20-1
1962-64	Jack Faulkner*	9-22-1
1964-66	Mac Speedie**	6-19-1
1966	Ray Malavasi	4-8-0
1967-71	Lou Saban***	20-42-3
1971	Jerry Smith	2-3-0
1972-76	John Ralston	34-33-3
1977-80	Robert (Red) Miller	42-25-0
1981-86	Dan Reeves	56-35-0

*Released after four games in 1964
**Resigned after two games in 1966
***Resigned after nine games in 1971

John Elway QB

REGULAR SEASONS

Year	W	L	T	Pct.	Pts	Opp.
1960	4	9	1	.308	309	393
1961	3	11	0	.214	251	432
1962	7	7	0	.500	353	334
1963	2	11	1	.154	301	473
1964	2	11	1	.154	240	438
1965	4	10	0	.286	303	392
1966	4	10	0	.286	196	381
1967	3	11	0	.214	256	409
1968	5	9	0	.357	255	404
1969	5	8	1	.385	297	344
1970	5	8	1	.385	253	264
1971	4	9	1	.308	203	275
1972	5	9	0	.357	325	350
1973	7	5	2	.571	354	296
1974	7	6	1	.536	302	294
1975	6	8	0	.429	254	307
1976	9	5	0	.643	315	206
1977‡	12	2	0	.857	274	148
1978†	10	6	0	.625	282	198
1979§	10	6	0	.625	289	262
1980	8	8	0	.500	310	323
1981	10	6	0	.625	321	289
1982	2	7	0	.222	148	226
1983§	9	7	0	.563	302	327
1984	13	3	0	.813	353	241
1985	11	5	0	.688	380	329
1986‡	11	5	0	.688	378	327
27 Years	178	202	9	.636	352	187

‡AFC Champion
†AFC Western Division Champion
§AFC Wild Card Qualifier for Playoffs

RECORD HOLDERS

Individual Records – Career

Category	Name	Performance
Rushing (Yds)	Floyd Little, 1967-1975	6323
Passing (Yds)	Craig Morton, 1977-1982	11,895
Passing (TDs)	Craig Morton, 1977-1982	74
Receiving (No.)	Lionel Taylor, 1960-1966	543
Receiving (Yds)	Lionel Taylor, 1960-1966	6072
Interceptions	Goose Gonsoulin, 1960-1966	43
Punting (Avg.)	Jim Fraser, 1962-1964	45.2
Punt Return (Avg.)	Rick Upchurch, 1975-1983	12.1
Kickoff Return (Avg.)	Abner Haynes, 1965-1966	26.3
Field Goals	Jim Turner, 1971-1979	151
Touchdowns (Tot.)	Floyd Little, 1967-1975	54
Points	Jim Turner, 1971-1979	742

Individual Records – Single Season

Category	Name	Performance
Rushing (Yds)	Otis Armstrong, 1974	1407
Passing (Yds)	John Elway, 1985	3891
Passing (TDs)	Frank Tripucka, 1960	24
Receiving (No.)	Lionel Taylor, 1961	100
Receiving (Yds)	Steve Watson, 1981	1244
Interceptions	Goose Gonsoulin, 1960	11
Punting (Avg.)	Jim Fraser, 1963	46.1
Punt Return (Avg.)	Floyd Little, 1967	16.9
Kickoff Return (Avg.)	Bill Thompson, 1969	28.5
Field Goals	Gene Mingo, 1962	27
Touchdowns (Tot.)	Floyd Little, 1972, 1973	13
	Steve Watson, 1981	13
Points	Gene Mingo, 1962	137

Individual Records – Single Game

Category	Name	Performance
Rushing (Yds)	Otis Armstrong, 8.12.74	183
Passing (Yds)	Frank Tripucka 15.9.62	447
Passing (TDs)	Frank Tripucka 28.10.62	5
	John Elway, 18.11.84	5
Receiving (No.)	Lionel Taylor, 29.11.64	13
	Bobby Anderson, 30.9.73	13
Receiving (Yds)	Lionel Taylor, 27.11.60	199
Interceptions	Goose Gonsoulin, 18.9.60	4
	Willie Brown, 15.11.64	4
Field Goals	Gene Mingo, 6.10.63	5
	Rich Karlis, 20.11.83	5
Touchdowns (Tot.)	Many times	3
	Last time by Steve Watson, 20.9.81	
Points	Gene Mingo, 10.12.60	21

Floyd Little RB

Steve Watson WR

1986 SEASON

	Off.	Def.
Total First Downs	339	291
Rushing	94	93
Passing	184	177
Penalty	41	21
Third Down Efficiency	41.7	34.2
Total Net Yards	5216	4947
Avg. Per Game	326.0	309.2
Total Plays	1042	1026
Avg. Per Play	5.0	4.8
Net Yards Rushing	1678	1651
Avg. Per Game	104.9	103.2
Total Rushes	455	432
Net Yards Passing	3538	3296
Avg. Per Game	221.1	206.0
Tackled/Yards Lost	38/273	49/459
Gross Yards	3811	3755
Att./Completions	549/306	545/301
Completion Pct.	55.7	55.2
Had Intercepted	16	18
Punts/Avg.	86/39.3	86/42.9
Punting Yds.	3376	3689
Penalties/Yards Lost	104/910	127/1034
Fumbles/Ball Lost	24/13	32/17
Touchdowns	45	36
Rushing	17	13
Passing	22	21
Returns	6	2
Avg. Time of Possession	30:30	29:30

W	L	T
11	5	0

ALL-TIME GREATS

The Broncos can boast the greatest quarterback in their history in John Elway. He set club records in 1985 for pass attempts (605), completions (327), and yards (3891). During the years 1975-83, Denver had the services of the finest punt returner of his era, Rick Upchurch, a potential Hall of Famer with 3008 yards gained, career, and an NFL-record eight touchdowns, career.

Receiver Lionel Taylor was Denver's star performer in their early years (1960-65), setting NFL records for most seasons, 50 or more pass receptions (six), most pass receptions, season (100), and most seasons 1000 or more yards, pass receiving (4).

He also led the league for five seasons with his pass receiving in 1960-63 and 1965. The years 1960-63 puts him second in the NFL for consecutive years leading the league with receptions, with four years.

In 1980, kicker Fred Steinfort set an all-time NFL record for the number of field goals of 50 or more yards in a season with 5.

Another all-time record holder for the Broncos is Bill Thompson who has the most touchdowns from fumbles with a career record of four.

THE FALCONS STATISTICS

RECORD HOLDERS

Individual Records – Career

Category	Name	Performance
Rushing (Yds)	William Andrews, 1979-1983	5772
Passing (Yds)	Steve Bartkowski, 1975-1985	23,468
Passing (TDs)	Steve Bartkowski, 1975-1985	154
Receiving (No.)	Alfred Jenkins, 1975-1983	359
Receiving (Yds)	Alfred Jenkins, 1975-1983	6257
Interceptions	Rolland Lawrence, 1973-1981	39
Punting (Avg.)	Billy Lothridge, 1966-1971	41.3
Punt Return (Avg.)	Al Dodd, 1973-74	11.8
Kickoff Return (Avg.)	Ron Smith, 1966-67	24.3
Field Goals	Mick Luckhurst, 1981-85	92
Touchdowns (Tot.)	Alfred Jenkins, 1975-1983	40
	William Andrews, 1979-1983	40
Points	Mick Luckhurst, 1981-85	451

Individual Records – Single Season

Category	Name	Performance
Rushing (Yds)	Gerald Riggs, 1985	1719
Passing (Yds)	Steve Bartkowski, 1981	3830
Passing (TDs)	Steve Bartkowski, 1980	31
Receiving (No.)	William Andrews, 1981	81
Receiving (Yds)	Alfred Jenkins, 1981	1358
Interceptions	Rolland Lawrence, 1975	9
Punting (Avg.)	Billy Lothridge, 1968	44.3
Punt Return (Avg.)	Gerald Tinker, 1974	13.9
Kickoff Return (Avg.)	Dennis Pearson, 1978	26.7
Field Goals	Nick Mike-Mayer, 1973	26
Touchdowns (Tot.)	Alfred Jenkins, 1981	13
	Gerald Riggs, 1984	13
Points	Mick Luckhurst, 1981	114

Individual Records – Single Game

Category	Name	Performance
Rushing (Yds)	Gerald Riggs, 2-9-84	202
Passing (Yds)	Steve Bartkowski, 15-11-81	416
Passing (TDs)	Randy Johnson, 16-11-69	4
	Steve Bartkowski, 19-10-80	4
	Steve Bartkowski, 18-10-81	4
Receiving (No.)	William Andrews, 15-11-81	15
Receiving (Yds)	Alfred Jackson, 2-12-84	193
Interceptions	Many times	2
	Last time by Bobby Butler, 2-9-84	
Field Goals	Nick Mike-Mayer, 4-11-73	5
	Tim Mazzetti, 30-10-78	5
Touchdowns (Tot.)	Many times	3
	Last time by Gerald Riggs, 17-11-85	
Points	Many times	18
	Last time by Gerald Riggs, 17-11-85	

Tommy Nobis LB

COACHING HISTORY

(119-185-5)

1966-68	Norb Hecker*	4-26-1
1968-74	Norm Van Brocklin**	37-49-3
1974-76	Marion Campbell***	6-19-0
1976	Pat Peppler	3-6-0
1977-82	Leeman Bennett	47-44-0
1983-86	Dan Henning	22-41-1

*Released after three games in 1968
**Released after eight games in 1974
***Released after five games in 1976

REGULAR SEASONS

Year	W	L	T	Pct.	Pts	Opp.
1966	3	11	0	.214	204	437
1967	1	12	1	.077	175	422
1968	2	12	0	.143	170	389
1969	6	8	0	.429	276	268
1970	4	8	2	.333	206	261
1971	7	6	1	.538	274	277
1972	7	7	0	.500	269	274
1973	9	5	0	.643	318	224
1974	3	11	0	.214	111	271
1975	4	10	0	.286	240	289
1976	4	10	0	.286	172	312
1977	7	7	0	.500	179	129
1978§	9	7	0	.563	240	290
1979	6	10	0	.375	300	388
1980†	12	4	0	.750	405	272
1981	7	9	0	.438	426	355
1982***	5	4	0	.556	183	199
1983	7	9	0	.438	370	389
1984	4	12	0	.250	281	382
1985	4	12	0	.250	282	452
1986	7	8	1	.469	280	280
21 Years	118	182	5	.393	5361	6560

§NFC Wild Card Qualifier for Playoffs
†NFC Western Division Champion
***NFC Qualifier for Playoffs

Steve Bartkowski QB

ALL-TIME GREATS

A former All-American at the University of California at Berkeley, quarterback Steve Bartkowski came to Atlanta as the Falcons' 1975 first draft choice and proceeded to make every passing record in Falcons' history his own. Bartkowski holds the records for yards passing, career (23,468, 1975-1985), touchdowns passing, career (154), yards passing, season (3830, 1981), touchdowns passing, season (31, 1980), yards passing, game (416, 15 November 1981) and touchdowns passing, game (four, 19 October 1980 and 18 October 1981).

Tommy Nobis, the Outland Trophy-winning linebacker from the University of Texas became Atlanta's first-ever draft pick in 1965 when the Falcons entered the NFL as an expansion team. Even though playing for a club that could only win six games during its first three years in the league, Nobis was immediately hailed as one of the NFL's finest and fiercest defensive players. In 1967, Nobis returned an interception 41 yards to lead Atlanta over Minnesota 21-20 for the Falcons' only victory that season. He was named Atlanta's first all-pro.

A third excellent draft choice came in 1982 when Atlanta chose Gerald Riggs, a running back from Arizona State in the first round. Riggs became the NFL's most fumble-free runner and holds Falcons' rushing records for most yards, season (1719, 1985) and most yards, game (202, 2 September 1984). Riggs' 1985 rushing total led the NFC and overtook William Andrews' Atlanta record.

1986 SEASON

	Off.	Def.
Total First Downs	305	268
Rushing	149	111
Passing	137	139
Penalty	19	18
Third Down Efficiency	36.2	35.7
Total Net Yards	5106	4908
Avg. Per Game	319.1	306.8
Total Plays	1086	964
Avg. Per Play	4.7	5.1
Net Yards Rushing	2524	1916
Avg. Per Game	157.8	119.8
Total Rushes	578	485
Net Yards Passing	2582	2992
Avg. Per Game	161.4	187.0
Tackled/Yards Lost	56/464	26/177
Gross Yards	3046	3169
Att./Completions	452/246	453/241
Completion Pct.	54.4	53.2
Had Intercepted	17	22
Punts/Avg.	78/43.3	83/41.4
Punting Yds.	3421	3436
Penalties/Yards Lost	99/763	106/834
Fumbles/Ball Lost	31/16	30/14
Touchdowns	30	34
Rushing	12	10
Passing	14	19
Returns	4	5
Avg. Time of Possession	32:35	27:25

W	L	T
7	8	1

THE **BILLS** STATISTICS

RECORD HOLDERS

Individual Records – Career

Category	Name	Performance
Rushing (Yds)	O.J. Simpson, 1969-1977	10,183
Passing (Yds)	Joe Ferguson, 1973-1984	27,590
Passing (TDs)	Joe Ferguson, 1973-1984	181
Receiving (No.)	Elbert Dubenion, 1960-1967	296
Receiving (Yds)	Elbert Dubenion, 1960-1967	5304
Interceptions	George (Butch) Byrd, 1964-1970	40
Punting (Avg.)	Paul Maguire, 1964-1970	42.1
Punt Return (Avg.)	Keith Moody, 1976-1979	10.5
Kickoff Return (Avg.)	Wallace Francis, 1973-1974	27.2
Field Goals	John Leypoldt, 1971-1976	74
Touchdowns (Tot.)	O.J. Simpson, 1969-1977	70
Points	O.J. Simpson, 1969-1977	420

Individual Records – Single Season

Category	Name	Performance
Rushing (Yds)	O.J. Simpson, 1973	2003
Passing (Yds)	Joe Ferguson, 1981	3652
Passing (TDs)	Joe Ferguson, 1983	26
Receiving (No.)	Frank Lewis, 1981	70
Receiving (Yds)	Frank Lewis, 1981	1244
Interceptions	Billy Atkins, 1961	10
	Tom Janik, 1967	10
Punting (Avg.)	Billy Atkins, 1961	44.5
Punt Return (Avg.)	Keith Moody, 1977	13.1
Kickoff Return (Avg.)	Ed Rutkowski, 1963	30.2
Field Goals	Pete Gogolak, 1965	28
Touchdowns (Tot.)	O.J. Simpson, 1975	23
Points	O.J. Simpson, 1975	138

Individual Records – Single Game

Category	Name	Performance
Rushing (Yds)	O.J. Simpson, 25-11-76	273
Passing (Yds)	Joe Ferguson, 9-10-83	419
Passing (TDs)	Joe Ferguson, 23-9-79	5
	Joe Ferguson, 9-10-83	5
Receiving (No.)	Greg Bell, 8-9-85	13
Receiving (Yds)	Jerry Butler, 23-9-79	255
Interceptions	Many times	3
	Last time by Jeff Nixon, 7-9-80	
Field Goals	Pete Gogolak, 5-12-65	5
Touchdowns (Tot.)	Cookie Gilchrist, 8-12-63	5
Points	Cookie Gilchrist, 8-12-63	30

REGULAR SEASONS

Year	W	L	T	Pct.	Pts	Opp.
1960	5	8	1	.385	296	303
1961	6	8	0	.429	294	342
1962	7	6	1	.538	309	272
1963	7	6	1	.538	304	291
1964□	12	2	0	.857	400	242
1965□	10	3	1	.769	313	226
1966△	9	4	1	.692	358	255
1967	4	10	0	.286	237	285
1968	1	12	1	.077	199	367
1969	4	10	0	.286	230	359
1970	3	10	1	.231	204	337
1971	1	13	0	.071	184	394
1972	4	9	1	.321	257	377
1973	9	5	0	.643	259	230
1974§	9	5	0	.643	264	244
1975	8	6	0	.571	420	355
1976	2	12	0	.143	245	363
1977	3	11	0	.214	160	313
1978	5	11	0	.313	302	354
1979	7	9	0	.438	268	279
1980†	11	5	0	.688	320	260
1981§	10	6	0	.625	311	276
1982	4	5	0	.444	150	154
1983	8	8	0	.500	283	351
1984	2	14	0	.125	250	454
1985	2	14	0	.125	200	381
1986	4	12	0	.250	287	348
27 Years	157	224	8	.412	7304	8412

□AFL Champion
△AFL Eastern Division Champion
§AFC Wild Card Qualifier for playoffs
†AFC Eastern Division Champion

1986 SEASON

	Off.	Def.
Total First Downs	256	334
Rushing	101	100
Passing	152	204
Penalty	38	30
Third Down Efficiency	32.4	36.2
Total Net Yards	5017	5523
Avg. Per Game	313.6	345.2
Total Plays	963	1071
Avg. Per Play	5.2	5.2
Net Yards Rushing	1654	1721
Avg. Per Game	103.4	107.6
Total Rushes	409	465
Net Yards Passing	3363	3802
Avg. Per Game	210.2	237.6
Tackled/Yards Lost	45/334	36/267
Gross Yards	3697	4069
Att./Completions	499/294	570/343
Completion Pct.	58.9	60.2
Had Intercepted	19	10
Punts/Avg.	75/40.4	83/38.1
Punting Yds.	3031	3162
Penalties/Yards Lost	131/838	128/1088
Fumbles/Ball Lost	40/20	19/8
Touchdowns	34	48
Rushing	9	18
Passing	22	21
Returns	3	1
Avg. Time of Possession	28:02	31:58

W	L	T
4	12	0

COACHING HISTORY

(156-217-8)

1960-61	Buster Ramsey	11-16-1
1962-65	Lou Saban	38-18-3
1966-68	Joe Collier*	13-17-1
1968	Harvey Johnson	1-10-1
1969-70	John Rauch	7-20-1
1971	Harvey Johnson	1-13-0
1972-76	Lou Saban**	32-29-1
1976-77	Jim Ringo	3-20-0
1978-82	Chuck Knox	38-38-0
1983-84	Kay Stephenson***	10-26-0
1985	Hank Bullough	4-17-0
1986	Marv Levy	2-5-0

*Replaced after two games in 1968
**Resigned after five games in 1976
***Replaced after four games in 1985

Joe Ferguson QB

ALL-TIME GREATS

One of the most famous names in the history of football, O.J. Simpson is unquestionably the greatest player to wear the red, white and blue of the Buffalo Bills. His four seasons leading the league in rushing (1972-73, 1975-76) is surpassed only by Jim Brown, and his 2003 yards rushing in 1973, has been overtaken as a season record only by Eric Dickerson. But no one had overtaken his career record of six games with 200 or more yards rushing by the start of 1986.

Another great is QB Joe Ferguson, far and away the Bills' greatest passer with a 3652-yard total in 1981.

O.J. Simpson RB

THE **BEARS** STATISTICS

COACHING HISTORY

Chicago Staleys 1921
(490-328-42)

		W	L	T
1920-29	George Halas	84	31	19
1930-32	Ralph Jones	24	10	7
1933-42	George Halas*	89	24	4
1942-45	Hunk Anderson-Luke Johnsos**	23	12	2
1946-55	George Halas	76	43	2
1956-57	John (Paddy) Driscoll	14	10	1
1958-67	George Halas	76	53	6
1968-71	Jim Dooley	20	36	0
1972-74	Abe Gibron	11	30	1
1975-77	Jack Pardee	20	23	0
1978-81	Neil Armstrong	30	35	0
1982-86	Mike Ditka	54	24	0

*   Retired November 1 to re-enter Navy
**   Co-Coaches

Total		522-331-42

REGULAR SEASONS

YEAR	W	L	T	Pct.	Pts.	Opp.
1960	5	6	1	.455	194	299
1961	8	6	0	.571	326	302
1962	9	5	0	.643	321	287
1963**	11	1	2	.917	301	144
1964	5	9	0	.357	260	379
1965	9	5	0	.643	409	275
1966	5	7	2	.417	234	272
1967	7	6	1	.538	239	278
1968	7	7	0	.500	250	338
1969	1	13	0	.071	210	339
1970	6	8	0	.429	256	261
1971	6	8	0	.429	185	276
1972	4	9	1	.321	225	275
1973	3	11	0	.214	195	334
1974	4	10	0	.286	152	279
1975	4	10	0	.286	191	379
1976	7	7	0	.500	253	216
1977§	9	5	0	.643	255	253
1978	7	9	0	.438	253	274
1979§	10	6	0	.625	306	249
1980	7	9	0	.438	304	264
1981	6	10	0	.375	253	324
1982	3	6	0	.333	181	176
1983	8	8	0	.500	311	301
1984†	10	6	0	.625	325	248
1985*	15	1	0	.938	456	198
1986***	14	2	0	.875	352	187
27 Years	180	190	7	.486	7197	7340

*	Super Bowl Champion
**	NFL Champion
***	NFL Qualifier for Playoffs
§	NFC Wild Card Qualifier for Playoffs
†	NFC Central Division Champion

RECORD HOLDERS

Individual Records – Career

Category	Name	Performance
Rushing (Yds)	Walter Payton, 1975-1985	14,860
Passing (Yds)	Sid Luckman, 1939-1950	14,686
Passing (TDs)	Sid Luckman, 1939-1950	137
Receiving (No.)	Walter Payton, 1975-1985	422
Receiving (Yds)	Walter Payton, 1975-1985	5059
Interceptions	Richie Petitbon, 1959-1968	37
Punting (Avg.)	George Gulyanics, 1947-1952	44.5
Punt Return (Avg.)	Ray (Scooter) McLean, 1940-47	14.8
Kickoff Return (Avg.)	Gale Sayers, 1965-1971	30.6
Field Goals	Bob Thomas, 1975-1984	128
Touchdowns (Tot.)	Walter Payton, 1975-1984	109
Points	Walter Payton, 1975-1985	654

Individual Records – Single Season

Category	Name	Performance
Rushing (Yds)	Walter Payton, 1977	1852
Passing (Yds)	Bill Wade, 1962	3172
Passing (TDs)	Sid Luckman, 1943	28
Receiving (No.)	Johnny Morris, 1964	93
Receiving (Yds)	Johnny Morris, 1964	1200
Interceptions	Roosevelt Taylor, 1963	9
Punting (Avg.)	Bobby Joe Green, 1963	46.4
Punt Return (Avg.)	Harry Clark, 1943	15.8
Kickoff Return (Avg.)	Gale Sayers, 1967	37.7
Field Goals	Kevin Butler, 1985	31
Touchdowns (Tot.)	Gale Sayers, 1965	22
Points	Kevin Butler, 1985	144

Individual Records – Single Game

Category	Name	Performance
Rushing (Yds)	Walter Payton, 20.11.77	275
Passing (Yds)	Johnny Lujack, 11.12.49	468
Passing (TDs)	Sid Luckman, 14.11.43	7
Receiving (No.)	Jim Keane, 23.10.49	14
Receiving (Yds)	Harlon Hill, 31.10.54	214
Interceptions	Many times Last time by Ross Brupbacher, 12.12.76	3
Field Goals	Roger LeClerc, 3.12.61 Mac Percival, 20.10.68	5
Touchdown (Tot.)	Gale Sayers, 12.12.65	6
Points	Gale Sayers, 12.12.65	36

1986 SEASON

	Off.	Def.
Total First Downs	305	241
Rushing	166	67
Passing	118	151
Penalty	21	23
Third Down Efficiency	37.2	32.5
Total Net Yards	5459	4130
Avg. Per Game	341.2	258.1
Total Plays	1045	1002
Avg. Per Play	5.2	4.1
Net Yards Rushing	2700	1463
Avg. Per Game	168.8	91.4
Total Rushes	606	427
Net Yards Passing	2759	2667
Avg. Per Game	172.4	166.7
Tackled/Yards Lost	24/153	62/503
Gross Yards	2759	3170
Att./Completions	415/208	513/243
Completion Pct.	50.1	47.4
Had Intercepted	25	31
Punts/Avg.	70/40.7	100/40.9
Punting Yds.	2850	4090
Penalties/Yards Lost	98/765	111/866
Fumbles/Ball Lost	36/22	27/16
Touchdowns	38	20
Rushing	21	4
Passing	12	12
Returns	5	4
Avg. Time of Possession	32:35	27:39

W	L	T
14	2	0

Post-Season Victories:

New York Giants in conference semifinal **21-0**
Los Angeles Rams in conference final **24-0**
New England Patriots in Super Bowl **46-10**

ALL-TIME GREATS

The Bears have 24 Hall of Famers, but two men stand out even in this legendary crew. Running back Gale Sayers still holds NFL marks for most touchdowns scored, season (22, 1965), most touchdowns scored, game (six, vs San Francisco 12 Dec 1965) and highest average gain, career (5.00, 991-4956, 1965-1971).

Completing this dream backfield, running back (and future Hall of Famer) Walter Payton owns NFL rushing records for most yards gained, career (14,860, 1975-1985), most seasons 1000 or more yards gained (9,

1976-81, 1983-85), most yards gained, game (275, vs. Minnesota 20 Nov 1977) and most games 100 or more yards gained, career (73, 1975-1985).

Mike Ditka Coach

William Perry RT

Jim McMahon QB

THE **BENGALS** STATISTICS

Ken Anderson QB

REGULAR SEASONS

Year	W	L	T	Pct.	Pts	Opp.
1968	3	11	0	.214	215	329
1969	4	9	1	.308	280	367
1970†	8	6	0	.571	312	255
1971	4	10	0	.286	284	265
1972	8	6	0	.571	299	229
1973†	10	4	0	.714	286	231
1974	7	7	0	.500	283	259
1975§	11	3	0	.786	340	246
1976	10	4	0	.714	335	210
1977	8	6	0	.571	238	235
1978	4	12	0	.250	252	284
1979	4	12	0	.250	337	421
1980	6	10	0	.375	244	312
1981‡	12	4	0	.750	421	304
1982□	7	2	0	.778	232	177
1983	7	9	0	.438	346	302
1984	8	8	0	.500	339	339
1985	7	9	0	.438	441	437
1986	10	6	0	.625	409	394
19 Years	138	138	1	.500	5983	5596

† AFC Central Division Champion
§ AFC Wild Card Qualifier for Playoffs
‡ AFC Champion
□ AFC Qualifier for Playoffs

RECORD HOLDERS

Individual Records – Career

Category	Name	Performance
Rushing (Yds)	Pete Johnson, 1977-1983	5421
Passing (Yds)	Ken Anderson, 1973-1985	32,667
Passing (TDs)	Ken Anderson, 1973-1985	196
Receiving (No.)	Isaac Curtis, 1973-1984	420
Receiving (Yds)	Isaac Curtis, 1973-1984	7106
Interceptions (No.)	Ken Riley, 1969-1983	63
Punting (Avg.)	Dave Lewis, 1970-1973	43.9
Punt Return (Avg.)	Mike Martin, 1983-1985	12.8
Kickoff Return (Avg.)	Lemar Parrish, 1970-1978	24.7
Field Goals	Horst Muhlmann, 1969-1974	120
Touchdowns (Tot.)	Pete Johnson, 1977-1983	70
Points	Horst Muhlmann, 1969-1974	549

Individual Records – Single Season

Category	Name	Performance
Rushing (Yds)	Pete Johnson, 1981	1077
Passing (Yds)	Ken Anderson, 1981	3754
Passing (TDs)	Ken Anderson, 1981	29
Receiving (No.)	Dan Ross, 1981	71
Receiving (Yds)	Cris Collinsworth 1983	1130
Interceptions	Ken Riley, 1976	9
Punting (Avg.)	Dave Lewis, 1970	46.2
Punt Return (Avg.)	Mike Martin, 1984	15.7
Kickoff Return (Avg.)	Lemar Parrish, 1980	30.2
Field Goals	Horst Muhlmann, 1972	27
Touchdowns (Tot.)	Pete Johnson, 1981	16
Points	Jim Breech, 1985	120

Individual Records – Single Game

Category	Name	Performance
Rushing (Yds)	Pete Johnson, 17-12-78	160
Passing (Yds)	Ken Anderson, 17-11-75	447
Passing (TDs)	Many times	4
	Last time by Ken Anderson, 29-11-81	
Receiving (No.)	Many times	10
	Last time by Cris Collinsworth, 22-9-85	
Receiving (Yds)	Cris Collinsworth, 2-10-85	216
Interceptions	Many times	3
	Last time by Ken Riley, 28-11-83	
Field Goals	Horst Muhlmann, 8-11-70, 24-9-72	5
Touchdowns (Tot.)	Larry Kinnebrew, 28-10-84	4
Points	Larry Kinnebrew, 28-10-84	24

COACHING HISTORY

(140-143-1)

Years	Coach	Record
1968-75	Paul Brown	55-59-1
1976-78	Bill Johnson*	18-15-0
1978-79	Homer Rice	8-19-0
1980-83	Forrest Gregg	34-27-0
1984-86	Sam Wyche	25-23-0

*Resigned after five games in 1978

Lemar Parrish DB

1986 SEASON

	Off.	Def.
Total First Downs	344	336
Rushing	134	134
Passing	183	171
Penalty	31	31
Third Down Efficiency	39.7	38.5
Total Net Yards	6490	5274
Avg. Per Game	405.6	329.6
Total Plays	1046	1051
Avg. Per Play	6.2	5.0
Net Yards Rushing	2533	2122
Avg. Per Game	158.3	132.6
Total Rushes	521	514
Net Yards Passing	3957	3152
Avg. Per Game	247.3	197.0
Tackled/Yards Lost	28/203	42/368
Gross Yards	4160	3520
Att./Completions	497/287	495/278
Completion Pct.	57.7	56.2
Had Intercepted	20	17
Punts/Avg.	59/33.8	77/39.8
Punting Yds.	1996	3068
Penalties/Yards Lost	111/847	93/840
Fumbles/Ball Lost	31/16	30/11
Touchdowns	51	47
Rushing	24	23
Passing	25	17
Returns	2	7
Avg. Time of Possession	28:48	31:12

W	L	T
10	6	0

ALL-TIME GREATS

For over a decade quarterback Ken Anderson was Mr. Cincinnati in the eyes of Bengals fans – and for good reason. Entering the 1986 season Anderson owned every passing mark in the Bengals' record book. These include most yards passing, career (32,667 in 1973-85), most touchdowns passing, career (196), most yards passing, season (3754 in 1981), most touchdowns passing, season (29 in 1981), most yards passing, game (447 on 17 November 1975), and most touchdowns passing, game (4 on 29 November 1981).

In his seven seasons with Cincinnati, big (17 st 2 lb) fullback Pete Johnson was the man the Bengals counted on whenever they really needed to put six points up on the board. Johnson bulled his way to team records for most yards rushing, career (5421 in 1977-1983), most total touchdowns, career (70), most yards rushing, season (1077 in 1981), most total touchdowns, season (16 in 1981), and most yards rushing, game (160 on 17 December 1978).

For a dozen years Ken Anderson's favourite target for his fabulous and reliable arm was steadfast wide receiver Isaac Curtis. Reliable, tough, and seemingly immune to injury, Curtis remains the Bengal's main man for career receiving records which include most yards (7106 in 1973-1984), and most number of receptions (420).

Cris Collinsworth WR

THE **BROWNS** STATISTICS

REGULAR SEASONS

Year	W	L	T	Pct.	Pts	Opp.
1960	8	3	1	.727	362	217
1961	8	5	1	.615	319	270
1962	7	6	1	.538	291	257
1963	10	4	0	.714	343	262
1964**	10	3	1	.769	415	293
1965△	11	3	0	.786	363	325
1966	9	5	0	.643	403	259
1967△	9	5	0	.643	334	297
1968△	10	4	0	.714	394	273
1969△	10	3	1	.769	351	300
1970	7	7	0	.500	286	265
1971†	9	5	0	.643	285	273
1972	10	4	0	.714	268	249
1973	7	5	2	.571	234	255
1974	4	10	0	.286	251	344
1975	3	11	0	.214	218	372
1976	9	5	0	.643	267	287
1977	6	8	0	.429	269	267
1978	8	8	0	.500	334	356
1979	9	7	0	.563	359	352
1980†	11	5	0	.688	357	310
1981	5	11	0	.313	276	375
1982□	4	5	0	.444	140	182
1983	9	7	0	.563	356	342
1984	5	11	0	.313	250	297
1985†	8	8	0	.500	287	294
1986†	12	4	0	.750	391	310
27 Years	218	162	7	.574	8403	7883

**NFL Champion
△ NFL Division/Conference Champion
□ AFC Qualifier for Playoffs
† AFC Central Division Champion

Len Ford DE

COACHING HISTORY

(311-208-9)
1950-62	Paul Brown	115-49-5
1963-70	Blanton Collier	79-38-2
1971-74	Nick Skorich	30-26-2
1975-77	Forrest Gregg*	18-23-0
1977	Dick Modzelewski	0-1-0
1978-84	Sam Rutigliano**	47-52-0
1984-86	Marty Schottenheimer	22-19-0

*Resigned after 13 games in 1977
**Released after eight games in 1984

RECORD HOLDERS

Individual Records – Career

Category	Name	Performance
Rushing (Yds)	Jim Brown, 1957-1965	12,312
Passing (Yds)	Brian Sipe, 1974-1983	23,713
Passing (TDs)	Brian Sipe, 1974-1983	154
Receiving (No.)	Ozzie Newsome, 1978-1985	502
Receiving (Yds)	Ozzie Newsome, 1978-1985	6281
Interceptions	Thom Darden, 1972-74, 1976-1981	45
Punting (Avg.)	Horace Gillom, 1950-56	43.8
Punt Return (Avg.)	Greg Pruitt, 1973-1981	11.8
Kickoff Return (Avg.)	Greg Pruitt, 1973-1981	26.3
Field Goals	Lou Groza, 1950-59, 1961-67	234
Touchdowns (Tot.)	Jim Brown, 1957-1965	126
Points	Lou Groza, 1950-59, 1961-67	1349

Individual Records – Single Season

Category	Name	Performance
Rushing (Yds)	Jim Brown, 1963	1863
Passing (Yds)	Brian Sipe, 1980	4132
Passing (TDs)	Brian Sipe, 1980	30
Receiving (No.)	Ozzie Newsome, 1983, 1984	89
Receiving (Yds)	Paul Warfield, 1968	1067
Interceptions	Thom Darden, 1978	10
Punting (Avg.)	Gary Collins, 1965	46.7
Punt Return (Avg.)	Leroy Kelly, 1965	15.6
Kickoff Return (Avg.)	Billy Reynolds, 1954	29.5
Field Goals	Matt Bahr, 1984	24
Touchdowns (Tot.)	Jim Brown, 1965	21
Points	Jim Brown, 1965	126

Individual Records – Single Game

Category	Name	Performance
Rushing (Yds)	Jim Brown, 24-11-57	237
	Jim Brown, 19-11-61	237
Passing (Yds)	Brian Sipe, 25-10-81	444
Passing (TDs)	Frank Ryan, 12-12-64	5
	Bill Nelsen, 2-11-69	5
	Brian Sipe, 7-10-79	5
Receiving (No.)	Ozzie Newsome, 14-10-84	14
Receiving (Yds)	Ozzie Newsome, 14-10-84	191
Interceptions	Many times	3
	Last time by Hanford Dixon, 19-12-82	
Field Goals	Don Cockroft, 19-10-75	5
Touchdowns (Tot.)	Dub Jones, 25-11-51	6
Points	Dub Jones, 25-11-51	36

Sam Rutigliano Coach

Marion Motley FB

1986 SEASON

	Off.	Def.
Total First Downs	271	302
Rushing	102	113
Passing	175	171
Penalty	25	18
Third Down Efficiency	36.8	37.4
Total Net Yards	5394	5269
Avg. Per Game	337.1	329.3
Total Plays	1047	1047
Avg. Per Play	5.2	5.0
Net Yards Rushing	1650	1981
Avg. Per Game	103.1	123.8
Total Rushes	470	494
Net Yards Passing	3744	3288
Avg. Per Game	234.0	205.5
Tackled/Yards Lost	39/274	35/258
Gross Yards	4018	3546
Att./Completions	538/315	518/291
Completion Pct.	58.6	56.2
Had Intercepted	11	18
Punts/Avg.	83/41.2	80/37.9
Punting Yds.	3423	3033
Penalties/Yards Lost	101/807	101/754
Fumbles/Ball Lost	31/13	36/19
Touchdowns	45	36
Rushing	20	12
Passing	18	21
Returns	7	3
Avg. Time of Possession	29:42	30:18

W	L	T
10	6	0

ALL-TIME GREATS

With 14 players in the Hall of Fame – including defensive end Len Ford and fullback 'Big' Marion Motley – Cleveland can boast some of the NFL's finest stars. Top of the list must be Jim Brown, perhaps the greatest running back ever. His eight seasons leading the league in rushing is still all time highest, as is his six seasons leading the league in rushing attempts. Over 700 attempts, no one has a higher average gain than Brown's 5.22 yards. But most impressive is his unbroken record of 106 rushing touchdowns.

Jim's namesake, Paul Brown, is another Hall of Famer through the strength of his outstanding 115-49-5 coaching record, including no less than three NFL Championships. Kicker Lou Groza was central to those successes with his unbroken record of five seasons leading the league in field goals in 17 years playing for the Browns. Tight end Ozzie Newsome proves that not all Browns heroes are in the past, with his current club record of 6281 receiving yards in 502 receptions.

THE **COWBOYS** STATISTICS

REGULAR SEASONS

YEAR	W	L	T	Pct.	Pts.	Opp.
1960	0	11	1	.000	177	369
1961	4	9	1	.308	236	380
1962	5	8	1	.385	398	402
1963	4	10	0	.286	305	378
1964	5	8	1	.385	250	289
1965	7	7	0	.500	325	280
1966△	10	3	1	.769	445	239
1967△	9	5	0	.643	342	268
1968□	12	2	0	.857	431	186
1969□	11	2	1	.846	369	223
1970‡	10	4	0	.714	299	221
1971*	11	3	0	.786	406	222
1972§	10	4	0	.714	319	240
1973△	10	4	0	.714	382	203
1974	8	6	0	.571	297	235
1975‡	10	4	0	.714	350	266
1976†	11	3	0	.786	296	194
1977*	12	2	0	.857	345	212
1978‡	12	4	0	.750	384	208
1979†	11	5	0	.688	371	313
1980§	12	4	0	.750	454	311
1981†	12	4	0	.750	367	277
1982	6	3	0	.667	226	145
1983§	12	4	0	.750	479	360
1984	9	7	0	.563	308	308
1985	10	6	0	.625	357	333
1986	7	9	0	.438	346	337
27 Years	240	141	6	.630	9264	7399

△ NFL Eastern Conference Champion
□ NFL Capitol Division Champion
‡ NFC Champion
* Super Bowl Champion
§ NFC Wild Card Qualifier for playoffs
† NFC Eastern Division Champions

COACHING HISTORY

1960-86	Tom Landry	240-141-6

As the only coach in the Cowboys' 26 year history, Tom Landry is responsible for the impressive 233-132-6 win/lose/tie record of 'America's Team'.

RECORD HOLDERS

Individual Records – Career

Category	Name	Performance
Rushing (Yds)	Tony Dorsett, 1977-1985	10,832
Passing (Yds)	Roger Staubach, 1969-1979	22,700
Passing (TDs)	Roger Staubach, 1969-1979	153
Receiving (No.)	Drew Pearson, 1973-1983	489
Receiving (Yds)	Drew Pearson, 1973-1983	7822
Interceptions	Mel Renfro, 1964-1977	52
Punting (Avg.)	Sam Baker, 1962-63	45.1
Punt Return (Avg.)	Bob Hayes, 1965-1974	11.1
Kickoff Return (Avg.)	Mel Renfro, 1964-1977	26.4
Field Goals	Rafael Septien, 1978-1985	147
Touchdowns Tot.)	Tony Dorsett 1977-1985	79
Points	Rafael Septien, 1978-1985	786

Individual Records – Single Season

Category	Name	Performance
Rushing (Yds)	Tony Dorsett, 1981	1646
Passing (Yds)	Danny White, 1983	3980
Passing (TDs)	Danny White, 1983	29
Receiving (No)	Tony Hill, 1985	74
Receiving (Yds)	Bob Hayes, 1966	1232
Interceptions	Everson Walls, 1981	11
Punting (Avg.)	Sam Baker, 1962	45.4
Punt Return (Avg.)	Bob Hayes, 1968	20.8
Kickoff Return (Avg.)	Mel Renfro, 1965	30.0
Field Goals	Rafael Septien, 1981	27
Touchdowns Tot.)	Dan Reeves, 1966	16
Points	Rafael Septien, 1983	123

Individual Records – Single Game

Category	Name	Performance
Rushing (Yds)	Tony Dorsett, 4.12.77	206
Passing (Yds)	Don Meredith, 10.11.63	460
Passing (TDs)	Many times	5
	Last time by Danny White, 30.10.83	
Receiving (No.)	Lance Rentzel, 19.11.67	13
Receiving (Yds)	Bob Hayes, 13.11.66	246
Interceptions	Herb Adderley, 26.9.71	3
	Lee Roy Jordan, 4.11.73	3
	Dennis Thurman, 13.12.81	3
Field Goals	Many times	4
	Last time by Rafael Septien, 21.9.81	
Touchdowns (Tot.)	Many times	4
	Last time by Duane Thomas, 18.12.71	
Points	Many times	24
	Last time by Duane Thomas, 18.12.71	

1986 SEASON

	Off.	Def.
Total First Downs	325	286
Rushing	98	118
Passing	199	148
Ponalty	28	20
Third Down Efficiency	37.6	39.4
Total Net Yards	5474	4985
Avg. Per Game	342.1	311.6
Total Plays	1054	1017
Avg. Per Play	5.2	4.9
Net Yards Rushing	1969	2200
Avg. Per Game	123.1	137.5
Total Rushes	447	500
Net Yards Passing	3505	2785
Avg. Per Game	219.1	174.1
Tackled/Yards Lost	60/498	53/364
Gross Yards	4003	3149
Att./Completions	547/319	464/226
Completion Pct.	58.3	48.7
Had Intercepted	24	17
Punts/Avg.	87/40.2	87/41.6
Punting Yds.	3498	3620
Penalties/Yards Lost	112/936	91/822
Fumbles/Ball Lost	44/17	29/18
Touchdowns	43	41
Rushing	21	17
Passing	21	21
Returns	1	3
Avg. Time of Possession	31:14	28:46

W	L	T
7	9	0

Lost to L.A. Rams in conference semifinal

ALL-TIME GREATS

Quarterback Roger Staubach was the Cowboys' star of the '70s, but running back Tony Dorsett owns the '80s, with records for the most seasons 1000 or more yards rushing (eight, 1977-81, 1983-85) and most consecutive seasons 1000 or more yards rushing (five, '77-81).

Tony Dorsett RB

Tom Landry Coach

Danny White QB

THE LIONS STATISTICS

RECORD HOLDERS

Individual Records – Career

Category	Name	Performance
Rushing (Yds)	Billy Sims, 1980-1984	5106
Passing (Yds)	Bobby Layne, 1950-1958	15,710
Passing (TDs)	Bobby Layne, 1950-1958	118
Receiving (No.)	Charlie Sanders, 1968-1977	336
Receiving (Yds)	Gail Cogdill, 1960-1968	5220
Interceptions	Dick LeBeau, 1959-1972	62
Punting (Avg.)	Yale Lary, 1952-53, 1956-1964	44.3
Punt Return (Avg.)	Jack Christiansen, 1951-1958	12.8
Kickoff Return (Avg.)	Pat Studstill, 1961-1967	25.7
Field Goals	Errol Mann, 1969-1976	141
Touchdowns (Tot.)	Billy Sims, 1980-1984	47
Points	Errol Mann, 1969-1976	636

Individual Records – Single Season

Category	Name	Performance
Rushing (Yds)	Billy Sims, 1981	1437
Passing (Yds)	Gary Danielson, 1980	3223
Passing (TDs)	Bobby Layne, 1951	26
Receiving (No.)	James Jones, 1984	77
Receiving (Yds)	Pat Studstill, 1966	1266
Interceptions	Don Doll, 1950	12
	Jack Christiansen, 1953	12
Punting (Avg.)	Yale Lary, 1963	48.9
Punt Return (Avg.)	Jack Christiansen, 1952	21.5
Kickoff Return (Avg.)	Tom Watkins, 1965	34.4
Field Goals	Eddie Murray, 1980	27
Touchdowns (Tot.)	Billy Sims, 1980	16
Points	Doak Walker, 1950	128

Yale Lary P & S   Bobby Layne QB

Individual Records – Single Game

Category	Name	Performance
Rushing (Yds)	Bob Hoernschemeyer, 23-11-50	198
Passing (Yds)	Bobby Layne, 5-11-50	374
Passing (TDs)	Gary Danielson, 9-12-78	5
Receiving (No.)	Cloyce Box, 3-12-50	12
Receiving (Yds)	Cloyce Box, 3-12-50	302
Interceptions	Don Doll, 23-10-49	4
Field Goals	Garo Yepremian, 13-11-66	6
Touchdowns (Tot.)	Cloyce Box, 3-12-50	4
Points	Cloyce Box, 3-12-50	24

REGULAR SEASONS

Year	W	L	T	Pct.	Pts	Opp.
1960	7	5	0	.583	239	212
1961	8	5	1	.615	270	258
1962	11	3	0	.786	315	177
1963	5	8	1	.385	326	265
1964	7	5	2	.583	280	260
1965	6	7	1	.462	257	295
1966	4	9	1	.308	206	317
1967	5	7	2	.417	260	259
1968	4	8	2	.333	207	241
1969	9	4	1	.692	259	188
1970§	10	4	0	.714	347	202
1971	7	6	1	.538	341	286
1972	8	5	1	.607	339	290
1973	6	7	1	.464	271	247
1974	7	7	0	.500	256	270
1975	7	7	0	.500	245	262
1976	6	8	0	.429	262	220
1977	6	8	0	.429	183	252
1978	7	9	0	.438	290	300
1979	2	14	0	.125	219	365
1980	9	7	0	.563	334	272
1981	8	8	0	.500	397	322
1982***	4	5	0	.444	181	176
1983†	9	7	0	.563	347	286
1984	4	11	1	.281	283	408
1985	7	9	0	.438	307	366
1986	5	11	0	.313	277	326
27 Years	178	194	15	.478	7498	7322

§NFC Wild Card Qualifier
†NFC Central Division Champion
***NFC Qualifier for Playoffs

COACHING HISTORY

Portsmouth Spartans 1930-33
(360-356-32)

1930-36	George (Potsy) Clark	54-26-9
1937-38	Earl (Dutch) Clark	14-8-0
1939	Gus Henderson	6-5-0
1940	George (Potsy) Clark	5-5-1
1941-42	Bill Edwards*	4-9-1
1942	John Karcis	0-8-0
1943-47	Charles (Gus) Dorais	20-31-2
1948-50	Alvin (Bo) McMillin	12-24-0
1951-56	Raymond (Buddy) Parker	50-24-2
1957-64	George Wilson	55-45-6
1965-66	Harry Gilmer	10-16-2
1967-72	Joe Schmidt	43-35-7
1973	Don McCafferty	6-7-1
1974-76	Rick Forzano**	15-17-0
1976-77	Tommy Hudspeth	11-13-0
1978-84	Monte Clark	43-63-1
1985-86	Darryl Rogers	13-20-0

*Resigned after three games in 1942
**Resigned after four games in 1976

1986 SEASON

	Off.	Def.
Total First Downs	287	286
Rushing	100	118
Passing	156	148
Penalty	31	20
Third Down Efficiency	38.5	39.4
Total Net Yards	4555	4985
Avg. Per Game	284.7	311.6
Total Plays	1009	1017
Avg. Per Play	4.5	4.9
Net Yards Rushing	1771	2200
Avg. Per Game	110.7	137.5
Total Rushes	470	500
Net Yards Passing	2784	2785
Avg. Per Game	174.0	174.1
Tackled/Yards Lost	39/323	53/364
Gross Yards	3107	3149
Att./Completions	500/286	464/226
Completion Pct.	57.2	48.7
Had Intercepted	20	17
Punts/Avg.	85/39.9	87/41.6
Punting Yds.	3389	3620
Penalties/Yards Lost	84/658	91/822
Fumbles/Ball Lost	30/17	29/18
Touchdowns	32	36
Rushing	13	15
Passing	18	14
Returns	1	7
Avg. Time of Possession	29:42	28:46

W	L	T
5	11	0

ALL-TIME GREATS

Hall of Famer Bobby Layne, the brilliant QB who inspired the team for most of the 1950s, still holds the Lions career record for passing yards (15,710) and passing touchdowns (118), and the single season passing touchdown record (26 in 1951).

Jack Christiansen, another Hall of Famer from that era, holds the Lions' career record for punt return average (12.8), individual single season records for interceptions (12 in 1953), punt return average (21.5 in 1952) and retains the NFL's all-time career record for most touchdowns from punt returns (8).

Another all-time record holder is Don Doll, for most yards gained (301) through interceptions in a rookie season (1949), and he also shares the Lions' single season record for interceptions (12) with Christiansen.

Outstanding performers of recent times include Billy Sims, one of the league's best runners, who had his third season rushing for more than 1000 yards in 1983. Ed Murray led the NFC with most field goals (27), in 1980 and was the National Football Conference's annual scoring leader with 116 points in the same year.

THE **PACKERS** STATISTICS

RECORD HOLDERS

Individual Records – Career

Category	Name	Performance
Rushing (Yds)	Jim Taylor, 1958-1966	8207
Passing (Yds)	Bart Starr, 1956-1971	23,718
Passing (TDs)	Bart Starr, 1956-1971	152
Receiving (No)	Don Hutson, 1935-1945	488
Receiving (Yds)	James Lofton, 1978-1985	8816
Interceptions	Bobby Dillon, 1952-1959	52
Punting (Avg)	Bucky Scribner, 1983-1984	42.0
Punt Return (Avg)	Billy Grimes, 1950-1952	13.2
Kickoff Return (Avg)	Dave Hampton, 1970-1971	28.9
Field Goals	Chester Marcol, 1972-1980	120
Touchdowns (Tot)	Don Hutson, 1935-1945	105
Points	Don Hutson, 1935-1945	823

Lynn Dickey QB

Paul Hornung RB

Individual Records – Single Season

Category	Name	Performance
Rushing (Yds)	Jim Taylor, 1962	1407
Passing (Yds)	Lynn Dickey, 1983	4458
Passing (TDs)	Lynn Dickey, 1983	32
Receiving (No)	Don Hutson, 1942	74
Receiving (Yds)	James Lofton, 1984	1361
Interceptions	Irv Comp, 1943	10
Punting (Avg)	Jerry Norton, 1963	44.7
Punt Return (Avg)	Billy Grimes, 1950	19.1
Kickoff Return (Avg)	Travis Williams, 1967	44.1
Field Goals	Chester Marcol, 1972	33
Touchdowns (Tot)	Jim Taylor, 1962	19
Points	Paul Hornung, 1960	176

Individual Records – Single Game

Category	Name	Performance
Rushing (Yds)	Jim Taylor, 3-12-61	186
Passing (Yds)	Lynn Dickey, 12-10-80	418
Passing (TDs)	Many times	
	Last time by Lynn Dickey, 4-9-83	5
Receiving (No)	Don Hutson, 22-11-42	14
Receiving (Yds)	Bill Howton, 21-10-56	257
Interceptions	Bobby Dillon, 26-11-53	4
	Willie Buchanon, 24-9-78	4
Field Goals	Many times.	
	Last time by Al Del Greco, 15-12-85	4
Touchdowns (Tot)	Paul Hornung, 12-12-65	5
Points	Paul Hornung, 8-10-61	33

REGULAR SEASON

Year	W	L	T	Pct.	Pts.	Opp.
1960△	8	4	0	.667	332	209
1961**	11	3	0	.786	391	223
1962**	13	1	0	.929	415	148
1963	11	2	1	.846	369	206
1964	8	5	1	.615	342	245
1965**	10	3	1	.769	316	224
1966*	12	2	0	.857	335	163
1967*	9	4	1	.692	332	209
1968	6	7	1	.462	281	227
1969	8	6	0	.571	269	221
1970	6	8	0	.429	196	293
1971	4	8	2	.333	274	298
1972†	10	4	0	.714	304	226
1973	5	7	2	.429	202	259
1974	6	8	0	.429	210	206
1975	4	10	0	.286	226	285
1976	5	9	0	.357	218	299
1977	4	10	0	.286	134	219
1978	8	7	1	.531	249	269
1979	5	11	0	.313	246	316
1980	5	10	1	.344	231	371
1981	8	8	0	.500	324	361
1982□	5	3	1	.611	226	169
1983	8	8	0	.500	429	439
1984	8	8	0	.500	390	309
1985	8	8	0	.500	337	355
1986	4	12	0	.250	254	418
27 Years	199	176	12	.531	7832	7067

**NFL Champion
△NFL Western Conference Champion
*Super Bowl Champion
†NFC Central Division Champion
□NFC Qualifier for Playoffs

1986 SEASON

	Off.	Def.
Total First Downs	286	313
Rushing	96	135
Passing	172	151
Penalty	18	27
Third Down Efficiency	35.6	43.3
Total Net Yards	5061	5015
Avg. Per Game	316.3	313.4
Total Plays	1026	1041
Avg. Per Play	4.9	4.8
Net Yards Rushing	1614	2095
Avg. Per Game	100.9	130.9
Total Rushes	424	565
Net Yards Passing	3447	2920
Avg. Per Game	215.4	182.5
Tackled/Yards Lost	37/261	28/222
Gross Yards	3708	3142
Att./Completions	565/305	448/267
Completion Pct.	54.0	59.6
Had Intercepted	27	20
Punts/Avg.	75/37.7	70/39.6
Punting Yds.	2825	2769
Penalties/Yards Lost	128/949	79/657
Fumbles/Ball Lost	35/18	31/12
Touchdowns	29	52
Rushing	8	16
Passing	18	31
Returns	3	5
Avg. Time of Possession	28:11	31:49

W	L	T
4	12	0

COACHING HISTORY

Bart Starr QB

(460-364-35)

1921-49	Earl (Curly) Lambeau	212-106-21
1950-53	Gene Ronzani*	14-31-1
1953	Hugh Devore,	
	Ray (Scooter) McLean**	0-2-0
1954-57	Lisle Blackbourn	17-31-0
1958	Ray (Scooter) McLean	1-10-1
1959-67	Vince Lombardi	98-30-4
1968-70	Phil Bengtson	20-21-1
1971-74	Dan Devine	25-28-4
1975-83	Bart Starr	53-77-3
1984-86	Forrest Gregg	20-28-0

*Released after 10 games in 1953
**Co-coaches for 2 games in 1953

ALL-TIME GREATS

They don't come much better than Don Hutson, Green Bay's Hall of Fame wide receiver of the 1930s and '40s. Few of the records he set then have ever been broken. They include: most seasons and most consecutive seasons leading the league in scoring, touchdowns and yards gained. His grand total of 99 career touchdowns is another all-time record.

Bart Starr, the Packers' QB during their heyday of the 1960s and another Hall of Famer, has had the greatest number of consecutive passes without interceptions (294) and the highest postseason pass rating with 108.4. Starr's teammate, the place-kicking running back Paul Hornung, holds the record for scoring the most points in a season, having totalled a massive 176 points in 1960.

Wide receiver James Lofton achieved 8816 receiving yards between 1978-85 – a record.

THE OILERS STATISTICS

COACHING HISTORY

(170-225-6)

Year	Coach	Record
1960-61	Lou Rymkus*	12-7-1
1961	Wally Lemm	10-0-0
1962-63	Frank (Pop) Ivy	17-12-0
1964	Sammy Baugh	4-10-0
1965	Hugh Taylor	4-10-0
1966-70	Wally Lemm	28-40-0
1971	Ed Hughes	4-9-1
1972-73	Bill Peterson**	1-18-0
1973-74	Sid Gillman	8-15-0
1975-80	O.A. (Bum) Phillips	59-38-0
1981-83	Ed Biles***	8-23-0
1983	Chuck Studley	2-8-0
1984-85	Hugh Campbell****	8-22-0
1985-86	Jerry Glanville	5-13-0

*Released after five games in 1961
**Released after five games in 1973
***Resigned after six games in 1983
****Released after 14 games in 1985

Bum Phillips Coach

REGULAR SEASONS

Year	W	L	T	Pct.	Pts	Opp.
1960□	10	4	0	.714	379	285
1961□	10	3	1	.769	513	242
1962△	11	3	0	.786	387	270
1963	6	8	0	.429	302	372
1964	4	10	0	.286	310	355
1965	4	10	0	.286	298	429
1966	3	11	0	.214	335	396
1967△	9	4	1	.692	258	199
1968	7	7	0	.500	303	248
1969	6	6	2	.500	278	279
1970	3	10	1	.231	217	352
1971	4	9	1	.308	251	330
1972	1	13	0	.071	164	380
1973	1	13	0	.071	199	447
1974	7	7	0	.500	236	282
1975	10	4	0	.714	293	226
1976	5	9	0	.357	222	273
1977	8	6	0	.571	299	230
1978§	10	6	0	.625	283	298
1979§	11	5	0	.688	362	331
1980§	11	5	0	.688	295	251
1981	7	9	0	.438	281	355
1982	1	8	0	.111	136	245
1983	2	14	0	.125	288	460
1984	3	13	0	.188	240	437
1985	5	11	0	.313	284	412
1986	5	11	0	.313	274	329
27 Years	164	219	6	.428	7687	8713

□AFL Champion
△AFL Eastern Division Champion
§AFC Wild Card Qualifier for Playoffs

1986 SEASON

	Off.	Def.
Total First Downs	270	285
Rushing	101	102
Passing	179	137
Penalty	19	46
Third Down Efficiency	37.8	35.4
Total Net Yards	5149	5034
Avg. Per Game	321.8	314.6
Total Plays	1089	1054
Avg. Per Play	4.7	4.8
Net Yards Rushing	1700	2035
Avg. Per Game	106.3	127.2
Total Rushes	490	532
Net Yards Passing	3449	2999
Avg. Per Game	215.6	187.4
Tackled/Yards Lost	48/394	32/201
Gross Yards	3843	3200
Att./Completions	551/288	490/228
Completion Pct.	52.3	46.5
Had Intercepted	31	16
Punts/Avg.	89/41.1	86/42.9
Punting Yds.	3659	3689
Penalties/Yards Lost	121/1018	127/1034
Fumbles/Ball Lost	28/12	32/17
Touchdowns	30	36
Rushing	13	13
Passing	14	21
Returns	3	2
Avg. Time of Possession	30:33	29:27

W	L	T
5	11	0

Earl Campbell RB

RECORD HOLDERS

Individual Records – Career

Category	Name	Performance
Rushing (Yds)	Earl Campbell, 1978-1984	8574
Passing (Yds)	George Blanda, 1960-66	19,149
Passing (TDs)	George Blanda, 1960-66	165
Receiving (No.)	Charley Hennigan, 1960-66	410
Receiving (Yds)	Ken Burrough, 1971-1982	6907
Interceptions	Jim Norton, 1960-68	45
Punting (Avg.)	Jim Norton, 1960-68	42.3
Punt Return (Avg.)	Billy Johnson, 1974-1980	13.2
Kickoff Return (Avg.)	Bobby Jancik, 1962-67	26.4
Field Goals	George Blanda, 1960-66	91
Touchdowns (Tot.)	Earl Campbell, 1978-1984	73
Points	George Blanda, 1960-66	596

Individual Records – Single Season

Category	Name	Performance
Rushing (Yds)	Earl Campbell, 1980	1934
Passing (Yds)	Warren Moon, 1984	3338
Passing (TDs)	George Blanda, 1961	36
Receiving (No.)	Charley Hennigan, 1964	101
Receiving (Yds)	Charley Hennigan, 1961	1746
Interceptions	Fred Glick, 1963	12
	Mike Reinfeldt, 1979	12
Punting (Avg.)	Jim Norton, 1965	44.2
Punt Return (Avg.)	Billy Johnson, 1977	15.4
Kickoff Return (Avg.)	Ken Hall, 1960	31.2
Field Goals	Toni Fritsch, 1979	21
	Tony Zendejas, 1985	21
Touchdowns (Tot.)	Earl Campbell, 1979	19
Points	George Blanda, 1960	115

Individual Records – Single Game

Category	Name	Performance
Rushing (Yds)	Billy Cannon, 10-12-61	216
Passing (Yds)	George Blanda, 29-10-61	464
Passing (TDs)	George Blanda, 19-11-61	7
Receiving (No.)	Charley Hennigan, 13-10-61	13
Receiving (Yds)	Charley Hennigan, 13-10-61	272
Interceptions	Many times	3
	Last time by Willie Alexander, 14-11-71	
Field Goals	Skip Butler, 12-10-75	6
Touchdowns (Tot.)	Billy Cannon, 10-12-61	5
Points	Billy Cannon, 10-12-61	30

ALL-TIME GREATS

No other player in the history of the NFL lasted as long as the Houston Oilers' legendary quarterback George Blanda, who played for an incredible 26 seasons. Blanda's career spanned four decades, beginning in 1949 and ending in 1975. Blanda holds the all-time NFL record for games played in a career (340), but he isn't in the record books for his longevity alone. Blanda was also a superbly accurate kicker. He holds the all-time record for most points in a career (2002, nine-TD, 943-PAT, 335-FG), most seasons leading the league in points after touchdown (eight), and most points after touchdown, career (943).

The man Blanda threw so successfully to during his early years with the Oilers

George Blanda QB

was Charley Hennigan. He holds a fistful of all-time NFL pass receiving records, including most yards gained in a season with 1746 in 1961, most games with 200 or more yards pass receiving in a season (three in 1961), most games 100 or more yards pass receiving in a season (10 in 1961), and most consecutive games with 100 or more yards pass receiving (seven in 1961).

Earl Campbell was Houston's number-one draft choice in 1978. For the next seven seasons Campbell proceeded to tear up the league, leading the NFL in rushing for four straight years (1978-81). He now holds Oiler records for career rushing (8574 yards, 1978-84) and single season rushing (1934 yards, 1980).

THE COLTS STATISTICS

1986 SEASON

	Off.	Def.
Total First Downs	282	334
Rushing	77	123
Passing	173	185
Penalty	28	26
Third Down Efficiency	34.7	41.6
Total Net Yards	4700	5701
Avg. Per Game	293.8	356.3
Total Plays	1046	1051
Avg. Per Play	4.5	5.4
Net Yards Rushing	407	1962
Avg. Per Game	93.2	122.6
Total Rushes	407	517
Net Yards Passing	3209	3739
Avg. Per Game	200.6	233.7
Tackled/Yards Lost	53/406	24/194
Gross Yards	3615	3933
Att./Completions	586/300	510/306
Completion Pct.	51.2	60.0
Had Intercepted	24	16
Punts/Avg.	81/44.7	67/40.7
Punting Yds.	3622	2725
Penalties/Yards Lost	99/880	100/728
Fumbles/Ball Lost	41/20	41/19
Touchdowns	27	47
Rushing	10	14
Passing	16	28
Returns	1	5
Avg. Time of Possession	29:12	30:48

W	L	T
3	13	0

Johnny Unitas QB

ALL-TIME GREATS

Three of the finest offensive players in NFL annals played for the Colts. Johnny Unitas, perhaps the greatest quarterback ever, held NFL records for most seasons with one club (17, 1956-72), most yards gained, passing, career (40,239) and most passes completed, career (2830). The flashy and brilliant flanker, Lenny Moore, established NFL bests for most consecutive games scoring TDs (18, 1963-65) and most touchdowns in his career (113, 1956-67). And the man with hands of glue, receiver Raymond Berry, set records for most seasons, 50 or more pass receptions (7, 1958-62 and 1965-66) and finished 2nd in most seasons leading the league in yards gained (3, 1957 and 1959-60).

RECORD HOLDERS

Individual Records – Career

Category	Name	Performance
Rushing (Yds)	Lydell Mitchell, 1972-1977	5487
Passing (Yds)	Johnny Unitas, 1956-1972	39,768
Passing (TDs)	Johnny Unitas, 1956-1972	287
Receiving (No.)	Raymond Berry, 1955-1967	631
Receiving (Yds)	Raymond Berry, 1955-1967	9275
Interceptions	Bob Boyd, 1960-1968	57
Punting (Avg.)	Rohn Stark, 1982-1985	45.2
Punt Return (Avg.)	Wendell Harris, 1964	12.6
Kickoff Return (Avg.)	Jim Duncan, 1969-1971	32.5
Field Goals	Lou Michaels, 1964-1969	107
Touchdowns (Tot.)	Lenny Moore, 1956-1967	113
Points	Lenny Moore, 1956-1967	678

Individual Records – Single Season

Category	Name	Performance
Rushing (Yds)	Lydell Mitchell, 1976	1200
Passing (Yds)	Johnny Unitas, 1963	3481
Passing (TDs)	Johnny Unitas, 1959	32
Receiving (No.)	Joe Washington, 1979	82
Receiving (Yds)	Raymond Berry, 1960	1298
Interceptions	Tom Keane, 1953	11
Punting (Avg.)	Rohn Stark, 1985	45.9
Punt Return (Avg.)	Wendell Harris, 1964	12.6
Kickoff Return (Avg.)	Jim Duncan, 1970	35.4
Field Goals	Raul Allegre, 1983	30
Touchdowns (Tot.)	Lenny Moore, 1964	20
Points	Lenny Moore, 1964	120

Individual Records – Single Game

Category	Name	Performance
Rushing (Yds)	Norm Bulaich, 19-9-71	198
Passing (Yds)	Johnny Unitas, 17-9-67	401
Passing (TDs)	Gary Cuozzo, 14-11-65	5
Receiving (No.)	Lydell Mitchell, 15-12-74	13
	Joe Washington, 2-9-79	13
Receiving (Yds)	Raymond Berry, 10-11-57	224
Interceptions	Many times.	
	Last time by Eugene Daniel, 27-10-85	3
Field Goals	Many times.	
	Last time by Raul Allegre, 30-10-83	5
Touchdowns (Tot.)	Many times.	
	Last time by Lydell Mitchell, 12-10-75	4
Points	Many times.	
	Last time by Lydell Mitchell, 12-10-75	24

Raymond Berry WR

REGULAR SEASONS

Year	W	L	T	Pct.	Pts	Opp.
1960	6	6	0	.500	288	234
1961	8	6	0	.571	302	307
1962	7	7	0	.500	293	288
1963	8	6	0	.571	316	285
1964 △	12	2	0	.857	428	225
1965	10	3	1	.769	389	284
1966	9	5	0	.643	314	226
1967	11	1	2	.917	394	198
1968**	13	1	0	.929	402	144
1969	8	5	1	.615	279	268
1970*	11	2	1	.846	321	234
1971§	10	4	0	.714	313	140
1972	5	9	0	.357	235	252
1973	4	10	0	.286	226	341
1974	2	12	0	.143	190	329
1975†	10	4	0	.714	395	269
1976†	11	3	0	.786	417	246
1977†	10	4	0	.714	295	221
1978	5	11	0	.313	239	421
1979	5	11	0	.313	271	351
1980	7	9	0	.438	355	387
1981	2	14	0	.125	259	533
1982	0	8	1	.056	113	236
1983	7	9	0	.438	264	354
1984	4	12	0	.250	239	414
1985	5	11	0	.313	320	386
1986	3	13	0	.188	229	400
27 Years	193	188	6	.507	8086	7623

△ NFL Western Conference Champion
** NFL Champion
* Super Bowl Champion
§ AFC Wild Card Qualifier for Playoffs
† Eastern Division Champion

COACHING HISTORY

(241-237-7)

Year	Coach	Record
1953	Keith Molesworth	3-9-0
1954-62	Weeb Ewbank	61-52-1
1963-69	Don Shula	73-26-4
1970-72	Don McCafferty*	26-11-1
1972	John Sandusky	4-5-0
1973-74	Howard Schnellenberger**	4-13-0
1974	Joe Thomas	2-9-0
1975-79	Ted Marchibroda	41-36-0
1980-81	Mike McCormack	9-23-0
1982-84	Frank Kush***	11-28-1
1984	Hal Hunter	0-1-0
1985-86	Rod Dowhower****	5-24-0
1986	Ron Meyer	3-0-0

*Released after five games in 1972
**Released after three games in 1974
***Resigned after 15 games in 1984
****Released after 13 games in 1986

Lydell Mitchell RB

Rohn Stark P

THE CHIEFS STATISTICS

RECORD HOLDERS

Individual Records – Career

Category	Name	Performance
Rushing (Yds)	Ed Podolak, 1969-1977	4451
Passing (Yds)	Len Dawson, 1962-1975	28,507
Passing (TDs)	Len Dawson, 1962-1975	237
Receiving (No.)	Otis Taylor, 1965-1975	410
Receiving (Yds)	Otis Taylor, 1965-1975	7306
Interceptions	Emmitt Thomas, 1966-1978	58
Punting (Avg.)	Jerrel Wilson, 1963-1977	43.5
Punt Return (Avg.)	J. T. Smith, 1979-1984	10.6
Kickoff Return (Avg.)	Noland Smith, 1967-1969	26.8
Field Goals	Jan Stenerud, 1967-1979	279
Touchdowns (Tot.)	Otis Taylor, 1965-1975	60
Points	Jan Stenerud, 1967-1979	1231

Individual Records – Single Season

Category	Name	Performance
Rushing (Yds)	Joe Delaney, 1981	1121
Passing (Yds)	Bill Kenney, 1983	4348
Passing (TDs)	Len Dawson, 1964	30
Receiving (No.)	Carlos Carson, 1983	80
Receiving (Yds)	Carlos Carson, 1983	1351
Interceptions	Emmitt Thomas, 1974	12
Punting (Avg.)	Jerrel Wilson, 1965	46.0
Punt Return (Avg.)	Abner Haynes, 1960	15.4
Kickoff Return (Avg.)	Dave Grayson, 1962	29.7
Field Goals	Jan Stenerud, 1968, 1970	30
Touchdowns (Tot.)	Abner Haynes, 1962	19
Points	Jan Stenerud, 1968	129

Individual Records – Single Game

Category	Name	Performance
Rushing (Yds)	Joe Delaney, 15-11-81	193
Passing (Yds)	Len Dawson, 1-11-64	435
Passing (TDs)	Len Dawson, 1-11-64	6
Receiving (No.)	Ed Podolak, 7-10-73	12
Receiving (Yds)	Stephone Paige, 22-12-85	309
Interceptions	Bobby Ply, 16-12-62	4
	Bobby Hunt, 4-12-64	4
Field Goals	Jan Stenerud, 2-11-69	5
	Jan Stenerud, 7-12-69	5
	Jan Stenerud, 19-12-71	5
Touchdowns (Tot.)	Abner Haynes, 26-11-61	5
Points	Abner Haynes, 26-11-61	30

REGULAR SEASONS

Year	W	L	T	Pct.	Pts	Opp.
1960	8	6	0	.571	362	253
1961	6	8	0	.429	334	343
1962□	11	3	0	.786	389	233
1963	5	7	2	.417	347	263
1964	7	7	0	.500	366	306
1965	7	5	2	.583	322	285
1966□	11	2	1	.846	448	276
1967	9	5	0	.643	408	254
1968	12	2	0	.857	371	170
1969*	11	3	0	.786	359	177
1970	7	5	2	.583	272	244
1971†	10	3	1	.769	302	208
1972	8	6	0	.571	287	254
1973	7	5	2	.571	231	192
1974	5	9	0	.357	233	293
1975	5	9	0	.357	282	341
1976	5	9	0	.357	290	376
1977	2	12	0	.143	225	349
1978	4	12	0	.250	243	327
1979	7	9	0	.438	238	262
1980	8	8	0	.500	319	336
1981	9	7	0	.563	343	290
1982	3	6	0	.333	176	184
1983	6	10	0	.375	386	367
1984	8	8	0	.500	314	324
1985	6	10	0	.375	317	360
1986	10	6	0	.625	358	326
27 Years	197	182	10	.519	8522	7593

□ AFL Champion
* Super Bowl Champion
† AFC Western Division Champion

ALL-TIME GREATS

The finest quarterback ever to don a Kansas City uniform was Len Dawson. In a Chiefs' career that spanned 14 seasons, Dawson broke and still holds almost every Kansas City passing record. They include most yards passing, career (28,507, 1962-1975), most touchdowns passing, career (237), most touchdowns passing, season (30, 1964), most yards passing, game (435, 1 November 1964), and most touchdowns passing, game (six, 1 November 1964).

The Norwegian placekicker Jan Stenerud can find his name in the Chiefs' record book more times than any other player in Kansas City annals. He holds a slew of records which include most field goals, career (279, 1967-1979), most points, career (1231), most field goals, season (30, 1968 and 1970), most points, season (129, 1968), and most field goals, game (five, 2 November 1969, 7 December 1969, and 19 December 1971).

The Chiefs have had a number of excellent receivers throughout the years, but none better than Otis Taylor. Despite being somewhat injury-prone, Taylor owns Kansas City records for most number of receptions, career (410, 1965-1975), most yards receiving, career (7306), and most total touchdowns, career (60).

COACHING HISTORY

Dallas Texans 1960-62 (202-185-10)		
1960-74 Hank Stram	129-79-10	
1975-77 Paul Wiggin*	11-24-0	
1977 Tom Bettis	1-6-0	
1978-82 Marv Levy	31-42-0	
1983-86 John Mackovic	30-34-0	

*Replaced after seven games in 1977

1986 SEASON

	Off.	Def.
Total First Downs	258	310
Rushing	83	111
Passing	152	173
Penalty	29	26
Third Down Efficiency	33.6	35.7
Total Net Yards	4218	4934
Avg. Per Game	263.6	308.4
Total Plays	1003	1098
Avg. Per Play	4.2	4.5
Net Yards Rushing	1468	1739
Avg. Per Game	91.8	108.7
Total Rushes	432	485
Net Yards Passing	2750	3195
Avg. Per Game	171.9	199.7
Tackled/Yards Lost	50/372	44/360

	Off.	Def.
Gross Yards	3122	3555
Att./Completions	521/257	569/303
Completion Pct.	49.3	53.3
Had Intercepted	18	31
Punts/Avg.	99/40.7	83/37.0
Punting Yds.	4033	3067
Penalties/Yards Lost	97/829	114/965
Fumbles/Ball Lost	27/17	26/18
Touchdowns	43	38
Rushing	10	13
Passing	23	21
Returns	10	4
Avg. Time of Possession	28:29	31:31

W	L	T
10	6	0

During one of their 10 losing games, Scott Radecic makes a successful tackle on Chargers' Pete Holohan.

THE **RAIDERS** STATISTICS

COACHING HISTORY

Years	Coach	Record
1960-61	Eddie Erdelatz	6-10-0
1961-62	Marty Feldman	2-15-0
1962	William (Red) Conkright	1-8-0
1963-65	Al Davis	23-16-3
1966-68	John Rauch	35-10-1
1969-78	John Madden	112-39-7
1979-86	Tom Flores	86-46-0

1986 SEASON

	Off.	Def.
Total First Downs	304	283
Rushing	97	85
Passing	186	168
Penalty	19	30
Third Down Efficiency	38.9	37.7
Total Net Yards	5299	4804
Avg. Per Game	331.2	300.3
Total Plays	1069	1003
Avg. Per Play	5.0	4.8
Net Yards Rushing	1790	1728
Avg. Per Game	111.9	108.0
Total Rushes	475	439
Net Yards Passing	3509	3076
Avg. Per Game	219.3	192.3
Tackled/Yards Lost	64/464	63/463
Gross Yards	3973	3539
Att./Completions	530/281	501/271
Completion Pct.	53.0	54.1
Had Intercepted	25	26
Punts/Avg.	90/40.2	97/41.4
Punting Yds.	3620	2648
Penalties/Yards Lost	114/951	118/868
Fumbles/Ball Lost	36/24	33/12
Touchdowns	37	43
Rushing	6	19
Passing	27	21
Returns	4	3
Avg. Time of Possession	30:40	29:20

W	L	T
8	8	0

Lost to New England in conference semifinal

RECORD HOLDERS

Individual Records – Career

Category	Name	Performance
Rushing (Yds)	Mark van Eeghen, 1974-1981	5907
Passing (Yds)	Ken Stabler, 1970-79	19,078
Passing (TDs)	Ken Stabler, 1970-79	150
Receiving (No.)	Fred Biletnikoff, 1965-1978	589
Receiving (Yds)	Fred Biletnikoff, 1965-1978	8974
Interceptions	Willie Brown, 1967-1978	39
Punting (Avg.)	Ray Guy, 1973-1985	42.6
Punt Return (Avg.)	Claude Gibson, 1963-65	12.6
Kickoff Return (Avg.)	Jack Larscheid, 1960-61	28.4
Field Goals	George Blanda, 1967-1975	156
Touchdowns (Tot.)	Fred Biletnikoff, 1965-1978	77
Points	George Blanda, 1967-1975	863

Individual Records – Single Season

Category	Name	Performance
Rushing (Yds)	Marcus Allen, 1985	1759
Passing (Yds)	Ken Stabler, 1979	3615
Passing (TDs)	Daryle Lamonica, 1969	34
Receiving (No.)	Todd Christensen, 1983	92
Receiving (Yds)	Art Powell, 1964	1,361
Interceptions	Lester Hayes, 1980	13
Punting (Avg.)	Ray Guy, 1973	45.3
Punt Return (Avg.)	Claude Gibson, 1963	14.4
Kickoff Return (Avg.)	Harold Hart, 1975	30.5
Field Goals	George Blanda, 1973	23
Touchdowns (Tot.)	Marcus Allen, 1984	18
Points	George Blanda, 1968	117

Individual Records – Single Game

Category	Name	Performance
Rushing (Yds)	Clem Daniel, 20-10-63	200
Passing (Yds)	Cotton Davidson, 25-10-64	427
Passing (TDs)	Tom Flores, 22-12-63	6
	Daryle Lamonica, 19-10-69	6
Receiving (No.)	Dave Casper, 3-10-76	12
Receiving (Yds)	Art Powell, 22-12-63	247
Interceptions	Many times	3
	Last time by Charles Phillips, 8-12-75	
Field Goals	Many times	4
	Last time by Chris Bahr, 6-10-85	
Touchdowns (Tot.)	Art Powell, 22-12-63	4
	Marcus Allen, 24-9-84	4
Points	Art Powell, 22-12-63	24
	Marcus Allen, 24-9-84	24

REGULAR SEASONS

Year	W	L	T	Pct.	Pts.	Opp.
Oakland Raiders						
1960	6	8	0	.429	319	388
1961	2	12	0	.143	237	458
1962	1	13	0	.071	213	370
1963	10	4	0	.714	363	288
1964	5	7	2	.417	303	350
1965	8	5	1	.615	298	239
1966	8	5	1	.615	315	288
1967**	13	1	0	.929	468	233
1968△	12	2	0	.857	453	233
1969△	12	1	1	.923	377	242
1970†	8	4	2	.667	300	293
1971	8	4	2	.667	344	278
1972†	10	3	1	.750	365	248
1973†	9	4	1	.679	292	175
1974†	12	2	0	.857	355	228
1975†	11	3	0	.786	375	255
1976*	13	1	0	.929	350	237
1977§	11	3	0	.786	351	230
1978	9	7	0	.563	311	283
1979	9	7	0	.563	365	337
1980*	11	5	0	.688	364	306
1981	7	9	0	.438	273	343
Los Angeles Raiders						
1982†	8	1	0	.889	260	200
1983*	12	4	0	.750	442	338
1984§	11	5	0	.688	368	278
1985†	12	4	0	.750	354	308
1986	8	8	0	.500	323	346
27 Years	246	132	11	.651	9108	8072

** AFL Champion
△ AFL Western Division Champion
† AFC Western Division Champion
* Super Bowl Champion
§ AFC Wild Card Qualifier for Playoffs

ALL-TIME GREATS

Marcus Allen, the MVP of Super Bowl XVIII, holds Super Bowl records for highest average gain (9.6), most yards gained in a game (191) and longest run from scrimmage (74). Kicker George Blanda, who played eight of his 26 seasons with the Raiders, has scored the most PATs ever and punter Ray Guy has led the NFL for three seasons.

Howie Long DE

Marcus Allen QB

Tom Flores Coach

THE **RAMS** STATISTICS

RECORD HOLDERS

Individual Records – Career

Category	Name	Performance
Rushing (Yds)	Lawrence McCutcheon, 1973-1979	6186
Passing (Yds)	Roman Gabriel, 1962-1972	22,223
Passing (TDs)	Roman Gabriel, 1962-1972	154
Receiving (No.)	Tom Fears, 1948-1956	400
Receiving (Yds)	Elroy Hirsch, 1949-1957	6289
Interceptions	Ed Meador, 1959-1970	46
Punting (Avg.)	Danny Villanueva, 1960-1964	44.2
Punt Return (Avg.)	Henry Ellard, 1983-85	13.5
Kickoff Return (Avg.)	Ron Brown, 1984-85	32.8
Field Goals	Bruce Gossett, 1964-69	120
Touchdowns (Tot.)	Elroy Hirsch, 1949-1957	55
Points	Bob Waterfield, 1946-1952	573

Vince Ferragmo QB

Lawrence McCutcheon RB

Individual Records – Single Season

Category	Name	Performance
Rushing (Yds)	Eric Dickerson, 1984	2105
Passing (Yds)	Vince Ferragamo, 1983	3276
Passing (TDs)	Vince Ferragamo, 1980	30
Receiving (No.)	Tom Fears, 1950	84
Receiving (Yds)	Elroy Hirsch, 1951	1425
Interceptions	Dick (Night Train) Lane, 1952	14
Punting (Avg.)	Danny Villanueva, 1962	45.5
Punt Return (Avg.)	Woodley Lewis, 1952	18.5
Kickoff Return (Avg.)	Verda (Vitamin T) Smith, 1950	33.7
Field Goals	David Ray, 1973	30
Touchdowns (Tot.)	Eric Dickerson, 1983	20
Points	David Ray, 1973	130

Individual Records – Single Game

Category	Name	Performance
Rushing (Yds)	Eric Dickerson, 4-1-86	248
Passing (Yds)	Norm Van Brocklin, 28-9-51	554
Passing (TDs)	Many times	5
	Last time by Vince Ferragamo, 23-10-83	
Receiving (No.)	Tom Fears, 3-12-50	18
Receiving (Yds)	Jim Benton, 22-11-45	303
Interceptions	Many times	3
	Last time by Pat Thomas, 7-10-79	
Field Goals	Bob Waterfield, 9-12-51	5
Touchdowns (Tot.)	Bob Shaw, 11-12-49	4
	Elroy Hirsch, 28-9-51	4
	Harold Jackson, 14-10-73	4
Points	Bob Shaw, 11-12-49	24
	Elroy Hirsch, 28-9-51	24
	Harold Jackson, 14-10-73	24

COACHING HISTORY

Cleveland 1937-45
(359-291-20)

1937-38	Hugo Bezdek*	1-13-0
1938	Art Lewis	4-4-0
1939-42	Earl (Dutch) Clark	16-26-2
1944	Aldo (Buff) Donelli	4-6-0
1945-46	Adam Walsh	16-5-1
1947	Bob Snyder	6-6-0
1948-49	Clark Shaughnessy	14-8-3
1950-52	Joe Stydahar**	19-9-0
1952-54	Hamp Pool	23-11-2
1955-59	Sid Gillman	28-32-1
1960-62	Bob Waterfield***	9-24-1
1962-65	Harland Svare	14-31-3
1966-70	George Allen	49-19-4
1971-72	Tommy Prothro	14-12-2
1973-77	Chuck Knox	57-20-1
1978-82	Ray Malavasi	43-36-0
1983-86	John Robinson	42-27-0

*Released after three games in 1938
**Resigned after one game in 1952
***Resigned after eight games in 1962

Roman Gabriel QB

ALL-TIME GREATS

In a half-century of football, the Rams have never had a greater running back than Eric Dickerson. He holds the all-time NFL record for most yards gained in a single season (2105, 1984) and for most yards gained in a playoff game (248 Rams vs Dallas, 4 January 1986).

Elroy (Crazylegs) Hirsch was the Rams' shining light in the 1950s. His bandy-legged gait earned Hirsch his nickname but his hands never wavered. He holds Rams records for most yards receiving, career (6289, 1949-1957), most touchdowns, career (55), and most yards receiving, season (1425 in 1951). Hirsch was inducted into the Hall of Fame in 1968.

Another Hall of Famer was the Rams' fiercest defensive tackle, Merlin Olsen. A first-round draft choice in 1962, Olsen joined the 1960s finest defensive front four (with Deacon Jones, Roosevelt Grier, and Lamar Lundy) and became their leader.

REGULAR SEASON

Year	W	L	T	Pct.	Pts	Opp.
1960	4	7	1	.364	265	297
1961	4	10	0	.286	263	333
1962	1	12	1	.077	220	334
1963	5	9	0	.357	210	350
1964	5	7	2	.417	283	339
1965	4	10	0	.286	269	328
1966	8	6	0	.571	289	212
1967☐	11	1	2	.917	398	196
1968	10	3	1	.769	312	200
1969☐	11	3	0	.786	320	243
1970	9	4	1	.692	325	202
1971	8	5	1	.615	313	260
1972	6	7	1	.464	291	286
1973†	12	2	0	.857	388	178
1974†	10	4	0	.714	263	181
1975†	12	2	0	.857	312	135
1976†	10	3	1	.750	351	190
1977†	10	4	0	.714	302	146
1978†	12	4	0	.750	316	245
1979‡	9	7	0	.563	323	309
1980§	11	5	0	.688	424	289
1981	6	10	0	.375	303	351
1982	2	7	0	.222	200	250
1983§	9	7	0	.563	361	344
1984§	10	6	0	.625	346	316
1985†	11	5	0	.688	340	277
1986	10	6	0	.625	309	267
27 Years	220	166	11	.580	8296	7058

☐ NFL Coastal Division Champion
† NFC Western Division Champion
‡ NFC Champion
§ NFC Wild Card Qualifier

1986 SEASON

	Off.	Def.
Total First Downs	269	272
Rushing	139	93
Passing	105	169
Penalty	25	10
Third Down Efficiency	33.3	31.1
Total Net Yards	4653	4871
Avg. Per Game	290.8	304.4
Total Plays	1008	1038
Avg. Per Play	4.6	4.7
Net Yards Rushing	2457	1681
Avg. Per Game	153.6	105.1
Total Rushes	578	460
Net Yards Passing	2196	3190
Avg. Per Game	137.3	199.4
Tackled/Yards Lost	27/184	39/292
Gross Yards	2380	3482
Att./Completions	403/194	539/313
Completion Pct.	48.1	58.1
Had Intercepted	15	28
Punts/Avg.	98/38.2	96/41.4
Punting Yds.	3740	3975
Penalties/Yards Lost	84/603	92/804
Fumbles/Ball Lost	39/22	25/15
Touchdowns	37	28
Rushing	16	9
Passing	15	17
Returns	6	2
Avg. Time of Possession	29:41	30:19

W	L	T
10	6	0

THE *Dolphins* STATISTICS

REGULAR SEASONS

Year	W	L	T	Pct.	Pts	Opp.
1966	3	11	0	.214	213	362
1967	4	10	0	.286	219	407
1968	5	8	1	.385	276	355
1969	3	10	1	.231	233	332
1970§	10	4	0	.714	297	228
1971‡	10	3	1	.769	315	174
1972*	14	0	0	1,000	385	171
1973*	12	2	0	.857	343	150
1974△	11	3	0	.786	327	216
1975	10	4	0	.714	367	422
1976	6	8	0	.429	263	264
1977	10	4	0	.714	313	197
1978§	11	5	0	.688	372	254
1979△	10	6	0	.625	341	257
1980	8	8	0	.500	266	305
1981△	11	4	1	.719	345	275
1982‡	7	2	0	.778	198	131
1983△	12	4	0	.750	389	250
1984‡	14	2	0	.875	513	298
1985△	12	4	0	.750	428	320
1986	8	8	0	.500	430	405
27 Years	191	110	4	.635	6843	5573

§ AFC Wild Card qualifier for play offs
‡ AFC Champion
* Super Bowl Champion
△ AFC Eastern Division Champion

ALL-TIME GREATS

Two greats of the Dolphins are Dan Marino and Mark Clayton. Magic Marino holds the NFL rookie pass rating record with 96.0 in 1983, the most yards gained in a season with 5084 in 1984, and has the most games with 300 or more yards gained consecutively, with 5 in the 1984 season. Mark Clayton has the record for most touchdowns in a season with 18 in 1984.

RECORD HOLDERS

Individual Records — Career

Category	Name	Performance
Rushing (Yds)	Larry Csonka, 1968-1974, 1979	6737
Passing (Yds)	Bob Griese, 1967-1980	25,092
Passing (TDs)	Bob Griese, 1967-1980	192
Receiving (No.)	Nat Moore, 1974-1985	472
Receiving (Yds)	Nat Moore 1974-1980	7116
Interceptions	Jake Scott, 1970-75	35
Punting (Avg.)	Reggie Roby, 1983-85	43.7
Punt Return (Avg.)	Freddie Solomon, 1975-77	11.4
Kickoff Return (Avg.)	Mercury Morris, 1969-1975	26.5
Field Goals	Garo Yepremian, 1970-78	165
Touchdowns (Tot.)	Nat Moore, 1974-85	68
Points	Garo Yepremian, 1970-78	830

Individual Records — Single Season

Category	Name	Performance
Rushing (Yds)	Delvin Williams, 1978	1258
Passing (Yds)	Dan Marino, 1984	5084
Passing (TDs)	Dan Marino, 1984	48
Receiving (No.)	Mark Clayton, 1984	73
Receiving (Yds)	Mark Clayton, 1984	1389
Interceptions	Dick Westmoreland, 1967	10
Punting (Avg.)	Reggie Roby, 1984	44.7
Punt Return (Avg.)	Freddie Solomon, 1975	12.3
Kickoff Return (Avg.)	Durial Harris, 1976	32.9
Field Goals	Garo Yepremian, 1971	28
Touchdowns (Tot.)	Mark Clayton, 1984	18
Points	Garo Yepremian, 1971	117

Individual Records — Single Game

Category	Name	Performance
Rushing (Yds)	Mercury Morris, 30.9.73	197
Passing (Yds)	Dan Marino, 2.12.84	470
Passing (TDs)	Bob Griese, 24.11.77	6
Receiving (No.)	Duriel Harris, 28.10.79, Tony Nathan 29.9.85	10
Receiving (Yds)	Mark Duper, 10.11.85	217
Interceptions	Dick Anderson, 3.12.73	4
Field Goals	Garo Yepremian, 26.9.71	5
Touchdowns (Tot.)	Paul Warfield, 15.12.73	4
Points	Paul Warfield, 15.12.73	24

1986 SEASON

	Off.	Def.
Total First Downs	361	337
Rushing	84	144
Passing	250	177
Penalty	17	16
Third Down Efficiency	50.8	41.1
Total Net Yards	6374	6050
Avg. Per Game	395.3	378.1
Total Plays	1011	1058
Avg. Per Play	6.3	5.7
Net Yards Rushing	1545	2493
Avg. Per Game	96.6	155.8
Total Rushes	349	540
Net Yards Passing	4779	3557
Avg. Per Game	298.7	222.3
Tackled/Yards Lost	17/119	33/268
Gross Yards	4898	3825
Att./Completions	645/392	485/290
Completion Pct.	60.8	59.8
Had Intercepted	23	13
Punts/Avg.	56/44.2	64/41.4
Punting Yds.	2476	2648
Penalties/Yards Lost	72/609	82/596
Fumbles/Ball Lost	37/14	32/14
Touchdowns	56	47
Rushing	9	23
Passing	46	22
Returns	1	2
Avg. Time of Possession	29:24	30:36

W	L	T
8	8	0

Lost to New England in AFC Championship

COACHING HISTORY

1966-69 George Wilson 15-39-2
1970-86 Don Shula 190-81-2

Dan Marino QB

Don Shula Coach

Bob Griese QB

THE VIKINGS STATISTICS

1986 SEASON

	Off.	Def.
Total First Downs	321	286
Rushing	114	106
Passing	186	155
Penalty	21	25
Third Down Efficiency	42.0	36.9
Total Net Yards	5651	5012
Avg. Per Game	353.2	313.3
Total Plays	1024	1013
Avg. Per Play	5.5	4.9
Net Yards Rushing	1738	1796
Avg. Per Game	108.6	112.3
Total Rushes	461	481
Net Yards Passing	3913	3216
Avg. Per Game	244.6	201.0
Tackled/Yards Lost	44/272	38/259
Gross Yards	4185	3475
Att./Completions	519/290	494/276
Completion Pct.	55.9	55.9
Had Intercepted	15	24
Punts/Avg.	73/40.0	75/40.3
Punting Yds.	2922	3021
Penalties/Yards Lost	96/890	99/806
Fumbles/Ball Lost	31/14	32/18
Touchdowns	48	28
Rushing	14	10
Passing	31	16
Returns	3	2
Avg. Time of Possession	30:15	29:45

W	L	T
9	7	0

Ahmad Rashad WR

RECORD HOLDERS

Individual Records – Career

Category	Name	Performance
Rushing (Yds)	Chuck Foreman, 1973-1979	5879
Passing (Yds)	Frank Tarkenton, 1961-1966, 1972-1978	33,098
Passing (TDs)	Frank Tarkenton, 1961-1966, 1972-1978	239
Receiving (No.)	Ahmad Rashad, 1976-1982	400
Receiving (Yds)	Sammy White, 1976-1985	5925
Interceptions	Paul Krause, 1968-1979	53
Punting (Avg.)	Bobby Walden, 1964-1967	42.9
Punt Return (Avg.)	Tommy Mason, 1961-1966	10.5
Kickoff Return (Avg.)	Bob Reed, 1962-1963	27.1
Field Goals	Fred Cox, 1963-1967	282
Touchdowns (Tot.)	Bill Brown, 1962-1974	76
Points	Fred Cox, 1963-1977	1365

Individual Records – Single Season

Category	Name	Performance
Rushing (Yds)	Chuck Foreman, 1976	1155
Passing (Yds)	Tommy Kramer, 1981	3912
Passing (TDs)	Tommy Kramer, 1981	26
Receiving (No.)	Rickey Young, 1978	88
Receiving (Yds)	Ahmad Rashad, 1979	1156
Interceptions	Paul Krause, 1975	10
Punting (Avg.)	Bobby Walden, 1964	46.4
Punt Return (Avg.)	Billy Butler, 1963	10.5
Kickoff Return (Avg.)	John Gilliam, 1972	26.3
Field Goals	Fred Cox, 1970	30
Touchdowns (Tot.)	Chuck Foreman, 1975	22
Points	Chuck Foreman, 1975	132

Individual Records – Single Game

Category	Name	Performance
Rushing (Yds)	Chuck Foreman, 24.10.76	200
Passing (Yds)	Tommy Kramer, 14.12.80	456
Passing (TDs)	Joe Kapp, 28.9.69	7
Receiving (No.)	Rickey Young, 16.12.79	15
Receiving (Yds)	Sammy White, 7.11.76	210
Interceptions	Many times	3
	Last time by Willie Teal, 28.11.82	
Field Goals	Fred Cox, 23.9.73	5
	Jan Stenerud, 23.9.74	5
Touchdowns (Tot.)	Chuck Foreman, 20.12.75	4
	Ahmad Rashad, 2.9.79	4
Points	Chuck Foreman, 20.12.75	24
	Ahmad Rashad, 2.9.79	24

REGULAR SEASONS

Year	W	L	T	Pct.	Pts	Opp.
1961	3	11	0	.214	285	407
1962	2	11	1	.154	254	410
1963	5	8	1	.385	309	390
1964	8	5	1	.615	355	296
1965	7	7	0	.500	383	403
1966	4	9	1	.308	292	304
1967	3	8	3	.273	233	294
1968 △	8	6	0	.571	282	242
1969**	12	2	0	.857	379	133
1970†	12	2	0	.857	335	143
1971†	11	3	0	.786	245	139
1972	7	7	0	.500	301	252
1973‡	12	2	0	.857	296	168
1974‡	10	4	0	.714	310	195
1975†	12	2	0	.857	377	180
1976‡	11	2	1	.821	305	176
1977†	9	5	0	.643	231	227
1978†	8	7	1	.531	294	306
1979	7	9	0	.438	259	337
1980†	9	7	0	.563	317	308
1981	7	9	0	.438	325	369
1982	5	4	0	.556	187	198
1983	8	8	0	.500	316	348
1984	3	13	0	.188	276	484
1985	7	9	0	.438	346	359
1986	9	7	0	.563	398	273
27 Years	199	167	9	.544	7890	7341

△ NFL Central Division Champion
** NFL Champion
† NFC Central Division Champion
‡ NFC Champion

COACHING HISTORY

(209-179-0)

1961-66	Norm Van Brocklin	29-51-4
1967-83	Bud Grant	161-99-5
1984	Les Steckel	3-13-0
1985	Bud Grant	7-9-0
1986	Jerry Burns	9-7-0

ALL-TIME GREATS

Fran Tarkenton, the Vikings' star quarterback of the '60s and '70s, still leads the record books as one of the greatest offensive players of all time. His unbeaten records include: most passes attempted (6467), most yards completed (3686), and most yards gained (47,003). He was elected to the Hall of Fame in 1986, joining halfback Hugh McElhenny.

Chuck Foreman still holds the Vikings' club record for career rushing yards, having totalled a massive 5897 yards between 1973 and 1979. He was only the third player in NFL history to have scored 22 touchdowns in a season (1975).

Bud Grant is the Vikings' most successful coach ever, with a 168-108-5 record, accumulated over 17 years. Receiver Ahmad Rashad leads the club in receptions (400) and for gaining 1156 receiving yards in 1979.

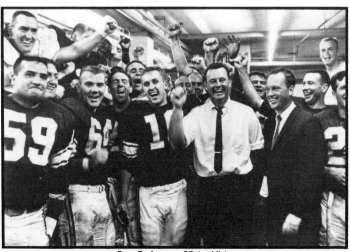

Fran Tarkenton QB (middle)

Bud Grant, Head Coach

THE PATRIOTS STATISTICS

RECORD HOLDERS

Individual Records – Career

Category	Name	Performance
Rushing (Yds)	Sam Cunningham, 1973-1979, 1981-1982	5453
Passing (Yds)	Steve Grogan, 1975-1985	21,581
Passing (TDs)	Steve Grogan, 1975-1985	146
Receiving (No.)	Stanley Morgan, 1977-1985	351
Receiving (Yds)	Stanley Morgan, 1977-1985	7201
Interceptions	Ron Hall, 1961-1967	29
Punting (Avg.)	Rich Camarillo, 1981-1985	43.2
Punt Return (Avg.)	Mack Herron, 1973-1975	12.0
Kickoff Return (Avg.)	Horace Ivory, 1977-1981	27.6
Field Goals	Gino Cappelletti, 1960-1970	176
Touchdowns (Tot.)	Sam Cunningham, 1973-1979, 1981-1982	49
Points	Gino Cappelletti, 1960-1970	1130

Individual Records – Single Season

Category	Name	Performance
Rushing (Yds)	Jim Nance, 1966	1458
Passing (Yds)	Vito (Babe) Parilli, 1964	3465
Passing (TDs)	Vito (Babe) Parilli, 1964	31
Receiving (No.)	Derrick Ramsey, 1984	66
Receiving (Yds)	Stanley Morgan, 1981	1029
Interceptions	Ron Hall, 1964	11
Punting (Avg.)	Rich Camarillo, 1983	44.6
Punt Return (Avg.)	Mack Herron, 1974	14.8
Kickoff Return (Avg.)	Raymond Clayborn, 1977	31.0
Field Goals	John Smith, 1980	26
Touchdowns (Tot.)	Steve Grogan, 1976	13
	Stanley Morgan, 1979	13
Points	Gino Cappelletti, 1964	155

Individual Records – Single Game

Category	Name	Performance
Rushing (Yds)	Tony Collins, 18-9-83	212
Passing (Yds)	Vito (Babe) Parilli, 16-10-64	400
Passing (TDs)	Vito (Babe) Parilli, 15-11-64	5
	Vito (Babe) Parilli, 15-10-67	5
	Steve Grogan, 9-9-79	5
Receiving (No.)	Art Graham, 20-11-66	11
Receiving (Yds)	Stanley Morgan, 8-11-81	182
Interceptions	Many Times	3
	Last time by Roland James, 23-10-83	
Field Goals	Gino Cappelletti, 4-10-64	6
Touchdowns (Tot.)	Many times	3
	Last time by Derrick Ramsey, 18-11-84	
Points	Gino Cappelletti, 18-12-65	28

REGULAR SEASONS

Year	W	L	T	Pct.	Pts	Opp.
1960	5	9	0	.357	286	349
1961	9	4	1	.692	413	313
1962	9	4	1	.692	346	295
1963 △	7	6	1	.538	317	257
1964	10	3	1	.769	365	297
1965	4	8	2	.333	244	302
1966	0	4	2	.667	315	203
1967	3	10	1	.231	280	389
1968	4	10	0	.286	229	406
1969	4	10	0	.286	266	316
1970	2	12	0	.143	149	361
1971	6	8	0	.429	238	325
1972	3	11	0	.214	192	446
1973	5	9	0	.357	258	300
1974	7	7	0	.500	348	289
1975	3	11	0	.214	258	358
1976 §	11	3	0	.786	376	236
1977	9	5	0	.643	278	217
1978 †	11	5	0	.688	358	286
1979	9	7	0	.563	411	326
1980	10	6	0	.625	441	325
1981	2	14	0	.125	322	370
1982 □	5	4	0	.556	143	157
1983	8	8	0	.500	274	289
1984	9	7	0	.563	362	352
1985 ‡	11	5	0	.688	362	290
1986 †	11	5	0	.688	412	307
27 Years	185	195	0	.487	8243	8441

△ AFL Eastern Division Champion
§ AFC Wild Card Qualifier for Playoffs
† AFC Eastern Division Champion
□ AFC Qualifier for Playoffs
‡ AFC Champion

1986 SEASON

	Off.	Def.
Total First Downs	294	286
Rushing	77	118
Passing	202	153
Penalty	35	15
Third Down Efficiency	33.9	35.6
Total Net Yards	5327	5181
Avg. Per Game	332.9	323.8
Total Plays	1073	1031
Avg. Per Play	5.0	5.0
Net Yards Rushing	1373	2203
Avg. Per Game	85.8	137.7
Total Rushes	469	510
Net Yards Passing	3954	2978
Avg. Per Game	247.1	186.1
Tackled/Yards Lost	47/367	48/346
Gross Yards	4321	3324
Att./Completions	557/340	473/255
Completion Pct.	61.0	53.9
Had Intercepted	13	21
Punts/Avg.	92/40.7	90/39.8
Punting Yds.	3746	3585
Penalties/Yards Lost	87/672	106/866
Fumbles/Ball Lost	27/11	38/19
Touchdowns	45	35
Rushing	10	19
Passing	29	15
Returns	6	1
Avg. Time of Possession	30:29	29:31

W	L	T
11	5	0

In the 1985 Postseason New England went 3-1.

ALL-TIME GREATS

Entering '86, quarterback Steve Grogan held many Patriots' passing records. Included were the records for most yards passing career (21,581 in 1975-1985), most touchdowns passing, career (146) and most touchdowns passing, single game (5 on 9 September 1979).

Vito (Babe) Parilli set four records: most yards passing, single season (3465 in 1964), most touchdowns passing, single seasons (31 in 1964), most yards passing, single game (400 on 16 October 1964), and most touchdowns passing, single game (5 on 15 November 1964 and 15 October 1967).

Entering '86, Stanley Morgan holds Patriots records for most number of receptions, career (351 in 1977-1985), most yards receiving, career (7201), most yards receiving, single season (1029 in 1981), and most yards receiving, single game (182 on 8 November 1981).

COACHING HISTORY

(189-200-9)

1960-61	Lou Saban*	7-12-0
1961-68	Mike Holovak	53-47-9
1969-70	Clive Rush**	5-16-0
1970-72	John Mazur***	9-21-0
1972	Phil Bengtson	1-4-0
1973-78	Chuck Fairbanks****	46-41-0
1978	Hank Bullough-Ron Erhardt††	0-1-0
1979-81	Ron Erhardt	21-27-0
1982-84	Ron Meyer††	18-16-0
1984-86	Raymond Berry	29-15-0

*Released after five games in 1961
**Released after seven games in 1970
***Released after nine games in 1972
****Resigned after 15 games in 1978
†Co-coaches
††Released after eight games in 1984

Record breaking quarterback Steve Grogan tells the team what to do.

THE **SAINTS** STATISTICS

RECORD HOLDERS

Individual Records – Career

Category	Name	Performance
Rushing (Yds)	George Rogers, 1981-1984	4267
Passing (Yds)	Archie Manning, 1971-1982	21,734
Passing (TDs)	Archie Manning, 1971-1982	115
Receiving (No.)	Dan Abramowicz, 1967-1973	309
Receiving (Yds)	Dan Abramowicz, 1967-1973	4875
Interceptions	Tommy Myers, 1972-1982	36
Punting (Avg.)	Tom McNeill, 1967-1969	42.3
Punt Return (Avg.)	Gil Chapman, 1975	12.2
Kickoff Return (Avg.)	Walt Roberts, 1967	26.3
Field Goals	Morten Andersen, 1982-1985	71
Touchdowns (Tot.)	Dan Abramowicz, 1967-1973	37
Points	Morten Andersen, 1982-1985	317

Individual Records – Single Season

Category	Name	Performance
Rushing (Yds)	George Rogers, 1981	1674
Passing (Yds)	Archie Manning, 1980	3716
Passing (TDs)	Archie Manning, 1980	23
Receiving (No.)	Tony Galbreath, 1978	74
Receiving (Yds)	Wes Chandler, 1979	1069
Interceptions	Dave Whitsell, 1967	10
Punting (Avg.)	Brian Hansen, 1984	43.8
Punt Return (Avg.)	Gil Chapman, 1975	12.2
Kickoff Return (Avg.)	Don Shy, 1969	27.9
Field Goals	Morten Andersen, 1985	31
Touchdowns (Tot.)	George Rogers, 1981	13
Points	Morten Andersen, 1985	120

Individual Records – Single Game

Category	Name	Performance
Rushing (Yds)	George Rogers, 4-9-83	206
Passing (Yds)	Archie Manning, 7-12-80	377
Passing (TDs)	Billy Kilmer, 2-11-69	6
Receiving (No.)	Tony Galbreath, 10-9-78	14
Receiving (Yds)	Wes Chandler, 2-9-79	205
Interceptions	Tommy Myers, 3-9-78	3
Field Goals	Morten Andersen, 1-12-85	5
Touchdowns (Tot.)	Many times	3
	Last time by Wayne Wilson, 2-1-83	
Points	Many times	18
	Last time by Wayne Wilson, 2-1-83	

COACHING HISTORY

(90-196-5)

1967-70	Tom Fears*	13-34-2
1970-72	J. D. Roberts	7-25-3
1973-75	John North**	11-23-0
1975	Ernie Hefferie	1-7-0
1976-77	Hank Stram	7-21-0
1978-80	Dick Nolan***	15-29-0
1980	Dick Stanfel	1-3-0
1981-85	O. A. (Bum) Phillips****	27-42-0
1985	Wade Phillips	1-3-0
1986	Jim Mora	7-9-0

*Released after seven games in 1970
**Released after six games in 1975
***Released after 12 games in 1980
****Resigned after 12 games in 1985

Tommy Myers S

REGULAR SEASONS

Year	W	L	T	Pct.	Pts	Opp.
1967	3	11	0	.214	233	379
1968	4	9	1	.308	246	327
1969	5	9	0	.357	311	393
1970	2	11	1	.154	172	347
1971	4	8	2	.333	266	347
1972	2	11	1	.179	215	361
1973	5	9	0	.357	163	312
1974	5	9	0	.357	166	263
1975	2	12	0	.143	165	360
1976	4	10	0	.286	253	346
1977	3	11	0	.214	232	336
1978	7	9	0	.438	281	298
1979	8	8	0	.500	370	360
1980	1	15	0	.063	291	487
1981	4	12	0	.250	207	378
1982	4	5	0	.444	129	160
1983	8	8	0	.500	319	337
1984	7	9	0	.438	298	361
1985	5	11	0	.313	294	401
1986	7	9	0	.438	288	286
20 Years	90	196	0	.484	4899	6839

O. A. (Bum) Phillips

1986 SEASON

	Off.	Def.
Total First Downs	275	331
Rushing	109	104
Passing	137	197
Penalty	29	30
Third Down Efficiency	29.9	42.2
Total Net Yards	4742	4757
Avg. Per Game	296.4	297.3
Total Plays	957	996
Avg. Per Play	5.0	4.8
Net Yards Rushing	2074	1284
Avg. Per Game	129.6	80.3
Total Rushes	505	350
Net Yards Passing	2668	3473
Avg. Per Game	166.8	217.1
Tackled/Yards Lost	27/225	59/414
Gross Yards	2893	3887
Att./Completions	425/232	587/334
Completion Pct.	54.6	56.9
Had Intercepted	25	24
Punts/Avg.	82/42.1	89/39.3
Punting Yds.	3456	3499
Penalties/Yards Lost	109/355	119/988
Fumbles/Ball Lost	33/18	36/19
Touchdowns	30	26
Rushing	15	10
Passing	13	15
Returns	2	1
Avg. Time of Possession	27:59	28:10

W	L	T
7	9	0

ALL-TIME GREATS

For just over a decade, quarterback Archie Manning was the darling of New Orleans. Manning commandeered every throwing record in Saints history, including most yards passing, career (21,734, 1971-1982), most touchdowns passing, career (115), most yards passing, season (3716, 1980), most touchdowns passing, season (23, 1980), and most touchdowns passing, season (23, 1980).

The end with all the records in New Orleans is Danny Abramowicz, a brilliant receiver with the Saints for eight seasons. Though finishing his career with the Saints in the early '70s, Abramowicz still holds the records for most number of receptions, career (309, 1967-1973), most yards receiving, career (4875), and total touchdowns, career (37).

Dan Abramowicz WR

Archie Manning QB

THE JETS STATISTICS

COACHING HISTORY

(181-209-7)

Year	Coach	Record
1960-61	Sammy Baugh	14-14-0
1962	Clyde (Bulldog) Turner	5-9-0
1963-73	Weeb Ewbank	73-78-6
1974-75	Charley Winner*	9-14-0
1975	Ken Shipp	1-4-0
1976	Lou Holtz**	3-10-0
1976	Mike Holovak	0-1-0
1977-82	Walt Michaels	41-49-1
1983-86	Joe Walton	35-30-0

*Released after nine games in 1975
**Resigned after 13 games in 1976

Joe Namath QB

1986 SEASON

	Off.	Def.
Total First Downs	344	349
Rushing	104	92
Passing	191	216
Penalty	24	41
Third Down Efficiency	38.8	42.9
Total Net Yards	5375	6050
Avg. Per Game	335.9	378.1
Total Plays	1072	1081
Avg. Per Play	5.0	5.6
Net Yards Rushing	1729	1661
Avg. Per Game	108.1	103.8
Total Rushes	490	450
Net Yards Passing	3646	4389
Avg. Per Game	227.9	274.3
Tackled/Yards Lost	45/386	28/178
Gross Yards	4032	4567
Att./Completions	537/334	603/348
Completion Pct.	62.2	57.7
Had Intercepted	21	20
Punts/Avg.	85/39.4	90/39.8
Punting Yds.	3353	3585
Penalties/Yards Lost	131/981	106/866
Fumbles/Ball Lost	37/16	48/18
Touchdowns	45	48
Rushing	15	12
Passing	27	35
Returns	2	1
Avg. Time of Possession	29:51	30:09

W	L	T
10	6	0

Lost 26-14 to New England in Wild-Card Game.

RECORD HOLDERS

Individual Records – Career

Category	Name	Performance
Rushing (Yds)	Emerson Boozer, 1966-1975	5104
Passing (Yds)	Joe Namath, 1965-1976	27,057
Passing (TDs)	Joe Namath, 1965-1976	170
Receiving (No.)	Don Maynard, 1960-1972	627
Receiving (Yds)	Don Maynard, 1960-1972	11,732
Interceptions	Bill Baird, 1963-1969	34
Punting (Avg.)	Curley Johnson, 1961-1968	42.8
Punt Return (Avg.)	Dick Christy, 1961-1963	16.2
Kickoff Return (Avg.)	Bobby Humphery, 1984-1985	26.6
Field Goals	Pat Leahy, 1974-1985	184
Touchdowns (Tot.)	Don Maynard, 1960-1972	88
Points	Pat Leahy, 1974-1985	901

Individual Records – Single Season

Category	Name	Performance
Rushing (Yds)	Freeman McNeil, 1985	1331
Passing (Yds)	Joe Namath, 1967	4007
Passing (TDs)	Al Dorow, 1960	26
	Joe Namath, 1967	26
Receiving (No.)	Mickey Shuler, 1985	76
Receiving (Yds)	Don Maynard, 1967	1434
Interceptions	Dainard Paulson, 1964	12
Punting (Avg.)	Curley Johnson, 1965	45.3
Punt Return (Avg.)	Dick Christy, 1961	21.3
Kickoff Return (Avg.)	Bobby Humphery, 1984	30.7
Field Goals	Jim Turner, 1968	34
Touchdowns (Tot.)	Art Powell, 1960	14
	Don Maynard, 1965	14
	Emerson Boozer, 1972	14
Points	Jim Turner, 1968	145

Individual Records – Single Game

Category	Name	Performance
Rushing (Yds)	Freeman McNeil, 15-9-85	192
Passing (Yds)	Joe Namath, 24-9-72	496
Passing (TDs)	Joe Namath, 24-9-72	6
Receiving (No.)	Clark Gaines, 21-9-80	17
Receiving (Yds)	Don Maynard, 17-11-68	228
Interceptions	Dainard Paulson, 28-9-63	3
	Bill Baird, 31-10-64	3
	Rich Sowells, 23-9-73	3
Field Goals	Jim Turner, 3-11-68	6
	Bobby Howfield, 3-12-72	6
Touchdowns (Tot.)	Many times.	3
	Last time by Mickey Shuler, 17-11-85	
Points	Jim Turner, 3-11-68	19
	Pat Leahy, 16-9-84	19

Emerson Boozer RB

Don Maynard WR

REGULAR SEASONS

Year	W	L	T	Pct.	Pts	Opp.
New York Titans						
1960	7	7	0	.500	382	399
1961	7	7	0	.500	301	390
1962	5	9	0	.357	278	423
New York Jets						
1963	5	8	1	.385	249	399
1964	5	8	1	.385	278	315
1965	5	8	1	.385	285	303
1966	6	6	2	.500	322	312
1967	8	5	1	.615	371	329
1968*	11	3	0	.786	419	280
1969△	10	4	0	.714	353	269
1970	4	10	0	.286	255	286
1971	6	8	0	.429	212	299
1972	7	7	0	.500	367	324
1973	4	10	0	.286	240	306
1974	7	7	0	.500	279	300
1975	3	11	0	.214	256	433
1976	3	11	0	.214	169	383
1977	3	11	0	.214	191	300
1978	8	8	0	.500	359	364
1979	8	8	0	.500	337	383
1980	4	12	0	.250	302	395
1981§	10	5	1	.656	355	287
1982□	6	3	0	.667	245	166
1983	7	9	0	.438	313	331
1984	7	9	0	.438	332	364
1985§	11	5	0	.688	393	264
1986§	10	6	0	.625	364	386
27 Years	177	205	0	.463	8207	8990

*Super Bowl Champion
△ AFL Eastern Division Champion
§AFC Wild Card Qualifier for Playoffs
□AFC Qualifier for Playoffs

ALL-TIME GREATS

One of football's most colourful personalities off the field, quarterback Joe Namath was also one of its greatest players. In 1967, he was the first QB to throw for more than 4000 yards in a season and his 17.71 average gain against Baltimore on 24 September 1972, is still the third highest ever. His 28 attempts without interceptions in Super Bowl III, has been surpassed in only one other Super Bowl.

Don Maynard is one of the highest ranking wide receivers in NFL annals. His career total of 11,834 receiving is an all-time best, as is his record of 50 games with 100 or more yards pass receiving. Emerson Boozer was another star Jet with his career total of 5104 rushing yards, and season record of 14 touchdowns. But not all New York's fine players are in the past. Running back Freeman McNeil's 1331 rushing yards in '85 set an impressive club record, as did the receiving power of Mickey Shuler, who picked up a massive 76 receptions.

THE *EAGLES* STATISTICS

RECORD HOLDERS

Individual Records – Career

Category	Name	Performance
Rushing (Yds)	Wilbert Montgomery, 1977-1984	6538
Passing (Yds)	Ron Jaworski, 1977-1985	25,558
Passing (TDs)	Ron Jaworski, 1977-1985	167
Receiving (No.)	Harold Carmichael, 1971-1983	589
Receiving (Yds)	Harold Carmichael, 1971-1983	8978
Interceptions	Bill Bradley, 1969-1976	34
Field Goals	Sam Baker, 1964-1969	90
Touchdowns (Tot.)	Harold Carmichael, 1971-1983	79
Points	Bobby Walston, 1951-1962	881

Individual Records – Single Season

Category	Name	Performance
Rushing (Yds)	Wilbert Montgomery, 1979	1512
Passing (Yds)	Sonny Jurgensen, 1961	3723
Passing (TDs)	Sonny Jurgensen, 1961	32
Receiving (No.)	Mike Quick, 1985	71
Receiving (Yds)	Mike Quick, 1983	1409
Interceptions	Bill Bradley, 1971	11
Field Goals	Paul McFadden, 1984	30
Touchdowns (Tot.)	Steve Van Buren, 1945	18
Points	Paul McFadden, 1984	116

Individual Records – Single Game

Category	Name	Performance
Rushing (Yds)	Steve Van Buren, 27-11-49	205
Passing (Yds)	Bobby Thomason, 18-11-53	437
Passing (TDs)	Adrian Burk, 17-10-54	7
Receiving (No.)	Don Looney, 1-12-40	14
Receiving (Yds)	Tommy McDonald, 10-12-60	237
Interceptions	Russ Craft, 24-9-50	4
Field Goals	Tom Dempsey, 12-11-72	6
Touchdowns (Tot.)	Many times	4
	Last time by Wilbert Montgomery, 7-10-79	
Points	Bobby Walston, 17-10-54	25

REGULAR SEASON

Year	W	L	T	Pct.	Pts	Opp.
1960**	10	2	0	.833	321	246
1961	10	4	0	.714	361	297
1962	3	10	1	.231	282	356
1963	2	10	2	.167	242	381
1964	6	8	0	.429	312	313
1965	5	9	0	.357	363	359
1966	9	5	0	.643	326	340
1967	6	7	1	.462	351	409
1968	2	12	0	.143	202	351
1969	4	9	1	.308	279	377
1970	3	10	1	.231	241	332
1971	6	7	1	.462	221	302
1972	2	11	1	.179	145	352
1973	5	8	1	.393	310	393
1974	7	7	0	.500	242	217
1975	4	10	0	.286	225	302
1976	4	10	0	.286	165	286
1977	5	9	0	.357	220	207
1978§	9	7	0	.563	270	250
1979§	11	5	0	.688	339	282
1980△	12	4	0	.750	384	222
1981§	10	6	0	.625	368	221
1982	3	6	0	.333	191	195
1983	5	11	0	.313	233	322
1984	6	9	1	.406	278	320
1985	7	9	0	.438	286	310
1986	5	10	1	.344	256	312
27 Years	161	215	11	.428	7413	8254

**NFL Champion
§NFC Wild Card Qualifier for Playoffs
△NFC Champion

1986 SEASON

	Off.	Def.
Total First Downs	287	278
Rushing	113	97
Passing	150	156
Penalty	24	25
Third Down Efficiency	38.5	34.3
Total Net Yards	4542	5224
Avg. Per Game	283.9	326.5
Total Plays	1117	1043
Avg. Per Play	4.1	5.0
Net Yards Rushing	2002	1989
Avg. Per Game	125.1	124.3
Total Rushes	499	458
Net Yards Passing	2540	3235
Avg. Per Game	158.8	202.2
Tackled/Yards Lost	104/708	53/406
Gross Yards	3248	3641
Att./Completions	514/268	532/260
Completion Pct.	52.1	48.9
Had Intercepted	17	23
Punts/Avg.	111/41.0	97/38.7
Punting Yds.	4547	3751
Penalties/Yards Lost	102/901	115/884
Fumbles/Ball Lost	34/10	30/13
Touchdowns	28	39
Rushing	8	14
Passing	19	21
Returns	1	4
Avg. Time of Possession	31:57	28:03

W	L	T
5	10	1

Harold Carmichael WR

Ron Jaworski QB

COACHING HISTORY

(295-386-24)

Years	Coach	Record
1933-35	Lud Wray	9-21-1
1936-40	Bert Bell	10-44-2
1941-50	Earle (Greasy) Neale*	66-44-5
1951	Alvin (Bo) McMillin**	2-0-0
1951	Wayne Millner	2-8-0
1952-55	Jim Trimble	25-20-3
1956-57	Hugh Devore	7-16-1
1958-60	Lawrence (Buck) Shaw	20 16 1
1961-63	Nick Skorich	15-24-3
1964-68	Joe Kuharich	28-41-1
1969-71	Jerry Williams***	7-22-2
1971-72	Ed Khayat	8-15-2
1973-75	Mike McCormack	16-25-1
1976-82	Dick Vermeil	57-51-0
1983-85	Marion Campbell****	17-29-1
1985	Fred Bruney	1-0-0
1986	Buddy Ryan	5-10-1

*Co-coach with Walt Kiesling in
Philadelphia-Pittsburgh merger in 1943
**Retired after two games in 1951
***Released after three games in 1971
****Released after 15 games in 1985

ALL-TIME GREATS

Steve Van Buren HB

Steve Van Buren, the Eagles' star rusher of the '40s, is one of the greatest halfbacks ever. No one has ever led the NFL in rushing attempts for more than four consecutive seasons – Van Buren's achievement between 1947 and 1950. Only Cleveland's Jim Brown has led the league for more seasons in rushing, or in rushing touchdowns.

Quarterback Sonny Jurgensen still holds the record for the most league-leading seasons in passing yards – five of which were for 3000 yards or more. His 82.6 pass rating over 1500 attempts makes him the third highest ranked QB ever, and his four seasons leading the league is surpassed only by Washington's Sammy Baugh.

THE Steelers STATISTICS

RECORD HOLDERS

Individual Records – Career

Category	Name	Performance
Rushing (Yds)	Franco Harris, 1972-1983	11,950
Passing (Yds)	Terry Bradshaw, 1970-1983	27,989
Passing (TDs)	Terry Bradshaw, 1970-1983	212
Receiving (No.)	John Stallworth, 1974-1985	462
Receiving (Yds)	John Stallworth, 1974-1985	7736
Interceptions	Mel Blount, 1971-1983	57
Punting (Avg.)	Bobby Joe Green, 1960-1961	45.7
Punt Return (Avg.)	Bobby Gage, 1949-1950	14.9
Kickoff Return (Avg.)	Lynn Chandnois, 1950-1956	29.6
Field Goals	Roy Gerela, 1971-1983	146
Touchdowns (Tot.)	Franco Harris, 1972-1983	100
Points	Roy Gerela, 1971-1978	731

Individual Records – Single Season

Category	Name	Performance
Rushing (Yds)	Franco Harris, 1975	1246
Passing (Yds)	Terry Bradshaw, 1979	3724
Passing (TDs)	Terry Bradshaw, 1979	28
Receiving (No.)	John Stallworth, 1984	80
Receiving (Yds)	John Stallworth, 1984	1395
Interceptions	Mel Blount, 1975	11
Punting (Avg.)	Bobby Joe Green, 1961	47.0
Punt Return (Avg.)	Bobby Gage, 1949	16.0
Kickoff Return (Avg.)	Lynn Chandnois, 1952	35.2
Field Goals	Gary Anderson, 1985	33
Touchdowns (Tot.)	Louis Lipps, 1985	15
Points	Gary Anderson, 1985	139

Individual Records – Single Game

Category	Name	Performance
Rushing (Yds)	John Fuqua, 20-12-70	218
Passing (Yds)	Bobby Layne, 3-12-58	409
Passing (TDs)	Terry Bradshaw, 15-11-81	5
	Mark Malone, 8-9-85	5
Receiving (No.)	J. R. Wilburn, 22-10-67	12
Receiving (Yds)	Buddy Dial, 22-10-67	235
Interceptions	Jack Butler, 13-12-53	4
Field Goals	Gary Anderson, 10-11-85	5
Touchdowns (Tot.)	Ray Mathews, 17-10-54	4
	Roy Jefferson, 3-11-68	4
Points	Ray Mathews, 17-10-54	24
	Roy Jefferson, 3-11-68	24

Mel Blount CB

ALL-TIME GREATS

The greatest quarterback in Steelers' history, Terry Bradshaw led Pittsburgh to four Super Bowl championships in the 1970s while taking over almost every Steeler career, single season, and single game record. Career marks include yards passing (27,989, 1970-1983), and touchdowns passing (212). His single season records are yards passing (3724 in 1979) and touchdowns passing (28 in 1978).

One of Bradshaw's favourite targets in those four Super Bowls was the superb wide receiver John Stallworth. Stallworth holds all Steeler career and single season receiving records including number of

receptions, career (462, 1974-1985) and yards receiving, career (7736). His single season marks are receptions (80, 1984), and total yards (1395 in 1984).

The heart of Pittsburgh's famous 'Steel Curtain' defense in their glory years was 6 ft 4 in, 19 st defensive tackle 'Mean' Joe Greene. Greene was named NFL defensive rookie of the year in 1969 and was a perennial All-Pro throughout the 1970s.

But one of the greatest Steelers players of the past was Franco Harris. Famed for his 'Immaculate Reception' in '72, Harris was one of the great rushers of the '70s, gaining a total of 11,950 yards in his 11 years for Pittsburgh.

REGULAR SEASONS

Year	W	L	T	Pct.	Pts	Opp.
1960	5	6	1	.455	240	275
1961	6	8	0	.429	295	287
1962***	9	5	0	.643	312	363
1963	7	4	3	.636	321	295
1964	5	9	0	.357	253	315
1965	2	12	0	.143	202	397
1966	5	8	1	.385	316	347
1967	4	9	1	.308	281	320
1968	2	11	1	.154	244	397
1969	1	13	0	.071	218	404
1970	5	9	0	.357	210	272
1971	6	8	0	.429	246	292
1972†	11	3	0	.786	343	175
1973§	10	4	0	.714	347	210
1974*	10	3	1	.750	305	189
1975*	12	2	0	.857	373	162
1976†	10	4	0	.714	342	138
1977●	9	5	0	.643	283	243
1978*	14	2	0	.875	356	195
1979*	12	4	0	.750	416	262
1980	9	7	0	.563	352	313
1981	8	8	0	.500	356	297
1982□	6	3	0	.667	204	146
1983●	10	6	0	.625	355	303
1984†	9	7	0	.563	387	310
1985	7	9	0	.438	379	355
1986	6	10	0	.375	307	336
27 Years	200	179	8	.528	8043	7598

***NFL Eastern Conference Runnerup. 0-1 in Playoff Bowl
†AFC Central Division Champion. 1-1 in Playoffs
§AFC Wild Card Qualifier for Playoffs: 0-1 in Playoffs
*Super Bowl Champion. 3-0 in Playoffs
●AFC Central Division Champion: 0-1 in Playoffs
□AFC Qualifier for Playoffs. 0-1 in Playoffs

Franco Harris RB

1986 SEASON

	Off.	Def.
Total First Downs	315	303
Rushing	125	97
Passing	140	176
Penalty	27	30
Third Down Efficiency	37.1	35.5
Total Net Yards	4811	5252
Avg. Per Game	300.7	328.3
Total Plays	1075	1050
Avg. Per Play	4.5	5.0
Net Yards Rushing	2223	1872
Avg. Per Game	138.9	117.0
Total Rushes	564	471
Net Yards Passing	2588	3380
Avg. Per Game	161.8	211.3
Tackled/Yards Lost	20/159	43/289
Gross Yards	2747	3669
Att./Completions	491/238	536/311
Completion Pct.	48.5	58.0
Had Intercepted	20	20
Punts/Avg.	89/38.7	82/39.0
Punting Yds.	3447	3194
Penalties/Yards Lost	104/853	109/904
Fumbles/Ball Lost	27/16	31/13
Touchdowns	35	39
Rushing	18¹	10
Passing	16	22
Returns	1	7
Avg. Time of Possession	29:45	30:15

W	L	T
6	10	0

COACHING HISTORY

(331-369-20)

1933	Forrest (Jap) Douds	3-6-2
1934	Luby DiMelio	2-10-0
1935-36	Joe Bach	10-14-0
1937-39	Johnny Blood (McNally)*	6-19-0
1939-40	Walter Kiesling	3-13-3
1941	Bert Bell**	0-2-0
	Aldo (Buff) Donelli***	0-5-0
1941-44	Walter Kiesling****	13-20-2
1945	Jim Leonard	2-8-0
1946-47	Jock Sutherland	13-10-1
1948-51	Johnny Michelosen	20-26-2
1952-53	Joe Bach	11-13-0
1954-56	Walter Kiesling	14-22-0
1957-64	Raymond (Buddy) Parker	51-47-6
1965	Mike Nixon	2-12-0
1966-68	Bill Austin	11-28-3
1969-86	Chuck Noll	170-114-1

*Replaced after three games in 1939
**Resigned after two games in 1941
***Replaced after five games in 1941
****Co-coach with Earl (Greasy) Neale in Philadelphia-Pittsburgh merger in 1943 and with Phil Handler in Chicago Cardinals-Pittsburgh merger in 1944.

THE **CARDINALS** STATISTICS

REGULAR SEASONS

Year	W	L	T	Pct.	Pts	Opp.
1960	6	5	1	.545	288	230
1961	7	7	0	.500	279	267
1962	4	9	1	.308	287	361
1963	9	5	0	.643	341	283
1964	9	3	2	.750	357	331
1965	5	9	0	.357	296	309
1966	8	5	1	.615	264	265
1967	6	7	1	.462	333	356
1968	9	4	1	.692	325	289
1969	4	9	1	.308	314	389
1970	8	5	1	.615	325	228
1971	4	9	1	.308	231	279
1972	4	9	1	.321	193	303
1973	4	9	1	.321	286	365
1974†	10	4	0	.714	285	218
1975†	11	3	0	.786	356	276
1976	10	4	0	.714	309	267
1977	7	7	0	.500	272	287
1978	6	10	0	.375	248	296
1979	5	11	0	.313	307	358
1980	5	11	0	.313	299	350
1981	7	9	0	.438	315	408
1982□	5	4	0	.556	135	170
1983	8	7	1	.531	374	428
1984	9	7	0	.563	423	345
1985	5	11	0	.313	278	414
1986	4	11	1	.281	218	351
27 Years	179	194	13	.480	7938	8423

† NFC Eastern Division champion
□ NFC Qualifier for Playoffs

1986 SEASON

	Off.	Def.
Total First Downs	273	304
Rushing	102	125
Passing	149	149
Penalty	22	30
Third Down Efficiency	32.7	36.4
Total Net Yards	4503	4864
Avg. Per Game	281.4	304.0
Total Plays	994	1037
Avg. Per Play	4.5	4.7
Net Yards Rushing	1787	2227
Avg. Per Game	111.7	139.2
Total Rushes	419	560
Net Yards Passing	2716	2637
Avg. Per Game	169.8	164.8
Tackled/Yards Lost	59/424	41/355
Gross Yards	3140	2992
Att./Completions	516/293	436/215
Completion Pct.	56.8	49.3
Had Intercepted	19	10
Punts/Avg.	92/37.1	83/42.3
Punting Yds.	3411	3514
Penalties/Yards Lost	116/932	86/682
Fumbles/Ball Lost	25/10	40/12
Touchdowns	27	40
Rushing	8	17
Passing	17	21
Returns	2	2
Avg. Time of Possession	29:18	30:42

W	L	T
4	11	1

RECORD HOLDERS

Individual Records – Career

Category	Name	Performance
Rushing (Yds)	Ottis Anderson, 1979-1985	7845
Passing (Yds)	Jim Hart, 1966-1983	34,639
Passing (TDs)	Jim Hart, 1966-1983	209
Receiving (No.)	Jackie Smith, 1963-1977	480
Receiving (Yds)	Jackie Smith, 1963-1977	7918
Interceptions	Larry Wilson, 1960-1972	52
Punting (Avg.)	Jerry Norton, 1959-1961	44.9
Punt Return (Avg.)	Charley Trippi, 1947-1955	13.7
Kickoff Return (Avg.)	Ollie Matson, 1952, 1954-1958	28.5
Field Goals	Jim Bakken, 1962-1978	282
Touchdowns (Tot.)	Sonny Randle, 1959-1966	60
Points	Jim Bakken, 1962-1978	1380

Individual Records – Single Season

Category	Name	Performance
Rushing (Yds)	Ottis Anderson, 1979	1605
Passing (Yds)	Neil Lomax, 1984	4614
Passing (TDs)	Charley Johnson, 1963	28
	Neil Lomax, 1984	28
Receiving (No.)	Roy Green, 1983, 1984	78
Receiving (Yds)	Roy Green, 1984	1555
Interceptions	Bob Nussbaumer, 1949	12
Punting (Avg.)	Jerry Norton, 1960	45.6
Punt Return (Avg.)	John (Red) Cochran, 1949	20.9
Kickoff Return (Avg.)	Ollie Matson, 1958	35.5
Field Goals	Jim Bakken, 1967	27
Touchdowns (Tot.)	John David Crow, 1962	17
Points	Jim Bakken, 1967	117
	Neil O'Donoghue, 1984	117

Individual Records – Single Game

Category	Name	Performance
Rushing (Yds)	John David Crow, 18-12-60	203
Passing (Yds)	Neil Lomax, 16-12-84	468
Passing (TDs)	Jim Hardy, 2-10-50	6
	Charley Johnson, 26-9-65	6
	Charley Johnson, 2-11-69	6
Receiving (No.)	Sonny Randle, 4-11-62	16
Receiving (Yds)	Sonny Randle, 4-11-62	256
Interceptions	Bob Nussbaumer, 13-11-49	4
	Jerry Norton, 20-11-60	4
Field Goals	Jim Bakken, 24-9-67	7
Touchdowns (Tot.)	Ernie Nevers, 28-11-29	6
Points	Ernie Nevers, 28-11-69	40

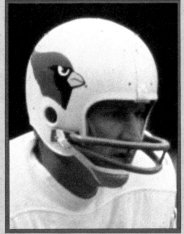

Larry Wilson S

Jim Hart QB

COACHING HISTORY

(343-453-38)

Years	Coach	Record
1920-22	John (Paddy) Driscoll	17-8-4
1923-24	Arnold Horween	13-8-1
1925-26	Norman Barry	16-8-2
1927	Guy Chamberlin	3-7-1
1928	Fred Gillies	1-5-0
1929	Dewey Scanlon	6-6-1
1930	Ernie Nevers	5-6-2
1931	LeRoy Andrews*	0-2-0
1931	Ernie Nevers	5-2-0
1932	Jack Chevigny	2-6-2
1933-34	Paul Schissler	6-15-1
1935-38	Milan Creighton	16-26-4
1939	Ernie Nevers	1-10-0
1940-42	Jimmy Conzelman	8-22-3
1943-45	Phil Handler**	1-29-0
1946-48	Jimmy Conzelman	27-10-0
1949	Phil Handler-Buddy Parker***	2-4-0
1950-51	Earl (Curly) Lambeau	8-16-0
1952	Joe Kuharich	4-8-0
1953-54	Joe Stydahar	3-20-1
1955-57	Ray Richards	14-21-1
1958-61	Frank (Pop) Ivy ****	17-29-2
1961	Chuck Drulis-Ray Prochaska-Ray Willsey†	2-0-0
1962-65	Wally Lemm	27-26-3
1966-70	Charley Winner	35-30-5
1971-72	Bob Hollway	8-18-2
1973-77	Don Coryell	42-29-1
1978-79	Bud Wilkinson††	9-20-0
1979	Larry Wilson	2-1-0
1980-85	Jim Hanifan	39-50-1
1986	Gene Stallings	4-11-1

*Resigned after two games in 1931
**Co-coach with Walt Kiesling
***Co-coaches for first six games in 1949
****Resigned after 12 games in 1961
† Co-coaches
†† Released after 13 games in 1979

ALL-TIME GREATS

The Cardinals' superb running back Ollie Matson holds the all-time NFL record for combined kick returns for TDs (9, 1952-1964) and touchdowns, career (6). He once held the Cardinals' records for longest kickoff return for a touchdown (105 yards, Cardinals vs Washington, 14 October 1956, now broken by Roy Green with 106 yards) and still has the highest average kickoff return, season (35.5, 1958).

From 1966 to 1983, quarterback Jim Hart was the soul of the Cardinals' offense. Besides leading St. Louis to two playoff appearances (1974 and 1975), Hart established records for most yards passing, career (34,639), and most touchdowns passing, career (209).

Hart set his records with the aid of tight end Jackie Smith who established Cardinals' records for number of receptions, career (480, 1963-1977) and most yards receiving, career (7918).

THE *CHARGERS* STATISTICS

Kellen Winslow TE

Earnest Jackson RB

1986 SEASON

	Off.	Def.
Total First Downs	380	308
Rushing	98	104
Passing	212	182
Penalty	24	22
Third Down Efficiency	42.4	43.0
Total Net Yards	5356	5366
Avg. Per Game	334.8	335.4
Total Plays	1107	1046
Avg. Per Play	4.8	5.1
Net Yards Rushing	1576	1678
Avg. Per Game	98.5	104.9
Total Rushes	471	475
Net Yards Passing	3780	3688
Avg. Per Game	236.3	230.5
Tackled/Yards Lost	32/265	62/440
Gross Yards	4045	4182
Att./Completions	604/339	509/288
Completion Pct.	56.1	56.6
Had Intercepted	33	15
Punts/Avg.	79/40.4	81/40.8
Punting Yds.	3193	3304
Penalties/Yards Lost	119/977	108/918
Fumbles/Ball Lost	29/16	42/22
Touchdowns	41	47
Rushing	19	14
Passing	21	27
Returns	1	6
Avg. Time of Possession	30:32	29:28

W	L	T
4	12	0

ALL TIME GREATS

Heading for an inevitable collision course with pro football's Hall of Fame, quarterback Dan Fouts holds a list of NFL records that reads like a football fact book. They include: most passes attempted in a season (609 in 1981), most consecutive seasons leading the league in passing yards (4), most games with 400 or more yards passing, career (6) and most games with 300 or more yards passing, career (47). Behind Fran Tarkenton, Fouts stands second with most passes completed in a career (2839) and second only to Miami's Dan Marino with most passes completed in a season (360), and most yards gained in a season (4802 in 1981). He now stands 9511 yards behind Fran Tarkenton's record for the most passing yards ever gained in a career. And he's still passing!

Other great Chargers' players are Lance Alworth, who gained 9585 receiving yards in his eight-year career in the '60s; kicker Rolf Bernischke, who kicked 130 field goals for 679 points between '77 and '85; and Earnest Jackson, now of the Philadelphia Eagles, who rushed for 1179 yards in 1984.

Hall of Fame head coach Sid Gillman led the Chargers to a ten-year record (1960-69) of 83-51-6, five playoff appearances (1960, '61, '62, '63, '64 and '65) and one AFL Championship.

RECORD HOLDERS

Individual Records – Career

Category	Name	Performance
Rushing (Yds)	Paul Lowe, 1960-1967	4963
Passing (Yds)	Dan Fouts, 1973-1985	37,492
Passing (TDs)	Dan Fouts, 1973-1985	228
Receiving (No.)	Charlie Joiner, 1976-1985	552
Receiving (Yds)	Lance Alworth, 1962-1970	9585
Interceptions	Dick Harris, 1960-1965	29
Punting (Avg.)	Maury Buford, 1982-1984	42.7
Punt Return (Avg.)	Leslie (Speedy) Duncan, 1964-1970	12.3
Kickoff Return (Avg.)	Leslie (Speedy) Duncan, 1964-1970	25.2
Field Goals	Rolf Benirschke, 1977-1985	130
Touchdowns (Tot.)	Lance Alworth, 1962-1970	83
Points	Rolf Benirschke, 1977-1985	679

Individual Records – Single Season

Category	Name	Performance
Rushing (Yds)	Earnest Jackson, 1984	1179
Passing (Yds)	Dan Fouts, 1981	4802
Passing (TDs)	Dan Fouts, 1981	33
Receiving (No.)	Kellen Winslow, 1980	89
Receiving (Yds)	Lance Alworth, 1965	1602
Interceptions	Charlie McNeil, 1961	9
Punting (Avg.)	Dennis Partee, 1969	44.6
Punt Return (Avg.)	Leslie (Speedy) Duncan, 1965	15.5
Kickoff Return (Avg.)	Keith Lincoln, 1962	28.4
Field Goals	Rolf Benirschke, 1980	24
Touchdowns (Tot.)	Chuck Muncie, 1981	19
Points	Rolf Benirschke, 1980	118

Individual Records – Single Game

Category	Name	Performance
Rushing (Yds)	Keith Lincoln, 5-1-64	206
Passing (Yds)	Dan Fouts, 19-10-80	444
	Dan Fouts, 11-12-82	444
Passing (TDs)	Dan Fouts, 22-11-81	6
Receiving (No.)	Kellen Winslow, 7-10-84	15
Receiving (Yds)	Wes Chandler, 20-12-82	260
Interceptions	Many times	3
	Last time by Pete Shaw, 2-11-80	
Field Goals	Many times	4
	Last time by Rolf Benirschke, 22-12-80	
Touchdowns (Tot.)	Kellen Winslow, 22-11-81	5
Points	Kellen Winslow, 22-11-81	30

REGULAR SEASONS

Year	W	L	T	Pct.	Pts	Opp.
Los Angeles Chargers						
1960 △	10	4	0	.714	373	336
San Diego Chargers						
1961 △	12	2	0	.857	396	219
1962	4	10	0	.286	314	392
1963 □	11	3	0	.786	399	256
1964 △	8	5	1	.615	341	300
1965 △	9	2	3	.818	340	227
1966	7	6	1	.538	335	284
1967	8	5	1	.615	360	352
1968	9	5	0	.643	382	310
1969	8	6	0	.571	288	276
1970	5	6	3	.455	282	278
1971	6	8	0	.429	311	341
1972	4	9	1	.321	264	344
1973	2	11	1	.179	188	386
1974	5	9	0	.357	212	285
1975	2	12	0	.143	189	345
1976	6	8	0	.429	248	285
1977	7	7	0	.500	222	205
1978	9	7	0	.563	355	309
1979 †	12	4	0	.750	411	246
1980 †	11	5	0	.688	418	327
1981 †	10	6	0	.625	478	390
1982 ***	6	3	0	.667	288	221
1983	6	10	0	.375	358	462
1984	7	9	0	.438	394	413
1985	8	8	0	.500	467	435
1986	4	12	0	.250	335	396
27 Years	196	182	11	.519	8948	8620

△ AFL Western Conference Champion
□ AFL Champion
† AFC Western Division Champion

Dan Fouts QB

COACHING HISTORY

(200-190-11)

1960-69	Sid Gillman*	83-51-6
1969-70	Charlie Waller	9-7-3
1971	Sid Gillman**	4-6-0
1971-73	Harland Svare***	7-17-2
1973	Ron Waller	1-5-0
1974-78	Tommy Prothro****	21-39-0
1978-86	Don Coryell****	72-60-0
1986	Al Saunders	3-5-0

**Resigned after 10 games in 1971
***Resigned after eight games in 1973
****Resigned after four games in 1978
****Released after eight games in 1986

THE 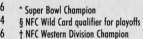 49ERS STATISTICS

1986 SEASON

	Off.	Def.
Total First Downs	346	285
Rushing	114	97
Passing	213	169
Penalty	19	19
Third Down Efficiency	35.7	30.3
Total Net Yards	6082	4880
Avg. Per Game	380.1	305.0
Total Plays	1118	1061
Avg. Per Play	5.4	4.6
Net Yards Rushing	1986	1555
Avg. Per Game	124.1	97.2
Total Rushes	510	406
Net Yards Passing	4096	3325
Avg. Per Game	256.0	207.8
Tackled/Yards Lost	26/203	51/448
Gross Yards	4299	3778
Att./Completions	582/353	604/324
Completion Pct.	60.7	53.6
Had Intercepted	20	39
Punts/Avg.	85/40.6	91/41.4
Punting Yds.	3450	3765
Penalties/Yards Lost	95/691	89/653
Fumbles/Ball Lost	32/9	31/10
Touchdowns	43	29
Rushing	16	8
Passing	21	18
Returns	6	3
Avg. Time of Possession	30:28	29:32

W	L	T
10	5	1

ALL-TIME GREATS

Quarterback Joe Montana has the highest pass rating in NFL history with a mammoth 92.4 rating over 1500 attempts. His five consecutive games with 300 or more yards passing is another all-time record. Tight end Earl Cooper cleared 83 pass receptions in 1980, the highest ever for a rookie. In Super Bowl XIX, running back Roger Craig's three touchdowns gave him a deserved Super Bowl record. Ray Wersching kicked no less than five field goals in the same game.

RECORD HOLDERS

INDIVIDUAL RECORDS – CAREER

Category	Name	Performance
Rushing (Yds)	Joe Perry, 1950-1960, 1963	7344
Passing (Yds)	John Brodie, 1957-1973	31,548
Passing (Tds)	John Brodie, 1957-1973	214
Receiving (No.)	Billy Wilson, 1951-1960	407
Receiving (Yds)	Gene Washington, 1969-1976	6664
Interceptions	Jimmy Johnson, 1961-1976	47
Punting (Avg.)	Tommy Davis, 1959-1969	44.7
Punt Return (Avg.)	Manfred Moore, 1974-1975	14.7
Kickoff Return (Avg.)	Abe Woodson, 1958-1964	29.4
Field Goals	Ray Wersching, 1977-1984	139
Touchdowns (Tot.)	Ken Willard, 1965-1973	61
Points	Tommy Davis, 1959-1969	738

INDIVIDUAL RECORDS – SINGLE SEASON

Category	Name	Performance
Rushing (Yds)	Wendell Tyler, 1984	1262
Passing (Yds)	Joe Montana, 1983	3910
Passing (Tds)	John Brodie, 1965	30
Receiving (No.)	Dwight Clark, 1981	85
Receiving (Yds)	Dave Parks, 1965	1334
Interceptions	Dave Baker, 1960	10
Punting (Avg.)	Tommy Davis, 1965	45.8
Punt Return (Avg.)	Dana McLemore, 1982	22.3
Kickoff Return (Avg.)	Joe Arenas, 1953	34.4
Field Goals	Bruce Gossett, 1973	26
Touchdowns (Tot.)	Joe Perry, 1953	13
Points	Ray Wersching, 1984	131

INDIVIDUAL RECORDS – SINGLE GAME

Category	Name	Performance
Rushing (Yds)	Delvin Williams, 31-10-76	194
Passing (Yds)	Joe Montana, 6-10-85	429
Passing (Tds)	John Brodie, 23-11-65	5
	Steve Spurrier, 19-11-72	5
	Joe Montana, 6-10-85	5
Receiving (No.)	Bernie Casey, 13-11-66	12
	Dwight Clark, 11-12-82	12
	Roger Craig, 6-10-85	12
Receiving (Yds)	Jerry Rice, 9-12-85	241
Interceptions	Dave Baker, 4-12-60	4
Field Goals	Ray Wersching, 16-10-83	6
Touchdowns (Tot.)	Billy Kilmer, 15-10-61	4
Points	Gordy Soltau, 27-10-51	26

COACHING HISTORY

(256-253-13)

1950-54	Lawrence (Buck) Shaw	33-25-2
1955	Norman (Red) Strader	4-8-0
1956-58	Frankie Albert	19-17-1
1959-63	Howard (Red) Hickey*	27-27-1
1963-67	Jack Christiansen	26-38-3
1968-75	Dick Nolan	56-56-5
1976	Monte Clark	8-6-0
1977	Ken Meyer	5-9-0
1978	Pete McCulley**	1-8-0
1978	Fred O'Connor	1-6-0
1979-86	Bill Walsh	76-53-1

* Resigned after three games in 1963
** Released after nine games in 1978

REGULAR SEASON

Year	W	L	T	Pct.	Pts.	Opp.
1960	7	5	0	.583	208	205
1961	7	6	1	.538	346	272
1962	6	8	0	.429	282	331
1963	2	12	0	.143	198	391
1964	4	10	0	.286	236	330
1965	7	6	1	.538	421	402
1966	6	6	2	.500	320	325
1967	7	7	0	.500	273	337
1968	7	6	1	.538	303	310
1969	4	8	2	.333	277	319
1970†	10	3	1	.769	352	267
1971†	9	5	0	.643	300	216
1972†	8	5	1	.607	353	249
1973	5	9	0	.357	262	319
1974	6	8	0	.429	226	236
1975	5	9	0	.357	255	286
1976	8	6	0	.571	270	190
1977	5	9	0	.357	220	260
1978	2	14	0	.125	219	350
1979	2	14	0	.125	308	416
1980	6	10	0	.375	320	415
1981*	13	3	0	.813	357	250
1982	3	6	0	.333	200	250
1983†	10	6	0	.625	432	293
1984*	15	1	0	.939	475	227
1985§	10	6	0	.625	411	263
1986†	10	5	1	.656	374	247
27 Years	174	187	10	.482	7355	7464

* Super Bowl Champion
§ NFC Wild Card qualifier for playoffs
† NFC Western Division Champion

Joe Montana QB

Roger Craig RB

THE Seahawks STATISTICS

COACHING HISTORY

(81-89-0)
1976-82	Jack Patera*	35-59-0
1982	Mike McCormack	4-3-0
1983-86	Chuck Knox	42-27-0

*Released after two games in 1982

Dave Brown CB

Kenny Easley S

Dave Krieg QB

RECORD HOLDERS

Individual Records – Career

Category	Name	Performance
Rushing (Yds)	Sherman Smith, 1976-1982	3429
Passing (Yds)	Jim Zorn, 1976-1984	20,042
Passing (TDs)	Jim Zorn, 1976-1984	107
Receiving (No)	Steve Largent, 1976-1985	624
Receiving (Yds)	Steve Largent, 1976-1985	10,059
Interceptions	Dave Brown, 1976-1985	45
Punting (Avg)	Herman Weaver, 1977-1980	40.0
Punt Return (Avg)	Paul Johns, 1981-84	11.2
Kickoff Return (Avg)	Zachary Dixon, 1983-84	23.4
Field Goals	Efren Herrera, 1978-1981	64
Touchdowns (Tot)	Steve Largent, 1976-1985	79
Points	Steve Largent, 1976-1985	475

Individual Records – Single Season

Category	Name	Performance
Rushing (Yds)	Curt Warner, 1983	1449
Passing (Yds)	Dave Krieg, 1984	3671
Passing (TDs)	Dave Krieg, 1984	32
Receiving (No)	Steve Largent, 1985	79
Receiving (Yds)	Steve Largent, 1985	1287
Interceptions	John Harris, 1981	10
	Kenny Easley, 1984	10
Punting (Avg)	Herman Weaver, 1980	41.8
Punt Return (Avg)	Kenny Easley, 1984	12.1
Kickoff Return (Avg)	Al Hunter, 1978	24.1
Field Goals	Efren Herrera, 1980	20
	Norm Johnson, 1984	20
Touchdowns (Tot)	David Sims, 1978	15
	Sherman Smith, 1979	15
Points	Norm Johnson, 1984	110

Individual Records – Single Game

Category	Name	Performance
Rushing (Yds)	Curt Warner, 27-11-83	207
Passing (Yds)	Dave Krieg, 20-11-83	418
Passing (TDs)	Dave Krieg, 2-12-84	5
	Dave Krieg, 15-9-85	5
Receiving (No)	David Hughes, 27-9-81	12
	Steve Largent, 25-11-84	12
Receiving (Yds)	Steve Largent, 25-11-84	191
Interceptions	Kenny Easley, 3-9-84	3
Field Goals	Efren Herrera, 5-10-80	4
	Norm Johnson, 9-3-84	4
Touchdowns (Tot)	Daryl Turner, 15-9-85	4
Points	Daryl Turner, 15-9-85	24

Curt Warner RB

1986 SEASON

	Off.	Def.
Total First Downs	299	310
Rushing	123	93
Passing	158	192
Penalty	10	25
Third Down Efficiency	43.4	37.3
Total Net Yards	5409	5341
Avg. Per Game	338.1	333.8
Total Plays	1005	1053
Avg. Per Play	5.4	5.1
Net Yards Rushing	2300	1759
Avg. Per Game	143.8	109.9
Total Rushes	513	471
Net Yards Passing	3109	3582
Avg. Per Game	194.3	223.9
Tackled/Yards Lost	39/315	47/306
Gross Yards	3424	3888
Att./Completions	453/268	535/301
Completion Pct.	59.2	56.3
Had Intercepted	14	22
Punts/Avg.	79/38.6	81/40.4
Punting Yds.	3048	3270
Penalties/Yards Lost	98/813	81/652
Fumbles/Ball Lost	29/13	26/14
Touchdowns	43	34
Rushing	15	12
Passing	24	20
Returns	4	2
Avg. Time of Possession	29:47	30:13

W	L	T
10	6	0

REGULAR SEASONS

Year	W	L	T	Pct.	Pts.	Opp.
1976	2	12	0	.143	229	429
1977	5	9	0	.357	282	373
1978	9	7	0	.563	345	358
1979	9	7	0	.563	378	372
1980	4	12	0	.250	291	408
1981	6	10	0	.375	322	388
1982	4	5	0	.444	127	147
1983*	9	7	0	.563	403	397
1984*	12	4	0	.750	418	282
1985	8	8	0	.500	349	303
1986	10	6	0	.625	366	293
11 Years	78	87	0	.472	3510	3750

*AFC Wild Card Qualifier for Playoffs.

Steve Largent WR

Jim Zorn QB

ALL-TIME GREATS

Brilliant wide receiver Steve Largent has already taken his place among the NFL immortals, 2nd behind Harold Carmichael for most consecutive games with a pass reception with 123 games from 1977 to the present, and has tied Lance Alworth with 1000 or more yards gained with seven.

Teaming with Largent to make one of the best one-two punches in football, all-pro quarterback Dave Krieg owns every Seattle Seahawk single season and single game passing mark, and is 2nd behind Johnny Unitas for most consecutive games with touchdown passes with 28.

THE **BUCCANEERS** STATISTICS

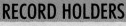

Jimmie Giles TE

Doug Williams QB

David Logan NI

RECORD HOLDERS

Individual Records – Career

Category	Name	Performance
Rushing (Yds)	James Wilder, 1981-85	4178
Passing (Yds)	Doug Williams, 1978-1982	12,648
Passing (TDs.)	Doug Williams, 1978-1982	73
Receiving (No.)	James Wilder, 1981-85	296
Receiving (Yds)	Kevin House, 1980-85	4722
Interceptions	Cedric Brown, 1977-1984	29
Punting (Avg.)	Frank Garcia, 1983-85	42.0
Punt Return (Avg.)	John Holt, 1981-83	7.5
Kickoff Return (Avg.)	Phil Freeman, 1985	22.6
Field Goals	Bill Capece, 1981-83	43
Touchdowns (Tot.)	James Wilder, 1981-85	38
Points	James Wilder, 1981-85	228

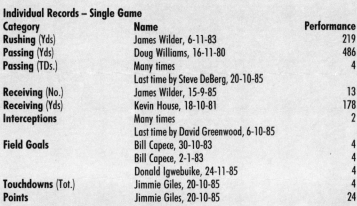

Individual Records – Single Season

Category	Name	Performance
Rushing (Yds)	James Wilder, 1984	1544
Passing (Yds)	Doug Williams, 1981	3563
Passing (TDs.)	Doug Williams, 1980	20
Receiving (No.)	James Wilder, 1984	85
Receiving (Yds)	Kevin House, 1981	1176
Interceptions	Cedric Brown, 1981	9
Punting (Avg.)	Larry Swider, 1981	42.7
Punt Return (Avg.)	Leon Bright, 1985	10.3
Kickoff Return (Avg.)	Isaac Hagins, 1977	23.5
Field Goals	Donald Igwebuike, 1985	22
Touchdowns (Tot.)	James Wilder, 1984	13
Points	Donald Igwebuike, 1985	96

Individual Records – Single Game

Category	Name	Performance
Rushing (Yds)	James Wilder, 6-11-83	219
Passing (Yds)	Doug Williams, 16-11-80	486
Passing (TDs.)	Many times	4
	Last time by Steve DeBerg, 20-10-85	
Receiving (No.)	James Wilder, 15-9-85	13
Receiving (Yds)	Kevin House, 18-10-81	178
Interceptions	Many times	2
	Last time by David Greenwood, 6-10-85	
Field Goals	Bill Capece, 30-10-83	4
	Bill Capece, 2-1-83	4
	Donald Igwebuike, 24-11-85	4
Touchdowns (Tot.)	Jimmie Giles, 20-10-85	4
Points	Jimmie Giles, 20-10-85	24

REGULAR SEASONS

Year	W	L	T	Pct.	Pts.	Opp.
1976	0	14	0	.000	125	412
1977	2	12	0	.143	103	223
1978	5	11	0	.313	241	259
1979†	10	6	0	.625	273	237
1980	5	10	1	.344	271	341
1981†	9	7	0	.563	315	268
1982	5	4	0	.556	158	178
1983	2	14	0	.125	241	380
1984	6	10	0	.375	335	380
1985	2	14	0	.125	294	448
1986	2	14	0	.125	239	473
11 Years	48	116	1	.293	2595	3599

†NFC Central Division Champion.

COACHING HISTORY

(51-133-1)
1976-84 John McKay 45-91-1
1985-86 Leeman Bennett 4-28-0

ALL-TIME GREATS

Running back James Wilder is the NFL's third-ranking rusher over the past two seasons with a total of 2844 yards. Quarterback Doug Williams took Tampa Bay to the playoffs in '81, with his mammoth 3653 passing yards and Frank Garcia led the NFC in punting in 1983.

1986 SEASON

	Off.	Def.
Total First Downs	273	362
Rushing	100	162
Passing	142	177
Penalty	31	23
Third Down Efficiency	30.6	46.6
Total Net Yards	4061	6333
Avg. Per Game	272.1	395.8
Total Plays	970	1061
Avg. Per Play	4.5	6.0
Net Yards Rushing	1863	2648
Avg. Per Game	116.4	165.5
Total Rushes	455	558
Net Yards Passing	2498	3685
Avg. Per Game	156.1	230.3
Tackled/Yards Lost	56/394	19/153
Gross Yards	2892	3838
Att./Completions	459/245	484/289
Completion Pct.	53.4	59.7
Had Intercepted	25	13
Punts/Avg.	78/40.2	59/41.3
Punting Yds.	3132	2438
Penalties/Yards Lost	83/661	116/941
Fumbles/Ball Lost	36/17	39/19
Touchdowns	27	59
Rushing	12	31
Passing	13	23
Returns	2	5
Avg. Time of Possession	28:40	31:20

W	L	T
2	14	0

Frank Garcia P

James Wilder RB

THE **REDSKINS** STATISTICS

Larry Brown RB

COACHING HISTORY

(875-328-26)

Year	Coach	Record
1932	Lud Wray	4-4-2
1933-34	William (Lone Star) Dietz	11-11-2
1935	Eddie Casey	2-8-1
1936-42	Ray Flaherty*	56-23-3
1943	Arthur (Dutch) Bergman	7-4-1
1944-45	Dudley DeGroot	14-6-1
1946-48	Glen (Turk) Edwards	16-18-1
1949	John (Billick) Whelchel**	2-4-1
1949-51	Herman Ball***	5-15-0
1951	Dick Todd	5-4-0
1952-53	Earl (Curly) Lambeau	10-13-1
1954-58	Joe Kuharich	26-32-2
1959-60	Mike Nixon	4-18-2
1961-65	Bill McPeak	21-46-3
1966-68	Otto Graham	17-22-3
1969	Vince Lombardi	7-5-2
1970	Bill Austin	6-8-0
1971-77	George Allen	69-35-1
1978-80	Jack Pardee	24-24-0
1981-86	Joe Gibbs	69-28-0

*Retired to enter Navy
**Released after seven games in 1949
**Replaced after seven games in 1949
***Replaced after three games in 1951

RECORD HOLDERS

Category	Name	Performance
Rushing (Yds)	John Riggins, 1976-79, 1981-85	7472
Passing (Yds)	Joe Theismann, 1974-1985	25,206
Passing (TDs)	Sonny Jurgensen, 1964-1974	209
Receiving (No.)	Charley Taylor, 1964-1977	649
Receiving (Yds)	Charley Taylor, 1964-1977	9140
Interceptions	Brig Owens, 1966-1977	36
Punting (Avg.)	Sammy Baugh, 1937-1952	45.1
Punt Return (Avg.)	Johnnie Williams, 1952-1953	12.8
Kickoff Return (Avg.)	Bobby Mitchell, 1962-68	28.5
Field Goals	Mark Moseley, 1974-1985	257
Touchdowns (Tot.)	Charley Taylor, 1964-1977	90
Points	Mark Moseley, 1974-1985	1176

Individual Records – Single Season

Category	Name	Performance
Rushing (Yds)	John Riggins, 1983	1347
Passing (Yds)	Sonny Jurgensen, 1967	3747
Passing (TDs)	Sonny Jurgensen, 1967	31
Receiving (No.)	Art Monk, 1984	106
Receiving (Yds)	Bobby Mitchell, 1963	1436
Interceptions	Dan Sandifer, 1948	13
Punting (Avg.)	Sammy Baugh, 1940	51.4
Punt Return (Avg.)	Johnny Williams, 1952	15.3
Kickoff Return (Avg.)	Mike Nelms, 1981	29.7
Field Goals	Mark Moseley, 1983	33
Touchdowns (Tot.)	John Riggins, 1983	24
Points	Mark Moseley, 1983	161

Individual Records – Single Game

Category	Name	Performance
Rushing (Yds)	George Rogers, 21-12-85	206
Passing (Yds)	Sammy Baugh, 31-10-43	446
Passing (TDs)	Sammy Baugh, 31-10-43	6
	Sammy Baugh, 23-11-47	6
Receiving (No.)	Art Monk, 15-12-85	13
Receiving (Yds)	Art Monk, 15-12-85	230
Interceptions	Sammy Baugh, 14-11-43	4
	Dan Sandifer, 31-10-48	4
Field Goals	Many times	5
	Last time by Mark Moseley, 26-10-80	
Touchdowns (Tot.)	Dick James, 17-12-61	4
	Larry Brown, 4-12-73	4
Points	Dick James, 17-12-61	24
	Larry Brown, 4-12-73	24

ALL-TIME GREATS

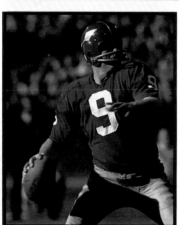

Sonny Jurgensen QB

Washington fans will not soon forget John Riggins. Retired at the age of 37, this human dynamo of a fullback set the Redskins' individual record for most yards rushing, career (7472 in 1976-79 and 1981-85), most yards rushing, single season (1347 in 1983), and total touchdowns, single season (24 in 1983).

One of the early Redskins' stars was Sammy Baugh. Drafted in 1937, Baugh led the league in passing in his rookie year, and went on to set a single season record for punting average in 1940 (51.4), single game records for passing yards (446 in 31-10-48) and passing touchdowns (6 in 31-10-43 and 23-11-47) and a team-high career record 45.1

punting average from 1937 to 1952.

The Redskins have had a number of excellent quarterbacks in their 54 year history, but none greater than Sonny Jurgensen who holds the Redskins' individual record for most touchdowns passing, career (209 in 1964-1974), most yards passing, single season (3747 in 1967), and most touchdowns passing, single season (31 in 1967).

One of the most accurate kickers in the history of the NFL is the Redskins' Mark Moseley. Besides holding every Redskins career, single season, and single game kicking record, Moseley is second on the all-time NFL list for most points scored, single season (161, 62-pat, 33-fg, 1983).

1986 SEASON

	Off.	Def.
Total First Downs	312	316
Rushing	112	103
Passing	177	181
Penalty	23	32
Third Down Efficiency	41.8	33.2
Total Net Yards	5601	5297
Avg. Per Game	350.1	331.1
Total Plays	1044	1046
Avg. Per Play	5.4	5.1
Net Yards Rushing	1732	1805
Avg. Per Game	108.3	112.3
Total Rushes	474	459
Net Yards Passing	3869	3492
Avg. Per Game	241.8	218.3
Tackled/Yards Lost	28/240	55/424
Gross Yards	4109	3916
Att./Completions	542/276	332/302
Completion Pct.	50.9	56.8
Had Intercepted	22	19
Punts/Avg.	75/43.6	95/41.3
Punting Yds.	3271	3923
Penalties/Yards Lost	94/860	115/1026
Fumbles/Ball Lost	29/10	21/9
Touchdowns	46	35
Rushing	23	14
Passing	22	21
Returns	1	0
Avg. Time of Possession	29:56	30:04

W	L	T
12	4	0

REGULAR SEASONS

Year	W	L	T	Pct.	Pts	Opp.
1960	1	9	2	.100	178	309
1961	1	12	1	.077	174	392
1962	5	7	2	.417	305	376
1963	3	11	0	.214	279	398
1964	6	8	0	.429	307	305
1965	6	8	0	.429	257	301
1966	7	7	0	.500	351	355
1967	5	6	3	.455	347	353
1968	5	9	0	.357	249	358
1969	7	5	2	.583	307	319
1970	6	8	0	.429	297	314
1971§	9	4	1	.692	276	190
1972‡	11	3	0	.786	336	218
1973§	10	4	0	.714	325	198
1974§	10	4	0	.714	320	196
1975	8	6	0	.571	325	276
1976§	10	4	0	.714	291	217
1977	9	5	0	.643	196	189
1978	8	8	0	.500	273	283
1979	10	6	0	.625	348	295
1980	6	10	0	.375	261	293
1981	8	8	0	.500	347	349
1982*	8	1	0	.889	190	128
1983‡	14	2	0	.875	541	332
1984†	11	5	0	.688	426	310
1985§	10	6	0	.625	297	312
1986	12	2	0	.875	371	236
27 Years	206	168	11	.551	8174	7802

§ Wild Card Qualifier
‡ NFC Champion
* Super Bowl Champion
† NFC Eastern Division Champion

PLAYER POWER

American Football is a team sport. It's all about strategy and concerted efforts by well-co-ordinated units. There is no room in any team for cowboys and mavericks who want to play their own way, apart from the rest of the team. But once the teamwork is going well, and the team is performing up to its potential, then that's the time when individual talent can shine. With the possible exception of OJ Simpson, whose Buffalo Bills' teammates never came close to tasting the glory of a Super Bowl, all the players listed in this chapter have played on teams that have either won a Super Bowl or have had the capability to do so. No matter how good you are, American Football is not the sport to really excel in if your teammates haven't got a winning attitude or first-class skill.

The chapter begins with a look at the New York Giants' superb linebacker Lawrence Taylor, whose performance in 1986 helped lead his team to the Super Bowl XXI championship. One of those rare talents, like most of the players listed here, whose ability and leadership stand out from the rest. Compared with the great Dick Butkus of the Chicago Bears, who reigned supreme for eight seasons in the 1960s, Taylor has few contemporaries at his position. New England's Andre Tippett is one, as well as Cleveland's Chip Banks. And then there is Taylor's counterpart from Denver, the big versatile Karl Mecklenburg. Equally potent as a linebacker and defensive lineman, Mecklenburg is highlighted here along with his teammate, John Elway.

To contrast Elway is the great Dan Marino of Miami, who, after only four years in the NFL, has shattered so many passing records that it seems as if he's been around for so much longer. Where these two quarterbacks differ is in their running abilities — Elway's elusive stride and Marino's willingness to let his arm do the talking.

As for great runners, what about the Jets' Freeman McNeil, a player who transformed his team from sole passing attacks to well-balanced and exciting offenses. Rounding out this series is a look at two of the best wide receivers in the NFL: Art Monk of the Washington Redskins and Mike Quick of the Philadelphia Eagles. Always one of the best yearly performers, Monk set an all-time NFL receiving record when he caught 106 passes in 1984. Quick, who has already broken several Philadelphia records set by the legendary Harold Carmichael, possesses Olympic sprint speed and a battery of moves enough to keep any defensive back off balance. He also shares the league record with five other players for catching a 99-yard pass for a touchdown in 1985.

Balancing out the positions a bit, one of the best offensive linemen to emerge in many years – Anthony Munoz of the Cincinnati Bengals is featured. The position has never been a glamorous one but with players grabbing the limelight like Munoz, this could change in a hurry.

TEAM: New York Giants
NFC Eastern Division

COLLEGE: University of North
Carolina 1977–1980

LAWRENCE TAYLOR

Twice voted Most Valuable Defensive Player

in the NFL, Taylor is the Giants' most honoured

linebacker – and he's still reaching for his peak

So far in his career with the Giants, Lawrence Taylor has played less than 100 regular season games (to the end of 1986). Yet in that relatively short period of time, he has reaped more individual honours than any other player in club history.

Through his first five seasons with the club, Taylor has been a unanimous All-NFL selection in each of those years, a Pro Bowl starter in all five of those seasons and has been voted the top linebacker in the NFL between 1981 and 1984 consecutively by the renowned Players' Association.

CREAM OF THE CROP

After an All-American career at the University of North Carolina, Taylor became one of the three 'special' linebackers available for the draft, the other two being Pittsburgh's Hugh Green and Alabama's E. J. Junior.

The consensus was, however, that while all three would be top 10 first-round selections, L.T. (Taylor's nickname) was

undoubtedly the leader.

Then there was the interesting survey conducted by an East Coast sportswriter. The New Orleans Saints held the first draft choice in 1981, so the survey dealt with the other 27 franchises.

'If you had first pick,' it said, 'which player would you draft for your team?'

All 27 teams responded and all but three said that Lawrence Taylor would have been their first choice.

IMPACT PLAYER

Giants' general manager George Young calls Taylor 'a player who has a great influence on an entire game, and had it from the first game he ever played as a pro.'

Mike Hickey, the personnel director of the New York Jets, has referred to Taylor as 'a real original at his position . . . the kind of guy other teams will be trying to emulate 10 years from now.'

Hickey's comments are of considerable interest because the Jets held the third choice in

With the strength of a gladiator, Lawrence Taylor (56) fights free of Philadelphia running back Michael Haddix during an '85 clash.

STAR POINTS

Born	4 February 1959
Height	6 ft 3 in
Weight	17 st 5 lb
College	University of North Carolina
Draft	New York Giants' 1st round choice, 1981
Team	New York Giants
Position	Linebacker
Number	56

BEST GAME

New York Giants vs Detroit Lions
26 November 1982
- Returned intercepted pass 97 yards for game-winning touchdown on Thanksgiving Day.

BEST SEASON

1983
- 125 total tackles
- 88 solo tackles
- 9 quarterback sacks
- 2 fumble recoveries
- 2 fumbles forced

HONOURS

Pro Bowl 1981-86
All-American 1980

POINTS TO WATCH

Taylor's reputation as a fierce intimidator derives from a combination of speed and strength. Weighing over 17 st, he can still run a 4.5 second 40-yard-dash.

PRO STATS

Year	TK/Solo	Sacks/Yds	Int./Yds
1981	133/94	9.5/87	1/1
1982	55/32	7.5/80	1/97t
1983	125/88	9/53	2/10
1984	114/88	11.5/84	1/–1
1985	83/104	13.5/102	0/0
1986	105/79	20.5/137	0/0
Tot.	615/485	71.5/549	5/107

the 1981 draft and used it to take future all-pro running back Freeman McNeil. But given the chance to move up, Hickey said that spring that it would be automatic. 'Hey, if we could have gotten L.T., we would have . . . well, it's useless to go on. The Giants would never have made any sort of trade.'

THE REAL THING

George Young said, 'Once you see Lawrence Taylor, you never forget him.'

Giants fans would agree. They saw Taylor shine in his

'There is no better linebacker in pro football,' said Dallas coach Tom Landry.
▶ Pittsburgh's Terry Long (74) obstructs Taylor's tackling thirst.

very first year (1981), making 133 tackles and 9.5 sacks to earn a trip to the Pro Bowl and become Associated Press's choice as NFL defensive player of the year.

Once again, statistics are faint measures. Moments of magnificence are not.

The Giants needed a sack to preserve their 10-7 lead late in the '81 season, so Taylor sacked everybody. He grabbed both

running backs, then reached over Wendell Tyler (now with the 49ers) and dropped quarterback Pat Haden with one arm. The lead was protected, the game won, and the Giants were on their way to the playoffs.

'A hitter, that's me,' said Taylor. 'In college, we'd hit people in practice. We'd even hit people in the lunchroom.'

The bunch of linebackers Taylor joined on the Giants team were hailed by many as the best in the league. Harry Carson, Brad Van Pelt and

TIME OUT

TAYLOR-MADE SACK
As a furious pass rusher and general all-purpose defensive weapon, Taylor has perfected the one-hand, reach-behind-the-blocker sack. It was believed that no one possessed the extraordinary strength to perform this feat, but that was BLT – Before Lawrence Taylor.

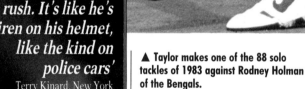

'You can tell when he's going to rush. It's like he's got a siren on his helmet, like the kind on police cars'
Terry Kinard, New York Giants' free safety

▲ Taylor makes one of the 88 solo tackles of 1983 against Rodney Holman of the Bengals.
◄ With a linebacker like L.T., it's no wonder that the Giants finished first in the NFL in sacks in '85.

Brian Kelley were all known as aggressive, gung-ho players.

GIANT INSPIRATION
What Taylor brought to the Giants was inspiration. Teammates and fans quickly began relying on him to make the big play when the big play had to be made.

Taylor happily admits he is not perfect. Telegraphing the oncoming blitz is a flaw in his technique. 'Anybody can tell what I'm going to do,' he said. 'I can see a lot of quarterbacks watching me, trying to see what I'm going to do. Sometimes I just wink at them.'

Taylor was born on 4 February 1959, in Williamsburg, Virginia. He believes the presence and guidance of his mother and father moulded his personality.

'My pop taught me a lot about sports,' he said, 'while my mom was always there to teach me values for life.'

As aggressive and quick-moving off the field as on, Taylor signed his contract with the Giants and immediately got married. Then he had two houses built – one for his parents in Williamsburg and another for him and his wife Linda in Chapel Hill, North Carolina.

THE GOOD NEWS
In five brilliant seasons of NFL play at his position of outside linebacker, L.T. has amassed over 500 tackles, added an amazing 51 quarterback sacks, and has recovered fumbles, forced fumbles, blocked PATs, run over blockers, and generally made life totally miserable for opposing quarterbacks and running backs.

And now for the good news. In terms of age Taylor is just reaching his prime. He promises to get even better . . . if that's possible.

KARL MECKLENBURG

The Denver Broncos' Mr Versatility excels almost

anywhere from linebacker to defensive

end. Mecklenburg is a one-man sack machine

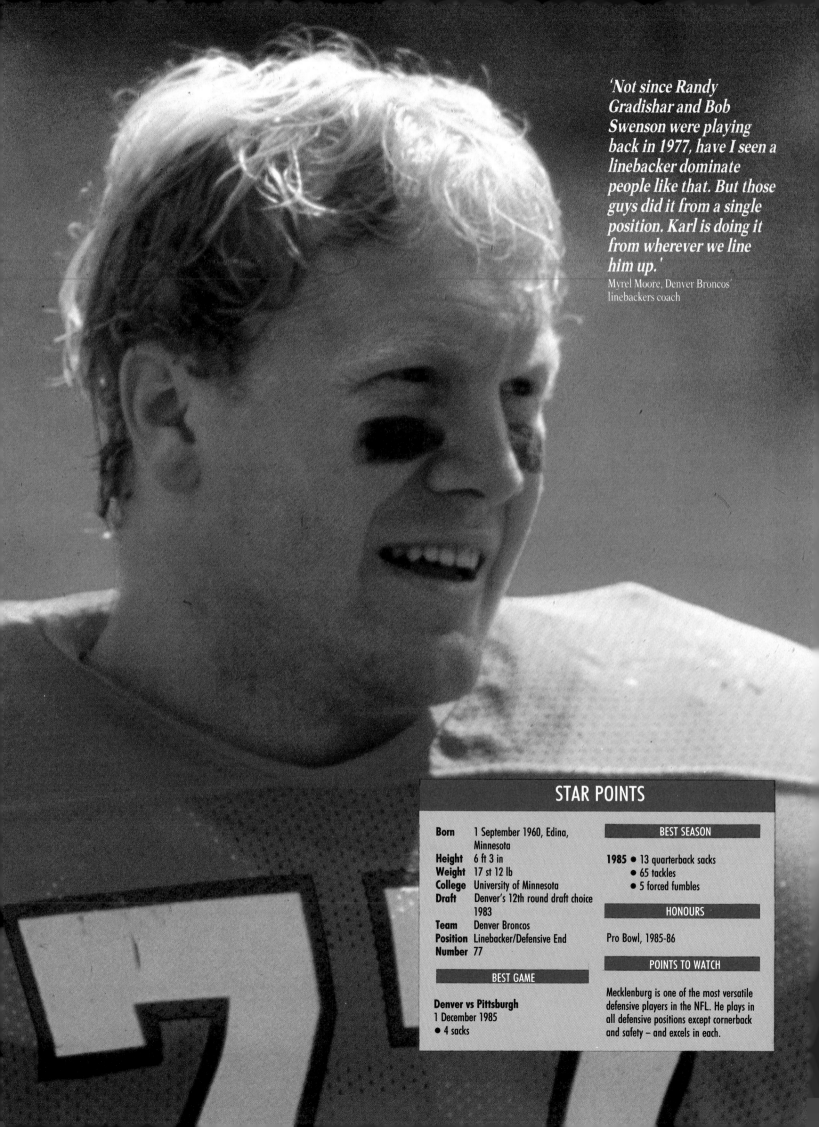

'Not since Randy Gradishar and Bob Swenson were playing back in 1977, have I seen a linebacker dominate people like that. But those guys did it from a single position. Karl is doing it from wherever we line him up.'

Myrel Moore, Denver Broncos'
linebackers coach

STAR POINTS

Born	1 September 1960, Edina, Minnesota
Height	6 ft 3 in
Weight	17 st 12 lb
College	University of Minnesota
Draft	Denver's 12th round draft choice 1983
Team	Denver Broncos
Position	Linebacker/Defensive End
Number	77

BEST GAME

Denver vs Pittsburgh
1 December 1985
● 4 sacks

BEST SEASON

1985 ● 13 quarterback sacks
● 65 tackles
● 5 forced fumbles

HONOURS

Pro Bowl, 1985-86

POINTS TO WATCH

Mecklenburg is one of the most versatile defensive players in the NFL. He plays in all defensive positions except cornerback and safety – and excels in each.

The Broncos' all-purpose defender is one of the NFL's most surprising successes. From being just a 12th round draft in 1983 as a defensive end, Karl Mecklenburg was named to his first Pro Bowl as a linebacker in 1986, led the AFC squad with 11 tackles and gained national acclaim as the Denver Broncos' leading sack specialist.

Associated Press, *Sports Illustrated*, *The Football News*, Pro Football Writers of America and Newspaper Enterprise Association named him All-NFL. *College and Pro Football Newsweekly* picked him for their second team. And UPI named him All-AFC – and all in just one season, 1985.

MORE SACKS THAN STARTS

Mecklenburg was a key part of Denver's revitalized 'Orange Crush' defense in '85 and set a new Broncos record with 13 sacks, despite the fact that he did not become a full-time starter until the tenth week. He also broke Denver's single-game sack record, dropping opposing quarterbacks four times against both New Orleans and Pittsburgh.

His great versatility enabled the coaching staff to move him around considerably in the Denver defense. Mecklenburg played seven positions during the 1985 campaign, leading the team in forced fumbles – with five – while posting 65 total tackles.

An extremely intelligent player, Mecklenburg learned the assignments of all four linebacker positions in Denver's complex defensive system. He demonstrated his versatility against Pittsburgh when he not only played at each linebacker spot, but also saw action at every position on the defensive line – which meant he played every defensive position except defensive back.

A MAN POSSESSED

After Mecklenburg's stellar performance against the Steelers, linebackers' coach Myrel Moore was ecstatic.

'He's a man possessed,' Moore said. 'I don't think I've ever been more excited watching a guy perform.'

Such praise is usually reserved for a first-round draft choice, or at least someone who has spent a better part of his life

Mecklenburg's tenacious pursuit of quarterbacks is famous. Miami's Dan Marino feels the full force, *right*, in Denver's 1985 loss to the Dolphins.

PRO STATS

	INTERCEPTIONS			
Year	No.	Yds	Avg.	Sacks
1983	0	0	0.0	2
1984	2	105	52.5	7
1985	0	0	0.0	13
1986	0	0	0.0	9.5
Tot.	2	105	52.5	31.5

San Diego's Dan Fouts (14) under pressure from Karl Mecklenburg and his all-pro teammate, defensive end Rulon Jones (75), *left*.

has been a hero to every Broncos fanatic.

Mecklenburg performed well in 1984, and in '85 he combined with defensive end Rulon Jones for 23 sacks, a new Broncos record for two players in a single season, also ranking high in club special teams statistics. Mecklenburg finished the season with seven sacks and two interceptions for a club-leading 105 yards.

DOING IT ALL FOR YOU

Along with his great playing Mecklenburg has been very active in the Denver community. He visits schools to talk to the students about the value of an education and the dangers of alcohol and drug abuse, and he and his wife Kathi have participated in fund-raising events for the Denver Opera and Denver's Samaritan Shelter.

When he finishes his pro-football career, Mecklenburg intends to go into business. If he is as good at crunching numbers as he is at crunching quarterbacks, he should do exceptionally well.

honing his skills at one position. But Mecklenburg was drafted only in the twelfth round in 1983 as a defensive end, and did not make the switch to linebacker until the 1984 training camp.

His progress as a linebacker was quietly successful until 'The Hit', when it became a loud roar. This occurred against the Los Angeles Raiders in the fifth week of the 1984 season when Mecklenburg laid a devastating tackle on Marcus Allen. From that moment he

TIME OUT

STAYING HEALTHY

For a man who specializes in mayhem on the field, Mecklenburg comes from an unlikely background. Both his parents are in the business of caring: his mother is a former Deputy Secretary of the Department of Health, and his father is a doctor with a practice in the Washington DC area.

JOHN ELWAY

Strong of arm and fleet of foot, the Broncos'

quarterback is surely destined for football greatness

The progress of John Elway would be considered spectacular if he were just another quarterback. But he's not. Bursting with talent, hope and promise, Elway entered the league in 1983 as the sport's new golden boy.

An exceptional pure passer, whose talents were honed by the pro-style offense employed by Stanford University, Elway inspired a Broncos' offense, which rated 23rd in passing in 1984, to sixth in 1985.

In his third year he set Denver single-season records for pass attempts (605), completions (327) and passing yards (3891). He threw 22 touchdown passes and rushed for more than 300

yards in three games, including a career-high 49 yards rushing in a 15-10 win over Indianapolis on 13 October.

'John made tremendous strides during the 1985 season,' says Broncos' head coach Dan Reeves. 'We didn't have a balanced running game and we had so many games decided in the final minutes. That puts a lot of pressure on your quarterback, and John did a great job leading us to 11 wins.'

TWO-SPORT STAR
Elway was the most highly sought-after prep athlete in the nation in 1979, after an unparalleled football-baseball career at Granada Hills High School, California.

He completed 129 of 200 attempts for 1837 yards and 19 touchdowns as a senior, as well as leading the baseball team to the Los Angeles City championship with a .491 batting average and a 4-2 pitching record. He completed 60 per cent of his high school passes for 5711 yards.

Kansas City Royals selected him in the 1979 summer draft, but Elway had already signed with Stanford. As a junior, he received All-American recognition and was the first

sophomore ever named Pac-10 (college conference) Player of the Year and the first sophomore ever named a first team All-American.

Elway compiled amazing 1980 statistics, completing 65.4 per cent of his attempts for 2889 yards.

In limited action as a freshman he completed 50 of 96 attempts for 544 yards, setting a school record by hurling six TD passes.

RECORD SETTER
As a senior, Elway was a consensus All-American and finished second in Heisman Trophy balloting, while setting virtually every Pac-10 and Stanford career record for total offense and passing.

Elway concluded his college career with five major NCAA Division 1-A records and nine major Pac-10 marks. He completed 62.1 per cent of his career passes (774 of 1243, both NCAA highs) for 9349 yards and 77 touchdowns, while setting an NCAA record for the lowest percentage of passes intercepted in a career (3.13 per cent).

GOLDEN BOY
Elway was the first player selected in the 1983 NFL draft

and joined the Broncos by trade with Baltimore on 2 May 1983, arriving on a tidal wave of publicity.

But coming into the league as the most publicized college prospect since Joe Namath in 1965 placed Elway under a tremendous strain. He struggled for much of the season before putting in outstanding performances to clinch a playoff spot for the Broncos.

Despite finishing a disappointing 17th among AFC passers, Elway set single game highs for his rookie year, completing 23 of 44 for 345 yards against Indianapolis.

LEADING OFFENDER
His rookie stats may not have been as impressive as he'd wished, but in his second season Elway took a major step forward in his development as an NFL quarterback. With 14 regular season starts, he helped the Broncos to a 13-3 record in 1984, and finished eighth among AFC passers.

Not only was Elway's passing a factor in his leadership of the offense, but he finished third on the team in rushing with 237 yards on 56 carries.

He tied the team record with five scoring passes in a single game (vs Minnesota on 18 November) and established a personal pro high in completions with 26 against New England on 4 November, also posting his only 300-yard game of the campaign against the Patriots (315).

His performance in 1986 is testimony to his efforts – and he aims to get bigger, faster and stronger.

TIME OUT

UNIVERSITY CHALLENGE
John Elway is the third player from Stanford to be chosen first overall in the yearly selection since the NFL player draft was instituted in 1936. Cleveland Browns chose Bobby Garrett in 1954, and New England Patriots chose Jim Plunkett in 1971. Only four other colleges have produced more than two players to be chosen first overall.

PRO STATS

PASSING

Year	Att.	Comp.	Pct.	Yds	TD	Int
1983	259	123	47.5	1663	7	14
1984	380	214	56.3	2598	18	15
1985	605	327	54.0	3891	22	23
1986	504	280	55.6	3485	19	13
Tot.	1748	944	54.0	11637	66	65

RUSHING

Year	Att.	Yds	Avg.	TD
1983	28	146	5.2	1
1984	56	237	4.2	1
1985	51	253	5.0	0
1986	52	257	4.9	1
Tot.	187	893	4.8	3

A shoulder injury kept Elway from starting two games and playing in a third in 1984, but work in the weight room has now developed his throwing arm.

STAR POINTS

Born 28 June 1960
Height 6 ft 3 in
Weight 15 st
College Stanford, California
Draft Baltimore Colts' 1st choice, 1983
Team Denver Broncos
Position Quarterback
Number 7

BEST GAME

Denver Broncos vs Seattle Seahawks
20 December 1985
- passed for 432 yards and 1 touchdown
- completed 24 of 42 passes

BEST SEASON

1985 • completed 327 of 605 passes
• passed for 3891 yards

HONOURS

All-American, 1980, Pro Bowl, 1986

POINTS TO WATCH

Elway puts unbelievable speed on the ball and his incredible mobility prevents him being sacked too often. When he goes to the air he looks for WRs Steve Watson, Vance Johnson and Clint Sampson.

'Nobody plays Denver without worrying if that could be the game Elway explodes. John is a time bomb waiting to go off.'
Sam Wyche, Cincinnati's head coach

ART MONK

'Less than an hour after signing the contract during his noon break, Art Monk was on the field at the Redskins' mini-camp and dazzled the coaches and players alike, repeatedly grabbing Joe Theismann's passes over the middle and then darting spectacularly downfield with his jets blazing.' So said the *Washington Star* of 14 May, 1980.

The Redskins' assistant general manager Bobby Mitchell watched closely. Having run with Jim Brown, caught passes from Sonny Jurgensen, and run patterns with Charley Taylor, he had seen greatness from up close. He was seeing it again.

ART ATTACK

'Once he and Theismann get their timing down, it's going to be like taking candy from a baby,' said Mitchell, a Pro Football Hall of Famer. 'Getting open for this guy won't be any problem.

'I just told him not to break all my records [1436 yards receiving in 1963, 72 catches in 1962] in his very first year.'

With all due respect, Monk waited until 1984 to write his name into the Redskins' records section. He did it in indelible ink, however, shattering the 20-year-old NFL receiving record of 101 receptions with 106 catches.

ART GALLERY

The quarterback who threw those passes, Joe Theismann, had almost predicted such a feat at that first workout: 'He's got all this raw talent and he can come across the middle – whooeee!!'

Art Monk found out in 1985 just how tough an act he is to follow. His 91-catch season has been bettered just six times in NFL history, yet it followed 106. A down year? Not at all. Redskins fans formed a rooting section at RFK Stadium called 'The Art Gallery'.

'You call his number, and he's there,' said head coach Joe Gibbs, following Monk's twin, team, single-game record-setting 13-catch, 230-yard performance against the Bengals in the '85 season. 'He's a star, an absolute star.'

But Redskins' brass wasn't the only group singing Monk's praises. His peers selected him to the AFC-NFC Pro Bowl for a second consecutive season. Other honours included first-team all-NFL nods from *Sporting News*, *Football News*, and TV commentator John Madden.

At Syracuse University, Monk played running back, possessing the size and speed to make him the eighteenth pick in the draft, and the Redskins' first number-one choice since 1968. Converted right away to wide receiver, the comparison was obvious.

'Art makes defenses do something; he makes the other receivers better,' says Mitchell. 'Same as CT [Charley Taylor] used to do.'

LAME IS THE SPUR

In six seasons, Monk has led the Redskins four times in both catches and yards. The only setbacks to this fabulous career have been a couple of injuries – one causing him to miss the 1982 playoffs, the other the first four games of 1983. Monk credits those setbacks for much of his drive.

'What was driving me was missing out on our first Super Bowl,' he said. 'I got a chance to play in the second after the 1983 season but we lost so badly that it left a bad taste in all our mouths. I wanted to get back to the Super Bowl and win one, so I could feel like I really accomplished something.'

FIRST FOR FIRSTS

'I'll tell you this, Art Monk has done more for this team than any receiver has done at any place I've ever been,' said head coach Joe Gibbs in 1985. Monk's 1984-85 totals of 197 receptions and 2598 yards are both NFL bests.

One statistic from 1985 best tells Monk's value. Of his 91 catches, 62 went for first downs, and, even more impressively, of 32 third-down catches, 31 went for first downs.

The best example of that came in the 1984 season finale against the Cardinals, with the Eastern Division title on the line. Down 27-26 with time running out, and faced with a third-and-19 play from their own territory, the Redskins rallied when Monk found a seam in the secondary to haul in Theismann's pass. The 20-yard catch led to a Mark Moseley field goal and a third straight division title.

Monk still has one goal.

'I want a Super Bowl ring,' he says. 'Sure, I have the one from Super Bowl XVII, when we beat Miami, but I missed the playoffs and the championships that year with an injury. I want one from when I contributed. And that's all I really want'.

> No other player in the NFL has ever caught more passes in successive seasons than the Redskins' super-tough wide receiver

TIME OUT

MONK'S HABIT OF SUCCESS
Many would have considered Art Monk a ridiculous choice as the NFL's comeback player of the year in 1984. 'Comeback' suggests having been away, and Monk had caught 47 passes in 1983 and averaged 49 receptions a year in his first four seasons.

Cowboys' safety Mike Downs feels the full force of Art Monk during Washington's 30-28 victory over Dallas in week 15 of the 1984 season.

STAR POINTS

Born	5 December 1957
Height	6 ft 3 in
Weight	14 st 13 lb
College	Syracuse University
Draft	Washington's 1st round choice, 1980
Team	Washington Redskins
Position	Wide receiver
Number	81

BEST GAME

Washington Redskins vs Cincinnati Bengals
15 December 1985
● 13 receptions for 230 yards

BEST SEASON

1984 ● 106 receptions, NFL all-time record
● 1372 yards
● 7 touchdowns

HONOURS

NFC Pro Bowl Squad 1985, 1986

POINTS TO WATCH

Monk's most conspicuous ability is to get out in the open and make the catch. He is especially good when under pressure and has the ability to make the clutch catch.

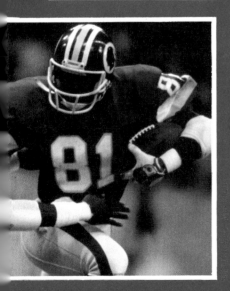

PRO STATS

	RECEIVING						RUSHING				
Year	**No.**	**Yds**	**Avg.**	**LG**	**TD**	**Year**	**No.**	**Yds**	**Avg.**	**LG**	**TD**
1980	58	797	13.7	54t	3	**1980**	0	0	0.0	0	0
1981	56	894	16.0	79t	5	**1981**	1	−5	−5.0	−5	0
1982	35	447	12.8	43	1	**1982**	7	21	3.0	14	0
1983	47	746	15.9	43t	5	**1983**	3	−19	−6.3	2	0
1984	106*	1372	12.9	72	7	**1984**	2	18	9.0	18	0
1985	91	1226	13.5	53	2	**1985**	7	51	7.3	16	0
1986	73	1068	14.6	69	4	**1986**	4	27	6.8	21	0
Tot.	466	6550	14.1	79t	27	**Tot.**	24	93	3.8	21	0

*NFL Record

'He's got to be the most awesome receiver in the league. He makes every tough catch that can be made. He's surrounded sometimes – and still gets free.'
Gary Clark, Washington Redskins' wide receiver

TEAM: Miami Dolphins
AFC Eastern Division

PLAYER POWER

Pitt

COLLEGE: University of
Pittsburgh 1979-1982

DAN MARINO

When Dan Marino became the Miami Dolphins' starting quarterback in 1983, he inherited an offense that was 27th in passing and 10th from last in scoring. That season he threw 20 touchdown passes on the way to taking the Dolphins to a 12-4 season. It was a spectacular debut.

Marino ended the season with 2210 yards and a rating of 96.0. In 1984, he set NFL single-season records for passes completed (362), passing yards (5084), and touchdown passes (48). It is not for nothing that American television commentator Fran Tarkenton called him the best young quarterback ever.

In 1985, the Dolphins went as far as the AFC Championship Game, where they were upset by the soaring New England Patriots. But the finest victory of the year was the Dolphins 38-24 win over the Chicago Bears on 2 December, the only defeat the Bears suffered all season. Marino was the architect of the victory, picking the Chicago defense apart to finish with 27 attempts, 14 receptions for 270 yards and three touchdowns.

At the close of 1985, Marino's ratio of touchdowns to interceptions (30-21) dropped from 1984's 48-17, and that sent his quarterback rating down from 108.9 to 84.1, fourth among AFC passers. But Marino still led the NFL in passing yardage (4137) and touchdown passes (30).

PASSING STRENGTH

If he continues in his present form, Marino looks set to become one of the greatest offensive players of all time. At 6 ft 4 in and 15 st 5 lb, Marino is bigger and beefier than most of his quarterback peers.

It is his strength, says Hall of Fame quarterback Sonny

Already a record breaker, Dolphin Dan seems destined to become one of the greatest quarterbacks of all time

The quarterback steps back before firing another fail-safe pass in his 1983 rookie season with the Dolphins.

Jurgensen, that is his greatest asset. 'Even a long pass of Dan's doesn't spend a long time in the air,' remarks Jurgensen. 'And he's smart enough not to be patterned; he throws when the defense tells him it's time, not after four steps or seven steps.'

SCHOOLBOY ATHLETE

Dan Marino first picked up a football when, aged 13, he went to junior high school. He displayed the talents of a born athlete. In his plain, working-class neighbourhood that meant a lot.

At high school, remembers college coach Andy Urbanic, 'He could seemingly do everything – football, baseball, basketball – and he was superb at all of them. He was actually too good for high school football. I've often wondered if he wasn't too good for college football as well.'

Certainly, Marino was heavily recruited by college football teams and the University of Pittsburgh was fortunate in welcoming the new star in 1979. It was then that the sports world began to pay attention. Marino's three-quarter throwing motion, with a strong, snappy wrist was considered perfect.

DRAFT PROBLEM

In spite of this, Marino's professional career got off to an uncertain start. NFL coaches were worried by rumours of Marino's 'attitude' problem and believed he would be a difficult player to build an offense around. As a result, five other quarterbacks were taken ahead of him in the 1983 draft. When Miami's first selection came around, however, coach Don Shula was confident enough to offer $2 million for a four-year contract for the gifted but potentially troublesome young quarterback.

It was one of the soundest decisions of Shula's career. 'Coaching is redundant for someone like Dan,' said Shula. 'As long as he listens, and knows what he has to do, you

TIME OUT

PRIME NUMBERS
The University of Pittsburgh team showed their gratitude to Marino by retiring his number, an honour bestowed only twice before by Pittsburgh University.

don't have to have him work on the whys and the mechanics.' Soon Marino's special skills were directing the Dolphins offensive approach.

Traditionally, Shula has favoured a slow but constant running play, with a powerful back like Larry Csonka bursting through to gain two or three yards on each carry. With Marino, new options became available. Says Shula, 'Marino is a pure passer, and I have no qualms about changing things around.' Gaining 30 or more yards on a single down was no longer an impossibility.

TEAM SPIRIT

It is a success that has lead Marino to endorsement perks and American media acclaim. But Marino is modest about his celebrity status: 'The attention is good now, but you have to realize that it might not be there always. I can't get too attached to it or even take it that seriously. I'm part of what's happening on the Dolphins, but I'm not the whole reason. Football isn't like tennis or baseball, an individual sport. It's a team sport, and being on this team puts me in a good situation.'

Certainly, Marino's relationship with his teammates has worked brilliantly. In the three years from 1983, Marino has led the Dolphins to three AFC East Championships and made an appearance at Super Bowl XIX.

If he has one cause for health concern, it is in the state of his knees which have already undergone two operations. But if this has limited his rushing play, Marino remains superlative as a passer and it would appear that everyone's expectations will be fulfilled as Marino is developing into a brilliant field general. Who knows, perhaps Dan will be the best QB the world will ever see.

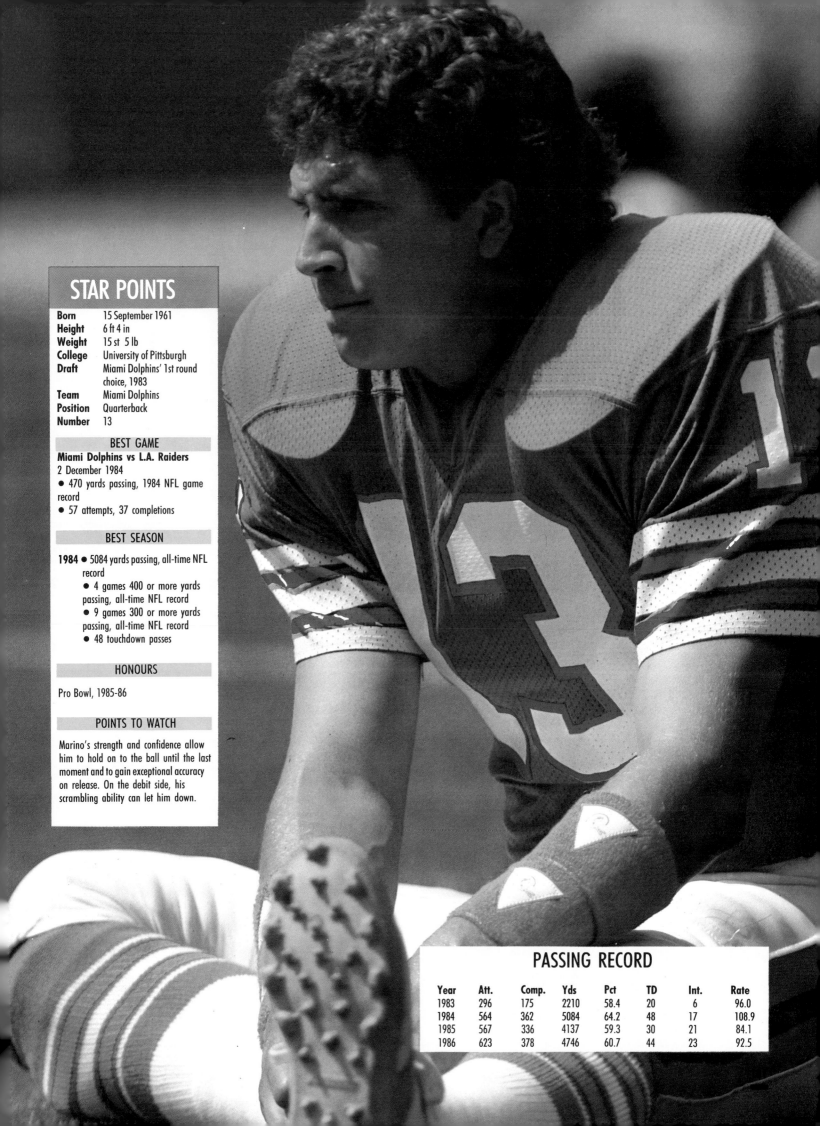

STAR POINTS

Born	15 September 1961
Height	6 ft 4 in
Weight	15 st 5 lb
College	University of Pittsburgh
Draft	Miami Dolphins' 1st round choice, 1983
Team	Miami Dolphins
Position	Quarterback
Number	13

BEST GAME

Miami Dolphins vs L.A. Raiders
2 December 1984
● 470 yards passing, 1984 NFL game record
● 57 attempts, 37 completions

BEST SEASON

1984 ● 5084 yards passing, all-time NFL record
● 4 games 400 or more yards passing, all-time NFL record
● 9 games 300 or more yards passing, all-time NFL record
● 48 touchdown passes

HONOURS

Pro Bowl, 1985-86

POINTS TO WATCH

Marino's strength and confidence allow him to hold on to the ball until the last moment and to gain exceptional accuracy on release. On the debit side, his scrambling ability can let him down.

PASSING RECORD

Year	Att.	Comp.	Yds	Pct	TD	Int.	Rate
1983	296	175	2210	58.4	20	6	96.0
1984	564	362	5084	64.2	48	17	108.9
1985	567	336	4137	59.3	30	21	84.1
1986	623	378	4746	60.7	44	23	92.5

FREEMAN McNEIL

Things such as records and glamour have little appeal for McNeil. For as long as he can remember, he has lived by his own standards and paid little attention to the popular notions of stardom. He has always had a firm handle on two things – his talent and his future – and that, for him, has been quite enough.

LET THE RECORD SPEAK

In McNeil's rookie season (1981) he had to sit out five games with a foot injury and still led the Jets in yards rushing with 623.

In the strike-shortened 1982 campaign, McNeil rushed for 116 yards in the opener against the Miami Dolphins. He had 106 yards the next week at New England and in the third game ran for 123 yards and two touchdowns against Baltimore.

It was the first time in Jets' history that a back had three consecutive 100-yard games.

In the nine regular-season games, McNeil churned for a total of 786 yards to lead the NFL. Then in the playoffs, he missed the all-time post season game rushing record by a scant four yards when his 202 yards helped bury Cincinnati 44-17. He followed that breathtaking performance with a 101-yard game in a 17-14 victory over the Los Angeles Raiders.

McNeil was selected by his teammates as MVP and earned his first starting berth in the Pro Bowl.

In 1983, despite missing seven games (due to a separated shoulder), McNeil still managed to lead the Jets in rushing with 654 yards, including three 100-yard performances.

JOB DONE

McNeil started 12 games in 1984, was hampered by sore ribs throughout the season, and finally broke a rib against the Giants on 5 December. He was placed on the Injured Reserve list, but still finished a remarkable fifth in the AFC in rushing with 1070 yards.

McNeil was selected again as the Jets' MVP and earned a second starting berth in the Pro Bowl (which he could not play in because of his injury).

'Freeman is one of the

While media attention focuses on such stars as Payton

and Dickerson, Freeman McNeil runs with the best

premier running backs in the NFL, and when healthy he is the pulse of our offense,' said Jets' head coach Joe Walton. 'He has also developed fine leadership qualities and he understands his role as a leader on the team. The younger players look to Freeman's practise habits and game preparation as their standard.'

Despite missing two full games and parts of two others in 1985, McNeil set the club single season rushing record with 1331 yards and produced the second most yards in the AFC. He was elected to the Pro Bowl as a starter for the third time, and was voted as the runner-up to Marcus Allen for AFC MVP in the *USA Today* Players' Poll.

McNeil produced the top two rushing performances in the AFC in 1985 with 192 yards against Buffalo (a Jets' club record) and 173 yards versus Miami. His four consecutive 100-yard days and his six for the season were also club records.

A MAN'S GOTTA DO

Obviously, McNeil's talent is proven and unassailable. His yearly penchant for sidelining

injuries, however, has produced worry-lines on the brows of McNeil's coaches, fellow players and fans alike.

'Getting hurt is no bed of roses,' McNeil said, 'but it's part of the business. Football is like the game of life. You can be on top of the world one minute, and flat on your back the next.

'No big thing. As long as I can see the sun shine tomorrow, I'll be okay'.

Freeman McNeil's quick feet, acceleration and mesmerizing moves have baffled defenses since 1981.

STAR POINTS

Born	22 April 1959
Height	5 ft 11 in
Weight	15 st 4 lb
College	UCLA
Draft	New York Jets' 1st round choice, 1981
Team	New York Jets
Position	Running back
Number	24

BEST GAME

New York Jets vs Buffalo Bills
15 September 1985
- 192 yards rushing
- 2 touchdown runs
- 69 yard run, career longest

BEST SEASON

1985
- 1331 yards rushing, Jets' all-time single season record
- 38 pass receptions for 427 yards, career best
- 5 touchdowns

HONOURS

Pro Bowl Starter, 1982, 1984, 1985

POINTS TO WATCH

McNeil doesn't possess great speed, but makes up for it with marvellous running instincts and competitiveness. Built low to the ground, McNeil's stocky frame makes him very tough to tackle.

PRO STATS

	RUSHING						RECEIVING				
Year	**Att.**	**Yds**	**Avg.**	**LG**	**TD**	**Year**	**No.**	**Yds**	**Avg.**	**LG**	**TD**
1981	137	623	4.5	43	2	1981	18	171	9.5	18	1
1982	151	786	5.2	48	6	1982	16	187	11.7	32t	1
1983	160	654	4.1	19	1	1983	21	172	8.2	21	3
1984	229	1070	4.7	53	5	1984	25	284	11.8	32	1
1985	294	1331	4.5	69	3	1985	38	427	11.2	25	2
1986	214	856	4.0	40	5	1986	49	410	8.4	26	1
Tot.	1185	5320	4.5	69	22	Tot.	157	1661	10.6	32t	9

ANTHONY MUNOZ

Anthony Munoz arrived in Cincinnati as a Bengals' rookie in the summer of 1980, and he must have thought he'd landed in another galaxy. He was a 6 ft 6 in 19 st 12 lb Mexican-American from Southern California, where he'd spent his entire life. Cincinnati is a straightforward, no nonsense city that didn't know quite what to make of him.

ACROSS STATE LINES

But when Munoz began knocking opposing linemen across the Ohio river into Kentucky, the fans began to like him. When he began showing how accommodating he could be by giving his time to nearly every charitable cause within driving distance of Riverfront Stadium, they decided he was their kind of player.

In 1981, the fans voted Munoz as their Man of the Year. This was the Bengals' Super Bowl season, and the team had a full complement of glittering heroes: quarterback Ken Anderson and super rookie wide receiver Cris Collinsworth to name only two others. Yet Munoz was the fans' decided favourite.

EXTRA SECONDS

Most would say that the addition of Munoz and Collinsworth was the most important factor in turning the Bengals' offense into one of the league's best. But Collinsworth would never have been as effective if Ken Anderson didn't have time to throw.

After the 1981 season, nine NFL assistant coaches combined to select the Seagrams' offensive Lineman of the Year award. All of the coaches listed Munoz on their ballots, and six of them gave their first place vote to him.

In the previous seven years of balloting, no lineman had

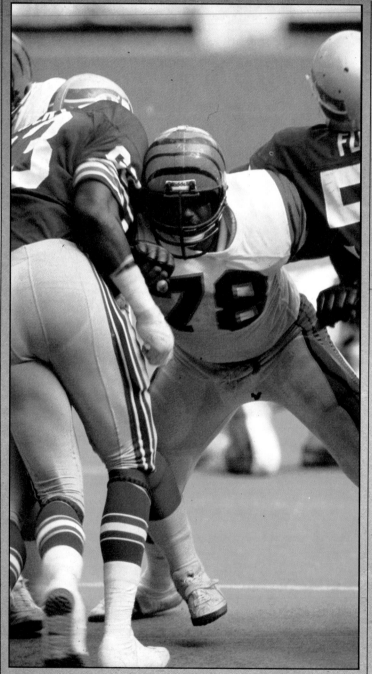

Cincinnati's sure-fire tackle moves with the agility

of a back and may well be the best offensive

lineman in the whole of the NFL

'He's as good an athlete as there is playing on any offensive line today. He may not be the biggest or the fastest or the quickest, but if you put them all together, he's got as good a combination as you'll find.'

Jim McNally, Bengals' offensive line coach

ever received more than four first-place votes. 'I can't believe how good this kid is at this stage,' one coach wrote on his ballot.

WATCH THIS GUY

Bengals' offensive line coach Jim McNally says, 'Anthony's one of the few guys I've seen who can move a guy 15 or 20 yards in the opposite direction. He just runs over them. I have to think it takes an opponent a full week to get mentally prepared for him. All the things they talk about at coaching clinics, he can do.'

Bengals' head coach Sam Wyche says, 'People who know football, the people who watch things other than the quarterback, watch this guy.'

THREE KNEE OPERATIONS

On New Year's Day, 1980, Ohio State was playing USC in the Rose Bowl (college's biggest game), and Munoz was in uniform for the first time since the season's opening game, when a Texas Tech defender smacked into the side of his left knee. Surgery was necessary; it was the third knee operation he'd undergone in four years. This planted doubts in the minds of the Bengals' management – until they saw the last quarter of the Rose Bowl.

With Munoz clearing out the left side of Ohio State's

defensive line time after time, running back Charles White swept down the field and gave USC a come-from-behind 17-16 victory. In Cincinnati, management watched and began laughing, licking their lips in anticipation.

PETRIFIED FORREST

The Bengals had the third pick in the draft that year, and after the Rose Bowl, they knew that if Munoz's knees were okay, he was their man. Forrest Gregg, a Hall of Fame tackle, was the Bengals' head coach at the time. He was dispatched to the west coast to check Munoz out. Upon meeting him, Gregg hunkered down his still-impressive frame into a defensive stance and rushed the kid a few times. Munoz stuck out one arm and knocked Gregg flat on his clipboard.

'When he did that,' Gregg says, 'I thought, "We've got to have this guy."'

After that impressive exhibition, it was a foregone conclusion that the Bengals would take Munoz if at all possible in the draft. He passed pre-draft physicals around the league and the Bengals selected him just behind Billy Sims and Johnny (Lam) Jones.

Since joining the Bengals,

Munoz has fulfilled Cincinnati's every expectation, becoming an all-pro offensive tackle and one of the very best offensive linemen in the NFL.

Munoz was chosen for the Pro Bowl for five consecutive years and in 1985 was named to the consensus All-NFL team. He did not miss a regular or postseason game in his first six years and had a consecutive game streak of 96 at the end of 1985.

The Houston Oilers' tough right tackle Bruce Matthews says of Munoz, 'He's the man I really try to model myself after. I think he's the premier player at his position. I try to incorporate the things he does best in my game.'

Perhaps the greatest praise of all comes from the Chicago Bears' incomparable defensive end Richard Dent who was named the MVP in Super Bowl XX. When asked who has given him the hardest time ever in a game, Dent (who tangled with Munoz in a pre-season game in 1984) said, 'That's easy. Anthony Munoz. I couldn't do anything with that guy.'

THE UPPER HAND

Munoz's dedication is characteristic of his temperament, which is calm

The most prominent highlight of Munoz's career was this touchdown pass from QB Boomer Esiason (7) against the Cleveland Browns on a tackle-eligible play in December 1984.

yet solidly devoted to self-improvement.

Anger in Munoz seldom surfaces, though he is trying to develop more intensity. 'That's something I have to work on,' he says. 'You have to have that meanness on the football field. You've got to go out there and take the upper hand because sometimes the only way you can quiet someone down is to physically quiet them down.'

Coach McNally doesn't argue.

'That's part of his success,' McNally says. 'It helps him think on the field, control his execution. If he were a little more aggressive, he would be so dominant you couldn't stop him, but it might mess up his game.

'And besides,' McNally adds with a grin, 'if he were a vicious guy you couldn't coach him. Right now, if I picked up this phone and said, "Let's look at some film," he'd be here in 10 minutes. He wants to improve himself every day, rather than become destructive.'

MIKE QUICK

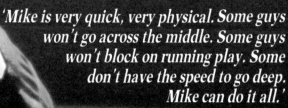

'Mike is very quick, very physical. Some guys won't go across the middle. Some guys won't block on running play. Some don't have the speed to go deep. Mike can do it all.'

John Spagnola, Philadelphia Eagles' tight end

When in 1986 Mike Quick was selected to play for the Pro Bowl for the fourth consecutive year, he was also the first Philadelphia Eagle in history to top 1000 yards receiving in three straight seasons missing a fourth by a mere 61 yards.

One of the premier players in the NFL, he is noted not just for his exceptional hands and his ability to get into the open on both short and long patterns, but also for what he does after making the catch. He can take any kind of pass all the way, and he is also a good downfield blocker. Entering the 1986 season Quick's four-year career statistics showed 213 receptions for 3864 yards – an 18.8-yard average – and 34 touchdowns. This ranked him fourth among the Eagles' all-time leaders in 100-yard receiving games and fourth on the all-time touchdown list.

HONOURED MAN

His 1985 honours included first team all-pro selections by Associated Press, the Newspaper Enterprise Association, *College and Pro Football, The Sporting News, Sports Illustrated* and NFL Films.

Quick played in all 16 games in the 1985 season and started

The wide receiver who lives up to his name. But he not only runs fast, he catches and blocks too. Quick adds up to a one man offense

PRO STATS

Year	No.	Yds	Avg.	LG	TD
1982	10	156	15.6	49t	1
1983	69	1409	20.4	83t	13
1984	61	1052	17.2	90t	9
1985	73	1247	17.1	99t	11
1986	60	939	15.7	75t	9
Total	273	4803	17.6	99t	43

Quick's speed has often been the downfall of opposing cornerbacks and safeties, vulnerable to his long patterns and his open-field running. *Right*, Quick burns Atlanta Falcons' cornerback Wendell Casson for a long gain in Philadelphia's dramatic overtime win in Week 10 of the 1985 campaign.

Quick excels over short, medium and long routes. He is also a fearless competitor, equally at home catching passes in open spaces, *left*, or in heavy traffic – abilities crucial to his success.

all of them except the season-opener against the New York Giants. His 1247 receiving yards led the NFC, ranked second in the NFL and third in the Eagles' history books. He also led the NFC with 11 touchdown receptions and set an Eagles' single season record for receptions with 73, surpassing his own record of 69 set in 1983 and ranking him fourth in the NFC.

He matched his own career high of eight receptions against Minnesota for 127 yards, Buffalo for 117 yards and Dallas for 81 yards. He surpassed 100 yards receiving four times, including a season-high of 146 on six catches against San Francisco. Also in 1985, he had a 99-yard touchdown reception from Ron Jaworski which defeated Atlanta in overtime, and was the longest pass play in Philadelphia's history, tying with five others for longest in NFL history.

Quick earned the game ball in that game and the one against Buffalo, when he had a 32-yard touchdown catch with just 1:55 left, capped a 21-point surge in the fourth quarter to beat the Bills.

SLOW STARTER

Quick was slow to get into the pro game. He caught only 10 passes for 156 yards as a rookie in 1982 when the Eagles drafted him from North Carolina State in the first round. But in 1983 and 1984 he had 130 receptions for 2461 yards and 22 touchdowns.

In 1983 Quick *was* the Eagles' offense. With running back Wilbert Montgomery out for

much of the season due to a knee injury, and John Spagnola sidelined for the entire year with a neck problem, Quick took over. He led the NFL with 1409 yards – the most in the league since 1967 – set an Eagles' season record for catches and 100-yard receiving games, and tied the club mark for touchdown catches.

In 1984, with Montgomery and Spagnola healthy again, Quick again topped the 1000-yard mark, despite frequent double coverage.

GREAT COMPETITOR

Quick is the complete offensive all-rounder.

'Mike can run under the bomb or make the tough catch over the middle,' says Eagles' quarterback Ron Jaworski. 'He's also a fine downfield blocker and a great competitor. It's not just "Throw me the ball". He'll do whatever you ask of him.'

When Quick was scouted, it was mainly for his blocking.

'The thing I remember most about Mike in college is his blocking,' says Eagles' head coach Marion Campbell. 'We had reel after reel of him blocking. We certainly knew he would not shy away from that part of the game. And he hasn't – he's stuck his head in there.'

Then there is the running.

'Mike lulls you to sleep the way he runs routes,' says Eagles' cornerback Herman Edwards who covers Quick in daily practice. 'He's so smooth, one of those long striders. You don't realize how much ground he is covering, and then all of a sudden he's by you. His speed is deceptive.'

FAME AND THE UNFORTUNATE

Mike Quick has put his college qualifications in speech communication to good use. He makes public service announcements for the Project Homeless Fund and the School Vote program. But his major charity work is fund raising for the fight against the blood disease sickle-cell anaemia.

He has also been honoured as one of 'The Fantastic Four' – along with Louis Breeden of the Cincinnati Bengals, Perry Williams of the New York Giants and Franklin Stubbs of the baseball team Los Angeles Dodgers. All four were born in the same tiny town of Hamlet, North Carolina.

TIME OUT

QUICK CHANGE ARTIST
Off the field, Quick is known as a fashionable dresser. He has a hat collection including fedoras, berets, baseball and painter's caps.

'I don't wear a hat on every occasion,' he says, 'but I *have* a hat for every occasion.' Many say he is better suited to the game of football.

Picture credits

This material was previously published in the Marshall Cavendish partwork *American Football.*